Ralph Russell was born in 1918. He read Classics and Geography at St. John's College, Cambridge, where he took his first degree in 1940. War service immediately followed, during which he served in India with the Indian Army and developed his first acquaintance with, and subsequent love for, Urdu — its language and its literature. In 1949 he took a second degree in Urdu and joined the staff of the School of Oriental and African Studies, eventually becoming Reader in Urdu.

Apart from his many articles in learned journals (including the *Encyclopaedia Britannica* entry on the subject of Urdu literature), he is (with Khurshidul Islam) the author of several books, including *Three Mughal Poets* (Harvard University Press and Allen & Unwin, 1968 and 1969). He is also the author of a range of volumes designed for teaching purposes: *Essential Urdu, Readings in Everyday Urdu, A New Course in Urdu and Spoken Hindi*, and *A Primer of Urdu Verse Metre*.

Since his retirement, he and Khurshidul Islam have completed a further literary volume, *Ghalib: Volume II: Urdu and Persian Ghazals* (Oxford University Press, New Delhi, forthcoming) and has continued to devote much time to developing teaching materials. His teaching, translations and writings about Urdu and its literature have earned him a high reputation both in the subcontinent, where he has spent much time lecturing and researching, and among his fellow Urdu scholars in North America and Europe. The present volume, *The Pursuit of Urdu Literature*, is the fruit of a lifetime's research and reflection and uniquely combines both introduction to and in-depth exploration of a language which for two centuries has been one of the major literary vehicles of the subcontinent.

Three Mughal Poets
Ralph Russell and Khurshidul Islam
(Cambridge, Massachusetts: Harvard University Press)

"This outstanding study . . . is one of great insight and sympathy and constitutes not only an excellent appreciation of Mir and his works, but also gives a brilliant introduction to medieval love and to the conventions of the *ghazal*, whether in Urdu, Persian or Turkish. . . Few will read it without experiencing the urge to know more of these poets' work."
British Book News, (September 1969)

"This book is an excellent introduction to eighteenth-century Urdu poetry, especially the *ghazal*, and can be read profitably not only by students of literature but also by those who are interested in the life and manners of the period."
C.M. Naim, *Journal of the American Oriental Society*, 92.1 (1972)

"The work is designed for fellow scholars and general readers alike, and deserves a very warm welcome from both."
V.G. Kiernan, *South Asia Review*, Vol. 4, No. 1, (Oct 1970)

"It is impossible to do justice to the riches of this book even in an extended review"
Simon Digby, *Asian Major*, Vol. XV, Pt. 2 (September 1970)

"This new substantial work on the three great Urdu poets is an event of great importance"
Ian Marck, *Der Islam*, Vol. 47, (1971)

Ghalib, 1797-1869: Volume 1: Life and Letters
Ralph Russell and Khurshidul Islam.
Unesco Collection of Representative Works (London: George Allen and Unwin, 1969)

"It furnishes the English-reading world for the first time with a detailed account of the personality of Ghalib, whose poetry is still on everybody's tongue in the Subcontinent."
Annemarie Schimmel, *Der Islam*, Vol. 47, (1971)

"A very rewarding and preservable volume. . . The authors should be congratulated as they have done a great service in offering to the English-speaking world an authentic biography and such excellent translations of Ghalib's letters in his centenary year."
P. Machwe, *The Indo-Asian Culture*, Vol. XIX, No. 4, (October 1970)

The Pursuit of
Urdu Literature

The Pursuit of Urdu Literature

A Select History

Ralph Russell

Zed Books Ltd
London and New Jersey

The Pursuit of Urdu Literature was first published by
Zed Books Ltd, 57 Caledonian Rd, London N1 9BU, UK, and
165 First Avenue, Atlantic Highlands, New Jersey 07716, USA;
and by Oxford University Press India, Oxford House, Apollo Bundar,
PO Box 31, Bombay 400 001, India, in 1992.

Cover designed by Sophie Buchet.
Typeset by Interpress Magazines Pvt. Ltd, New Delhi.
Printed in India by Seagull Books Pvt. Ltd, Calcutta

ISBN 1 85649 028 9 Hb
ISBN 1 85649 029 7 Pb

Contents

Note on Pronunciation

Urdu words (other than names) are given in italics and, on first mention, their meaning generally explained. I have not thought it necessary to indicate pronunciation in the main text, but those of you who wish to have a rough guide will find it indicated in the Index and in a note prefixed to the Notes and References which explains the Urdu sounds that English vowels and consonants have been used to represent.

Preface

This book is what might be called a select personal history of Urdu literature –
personal, because I have chosen to emphasize the things which, in the forty years
in which I have studied Urdu literature, have made the strongest appeal to me.
I have called it *The Pursuit of Urdu Literature* because my study of it often *was*
a pursuit, a pursuit of meanings which I knew I would find if I persevered in the
quest for them, and which in the end I did find.

The starting point for the book was a collection of articles written over the
past 20 and more years, all of them written out of a desire to share with others
the things of lasting value in a literature which is too little known outside the
Urdu-speaking world. While I am pleased that what I have had to say has been
of interest to scholars, I have always written primarily for that concentration of
many different persons into one conventionally known as the general reader. I
shall say a little more below about the different audiences to which I hope this
book will appeal. For the moment it will be enough to say that they comprise
all those people throughout the world who find it easiest to approach the study
of Urdu literature through the medium of English and also those who are already
familiar with Urdu but are interested in what may be, for them, a new approach
to it.

For those who do not yet know much about Urdu, some brief account may
be useful at this point. It is one of the dozen or so major modern languages of
the South Asian subcontinent. All of these have a literature, which, were it not
for the fact that so little of it has yet been translated into English, would be much
more widely known and valued than it is, and Urdu is one of the richest. Of most
of these languages it can be said that it is virtually the single language of a single
linguistic area, as, for example, Bengali is the language of the Indian state of
Bengal and of neighbouring Bangladesh. But the position of Urdu is different.
Its homeland – that is, the territory in which people speak it as their mother
tongue – extends over the vast area that comprises, roughly, the Indian states of
Rajasthan, Haryana, Uttar Pradesh, Bihar and Madhya Pradesh with a combined
population of something like 290 million. But it shares this homeland with
Hindi. The two languages are, linguistically, variants of each other, and at the
level of everyday spoken transactions are almost identical. Above that, however,
divergence is considerable. Urdu is written in a modified form of the Arabic
script and draws heavily on Persian and, through Persian, Arabic for its higher
vocabulary. It is spoken mainly by Muslims and the great bulk of its literature
portrays the life of the Muslims of the subcontinent. Millions of Muslims who
do not have it as their mother tongue have always used it as the language of

literacy and culture, and in Pakistan, where the mother tongues of the vast majority of the population are languages closely related to Urdu but distinct from it, it is the national language, understood by almost all Pakistanis and spoken by the great majority of them. Similarly throughout India millions of people, mainly but by no means exclusively Muslims, value it as their language of culture, and the popularity of its poetry extends to millions more. Many who understand very little of it will tell you that 'Urdu is a sweet language' and will listen enthusiastically to the Urdu songs which feature prominently in the mass circulation films of India's huge film industry.

Since independence, large scale migration of Urdu speakers has extended the range of the language far and wide – to the Arab countries, to Western Europe, and to North America. In Britain it is, after English, perhaps the language most widely spoken and understood, and the community of Urdu speakers is large enough to support a thriving national daily newspaper, more than one weekly, and numerous (often ephemeral) small literary periodicals.

All this has produced over the past few decades a new and growing audience of people who want to learn about Urdu literature, and it is to them that this book is addressed. In particular I hope that it will be useful to those young people of South Asian background who use English as their effective first language. In Britain alone there are many such people, born and brought up here, who have not had the chance they should have had to become confident speakers and readers of the language of their family and community. A growing number of them now feel a strong desire to learn more about the wealth of their literary heritage, but have no choice but to do this through the medium of English. Some of their younger brothers and sisters are now at last being offered the chance to learn Urdu as a school subject, and a small but significant number of them are going on to study Urdu at A level, and so have their first taste of its literature. There are also many thousands of English speakers who, through their friendship or work contact with Urdu speakers, have begun learning to speak Urdu at a simple level, and of these some will want to go on to find out about its literature.

Nor is it only in Britain, Canada, the United States and elsewhere that the need exists for a book in English which can help people learn about Urdu literature: tens of thousands of people in Pakistan and India whose parents are Urdu speakers have had their own education through the medium of English, and are likely to read English considerably more easily than Urdu. I know, and am very pleased to know, that a growing number among them regret that they have learnt less about Ghalib's poetry than about Wordsworth's, and would like to do something to change this situation. Finally, there are people throughout India, or wherever people of Indian origin have settled, who, while not themselves Urdu speakers, know that Urdu has a rich literature, look upon it as part of their wider South Asian heritage, and would like to know more about it.

None of these groups will find it a straightforward task to learn about Urdu literature through the medium of English, for good translations are rare, and there is very little published descriptive or critical material that would be of much use to them. Even those who have learnt to read Urdu with ease are likely to find that they need more background explanations than they get from books written for people who have grown up surrounded by Urdu cultural influences.

I hope that this book will help all such readers to understand the social and political setting out of which Urdu literature has grown at different times in history, to have a taste of some of the major forms and most significant writers, and to see what they have written not as museum pieces but as living literature full of challenge and stimulus. I hope that by removing some of the obstacles which new readers might encounter I will have enabled them to make a direct, personal response to what the authors have to say.

Before you read this book it may help if you know something about how the material in it has been arranged.

Each chapter is complete in itself, and chapters are grouped chronologically. If you are already familiar with Urdu literature you can read them in any order, turning first to the themes that interest you most; but if you are new to the subject, you should read the chapters in the order in which I have put them, because you will need to know things that I have explained in the earlier chapters if you are to understand the later ones. The Index will, I hope, help you to find key explanations. I have tried to give you a taste of the works I am discussing through translated extracts and summaries. All the translations are my own except for most of those in the chapter on Faiz, which are by Victor Kiernan.

The book does not attempt to be comprehensive – you will not find in it a treatment of every important author and every important theme; nor is every topic I have included treated in the same detail as every other. Many chapters contain substantial comprehensive studies, while others give little more than an outline of their subject. If you want to read further you will find suggestions at the end of the book covering each main period; more specific references have been included in the notes on each chapter, where I have felt these might be useful.

Over half the chapters consist of material written specifically for this book. The others are based on previously published articles, but few appear here in their original form. Some have been amalgamated to eliminate overlap; I have made alterations where necessary to reflect increases in my knowledge or changes in my views over the years, or to replace references to books or editions of books not now easily available by references to more recent publications; and I have added new passages, some of them quite lengthy.

One chapter, that on Akbar Ilahabadi, is adapted from an article which was the joint work of myself and my friend and colleague of nearly 40 years' standing, Khurshidul Islam. Even those which have borne only my name, and more particularly those on poetry, owed a great deal to him, for it was he who first enabled me to understand and appreciate much in Urdu poetry which had, in the years before I met him, been unintelligible to me.

The introductory essay by Marion Molteno has been included at my request because it covers ground that none of my own articles have done and makes a good starting point for the study of what follows. I am grateful to her not only for this but also for all the considerable help she has given me in editing and arranging the material for this book.

Ralph Russell
London

Approaching Urdu Poetry

Marion Molteno

Anyone who is interested in Urdu literature will soon discover that poetry is the form of expression Urdu speakers value most. For most English speakers this fact is not easy to absorb, because our own cultural attitude to poetry is very different. Most English speakers know a little poetry, because they have been introduced to it at school, but only a minority regularly read it for pleasure once their formal education is over. Though English has a rich poetic tradition, and we would expect someone who claimed to be familiar with British culture to have some acquaintance, however superficial, with a few of the great poets (Shakespeare, Keats, Wordsworth, and so on), we would be thinking of what might be called 'high culture' rather than 'popular culture'. You would learn more about the ways of thought and concerns of ordinary people in Britain today from the words of popular songs; and if you wanted an example of English verse which is part of *everyone's* culture, regardless of their educational level, you would be driven to nursery rhymes, or songs like Auld Lang Syne.

With Urdu poetry the situation is very different. Poetry is a part of the everyday life and thought of vast numbers of Urdu speakers to an extent quite unexpected to anyone from an English background.

Poetry and Daily Life

Urdu poetry is, like English poetry, part of established culture; as such it is of course studied at school, and those who have had higher education may well pride themselves on having a deeper understanding of it. But the taste for poetry, the awareness that it contributes something of value to one's life, extends far beyond those fortunate enough to have had the chance to study it.

People who cannot read get to know poetry in other ways. From childhood they will have heard poems quoted by their elders; even in a village where few people are literate there may be one person who can recite long extracts of classical narrative poems from memory, and other villagers will gather round to listen. In towns and cities it is not at all uncommon for thousands of people to attend poetry recitals, with illiterate labourers paying for tickets out of meagre wages.

A poetry recital is called a *mushaira*. A *mushaira* can be a huge affair where tens of thousands listen to famous poets reciting their latest works, or it can be a simple get-together in someone's home, where friends recite what they have composed. To compose poetry in the accepted forms one does, of course, need to have had a high level of education in Urdu – it is not technically easy. But a startling number of people do consider themselves poets. I once asked a friend what had made him start composing poetry. 'Well,' he said, 'as a young man I loved going to *mushairas,* and each time I went someone would say, "Come on, it's your turn to recite, show us what you have composed." It got to the point where I had a choice – to avoid this embarrassment I had to either give up the pleasure of going to *mushairas* or start composing poetry!'

Reciting poetry is a more important way for poets to reach their audience than getting their work published in books, and this oral tradition has been a vital means of keeping poetry alive in a society in which the majority cannot read. Some types of poetry are closely associated with religious worship, and at certain times of year people congregate in large numbers to hear long poems recited in honour of religious martyrs. Major poets are honoured as no political leader would be, and their influence has been at times more powerful; the chapters on Hali and Iqbal in this volume give vivid descriptions of the effect of a public recital on listeners, and the impact that major poems have made on the outlook of an entire generation. Quotations from poems are used as slogans, painted on the sides of buses, scattered through novels and magazine articles. And finally, everyone hears poetry sung, for many of the popular songs that blare out from radios all over India and Pakistan have words which derive from – and in some cases are – classical poetry. For an analogy in English we would have to imagine the latest rock groups choosing their lyrics from Wordsworth.

Because poetry is an everyday activity which people enjoy, the values most commonly expressed in classical poetry are unconsciously absorbed and exert a powerful influence. Anyone who wants to understand more about Urdu-speaking society needs to learn something about its poetry.

Urdu poetry had an aristocratic origin. Urdu developed as the language with which the Muslim rulers of north India, who came from Afghanistan, Iran, and Central Asia, communicated with their Indian subjects. The earliest Urdu poets were people from the aristocratic Muslim families attached to the courts. The young men in such families received an education in which poetry played an important part: they were all expected to try their hand at composing, much as in Jane Austen's day women of her class were all expected to be able to paint and play a musical instrument. Those who took poetry more seriously would attach themselves as a *shagird* – a pupil – to an established poet who would become their *ustad* – teacher – guiding their efforts and correcting their verses. Eventually they would themselves perhaps seek a wealthy patron, so that they would be assured the leisure to compose. The better-known poets were given places at court or in one of the princely states, where they provided poems for special occasions and improved upon the verses their patrons composed.

To those who excelled at poetry, society gave special respect and admiration. This being so there were naturally rivalries between poets. The *mushairas* at which poets and would-be poets gathered gave each his chance to prove his worth, and these events were keenly followed. In our society today only sport has captured people's interest in the same way. Just as events in Wimbledon are followed by tennis players and non-tennis players alike, and people talk appreciatively about the grace of one player's strokes or the force of another's backhand, in the same way each poet's special qualities were noted by an audience that was educated to appreciate the finer points. And just as spectators at a football match express their approval or disapproval instantly, not waiting till the end to applaud as theatre audiences do, so those present at a *mushaira* would instantly show that they liked a line.

Many of the detailed miniature paintings commissioned by the Mughal courts give us a picture of the atmosphere in which poetry was shared. Persian carpets would be spread on the floor, on which the poets and listeners sat, perhaps in a circle. In the background there would be musicians playing flutes or stringed instruments; rose water would be sprinkled to give the air fragrance, and candles set in niches of the walls. A candle would be placed in front of one of those present, signalling that it was his turn to recite; then the candle would be set in front of another, and so on, into the small hours of the morning.

The poetry of this period drew much of its imagery from such gatherings, in which – contrary to the prohibitions of Islam – wine was depicted as being freely available, served by a *saqi* who would go round the circle, filling people's glasses. Wine, and the intoxication it brought about, became a symbol for a heightened spiritual awareness, a disregard for worldly concerns and an openness to the deeper reality which poetry aimed to reflect.

The original, aristocratic *mushairas* have given way to modern ones, but many of the same conventions apply. *Mushairas* still are gatherings where a large number of those present recite their own works, and though the audiences are much less exclusive and include many who have no pretensions to compose, they still participate actively. There is still a strong element of competition, with the more illustrious poets appearing last in the programme, just as in pop concerts in the West, where lesser known groups are given a chance to perform early in the evening and the audience waits with growing impatience for the singers they have really come to hear. The recital may go on into the small hours of the morning; people wander in and out, but no one seems to get tired.

Both the form of poem and the style of recital make listening easy. The most popular form of poem is called a *ghazal*. It consists of a series of couplets – two lines – each containing a complete thought. Listeners have only to concentrate on two lines at a time; if their minds drift and they miss a few couplets, they can wake up for those thereafter and still be able to follow.

There are several common styles of reciting poetry. In the style called *taht-ul-lafz*, the words are spoken much as they would be in English poetry; but with both rhyme and rhythm being more prominent features, for Urdu is both richer in rhyming words than is English, and has a much wider range of poetic metres. Another style is called *tarannum*, a type of chant with a two-line tune, something like the chanting of psalms in a church service. To a modern Western ear *tarannum* has an effect not so much like that of a song, but of a repeated rise and fall of sound, like bees buzzing on a warm day. Eventually you cease to be aware of the tune, which becomes simply the backdrop against which the words stand out. Finally, there is song itself – sometimes accompanied, sometimes unaccompanied. Often the poet or singer will repeat a line which seems particularly significant, giving listeners a second chance to take it in. A common style is to return again and again to one or two lines, which then become a sort of refrain. By the end of the recital many listeners will already know bits of the poem by heart.

Poetry is, of course, also published in books, and has been since classical times. But people read and study the *divan* (collection of *ghazals*) of a classical poet as one might read a Shakespearean play, knowing that this is a transcription of something one should hear. Even the terminology reflects this: you cannot say 'to write poetry' – the idiom is *sher kahna* – 'to say poetry'.

Wherever Urdu speaking communities have settled they have taken the love of poetry with them. In Britain, the United States or Canada, thousands of miles from the home of Urdu culture, even people of moderate means will contribute to the cost of organizing a *mushaira*. Well-known poets from India or Pakistan who visit the West are immediately booked to recite their poetry, and may even be flown in specially. After the death of Faiz Ahmad Faiz, whose impact and popularity Ralph Russell analyses in *Faiz Ahmad Faiz – Poetry, Politics and Pakistan*, a commemorative meeting was called at short notice in London. The response was overwhelming; though there had been no time for advance publicity, over 700 people from all over Britain filled the hall, to listen to hours of speeches in honour of Faiz, and readings of his poetry. Only for something they passionately care about will people travel across country at short notice just to be a member of an audience.

Cultural organizations that have grown up among Urdu speakers settled abroad take it for granted that one of their functions should be to organize poetry events. One example is *bait bazi* – an activity which could have no equivalent in English because it relies on the fact that so many Urdu speakers have learnt by heart and can recite extraordinary amounts of poetry. It is a competition between two teams, where someone from one team recites a famous couplet and the other side has immediately to follow it with another couplet which begins with the letter of the alphabet with which the previous couplet ended. The competition may go on for hours, with neither side showing any signs of flagging in producing fresh couplets – and many people in the audience will know most of the couplets quoted.

Asking Urdu speakers whether they like poetry is somewhat like asking Western children whether they like Christmas. But the very fact that you are so unlikely to get the answer 'no' means that the attitude is a self-perpetuating one; people who have been told from their earliest years that Christmas – or poetry – is something special and wonderful, will almost certainly come to feel that it is so.

Naturally, for the second generation who have grown up in the West, hearing more English than Urdu and surrounded by Western attitudes, the influence of Urdu poetry is obviously weaker. In the West far more than in the subcontinent,

Urdu speakers' access to poetry is determined by their level of education, for there are so few opportunities to hear poetry in the natural course of events. Many British-born children, whose parents are from village communities in Pakistan or Kashmir, are growing up not even knowing that Urdu has a rich poetic tradition. Yet the influence of poetry may still be present in their lives in subtle ways – and one of the most powerful agents in keeping it alive has been the Indian film industry. Watching video films is a regular occupation of young and old alike in many British Asian homes; and though these films are often referred to as 'Hindi' films, Hindi and Urdu are, at the simple spoken level used in mass circulation films, almost the same language. Many of the scriptwriters have been Urdu speakers, and the concepts of poetry they were heir to have found their way quite naturally into the film songs they have composed.

Recordings of popular singers rendering well-loved classical poems sell briskly in Asian bookshops in many cities in Britain. A young sales assistant in London, whom I got to know because he overheard me speaking Urdu to my companion, was delighted by my interest and offered to lend me some of his own Urdu cassettes; it turned out that he had several hundred, and the majority were of poetry being sung. Popular British Asian musical groups, which play to audiences of teenagers born and brought up in Britain, sing songs in which the influence of Western rhythms and styles may be clear in the music, but the heritage of classical poetry is equally clear in the words. If the young people who listen appreciatively to such songs, and who know popular film songs by heart, were to be introduced to the best of classical poetry they would, without being aware of it, already have had much of the preparation necessary to enable them to enjoy it.

I received my own introduction to Urdu poetry from people who have come to live in Britain only once they were adults, and so grew up surrounded by the influences of Urdu-speaking culture. Some have had university or secondary education, but many have not; even among those who have, very few now have the time or opportunity to read, or to attend cultural events where they would continue to hear poetry. Yet all of them use the poetry they already know. Quoting couplets as a comment on daily events seems to be among Urdu speakers as much a cultural habit as talking about the weather is among the British. Perhaps the *ghazal* form has helped to encourage this close connection between poetry and daily life. *Ghazal* couplets are easy to memorize, because even complex thoughts are condensed into two lines; and since each couplet touches on a different topic, a few favourite *ghazals* memorized during schooldays can provide for years after a store of comments relevant to a wide range of situations.

I remember vividly my own first experience of this. In the middle of a quite ordinary conversation in Urdu with a colleague, he suddenly used a stream of words I didn't understand. From the rhythm and lilt I assumed that this must be poetry, but I was extremely surprised that this should be so because the subject we had been discussing, though important to both of us, was not to my way of thinking a poetic one. We were talking about how best to persuade the conservative head teachers of schools in our area that it was important for pupils of minority communities to be taught their home languages at school. I argued for starting with junior school teachers; he disagreed; if we could help just a few older pupils in secondary schools to gain good examination results in their own languages, he said, that would bring the school credit, and we would have no further difficulty persuading head teachers! It was then that he suddenly quoted this couplet:

خدا جب حسن دیتا ہے نزاکت آہی جاتی ہے

which means:

> When God bestows beauty delicacy follows of its own accord.

When he had explained what it meant I was for a moment confused. Who was this person, whom he described as having beauty and delicacy? Then it dawned on me – all he meant was that we should get the essential thing right and the rest would take care of itself. But I thought how unlikely it was that I would ever have associated examination passes with 'God-given beauty', or the opinions of the reluctant head teachers with 'delicacy'!

Since then I have become used to, and am continually delighted by, the direct connection people feel between poetry and the practicalities of everyday life. A friend recently wrote me a note to say it was a long time since we had seen each other, and to suggest that we should meet soon. She quoted:

تمہاری یاد جب آئی، تمہیں جب دیکھنا چاہا
فلک کے ماہ و تارے دیکھ کر حسرت مٹا ڈالی

This means:

> When I remembered you, when I longed to see you
> I gazed at the heavens at the moon and the stars and so banished my yearning.

The only context in which I could have imagined an English speaker quoting a couplet like this would be when speaking to a lover from whom he or she had been separated; who else would indulge in sentimental thoughts about the moon and stars? Yet to my friend there was nothing inappropriate about using a couplet composed for a highly charged emotional situation to say, simply, that she regretted not having seen me at a meeting! Her note went on in a completely matter-of-fact tone to comment that 'Here in Britain, of course, the sky is usually covered with cloud; so we can't even see the moon!'

It is the way she and many others use poetry – taking it seriously as a thing

of beauty, but also putting it to work to enliven their everyday thinking – which
made me want to learn more about Urdu poetry for myself.

The Language of Poetry

Poetry which is intended to be listened to, and so is a close relative of song, can
be enjoyed even by people who do not understand the words. Many English
speakers who know no Italian nevertheless love Italian opera – and may even
resist the idea of listening to a performance in English translation. A first
encounter with what the words mean can in fact be confusing; opera that was
once grand may begin to seem slightly ridiculous when you realize that in some
of the most beautiful musical lines the singers are only saying 'What is the time?'
or 'This champagne is good.'

People who have heard of the richness of Urdu poetry and try to read it in
translation may well face similar disappointment. In any language poetry is
difficult to translate well; but as Ralph Russell describes so well in *Understanding the Urdu Ghazal*, for an English speaker encountering Urdu poetry for
the first time there may be other sources of confusion. My own first impression,
even once I could begin to read it in the original Urdu, was that the poets whose
work I was reading seemed to have very little to say. Couplet after couplet
produced little but empty platitudes, or descriptions of emotion phrased in such
general terms that for me they lost all force. When I confessed to an Urdu-speaking friend that I could see no point in a *ghazal* she particularly liked, she smiled
and said – not unsympathetically – 'It must be hard for you enjoy our poetry. We
people love beauty too much.' And, by clear implication, 'you people' (non-Urdu
speakers) too little! To her the matter was simple. The lines were beautiful; if I
could not appreciate them, my sense of beauty was not well enough developed.

Of course people in all cultures respond to beauty; the question is, what
strikes you as beautiful, and what as 'too much'. Though as individuals we have
different tastes, certain responses are undoubtedly cultural – learnt from those
around us, unconsciously transmitted and unconsciously received. Fortunately
we are not limited for ever to the tastes so formed; we can add to that unconscious
training, can teach ourselves to become aware of what people from another
culture see as beautiful, and learn to see it in the same way too.

What sorts of words and images do Urdu speakers find beautiful in poetry?
And how does this differ from what most English speakers feel comfortable
with? One of the things that first struck me was the prevalence of abstract nouns
and lush adjectives. I soon discovered that many of these are words even Urdu
speakers never use. For instance, the everyday word for beautiful is *khubsurat*:
naturally there are other closely related words in common use, but in addition
there are in poetry special ways to describe beauty. A beautiful woman, for
instance, may be described as *pari-paikar* – which means formed like a fairy;
mah-ru – with a face like the moon, *mah-jabin* – with a brow like the moon; and
so on. People understand these words in poems, and like them, but keep them
for literary use only.

Most languages have a specifically poetic vocabulary. In English we wouldn't dream of saying in conversation 'Much have I travelled in the realms of gold...' but we feel it is appropriate in a poem. Yet even in poetry the tendency in English nowadays is to prefer words which are simple and direct rather than gorgeous. We accept that earlier poets used a vocabulary not in common use today, but if a modern poet writes in a highly poetic vocabulary many readers think it slightly ridiculous.

This is not the case with Urdu speakers; in fact the typical reaction is exactly the opposite. Listeners seem to feel that the richer the literary vocabulary, the more effective the poem. Speakers of other South Asian languages who describe Urdu as a particularly 'sweet' language, when pressed to say what they mean, often give examples of some of its rich store of poetic ways of saying things. In any language, part of the impact of words comes from their familiarity, from the associations that have built up around them; if a word is not used in daily life and the associations are therefore all poetic, that in itself may add to its appeal in a society in which poetry is so generally valued. 'Moon-browed' may sound absurd in English translation, but to an Urdu speaker who has heard *mah-jabin* many times – always in poetry, always in connection with someone beautiful, and usually associated with a situation of heightened emotion – it can have power to move.

A similar process happens with the standard images of classical Urdu poetry. Words such as *wine*, the *desert*, recur frequently, always symbolizing the same situations or feelings. Wine, as we have seen, represents intoxication, but usually intoxication of a spiritual kind; the desert too is a spiritual more than a physical area, where the poet who has defied the norms of worldly society is pictured as wandering alone, yet proud. To Western readers such stock images soon begin to sound like tired clichés, for our tastes have been formed in an individualistic society which puts a high value on originality, on a poet's ability to express things in quite unique ways. But this prejudice against reusing an image is clearly not universal. For people familiar with Urdu poetry an image becomes more meaningful, not less, through constant reuse. Each stock-in-trade image is like a technical term, a shorthand understood by poets and listeners alike, which enables poets to refer with extreme economy to a complex range of experience, still having space within the two brief lines of a *ghazal* couplet to add something specifically their own. When Ghalib, the great nineteenth century poet, uses the image of lightning in the following couplets (from two different *ghazals*), he draws on the standard connotation which his listeners will know without being told. Lightning is a metaphor for a sudden, highly-charged event, capable of bringing calamity into your personal life – particularly the calamity of falling in love when this is bound to bring rejection or disgrace:

رونقِ ہستی ہے عشقِ خانہ ویراں سازسے

انجمن بے شمع ہے گر برقِ خرمن میں نہیں

All that gives radiance to life comes from the love that ruins your home
Only the lightning that destroys the crops lights up this gathering.

سراپا پارہن عشق و ناگزیرِ الفتِ ہستی

عبادت برق کی کرتا ہوں اور افسوس حاصل کا

> I pledge myself entire to love – and love of life possesses me
> I worship lightning – and lament the lightning's handiwork.

Naturally no reader who is new to Urdu poetry can hope to receive the full impact of such lines. There are bound to be many couplets which to Urdu speakers are intensely meaningful, but which initially would make little sense to anyone else. The important thing to recognize is that the repeated images are tools for achieving that high concentration of thought and feeling which is one of the hallmarks of good poetry in any language. The route towards greater appreciation is simply more exposure, so as to become more familiar with this special poetic shorthand. I discovered this for myself early on in my reading of Urdu poetry, when I came across the use of the words *nightingale* and *rose* used symbolically in a couplet of Ghalib's, and realized that I had met them before in a simple but beautifully told parable by Oscar Wilde. In Wilde's tale the nightingale is a devoted lover, and the rose his imperious beloved, accepting the homage of the nightingale's song as her due, yet essentially unmoved by it. I can only assume Wilde must have encountered these images in Persian poetry (from which Urdu poetry derives) for he uses them in precisely the same way. Because I had been moved by Wilde's tale I had no difficulty in responding to similar images when I met them in Urdu poetry. Repetition, far from reducing the effectiveness of the images, had enhanced it.

Another aspect of Urdu's special poetic diction, to which English speakers may initially feel resistant, is that every experience is portrayed in extreme terms. Unpleasant states are described with words which refer to the utter depths – grief, lament, and so on; while pleasant states are at the other extreme such as joy, radiance. The poet appears to be either in a state of complete bliss, or despair. The eighteenth century poet, Mir, expresses desire like this:

کیا کیے کیا رکھیں ہیں ہم تجھ سے یار خواہش

یک جان و صد تمنا، یک دل ہزار خواہش

> My love, I cannot tell the tale of all the things I want of you.
> A hundred longings fill my soul, a thousand yearnings throng my heart.

and the suffering of the lover like this:

دل جلتے کچھ بن نہیں آتی، حال بگڑتے جاتے ہیں

جیسے چراغِ آخری شب ہم لوگ نبڑتے جاتے ہیں

When once our hearts catch fire, no power avails to save us from our fate
Like lamps that burn throughout the night, we too are steadily consumed.

How we respond to the expression of such extreme emotion is a personal matter – and also a cultural one. English speakers are used to a literary convention which understates rather than overstates. Humorous literature in English often depends on such understatement for its effect, and we are moved by the kind of writing about strong emotions in which very little is said, but much implied. This preference is not only literary; in daily life, too, our culture values those who can put up with discomfort without too much complaint; and if people do not channel their anger or disapproval through acceptably toned-down formulae, they are considered to be behaving impolitely. 'I don't get on very well with him' is quite likely to mean 'I dislike him intensely.'

Given this cultural bias towards understatement, English readers may well feel that to describe desire as 'a hundred longings...a thousand yearnings...' is somewhat over-the-top. The chapter on 'Mir – the Poet and the Man' may help to explain this intensity coming from someone who lived and loved under eighteenth century conditions. What may still be seen puzzling is that the expression of such extreme emotions appeals to ordinary Urdu speakers today, for many of whom life must surely be a more placid affair, those who do not look as if their hearts were consumed like lamps that burn all night. Their experiences seem seldom to be reflected in Urdu poetry – and yet apparently they don't feel that the poetry is any less relevant to them because of that.

Why does poetry have so powerful an impact on so many Urdu speakers, whatever their temperament? What function does it fulfil for them? Perhaps for English speakers a starting point in trying to understand this is to look in our own society for examples of a kind of literature that has a similar popularity, and consider what it is that people get out of that. Readers of thrillers of the James Bond type, or of Mills and Boon romantic novels, for example, do not necessarily expect to find in these books an accurate reflection of their own thoughts and feelings, yet this type of literature would not be as popular as it is unless it met some emotional need. Men who read racy thrillers are not necessarily themselves macho, successfully outwitting all comers, pandered to by an endless succession of willing women; but precisely because their lives are circumscribed, regulated by the demands of work, governed by habit, their unfulfilled adventurous instincts may look for the illusion of freedom and power in what they read. A woman whose life holds little more romantic than the usual round of domestic chores, yet who constantly reads romantic novels, may do so precisely because she needs to be lifted out of the confines of her own uneventful days by becoming absorbed in the fortunes of the beautiful heroine whose life is so unlike her own. Urdu has equivalent types of literature. The poor avidly watch films which depict lifestyles of extravagant wealth. Tragic novelettes in which young people fall in love against the wishes of their parents are popular among young and middle-aged readers alike – most of whom know that they would not dare thus to defy the expectations of the society around them.

Good poetry, of course, offers much more than such escapist literature, but there is one point of similarity – the appeal is often to what is hidden, or unexpressed, or perhaps inexpressible in daily life. Many English speakers, even though they are surrounded by a culture which divorces poetry from everyday life, have at moments in their lives taken to writing poetry (often secretly, as if it were a vice) to express the kinds of feelings that they are sure no one near them would understand. Among Urdu speakers, couplets which express intense emotion may have a special appeal to people in whose daily lives family needs take precedence over more personal feelings. A woman in a traditional extended family must defer to her mother-in-law and senior sisters-in-law, regardless of whether she genuinely thinks they know better than her; a man in such a family owes a similar deference to the advice of his older brother, who has the right to intervene in any aspect of his life; and in the vast majority of cases neither men nor women have the freedom, which Westerners take for granted, to make major decisions about their personal lives on the basis of their individual feelings rather than what is required by the family. But if people in such situations learn not to expect that they can openly express strong feelings, this does not, of course, mean that they do not have them.

Of all the emotions which are likely to have to be suppressed in daily life and seek expression in poetry, the commonest is love. This is certainly not something confined to Urdu poetry; any collection of poetry in any language is likely to contain a high proportion of love poems, and you have only to think of the words of popular songs in the West – generation after generation – to see how universal is this instinct to use verse to express every type of love, from the most casual to the most intense. Because love is universal, love poetry written centuries ago in languages we do not understand can still speak powerfully to us; but the social pressures on lovers vary greatly from society to society. In 'Understanding the Urdu Ghazal' Ralph Russell explains how the love expressed in Urdu poetry mirrors the society out of which it grew, in which lovers faced constraints unknown to most English speakers. Urdu love poetry appeals powerfully to anyone who has experienced the kind of love which brings disapproval from the society around them – and that may include young people of Pakistani or Indian origin growing up in Britain, even those who have had no previous exposure to Urdu poetry. I asked a friend from this kind of background who subsequently studied Urdu at university whether, as someone who had grown up in an English-speaking environment, she had had any difficulty learning to understand and like Urdu poetry. 'No,' she replied without any hesitation, 'because by the time I started reading it I was in love with someone I knew my family wouldn't let me marry.'

Whether the poetry in question is love poetry in this sense, or in the other senses described in 'Understanding the Urdu Ghazal', or on other themes altogether, the intensity that characterizes it is capable of addressing the deepest, most personal area in all of us. When Ghalib says:

نہ گل نغمہ ہوں نہ پردۂ ساز
میں ہوں اپنی شکست کی آواز

> I am no melody; I am no lute;
> I am the sound of my own breaking heart

we are aware of someone who writes poetry because the feelings inside him demand expression. Whether or not the daily lives of his listeners hold anything dramatic enough to cause a breaking heart, there will be many among them – Urdu and non-Urdu speakers alike – who will feel that the poet speaks for them.

Convention, and Beyond

The poetic language, the symbolic images that seem at first like clichés, the exaggerated expression, all these features, and much else in Urdu poetry that I have not touched on, are to some extent matters of convention. If at first encounter they do not appeal to you, part of the reason is almost certainly that they are not what you expect. The same may be true of much in the early prose writing in Urdu. But it is important to remember that any art form is governed by convention – and that by its nature any convention seems natural to people who are accustomed to it, and strange to those who are not. This is something most of us are familiar with in more mundane areas of life, wherever people of two cultures interact. Most Urdu speakers, for instance, find it decidedly odd that the English are not more hospitable, that one can know an English person for a long time without being invited home. To the English it is equally odd that Urdu speakers do not mind distant relatives arriving to stay in an already overcrowded home, without giving any indication of when they will leave. Most people make similar judgements about what is natural and what is strange in art, in music, in literature.

Approaching any new art form involves deliberately putting aside what we are accustomed to expect. You cannot hope to be moved by watching the ballet *Swan Lake* unless you can tranquilly accept the convention that the performers are telling a story without speaking at all, but instead are moving their bodies in highly stylized ways; and you will not discover what there is to enjoy in *The Sound of Music* if you allow yourself to be irritated by people suddenly bursting into song, in situations where in real life they would simply continue speaking. The conventions that underlie the rich variety of Urdu literature are no more odd – or more natural – than these. Nor are they in essence any more difficult to become used to, requiring only what Coleridge described as "the willing suspension of disbelief for the moment, which constitutes poetic faith".

This book provides an understanding of these conventions and of the society out of which they arose. It will help you share something of the pleasure which Urdu literature gives to the millions of people who have grown up surrounded by its influence – and to find in all its rich variety of forms much that is meaningful.

Part 1
Classical Poetry
(18th to mid-19th century)

1. The First Flowering of Urdu Literature

The first great flowering of Urdu literature took place in the early decades of the eighteenth century. For some centuries before that time Urdu had been used as a medium of prose writing, mainly in religious tracts, but these were not literature except in the very broadest sense that word can bear. Urdu poetry, too, had flourished in the sixteenth and seventeenth centuries under Muslim rulers in central India, but this formed, so to speak, a compact and isolated phenomenon, beginning and ending before the continuous history of mainstream Urdu literature began in the northern plains. What we may call the classical period of Urdu literature, then, begins in the early decades of the eighteenth century; and the great watershed of the revolt of 1857 provides a convenient closing date.

Readers who know something of Indian history as the British have written it will have a mental picture of the eighteenth century as a period in which nothing much happened, one in which, so to speak, real history had stopped until the British victory in the battle of Plassey in 1757 enabled it to get started again. (And thereafter until the coming of independence in 1947 the picture is one in which Indian history means the history of what the British did in India.) It is understandable that the British should have viewed Indian history in this way, but it is important to realize that this was not the picture as Indians saw it, and, no less important, that there were, within the subcontinent, different groups that saw historical developments from different standpoints, so that one could speak, for example, of a Maratha view, a Bengali view and a Muslim view of Indian history. For us it is the Muslim view that is important, for Urdu literature has always been, and still is, a Muslim literature – not in the sense that it expounds the teachings of Islam, but in the sense that it has always been overwhelmingly a literature that depicts the experiences of the Muslim community of the subcontinent.

The Muslim View of Indian History

The first thing to understand about the Muslim community's view of Indian history is that it had always felt itself to be the elite of the Indian population, ruling the land by virtue of the special qualities which God in His special grace had bestowed upon it. Muslim dynasties had dominated the North of the subcontinent for the greater part of five centuries, up to the death of Aurangzeb, the last great Mughal Emperor, in 1707. Their rule extended into the central plateau and, on occasion, penetrated far into the South. Muslims were, throughout this period, as they have always been, only a minority of the subcontinent's population – a large and powerful minority, but a minority nevertheless. They were always aware of their minority position and, in that awareness, all the more proud of the fact that they dominated the course of Indian history.

It is not difficult to envisage, then, the heart-searchings that began in the Muslim community when an empire that in 1707 had seemed to be at the height of its power and glory went into a period of precipitate, catastrophic decline with Delhi, the capital, repeatedly invaded and plundered and its citizens subjected to general massacre. The devastating impact these events had on those living at the time will be described in 'Mir – the Poet and the Man'; the expression of the emotions to which this impact gave rise dominates the literature of the eighteenth century. In the eyes of Mir and his fellow poets the picture was one of the universal, rapid erosion of the ideal values of what we may describe as a medieval social order. They thought that these values had once prevailed, and were inspired by an intense desire to restore them, and by a determination to do their part by holding fast to them even when most others had abandoned them. Any idea that a new approach to the world around them was now needed did not occur to them, and for understandable reasons.

In other parts of India a new historical force had begun to make its influence felt in literature. The emergence of the British as the dominant power had compelled people to respond to a radically different set of values. Thus in Bengal, where British ascendancy had been established since 1757, the influence of British rule and British values had increased rapidly and relatively smoothly. But the vast area over which Urdu was spoken was, culturally speaking, as yet barely affected by British rule. True, Avadh (the area around Lucknow) had become a client state of the British in 1765, but physical British presence in Avadh was minimal, and cultural influence almost nil. In Delhi it was not until 1803 that the British appeared on the scene, and here too the old Mughal court, though politically powerless, was allowed to continue as a centre of cultural life.

This was also a period in which the desire of many British administrators to acquire the cultural accomplishments of the Mughal elite was at least as marked as the desire of Urdu-speakers to acquaint themselves with British culture. Ghalib was the first of the great classical poets to form intimate contacts with the British, and his powerful intellect and exceptionally tolerant outlook made him receptive to some of the new ideas of which these encounters made him aware. But in his poetry too these influences find expression in the old traditional forms and in new interpretation of already familiar concepts.

A Literature of Medieval Values

In the eighteenth century and the first half of the nineteenth century, therefore, it was medieval values that prevailed in Urdu literature. Let me say at once that I do not use 'medieval' in any pejorative sense. In the modern West and in influential sections of society throughout the world, medieval values have been displaced by modern ones, but if this has been in the main a desirable process, it has also involved the destruction of some medieval values which it would have been better to preserve and maintain. These include the major values which the Urdu poets uphold and which enable them still to speak powerfully to us today.

It is a feature of medieval ways of thought that they establish norms, both for literature and life, which are conceived of as both ideal and eternal. Everything must be done in the forms which long-established precedent has prescribed. In poetry, therefore, one writes in already established forms, and the idea that one may break these moulds or abandon them, or introduce new ones, is unthinkable.

Urdu literature began, as the literatures of many other countries and communities have begun, as the literature of poetry. The poets used forms established by long tradition, drawn from the more western parts of the Islamic world, from Iran and from the Arab countries further west of Iran, but nevertheless embodying in those forms the experience of life in the subcontinent. Urdu poetry was thus in a very real sense the direct descendant of Persian poetry, and in order to understand the cultural atmosphere in which the first great Urdu poets lived and wrote, you need to know something about the relationship between Urdu and Persian in this period.

Urdu and Persian

Long before Urdu poetry in North India came into existence, northern India had been a part of that great area of the Islamic world in which Persian was equally the language of government and diplomacy and the language of culture. No cultured North Indian Muslim before about the beginning of the eighteenth century would have dreamed of writing poetry in any other language, and there in fact arose in India a whole school of Persian poetry and a distinctive poetic style which the Iranians themselves call *sabak-i-hindi*, 'the Indian style'.

In the course of time, however, it began to be felt that people for whom Persian was, after all, an acquired language, could not hope to write great poetry in it. This feeling was no doubt accentuated by the comments of Persian-born poets who emigrated to Mughal India and settled there. There is a story of a clash between the Persian-born poet Urfi and the Indian-born Abul Fazl, who was one of the outstanding figures at the court of the Mughal Emperor Akbar during the latter half of the sixteenth century. Abul Fazl was boasting to Urfi that he had studied Persian so thoroughly that his command of the language was complete. 'Well,' said Urfi, 'but I have one advantage that you cannot match; ever since I was old enough to understand, my ears have heard the Persian spoken by the old men and old women of my house.' Abul Fazl replied, 'So you learnt Persian from the old women, while I learnt it from the great masters of Persian, Anvari and Khaqani.' 'Yes,' said Urfi, 'and they learnt it from the old women.'[1]

By the early decades of the eighteenth century, a school of Urdu poets had established itself, and by the middle of the century the scene was dominated by two great names – those of Mir and Sauda. The pre-eminence of these two over their contemporaries has always been acknowledged right from their own day, and it was perhaps their genius more than anything else which finally decided the battle between Persian and Urdu. But Mir and Sauda were two of many, and Mir, who was an exacting critic, in an account of the Urdu poets which we know to have been written in 1751 finds over one hundred names worthy of mention.[2] In the same work he speaks briefly of his own aims as a poet, telling us, in effect, that he aspires to write poetry in Urdu of the same excellence as that achieved by Persian poetry after centuries of development.

Sauda, and all the other notable poets of the age, would have subscribed to this aim, and their close acquaintance with Persian poetry greatly helped them in achieving it. They had ready at hand all the rich tradition of Persian poetry, and they made full use of it. Urdu has in common with Persian poetry its metres, its verse forms, its delight in verbal conceits, its major themes, and its expression of the teachings of Islamic mysticism. But the use of the mother tongue helped Urdu speakers to convey an intensity in their poetry which they could not have expressed in Persian.

The Forms of Classical Poetry

The major forms which the poets of the classical period used were the *ghazal* (a love lyric), the *qasida* (a panegyric ode), the *masnavi* (a love narrative poem), and the *marsiya* (an elegy on the death of Imam Husain, the Prophet's grandson).

Of these, the *qasida* is of least interest to the general reader today, either in South Asia or in the English-speaking world. *Qasidas* were formal odes, usually in praise of the poet's patron, which the poet used as an opportunity to display his immense poetic skill. *Qasidas* are therefore characterized by intricate verbal conceits and complex flights of rhetoric, together with often absurdly exaggerated flattery of the patron.

The Urdu *masnavi* is of two kinds, but the theme of both kinds is love, and some of the most appealing poetry of the eighteenth and early nineteenth centuries is in this form. The word itself simply means a poem written in rhyming couplets. One kind is a realistic depiction of human love at what may be called short-story length. In the other kind – and *masnavis* of this kind are longer – there is, mingled in with this realistic depiction, an element of fantasy, and *jinns* and *peris* (men and beautiful women of supernatural powers) play a part in the story.

Marsiya means simply 'elegy', but the word is generally used to refer to the long poems lamenting the martyrdom of Husain and his companions at Karbala – an event of great significance in the history of Islam – and narrating the events to which this was the climax.

A full treatment of classical poetry would require a more detailed account of all these forms and of the major poets who wrote in them. But this section is almost entirely devoted to a detailed discussion of just one form, the *ghazal*, the love lyric, with some examples from the work of the two greatest *ghazal* poets

of the classical period, Mir and Ghalib. There are good reasons for concentrating
on the *ghazal*. It is the form which enjoys the widest popularity, now as in the
eighteenth century; it is the form in which the major themes of classical poetry
find their main expression; and it is also the form in which Urdu has produced
some of the greatest love poetry that the world can show.[3]

2. Understanding the Urdu *Ghazal*

I well remember my introduction to the Urdu *ghazal*–the classical Urdu lyric. My teacher began reading *ghazals* with me when all I knew about them was that they were love poems. I like love poetry, and went into class with pleasurable anticipation. I came out a sadder, but not, I am afraid, a very much wiser man, having found with something like dismay that there was almost nothing about the *ghazals* I had read which I understood and liked. From that day to this I have been convinced that to understand and appreciate the *ghazal* is the most difficult task that confronts the modern Western student of Urdu literature; and as my own understanding increased I have become equally convinced that this is a task which, once accomplished, brings the greatest reward.

That view is not shared by most of those who have written in English about Urdu literature. Thus Muhammad Sadiq wrote in his *History of Urdu Literature,* first published in 1964, that the *ghazal* 'stands very low in the hierarchy of literary forms' – a statement that recurs in the second edition published in 1984.[1] That judgement could hardly be more completely opposed to my own, and, what is more important, to the judgement of millions upon millions of South Asians of all social classes who have always loved the *ghazal* and still do.

First Encounter

I am writing primarily for English speakers who perhaps know little more about the *ghazal* than I did when I first encountered it, and I therefore make no apology for first giving something of the history of my own attempts to identify, and later to solve, the problems which the Urdu *ghazal* poses. For while every individual's experience differs in some measure from every other's, I do not think that my own has been markedly untypical.

I came to the systematic, full-time study of Urdu literature relatively late in life – to be precise, at the age of 28, having not only finished my school and university life, but having also spent six years in military service. (Three-and-a-half of these were spent in India, where I acquired an ability to speak and read Urdu.) At school and at university my main subjects of study had been Greek and Latin literature, and I had also acquired a reading knowledge of French and a taste for English literature and for the classics of other European languages which could be reached through English translations; and I had continued to read during the war years when, for me at any rate, short periods of all-engrossing activity alternated with long ones of relative idleness.

Thus I came to the Urdu *ghazal* with a moderately wide range of general reading in literature behind me. As I have already said, I liked love poetry, and expected to like the *ghazal*. Yet at my first encounter with it I was very much taken aback. In the first place, before I ever got to grips with its content, I was baffled by the oddness of its form. The *ghazal* is usually a relatively short poem, knit together by a unity of metre and by a strict rhyme scheme (AA, BA, CA, DA and so on). I could appreciate the rhyme, but the metres were exceedingly complex, and for the most part yielded no rhythmic pattern that was discernible to me. I was familiar with the stress-based metres of English, and with the quantity-based metres of Latin, Greek, and Sanskrit, but none of them gave me much help where Urdu was concerned. (I found T. Grahame Bailey's statement that Urdu metre is, like that of Latin and Greek, based on quantity, to be untrue – or rather if not wholly untrue, at any rate sufficiently incomplete to make it of little help to me.) More disconcerting still was the discovery that in the typical *ghazal* the close unity of form stood (to me) in glaring contrast with a complete disunity of content, in the sense that every couplet is an independent entity, not necessarily related even in mood to its neighbours.[2] I was told that the *ghazal* is commonly compared in this respect to a pearl necklace – beautiful, separate pearls held together on a single string; but to be quite honest, this is not an entirely apt comparison. In the first place, in the typical *ghazal*, including some of the very best ones, not every couplet is a pearl, or, indeed, a precious or semi-precious stone of any kind. It is not a string of pearls, but a string on which are threaded, in apparently haphazard order, pearls, rubies, pretty pebbles, and cheap beads of plain and coloured glass, uniform in size and shape, but not in anything else. And why is every verse a separate entity? No one could tell me.

Finally there was the problem of the gender of the beloved. All the great classical *ghazal* poets were men, but they always used masculine forms when referring to the beloved. This was the strict classical convention: women poets too wrote as if they were men, addressing a masculine beloved. (Respectable women did not generally write poetry, but it was a standard accomplishment of courtesans.) Why was the beloved always addressed in the masculine form? Was it because the *ghazal* is the poetry of male homosexual love? That in itself would have been no great obstacle to my appreciation of it, and I quickly realized that this was part of the answer – although people who knew very well that this was the case were generally reluctant to say so. But it was clear that though the *ghazal* poet always uses the masculine gender of his beloved, that beloved is often quite unmistakably female. (I was later to see that this convention holds even in such unconventional poets as Nazir Akbarabadi and in a modern poet like Akbar Ilahabadi.) Why? Again no one could give a clear, comprehensive explanation.

I turned, therefore, still puzzled by these conventions of form, to see what the content had to offer – and found it no less disconcerting than the form. The situations of love which it portrayed were generally far, far different from those in my own experience or from anything I had met in the love poetry of other literatures. Most of it I did not understand, and what I did understand (or thought I understood) had very little appeal for me. At the time I reacted at best with scepticism and at worst with derision. I said to myself, 'The beautiful girl whom a man loves but who does not love him is not, to me, a new phenomenon either in literature or in life, but in the *ghazal* the poet's mistress *always* seems to be like that. Moreover, her beauty is described in ridiculously exaggerated and ridiculously conventional terms. Then, I can understand a girl who does not return a poet's love being, in his eyes, cruel. But the beloved of the *ghazal* poet is not content to be cruel in this sense; she is a thoroughly nasty character who delights in being really and actively cruel and vindictive. And how does the lover react to all this? Not as any self-respecting man would, by trying to cure himself of so hopeless a love, or resolving by his persistent devotion to melt his beloved's heart, or by making up his mind at the very least to bear manfully and with dignity the lifelong burden of a love that he knows will never be requited. No, not in any of these ways, but with complete spinelessness, bewailing his lot in the most extravagant, unmanly self-pity, and taking it for granted that he is in a situation which he can never change.' In short, I found both the lover and his mistress singularly unsympathetic characters, people who could inspire in me no sense of fellow-feeling at all.

Beset by all these problems, I sought help from my British teacher. He was the kindest and most helpful of men but here he seemed powerless to help me, and the more I pressed him the more I came to feel that, though he did not like to confess it freely, the fact was that he too did not find much in the *ghazal* to appeal to him.

This situation made me pause to think, and to think pretty hard. By this time I had made a good number of friends among Urdu speakers. Most of them were postgraduate students at the various colleges of London University, and not all of them were particularly interested in the *ghazal*. But many of them were, and the majority of these subscribed to the view that the *ghazal*, as exemplified by the best exponents of the form, was poetry of high merit. I was very willing to be convinced that this was so, but for all my willingness, none of them was very successful in his attempts to enlighten me. Thus, they could not explain why it was that every couplet of the *ghazal* was independent of every other, or why an obviously female beloved should be spoken of in the masculine gender. (On the other hand, they were used to these conventions and did not find them odd.) In the matter of metre my talks with them were a little – a *very* little – more fruitful. They all knew that there was an elaborate system of prosody based ultimately on Arabic. None of them laid claim to more than the most rudimentary knowledge of it, but what they could nearly all do was recognize its rhythms where I could still discern none. It quite often happened that I would quote from memory to one of my friends some line which I liked, and would at once be told, 'You must have remembered it wrongly. It can't be that. It doesn't scan.' He would think a bit and say, 'It's probably this,' – and recite something which to my ear sounded identical in metre to what I had just said. Something like the following dialogue would ensue:

'But that sounds exactly the same metre to me.'

'Well, it's not.'

'What's the difference then?'

'I can't explain it to you, but the two lines *are* different. One scans and the other doesn't.'

Thus, I at any rate discovered that these complex metres in which *I* could discern no pattern were real enough to Urdu speakers, even if they could not help me much to understand them. I may say in passing that this experience led me to form the tentative conclusion that a study of Urdu verse would ultimately make it possible to make an analysis of Urdu metre in its own terms – without reference to English, Latin, Greek, Sanskrit, Arabic, or anything else. Subsequent work has fully convinced me that this is so, and I can now analyse the metres in terms which make them intelligible, at any rate to me and to my students, though I very much doubt whether the experts in the traditional system would accept my findings.[3]

But to return to the main line of my argument: I was compelled to conclude that I must wait a long time before I could hope to appreciate the *ghazal* as my Urdu-speaking friends did. I never ceased to think that I could one day hope to achieve this result. I reflected that the poet Mir, for instance, had been acclaimed now for two hundred years, and that cultured people whose taste and judgement I respected still acclaimed him as a great poet. It was possible that they were all wrong, but much more likely that the fault lay in me, in my continuing inability to understand exactly what the *ghazal* was all about. I determined therefore to persevere in the hope that I should one day learn what I needed to know; and this was still the situation when I went to India and Pakistan on a year's study leave at the end of 1949.

I did not at once realize how significantly different would be the experience of life in the subcontinent I was now to have from that which I had acquired hitherto. I had been in India for three-and-a-half years during the Second World War, but not for any significant length of time in any context which brought me into contact with aspects of life relevant to the understanding of Urdu poetry – poetry which in any case I would not have been able to read in those days. Later I had studied Urdu in London, and had made good friends among Urdu speakers there. But, in London, they were living in an environment which was not their own. I was now for the first time to meet on their own ground, so to speak, the class of Urdu speakers by whom and for whom the Urdu *ghazal* was produced.

Once again, the experience was not at first as fruitful as one might expect. I spent the first few months at Aligarh Muslim University, where I was most kindly received, and where all whom I approached, from MA students to lecturers and professors, were more than generous with their help. But there were still many problems to be solved – and some of them were new ones. None of the MA students I talked to seemed to me in the least like the lover portrayed in the Urdu *ghazal*; yet all of them admired the *ghazal*, and did not at all feel that the lover, as there portrayed, was an odd or an unsympathetic figure. My efforts to find out how this could be so did not meet with much success. Nor were lecturers appreciably more able to help me to see the light. I tried another tactic and decided to approach Urdu-speaking students of, and lecturers in, English. I thought to myself, 'English poeetry is in a tradition alien to them, just as Urdu poetry is in a tradition alien to me. Perhaps if I find out what impact it makes on them, this will give me some clues about their attitudes which will help me to understand *their* poetry.' Here too the results were disappointing. Only one experience gave me any encouragement; this was when I asked an MA student whether he could follow the metres of English poems. 'Oh no,' he replied, 'we read them as though they were prose.' 'Good!' I thought. 'I'm in a similar position in regard to Urdu poetry. No doubt the metres there all right; I just have to discover how it works.' But this was in the realms of form; in the realms of content – of themes, significance, interpretation – I did not discover what I had hoped, and, in time, I came to realize why.

I hope that I shall not offend any Urdu-speaking readers if I say that the tradition of their education for centuries has been one which has told them, 'Learn, accept, and repeat.' I would be the last to claim that this attitude is no longer to be found in the countries of the West, but it has at any rate been appreciably weakened since the replacement of medieval by modern society. Most teachers will tell their students, and a fair number will actively encourage them, to use their own intelligence and sensibility in the study of literature, and learn to express adequately their own thoughts and feelings about what they read. I hope things have changed for the better by now, but at the time of which I am speaking, most Aligarh students of English learned the opinions of the best English authorities of the day about English writers, and accepted and repeated them as their own. I found also that their reasons for studying English were generally not what, in my simplicity and inexperience, I had imagined. I know that if you read literature at a university you are bound to give due weight to the consideration that you have to pass examinations in it, and to recognize that this obliges you to study aspects that do not particularly interest you. But even so, you still have quite a lot of time to do what *does* interest you, and to experience the enjoyment that comes from reading the great works which add something to your whole being, enlarging both your capacity to enjoy life and your ability to understand more fully yourself, and other men and women, and the world around you. It is important that you learn what a great poem or play or novel meant to the person who wrote it and to the people and the age it was written for; but in a sense, it is even more important to think what it means to *you* – you, who belong to a different age and a different people, and who even as an individual are in some measure different from any other individual, regardless of the age and the people to which you belong – and who despite all these things find that the greatest works of literature can speak directly to you. In the last resort both the pleasure and the profit of reading derive from the sense of what the things you read mean to you personally, and I supposed that in India too most people who chose to study literature would be people who felt something like this about it, even if they could not easily put the feeling into words. Well, I found that this feeling for English literature was, in the words of the old cliché, conspicuous by its absence.

Here again, there is more than a century of history behind the attitudes which I found all too widely prevalent; but it is not too much to say that, for many, the motives for acquiring qualifications in English were to acquire the prestige (and the better jobs) which proficiency in English could give and to display their social superiority by, among other things, a lofty disdain for the languages of their own country and for those for whom these languages are the main medium of culture. For people so motivated the ideas of enjoyment of and learning from literature are alike only dimly comprehensible; they learn the 'right' answers to likely questions, and that is as far as it goes.

The unquestioning, unthinking acceptance of authority, including cultural authority, was to strike me forcibly many times. Attitudes to Urdu too are affected by it. I met, and still meet, lecturers and others who, when speaking of Mir, would evaluate the *ghazal* as the crowning glory of Urdu literature, and when speaking of Hali's *Sher o Shairi* (Poetry and Poetics) would echo his puritanical, Victorian strictures upon this same *ghazal*.[4], generally quite unaware that they were showing any inconsistency.

In short, for many months my difficulties remained unresolved, and I began to see light only when I made the acquaintance of Khurshidul Islam. I do not want to embarrass him with my praises; nor would I wish to suggest that had the chances of life not brought us together I should never have met anyone else who could have substantially helped my understanding. But at all events, it is to him above all others that I owe most of such understanding of the *ghazal* as I possess, and 1950 marked the beginning of a collaboration that has continued ever since.

It would take too long to describe the discussions between us from which an understanding of the *ghazal* evolved, and it is in any case time, having illustrated the difficulties which face students from the modern West as they approach the Urdu *ghazal,* to say how, in the light of my own experience, I believe it should be understood and assessed.

Love in a Medieval Society

It seems to me that in studying Urdu literature as a whole, three things need to be constantly borne in mind: firstly, that the greater part of it is a literature medieval in spirit rather than modern; secondly, that it is the literature of a community which has always regarded itself as an elite, and is therefore markedly aristocratic in its values; and thirdly, that it is largely (especially in its poetry) a literature of oral tradition – that is, a literature composed in the first instance to be spoken, and only afterwards to be written down and read. Where the *ghazal* is concerned, the reservations with which I have made the first and the third points can be dropped. These points are fully applicable to the *ghazal* without any qualification at all. In these respects, it differs a good deal from the bulk of the English literature with which English-speaking students are familiar, and the implications of each point will need spelling out fairly fully.

The central fact about Urdu love poetry is that it is the poetry of a medieval society. The parallels between the society and the love poetry of medieval Western Europe on the one hand and those of eighteenth century Mughal India on the other are very striking. As I have said in 'The First Flowering of Urdu Literature', I am well aware of the objections that can be made to the use of the term medieval; but all the same it seems to me that it is the most apt word to use, partly because it is not over-precise in its connotations. I, at any rate, cannot find a better word, and when I see how closely comparable are the concepts of the *ghazal* to those of European medieval literature, I am all the more content to adopt this description.

I have mentioned earlier my disagreement with Mohammed Sadiq's judgement of the *ghazal* in his *History of Urdu Literature.* His interpretation has one great merit in that he has clearly recognized the medieval character of the *ghazal.* What he has not been able to do is to muster any great sympathy for its values and its conventions. It is a curious fact that for those who are approaching classical Urdu poetry for the first time and whose previous reading in literature has been from books written in, or translated into, English, the easiest path to understanding it is through the writings of people who knew nothing about it. In books like J. Huizinga's *The Waning of the Middle Ages* or C. S. Lewis's *The Allegory of Love* and *The Discarded Image* you may see how a scholar may remain a modern and yet enter with insight, sympathy and understanding into the world of medieval men and women. Very few of the best known modern scholars of Urdu have yet achieved this kind of imaginative sympathy with their classical forebears; and until Urdu scholars do acquire it such writers as Huizinga and Lewis will remain the best guides into the world of classical Urdu poetry, which is strikingly – and sometimes, indeed, amazingly – similar to that of medieval Europe.

Imaginative sympathy is only one of the things that the would-be historian and critic of Urdu literature can learn from these writers. Another is the ability to recognize, and to be willing to state, the obvious central feature of the classical poetry they are presenting. The central theme of the *ghazal* is love; and the love which it celebrates is, and in the society which produces the *ghazal* can only be, illicit love.

Those who know something of European medieval love poetry will know that the *ghazal* is not exceptional in this respect. C. S. Lewis begins his account of the courtly love poetry of Western Europe with the words, 'Any idealisation of sexual love, in a society where marriage is purely utilitarian, must begin by being an idealisation of adultery.'[5] (I think his words are in a sense misleading – perhaps deliberately used to give the reader's preconceptions a violent jolt and prepare him for an unfamiliar concept of love. Medieval poetry is not the glorification of adultery as such; it is the glorification of love, which happens incidentally to be adultery.) Prominent scholars of Urdu do not seem to be willing to speak in similar terms. I well remember saying in a lecture I gave in 1958 at the University of Delhi that the *ghazal* was the poetry of illicit love, and finding to my surprise and perplexity that my statement was greeted with disapproval and even with resentment. I know Urdu-speaking society better now than I did then, and I feel surprise and perplexity no more. But I would still insist that my statement was true and that even those who disapproved of it must have sensed its truth to some extent. That being so, it is surely not too much to expect of serious scholars that they should find the courage to say so; but, be that as it may, anyone writing for the modern English-speaking world *must* say so. For only when readers realize that the love which the *ghazal* celebrates is illicit love can they even begin to understand what it is all about. Once they do realize this central fact they will not feel as I used to feel about the lover and the beloved that the *ghazal* portrays. They may still not understand them fully, but at any rate they will have made a start.

In a purdah society of the kind that produced the *ghazal* love has nothing to do with marriage.[6] Marriage is an alliance made on purely social and utilitarian considerations, and love or the absence of it is quite irrelevant to it. In fact, that is putting it too mildly: love is all too likely to make difficulties in what would otherwise be a smooth and straightforward process of arranging marriages, or to disrupt such marriages once they have been made. Where, therefore, modern Western society is sympathetic to love, medieval society is hostile to it. To obviate – as far as it *can* be obviated – the possibility of this disruptive force coming into play, a girl's marriage is arranged as soon as she is physically capable of childbearing, and it necessarily follows that, in the typical case, the girl with whom the poet-lover falls in love is already betrothed or married to someone else. This fact is so self-evident that the poet never even mentions it, and while the lover's rival is a familiar figure in his poetry, the beloved's fiancé or husband is too unimportant even to be referred to.

All the same, the fact that love necessarily involves the violation of the ties established by betrothal or marriage is important. In a society where marriage is an institution of much more fundamental social importance than it is in the modern West, it is protected by drastic measures against those who would violate it. The effect of this is that the lover therefore knows from the start that his beloved is likely to be unattainable, and this knowledge heightens the intensity of his longing and tinges it with desperation. In the Muslim society of eighteenth century India, the purdah system made things even worse for him. For in purdah society every girl approaching puberty is withdrawn completely from the society of all males except those who are too closely related to her for marriage to be possible. She lives in a separate part of the house, rarely goes out, and when she does so, wears a *burqa*,* which veils her completely from head to foot. In such a society a boy may grow to maturity without ever seeing a girl of his own community except his own close relatives, and one may imagine something of the intensity of his longings and frustrations, and the violence with which they burst forth when some chance happening provides them with an outlet. For accidents can happen to provide such outlets, and the convention of Urdu love poetry, that love is always love at first sight, is less remote from the reality of such a society than may at first appear. For example, a girl may stand unveiled before a window when she thinks she cannot be seen, and be seen by someone passing by. In many Urdu love stories this is how love begins.

---

* A loose, flowing garment worn by Muslim women who observe purdah, completely enveloping them from head to foot. The eyes are covered either by a cloth mesh or by material thin enough to be seen through from the inside. Some have a veil which may be thrown back over the head when not in use.

*lover +
beloved*

This kind of situation also explains to some extent another convention of Urdu poetry – that the beloved is cold and indifferent to her lover. If she becomes aware of his love she is likely to react with indignation and anger against one whose conduct is almost certain to cause *her* to be suspected of encouraging him. And if she reacts favourably, and begins to feel a responding attraction, her position is one of heart-rending difficulty. The danger in which her lover puts himself is grave enough, for discovery will certainly mean bitter social persecution and may even mean death. But a woman discovered in an illicit love affair faces hatred of such virulence that even if her life is spared, it may seem to her hardly worth living. Hence, before she surrenders herself she does all she can to test the strength of her lover's loyalty to her, pretending indifference even when she does not feel it, and even treating him with deliberate cruelty until she can be sure that nothing will shake his loyalty to her. Even if, having put her lover to the test, she finds him true to her, and responds accordingly, she may still vacillate, and indeed repent of her conduct and conclude that it is better to come to terms with a life without love than to face the terrible dangers that love involves. Or a sense of guilt, a deep conviction that her love is dishonourable, may urge her to the same course.

Her lover understands quite well that her cruelty or her refusal to respond does not necessarily mean that she does not love him, but this understanding does not save him from the spiritual agonies which this time of testing brings him, and he pours out his anguish in verse of extravagant, passionate self-pity.

This mood often adds to the difficulties of the modern English reader struggling to enter into the spirit of the Urdu *ghazal*, for to most of us today self-pity connotes unmanliness and other unsympathetic qualities. It takes an effort to realize that this connotation is a modern one: as Dorothy Sayers writes, in a rather similar context, 'There are fashions in sensibility as in everything else. The idea that a strong man should react to great personal and national calamities by a slight compression of the lips and by silently throwing his cigarette into the fireplace is of very recent origin.'[7] You will see the truth of this if you turn to Shakespeare's *Romeo and Juliet* and see how Romeo, whom Shakespeare portrays as a resolute and courageous man, reacts to the news of his banishment from Verona.[8]

It is understandable that where a man's love is likely to be a hopeless one, he can look to find spiritual peace only if he cultivates the ability to love for its own sake, without any expectation of return, and whatever the suffering his love may bring upon him. The experience of loving is in itself a priceless treasure. It reveals to him qualities in himself which have hitherto been dormant, and which love alone can rouse. The trials of love test the steadfastness of his heart, reveal to him his own spiritual strength, and bring him to the stage where he actually welcomes every cruelty which his mistress inflicts upon him, including even death, because it enables him to prove to her and to himself that he has the strength to love her to the end. Courage, constancy and complete dedication to love are the supreme qualities which the Urdu *ghazal* exalts, and because only the experience of love can develop these qualities, no suffering is too great a price to pay.

Some of those who know the Urdu *ghazal* argue that for the most part it is not really about this kind of experience at all – that most Urdu poets who depict their love experience in these terms are not writing direct, realistic accounts of what they have known but using those terms as conventional metaphors for the description of other experience. I would reply first, that some of the greatest *ghazal* poets – the outstanding example is Mir – evidently *are* writing of their personal experience of exactly this situation. Mir's *Masnavi Mamlat i Ishq* (Stages of Love) gives a frank and moving account of his own love affair, but this evidence has been passed over in discreet and respectable silence even by scholars who have written at length on his life and poetry. I am aware that the 'I' of a poem written in the first person is not necessarily in every respect the 'I' of the poet,[9] but in the absence of external evidence there is no reason not to assume that the two correspond, and it is at any rate clear that the poet identifies sufficiently with the 'I' of his poem to be ready to have his readers think that he is writing of himself.

Secondly, even those poets who are not writing of their own experience of love are nevertheless describing other experience in metaphors derived from this situation, and you can understand the metaphors only if you first understand their literal connotation. I repeat, therefore, that the key to the understanding of the *ghazal* is the realization that it is the poetry of illicit love, of the love of a man for another man's betrothed or another man's wife.

Mystic Love

But the *ghazal* is also the poetry of another kind of love – the passionate love of the mystic for God, his Divine Beloved. The poets called one kind *majazi*, 'symbolic', and the other *haqiqi*, 'real' – and, once again, the modern English reader is disconcerted to discover that 'symbolic' love is earthly love, and 'real' love mystic love – and not the other way round. In one and the same *ghazal* one will find some verses which one naturally takes in the earthly sense and others which one takes in the divine sense; and when one takes a second look there are many which could be taken in either sense or indeed in both at the same time.[10]

The second major task in learning to appreciate the *ghazal* thus becomes that of understanding the parallels between the two kinds of love. It is not easy for us to appreciate just *how* close, to the medieval mind, these parallels were. Once again, I use the historical term 'medieval' rather than one with regional connotations like 'Indian' or 'Muslim', because I think our difficulties in understanding the mystic themes of the *ghazal* spring not so much from the difference in outlook between East and West as from that between modern and medieval. I feel sure that one of the reasons why many people today jib at the parallelism with which human and divine love are treated in the *ghazal* is the long Protestant tradition of the modern West which tends to regard sexual love as sinful, or if not sinful, at least not religious, and for this and other reasons feels very uncomfortable with the symbolic identification of God with an irresistibly beautiful woman. Such readers would do well to remember that it did not occur to our ancestors – not even to some of our Protestant ancestors – that there was anything objectionable in the parallelism between sexual and divine love. You will find it in the Bible, in the *Song of Solomon*, where the chapter headings take the most sensuous descriptions of the beloved – her feet, her thighs, her belly, her navel, her breasts – as Christ's description of the graces of the Church.[11] This treatment is not exceptional. J. M. Cohen, in his *History of Western Literature*,[12] speaks of love poetry 'translated *a lo divino* for pious reading, according to the strange custom of the time, with a divine lover carefully substituted on all occasions for an earthly one'. In European medieval literature the lover is often God and the beloved his worshippers, but the symbolism of the *ghazal* is also commonly found. In Dante's *Divine Comedy* the figure of Beatrice appears both as Dante's earthly beloved and on other occasions as the symbol of Christ.[13] And Huizinga tells us that in the most celebrated treatment of love in the medieval literature of Western Europe, *The Romance of the Rose*, the rose was taken as the symbol both of the female genitals and of Christ.[14]

The starting point of mysticism is the soul's longing for God, a longing which owes as little to reason as does a man's involuntary, powerful attraction to a beautiful woman. It is this direct, deeply emotional relationship with God on which the whole structure of mysticism is built, and it is worth making the point at the outset that this in itself means that mysticism is potentially a doctrine subversive of medieval society, and therefore deeply suspect to it. If your one overriding aim in life is to draw ever closer to God, then the great ones of this world are unimportant in your eyes. And the great ones of this world do not like those who do not think them great. If you rely upon your love of God to guide you, you do not need the advice of learned divines and do not accept their pretensions to be in some special sense the guardians of true religion. And the spiritual pillars of the medieval order do not like this attitude any more than their temporal counterparts do.

Islamic mysticism has a wide range of expression and I do not want to give the impression that its most radical, potentially subversive trend was everywhere made explicit – still less that it was the dominant trend in Islamic mysticism as a whole. But in the convention of the Urdu *ghazal* it *does* dominate, and is not only made explicit, but like almost everything else in the *ghazal*, carried to an extreme. The hero of the Urdu *ghazal* poet, in his mystic role, is Mansur al Hallaj, who was crucified by the orthodox in 922 A.D. for crying out *'anal haq! anal haq!'* – 'I am God! I am God!' – words which to the mystic express his sense of the complete merging of the individual soul in the Divine Beloved, but which to the orthodox are unspeakable blasphemy. In the convention of the Urdu *ghazal* the poet's position is Mansur's position, and he takes it for granted that this exposes him to the same persecution from the pillars of society and of orthodox religion as Mansur himself had to face. Thus the eighteenth century poet Mir writes:

منصور کی حقیقت تم نے سُنی ہی ہوگی

حق جو کہے ہے اُس کو یاں دار کھینچتے ہیں

Have you not heard what happened to Mansur?
Here, if you speak the truth, they crucify you.[15]

There is a play on words here. In the original the word I have translated as
'the truth' is *haq,* and Mir uses it because it is the same word as Mansur used,
though in his cry '*anal haq*' it means 'God'.

If we piece together from the lines of the Urdu *ghazal* the essential doctrines
of the extreme mystics we can readily understand why the orthodox abhorred
and hated them, and why this hatred was most cordially returned. Some of the
leading ideas are these. The worship of God means the *love* of God, a love as
all-consuming as love for a beautiful mistress. Rituals of worship are of no
significance as compared with this. Of the 'Five Pillars' of Islam, the five
fundamental duties of faith, prayer, fasting, almsgiving and pilgrimage, only the
first is essential. Performance of the others *may* conceivably help you to draw
closer to God; but mostly they are harmful to true religion, for they lead you to
see religion as the hollow performance of external rituals, and, if you perform
them, to an arrogant self-satisfaction that you are 'not as other men are'. Far
better than such Muslims are Hindu idolators who love their God with all their
hearts, though they call him by another name. For God reveals Himself in many
forms and the worship of His true lovers is acceptable to Him, no matter in what
form they worship Him. God not only created the universe; He *is* the universe.
All that exists *is* He, and there is nothing beside Him. The worship of the beauty
of the universe is the worship of God, whether it be the beauty of nature, or of
a beautiful woman, or of a handsome boy. The finest of God's creations is
humankind, which in Islam is considered the noblest of created things.

The *ghazal* poet's ideal is a strongly humanist one. It stresses the greatness
of humankind, and proclaims the almost infinite potentialities of human beings,
urging their claims even against God himself. The cardinal religious commandment is to love other people, no matter what their creed and nationality. Hafiz,
the great fourteenth-century Persian poet, proclaimed this commandment in a
much-quoted verse

مباش در پئ آزار و هر چه خواهی کن

که در شریعت ما غیر ازین گناهے نیست

Do not distress you fellow men, and do what else you will
For in my Holy Law there is no other sin but this.

And Mir in one of his verses reproduces these words almost identically in an Urdu version.[16] He remembers how in his childhood a mystic had told him, 'Never on any account give pain to any man's heart, or break this phial with the stone of cruelty; for in the heart of man the Divine Beloved sits enthroned, and it is His special abode.'[17] And in many of his verses there is an echo of these words. The human heart which is so frail and brittle, once it is filled with love, becomes incomparably strong, strong enough to withstand any assault and sustain any burden, so much so that it holds up the heavens themselves. The loving heart is your surest guide as you go through life. Its generous impulses teach you to wage war on bigotry and narrow Pharisaical self-satisfaction, and to love your fellows regardless of their creed. The true lover of the Divine Beloved is the implacable foe of the *shaikh,* a word which originally meant simply 'an old man', but hence came to mean 'an elder', a man of moral authority, and is in the convention of the *ghazal*, the type of the Pharisee who is assailed with every weapon of ridicule and invective that the poet can command.

Because mystics consider the impulses of the heart to be their chief guide, they do not regard wine and music and love as forbidden, although the first is prohibited by Islam and the other two disapproved of by orthodox Muslims. On the contrary, these things are, so to speak, regarded as the mystics' allies, for they banish the cowardly inhibitions of worldly wisdom and the austere attitudes of Pharisaical pride, and stimulate all that is free and generous. (In the great majority of cases the self-portrait of the Muslim mystic as a wine-drinker is purely symbolic. Music, on the other hand, was in literal fact a common feature in mystic practice, as was the view that experience of earthly love was an aid to the attainment of divine love.) The heart teaches the mystic to war against the *dunyadar*, the worldly-wise, no less than against the *shaikh*. For their complacent 'practical wisdom' is essentially a cowardly prudence which makes people betray the principles which the heart teaches for the sake of making their way in the world. Unlike the worldly-wise, mystics are indifferent to wealth and social status, and to what the respectable may think of them. They are proud to call themselves *faqirs* (a word in which the senses of beggar and holy-man are still closely associated) and to live their lives true to their beliefs, trusting to God's love, and to the freely given charity of others, to sustain them. There has been much dispute about the extent to which the verses of the *ghazal* should be interpreted as the symbolic expression of mystic love. There is in the homelands of the *ghazal* an orthodox, conservative school of critics which asserts that all of Hafiz is to be understood in the mystic sense. Most people nowadays would regard this view as untenable, and, I think, rightly. Nazir Ahmad, the great nineteenth century Urdu prose writer, just about summed up the situation when he remarked scathingly that trying to read the whole of what Hafiz wrote in a mystic sense is like 'trying to touch your buttocks with your ears'.[18] This school is motivated by a desire to make respectable what in fact cannot *be* made respectable to orthodox Islam, and this vitiates the whole of its judgement. In contrast to this, some Western scholars have gone to the opposite extreme, and would agree with Gertrude Bell, who admired Hafiz and translated a selection of his verse into English, and who was reluctant to read a mystic meaning into any verse where, to quote her words, 'the simple meaning is clear enough and sufficient in itself'.[19] To do this, she says, is to remove Hafiz 'from the touch of human sympathies'. But this shows too limited a range of appreciation. (In another passage she writes, 'I am very conscious that my appreciation of the poet is that of the Western'[20] – of the *modern* Western, she might well have said.) It is significant that her words about remoteness from human sympathies imply the assumption that a verse read in the mystic sense *cannot* have the same immediacy of feeling as one on a purely human theme. This is perhaps true for a modern audience; but I do not think it was anything like so true for a medieval one. The feelings of medieval men and women about their religion were often as intense and immediate as any feeling arising from purely human relationships. Moreover, there seems to me to be no doubt that one of the main techniques of the *ghazal* poet was to write verse which should be capable of interpretation on several planes, so that of the very numerous verses which can be read without difficulty either in a literal or in a mystic sense, many were probably intended by the poet to be capable of either interpretation, or, if you like, of both simultaneously.

A modern audience perhaps understands the mystic aspect of the *ghazal* more readily if it is expressed in non-religious terms. The poets' beloved could be regarded as standing for the ideals of life in which they passionately believe, for the sake of which they would be ready to face every hardship, to withstand every persecution, and in the last resort to sacrifice even their lives. In a medieval society such ideals could only be conceived and expressed in religious form. But the essence of the mystic love which the *ghazal* portrays is a self-sacrificing devotion to an ideal which, conceived in modern terms, is not *necessarily* a religious ideal at all, though of course it *may* be that.

The *ghazal* poet does not spell out in any great detail what these ideals involve for one's personal and social life, but takes it for granted that to proclaim such an ideal and to act upon it consistently necessarily incurs the wrath of the pillars of society. To take one's stand uncompromisingly on humanist ideals and not to flinch from any of their practical implications means to face persecution throughout one's life and ultimately to suffer death at the hands of the upholders of the established order of things.

The range of possible mystic or quasi-mystic ideals is almost infinite. All who see themselves as struggling for a cause, whatever that cause may be, can express that commitment in the terms of the mystic symbolism of the *ghazal* and thus, so to speak, be potential *ghazal* poets.

The Poet's Experience

I said earlier that among the conventions of the *ghazal* is exaggeration – exaggeration of an order that modern readers accustom themselves to only with great difficulty. This exaggeration is evident in the depiction of the situations I have described. There are famous Urdu poets who indeed had illicit love affairs and suffered because of them; but none lived out his life as a cruelly persecuted social outcast, either because of such a love affair or because of his dedication to the ideals of the mystic lover. Nor did any of them end his life on the execution ground, on the gallows or the impaling stake. In other words, the *ghazal* picture is a conventional one – a picture through which poets portray in terms of the most extreme symbolism their dedication to the ideals of love and of mystic humanism in face of the hostility of the conventional and the worldly-wise who dominate the society in which they live.

The extent to which one is justified in reading meanings into the verse of any given poet depends on one's actual knowledge of that poet gained from a study of his work as a whole and wherever possible from other, external evidence. And this brings us to another much discussed question: to what extent do the poets' *ghazals* represent their real experience and real outlook?

Let us first take the situations of earthly (*majazi*) love. In cases where the beloved is not another man's betrothed or another man's wife, who is she – or he, or it? What other love experience could the poet have had? One has to look plainly at life in a purdah society to find the answers. First, as in any other society where the sexes are strictly segregated, love found one outlet in homosexuality, and *one* of the 'beloveds' of the Urdu *ghazal* is a beautiful male youth. There is nothing sensational about such a statement. In the modern West too there are few normal people who have not in similar situations experienced the stirrings of homosexual love, and both in Plato's Athens and in Shakespeare's England, homosexual love was accepted as one of the common forms of love. Most Urdu poets living in purdah society must have had at least some emotional experience of it, and this experience must have been part of the raw material of their poetry.

Second – and this is again true of other societies in history, besides that of Mughal India – sexual segregation, and along with it the low cultural level of the respectable women of society, called into being the courtesan – the woman who learned all the skills of love-making as a professional accomplishment, and added the cultural attainments which are also necessary to the satisfaction of the cultured man. Like homosexual love, resort to courtesans was formally frowned upon, but in the polite society in which the poets and their patrons moved courtesans were a normal part of the social scene, and many poets must have experienced some sort of relationship with them.

It is worth pointing out that all three of these situations of love have one feature in common – the lover knows that his love must in the last resort be hopeless. A girl married or betrothed to another man can never be his; a boy grows up; and a courtesan by the very nature of her calling cannot give herself to him alone. The desperation of the lover portrayed in the *ghazal* is, therefore, a desperation founded upon all the real-life experience of love.

A question which is bound to occur to the Western reader is whether the beloved is not perhaps in some cases modelled on the poet's wife. In the great majority of cases, I think the answer is No. (Aziz Ahmad's modern story *Tasavvur i Shaikh* is a remarkable and imaginative picture of a situation where the poet's wife *is* or at least *becomes*, his model, but this is not the typical situation.) It is true that (contrary to what modern Westerners tend to assume) an arranged marriage can be, and often is, as happy as one based upon mutual free choice. The two partners will in any case, even if only in their own interest, set themselves to win their spouse's love and devotion, and where they succeed, the difference between the arranged marriage and the free-choice marriage may be summed up in the words spoken to me by an Indian Muslim lady in 1958: 'With you courtship precedes marriage; with us, marriage precedes courtship.' But this love has never been thought of as having anything to do with the kind of love which the *ghazal* portrays. Even in modern societies, where for generations romantic love has generally been assumed to be the prelude to marriage, and where, conversely, a marriage is generally assumed to have been the outcome of romantic love, people know what is meant when the love between husband and wife is contrasted with that of lovers. In a medieval society, the two kinds of love were generally thought of as quite unrelated. In medieval Europe the 'theoreticians' of love considered the question of whether a man's beloved could be his own wife. Some, at least, were emphatic that this was quite out of the question.[21]

A man did not look for those qualities in his wife which he hoped to find in a mistress – or would have hoped to find if he had dared to have one or was able to find one.

These last words foreshadow a fourth possibility. If the poet is writing of actual experience of love for a real person, the real person is either another man's wife or betrothed, or a boy, or a courtesan. But in many cases the 'beloved' must have had no existence at all except in the poet's fantasy. In this case, the question of real-life experience and real-life models simply does not arise; all is the product of the poet's imagination, and in his 'beloved' he paints the portrait of someone who in his real-life experience never existed and probably never will exist. It may be remarked in passing that, free from the trammels of real-life experience he paints her in superlative terms, and that this is one of several factors which introduce into *ghazal* an exaggeration a good deal more extravagant than the modern Western student can easily accept.

Finally, just to complete the picture, there have no doubt always been *ghazal* poets who never had even a fantasy beloved. For a tolerable performance at *ghazal* composition was regarded by many as a necessary part of the social equipment of a gentleman, in much the same way as a tolerable ability to play bridge is so regarded in some circles in the modern West. At this level, the *ghazal* is nothing more than evidence that its author has successfully acquired certain techniques.

The deliberate universality of the *ghazal* determined perhaps more than any other factor the *ghazal* convention that the beloved should always be masculine, though there is more to the question than this. Hali quite sensibly draws attention to the fact that general statement in most languages has traditionally employed the masculine gender. (Usage in English has changed in recent years, but until recently if I had said 'The student needs a teacher in whom he can have confidence,' no one would have assumed that I meant thereby to exclude my girl students from the scope of this statement.) I would, however, also suggest that another general consideration lies behind this convention. First, of course, the poet's beloved could be male; homosexual love was to the *ghazal* poet as legitimate a form of love as heterosexual. But more important is the fact that the poet's mistress stood in a relationship to him which must have struck him as wholly exceptional in the overall pattern of medieval social relationships; in all other comparable relationships of service and allegiance in which he stood, her counterpart could only have been a man. The sort of feeling that lay behind masculine forms of address for a woman beloved is at any rate not confined to Urdu, nor indeed even to Islamic poetry. E. W. Lane in his classic *Manners and Customs of the Modern Egyptians* translates an extract from 'one of the grossest songs I have ever seen or heard even in the Arabic language' and adds the comment, 'In translating.... I have substituted the feminine for the masculine pronoun; for, in the original the former is meant, though the latter is used; as is commonly the case in similar compositions of the Egyptians.'[22] And C. S. Lewis remarks in passing in *The Allegory of Love* that 'midons,' the courtly lover's form of address to his lady 'etymologically represents not "my lady" but "my lord".'[23]

With mystic (*haqiqi*) love the range of experience that lay behind the poetry was probably as wide as with human (*majazi*) love. At one extreme stand first, those poets who really were mystics – Mir Dard is the example that comes most readily to mind – and, at the other, those who have no more loved their God than they have ever loved a woman, but who can handle the techniques with sufficient expertise to show that they are cultured gentlemen. In between, the possible diversity of range is great. In fact, even among the true mystics there is a certain diversity. None of them literally fits the *ghazal* portrait in every particular. Mystic lovers of God had at one time existed – and perhaps still did exist – of whom it could be said that the standard *ghazal* portrayal was more or less literally accurate. But certainly no prominent Urdu *ghazal* poet fits this bill. Still, one may be content to leave aside the more colourful trappings of the *ghazal* picture and wonder how much direct, actual, personal experience lay behind the symbols through which mystic love is expressed. Which of the mystic poets had indeed found their way to their intense love of God through the experience of passionate, sexual love for another man's wife, or through wine and its intoxication, or through music and the ecstasy it can bring? One would naturally like to know: and it is therefore all the more necessary to say quite bluntly that we do not know and that we almost certainly never will. We can assume that mystic poets must have ranged all the way from those who had had all these experiences to those who had had none of them. But at what point on the spectrum any particular poet stands we have no means of knowing; at the very best we can only surmise. Poets can make perfectly effective use of experiences which they have had only in fantasy, and even if they had experienced them in fact, the norms of Mughal society would in any case have forbidden them to avow this in completely unambiguous terms. Even today, the norms of Muslim society in India and Pakistan would operate to the same effect; no cultured audience would approve of a poet who spoke openly of this kind of intimate personal experience; and it would consider the attitude of a critic who tried to inquire into such experience quite reprehensible: such inquiries would be held to be neither necessary nor permissible. The modern West sees nothing impermissible in such inquiry, and neither do I; but I think I would agree with Muslim judgement in considering it unnecessary. I doubt very much whether a detailed, factual knowledge of what practical experience lies behind a poet's poem helps very significantly to an understanding of its impact. I think it probable that the great majority of those who respond to the poetry of Keats' *Ode to a Nightingale* have never heard a nightingale sing, and that most of those who have, myself included, would probably not recognize its song again if they heard it. They no doubt vaguely assume that Keats himself had heard it, and I expect he had. But if someone could prove to me conclusively that in fact he had not, this would not alter in any way my estimate of the greatness of his poem, just as it does not in any way lessen my opinion of people who like the poem if I know that they have never heard a real nightingale sing.

Though a few Urdu *ghazal* poets may really be mystics, with varying degrees of personal, or vicarious, or fantasy experience of the earthly emotional experiences which serve as symbols, the majority of them are not mystics in any very meaningful sense of the term. The best of them, like Mir, share with the mystics many of the values that guide them in their conduct toward their fellows; and what all the really worthwhile Urdu poets have in common with the mystics is a sense of dedication to ideals which they feel to be greater than themselves and for which they are prepared, in at least some measure, to sacrifice themselves. And, as in the case of earthly love, poets may not be people who can and do in real life sacrifice themselves to an ideal, but rather ones who wish that they had the strength to be such people, and in poetic fantasy present themselves as though they were. Linked to this situation is the sense that their devotion to the things they love makes them in some sense unique, brings them into inevitable conflict with the conventional ways of the mass of their fellows, and dooms them to a life and a death in which society rejects, despises and ultimately crucifies them.

We can now put in comprehensive form the question, 'Who, or what is the beloved of the Urdu *ghazal*?' and can answer, 'Any person, or any ideal to whom or to which the poet, whether in real life or in fantasy, is prepared to dedicate him or herself, sacrificing everything for its (her, his) sake and willingly accepting the hostility of conventional society as an inevitable consequence of this love.'[24]

The Dramatis Personae of the *Ghazal*

It is important to bear in mind that the experiences of such a person in all the situations which may confront him (or her – but I shall henceforth use the masculine form because it is in the role of the male lover that the *ghazal* poet speaks) and especially in that situation which demands the supreme sacrifice of him is *the* theme of the *ghazal*; and, necessarily, this involves portrayal of the ways in which society reacts to him. It is from his standpoint that the lover-poet surveys humankind. He sees that people like him form a small minority, hated and persecuted by that other small minority that holds temporal and spiritual power and is corrupted by that power. He sees that between these two minorities unceasing war rages, and that no reconciliation is, or ever will be, possible. He sees also how those who do not belong to either of these two minorities react to the battle between them. He identifies a number of common reactions, and in the stock characters of the *ghazal* drama he typifies these common reactions, so that each character represents in its purest form the qualities of each group that the lover-poet identifies.

He reserves his special enmity for the ideological leader of his enemies. This is the *shaikh*, 'the elder, the presbyter' the pillar of orthodox Islam and the zealous persecutor of the 'heresy' that lovers represent. Yet the *shaikh's* own 'religion', as evidenced not by his words, but by his deeds, will not stand even the mildest scrutiny. He is firmly on the side of the rich and powerful. About *their* sins he remains discreetly silent, while the 'sins' of those whom they oppress are proclaimed from the housetops. His reward is to share in their power and wealth and privilege, and to commit in secret all the sins of which he, often falsely, accuses others.

Between the lover and the *shaikh* stand the millions who constitute the rest of mankind. The lover sees clearly the positions they take up and recognizes equally clearly the consequences that flow from them.

Closest to him is the *razdan,* the confidant, or the *gham-khvar*, the 'sympathizer' – the man who is not himself a lover, who lacks the resolute courage to embrace a high ideal and serve it to the end, but whose sympathies lie with those who do, and who therefore strives to console or support the lover in the hardships he undergoes. Since in the last resort he lacks the capacity to be a lover himself, he necessarily lacks the capacity for complete and unfailing loyalty to the lover, and the *ghazal* is often blunt about his shortcomings.

Next in the scale comes the *nasih*, 'the counsellor'. He is the genuinely compassionate observer of the lover's aberrations from the norms of the medieval establishment, and wants to alleviate his distress; but he is totally ineffective, because the ideals of the lover are totally incomprehensible to him. Ghalib writes of him:

حضرتِ ناصح گر آویں دیدہ و دل فرشِ راہ
کوئی مجھ کو یہ تو سمجھا دو کہ سمجھاویں گے کیا

If it please his grace the preacher, let him come, with all my heart!
Only let someone persuade me: What will he persuade me of?

His own ideals are essentially those of the establishment, and he differs from the lover's enemies only in regretting the ferocity of the persecution which they practise against him.

More numerous are the *dunyadar*, 'the worldly' – that is, the worldly-wise, the 'practical' men, those who believe that high ideals are all very well, but....

— and whose whole life is governed by the unformulated concepts which follow the 'but', and which lead them, without positively harming others more than necessary, to 'look after number one'.*

A more subtle enemy of the lover is the *raqib,* the rival. This man professes love for the beloved, and she is often deceived into thinking that his professions are genuine. They are not. He is motivated only by his selfish lust for her, and his professions of love are the snares with which he hopes to entrap her. This concept too applies both at the level of love for a woman and at that of dedication to an ideal. Ghalib writes:

ہو گئی ہے غیر کی شیریں بیانی کارگر
عشق کا اس کو گماں ہم بے زبانوں پر نہیں

My rival's honeyed words have worked the spell that he intended.
And I am dumb; the thought 'He loves me' does not cross her mind.

These categories between them, in the *ghazal* poet's view, comprise all mankind in its reaction to the situations of love.

That is not to suggest that other, equally valid categories could not be established, and I should perhaps dwell on this point for a moment. Let me stress again that the *ghazal,* in its major themes, does not concern itself with *all* the multifarious activities and experiences that make up life as a whole. Its key theme presents only one sector of human experience. True, it regards this part of human experience — the experience of love — as the all-important one, and extends the term to embrace within a single complex phenomenon, subject to the same laws, *all* those loves which assume the capacity for the ultimate self-sacrifice. The *ghazal* is concerned with how people respond to this situation, and its dramatis personae are types of people, each of which embodies in its purest and most essential form each of the human attitudes to love and to the lover that come into play in the situation. This does not mean that the *ghazal* poet does not know that there is more to life than this. In the *ghazal* context, *shaikh* means a contemptible, vicious hypocrite; outside that context the *ghazal* poet knows as well as anyone else that *shaikh* does not *necessarily* mean that — just as the English reader knows that 'pharisee' in one context means one who thanks God that he is 'not as other men are' and in other contexts is a purely neutral term describing a member of a particular sect. Similarly, in the *ghazal* context, the *raqib,* the rival, is always an *insincere* lover; outside that context, the poet knows as well as anyone else that two rivals for a woman's love may both be equally sincere.

---

* The actual word *dunyadar* is not much used in the *ghazal,* but it is convenient term to apply to the character here described.

The Poet's Audience and the *Ghazal* Form

The modern reader will naturally wonder how it came about that, with these as its themes, the *ghazal* was the most popular, the most esteemed literary form in Mughal society. At first sight it seems an extraordinary fact. In the *ghazal* all the conventions of that society, all its accepted institutions, and all its leading figures – kings, nobles, and learned divines – are all held up to the most unrestrained, vituperative ridicule and condemnation, and God himself is sometimes the target of sarcastic attack for His injustice to His creation. Upon reflection, however, one comes to the conclusion that the *ghazal* won its pre-eminent prestige not in spite of, but because of its content. Medieval society is one of static ideals; its structure is hierarchical, its ideal 'a place for every man, and every man in his place,' its norms of conduct strictly prescribed, sanctioned by centuries of unquestioned tradition, explicitly founded upon a final, eternally valid religious revelation, and enforced by the overwhelming pressure of a public opinion of a kind which in the modern West survives in full force perhaps only in rural communities, in which people know nothing of the modern idea that your life is your own, but want to know, and *do* know most of what goes on in one another's lives, and react to any unorthodox pattern of behaviour with the mingled hatred and fear which people feel when confronted with anything strange, (to them) incomprehensible, and (therefore) vaguely menacing to their own sense of security. The cultivated, sensitive sections of such a society would have burst had there been no safety valve to reduce the pressure which their environment built up in them, and the rulers of society felt no great difficulty in giving the seal of their approval to the *ghazal* as a, so to speak, licensed, institutionalized form of passionate protest against the world in which poets and their audiences were alike confined. And from that day to this it is probably true to say that for the great majority of *ghazal* poets – I am not speaking only of the great ones, but of all – good, bad, and indifferent – and for the great majority of their audiences the *ghazal* has represented the release in socially approved fantasy of impulses which if released in action would bring drastic penalties to those who feel them, and disruption to social life as a whole.

This applies at both levels of interpretation. The novelist Rusva in his great novel *Umrao Jan Ada* comments aptly on this function of the *ghazal* at the level of earthly love. He makes Umrao remark that in poetry people can express without embarrassment – and in any company – things which they could never venture to speak of in ordinary conversation.[25] The words 'in any company' are significant: for the 'safety valve' function is made all the more immediate and effective by the fact that the *ghazal* was, and still is, a poem composed primarily not for presentation in writing but for recitation before a live audience.

This has had a marked effect on the form of the *ghazal*. This is the first, essential thing to understand about the *ghazal* form – it is a form moulded by a long tradition of oral transmission – a tradition in which poetry is composed to be recited by the poet, and only later to be read. Until one knows the whole context in which the poetry comes before its audience, and what the feelings, values and tastes of the audience are, much in the *ghazal* form is baffling and

Seems to ignore the Persian heritage. Urdu did not invent it.

inexplicable; but little in it remains so once these things are known.

Ghazal poets composed their *ghazal* for recitation at a *mushaira,* that is a gathering, sometimes small, sometimes quite large, at which poets assembled to recite their verse. An element of competition among them was always present, especially when, as was often the case, the host of the gathering prescribed beforehand a half-line of verse which had to be incorporated in their own poems by all poets attending, and so prescribed metre and rhyme scheme for them. Each couplet would be assessed by its hearers as the poet recited it, and approval, indifference, or disapproval politely but unmistakably expressed. Clearly, poets who composed in this tradition needed qualities which the poet who composes for a tradition of written transmission does not need at all. Besides the essential qualities of a poet as such, they needed, if they were to make their mark, something of the talents of an orator, a debater, and an actor. They must be able to hold the audience, and hold it, moreover, in competition with fellow poets, and must be able to react swiftly and sensitively to their hearers' changing moods. The *mushaira* is a long-drawn-out affair, and the poets' main enemy is monotony. If they are to participate effectively in a *mushaira* which will perhaps last for hours together, they cannot hope to do so without resort to variety. The audience knows as soon as a poet has recited the first couplet what the metre and rhyme scheme are. Unless the *ghazal* is one of quite exceptional force, it is perilous to adopt a uniformity of tone and of emotional pitch. Poets are more likely to strive to make their impact in two or three couplets only, and intersperse them with others which will be liked, but which will provide contrast to those on which the main effort has been concentrated, will ease the emotional tension they have engendered, and even on occasion provide a certain comic relief. They are assisted in their efforts by the characteristically medieval preoccupation with form (noted for example by C. S. Lewis in his discussion of the medieval and renaissance literature of Western Europe).[26] The audience would in general find adequate satisfaction in a couplet which has very little to say, but says it in a manner that demonstrates the poet's ability to manipulate with ease the metres, rhymes, and complex figures of speech and thought of which any poet was expected to be master. A poet sometimes wins the audience with a couplet designed mainly to enable them, given their prior knowledge of the rhyme scheme, to complete for themselves the second line of the couplet without needing to have it all recited; and those who have seen this happen know how much the audience enjoys the experience. Or the poet will aptly introduce a well-known saying which happens to fit the metre being used or use in the second line of a couplet a series of words which have well-tried associations with a parallel series in the first line, even though these associations may not here be relevant to the point. Verses like this are not of course great poetry; but we should not make the mistake of imagining that the people who composed them thought they were. Their purpose was, in the main, simply to heighten the impact of the verses into which they had put what they most wanted to convey.

All this is the unstated background to Hali's bare statement in his *Poetry and Poetics* that the great Urdu *ghazal* poets of the eighteenth and early nineteenth centuries thought that 'no *ghazal* would include more than one or two couplets of high quality, and that the rest would be padding.'[27] And it is a background which readers in the modern West, with their now long-standing tradition of poetry as a *written* literature, must be told if they are to make head or tail of the *ghazal* form as it appears on the silent, written page. This background alone explains the unevenness of quality, and diversity of mood and poetic intensity, of the couplets which make up the *ghazal*, and which stand in such marked and, to Western readers, disconcerting contrast with the poem's very close unity of form.[28]

The diversity of the poet's audience also makes its impact upon the *ghazal* form. The poet knows that some have come to be entertained simply by a display of mastery of poetic techniques; others will be entering for some hours into a world of pure fantasy; others – those with the greatest sensitivity and strength of spirit – will be responding to the message of a poetic tradition, enhanced by the great poet's own individual contribution, which sustains and glorifies people who, like themselves, strive to serve the beloved to whom, or the ideals to which, they have devoted themselves, no matter what suffering this may entail. The poet knows also that people's ideals vary, and even clash, and so speaks in words and symbols which will enable every individual in the varied audience to find in them what he or she is seeking. When Mir recites the verse:

اڑ گئے خاک ہوا اتنے ہی ترے کوچے سے

باز آتے نہیں پر تیرے ہوادار ہنوز

> The wind has blown away the dust of men
> unnumbered from your lane:
> Yet your true lovers are not daunted: men
> come to your threshold still.[29]

using as the conventional symbol of devotion the figure of the lover who waits at his mistress's door his whole life through and dies and turns to dust there, his hearers can identify the unspecified 'you' of the verse in their own terms. If one of the great secrets of the *ghazal*'s wide appeal is its being the perhaps unique socially approved means of release of the emotional pressures of a medieval society, the second is just this quality of universality – this ability to serve, in Olive Schreiner's words, as 'a little door that opens into an infinite hall where you may find what you please.'[30]

This deliberate universality of the *ghazal*'s modes of expression lies behind another of its features which modern readers find disconcerting to their sense of proprieties. The medieval poet uses a range of comparison – in simile, metaphor, and symbol – far wider and far less inhibited than modern readers are accustomed to. Not only may 'beloved' mean a purdah woman, a boy, a courtesan, God, or any one of a whole range of ideals; every comparison appropriate to any one of these may be freely used of any other. For example, a common picture in the *ghazal* is that of the beloved sitting in her *bazm*, 'assembly', surrounded by her admirers and exercising her imperious sway over them. The real life model for such a picture can only be that of the courtesan; but the lover of a purdah girl will freely use such an image of her if he wants to depict her exulting in the exercise of her power over him, and will do so without any sense that the comparison is in the least insulting to her. Nor will the poet shrink from comparing God to a beautiful women who distributes her favours as the whim takes her without discrimination between those who truly love her and those who do not. Linked with this universality is, once more, the exaggeration of *ghazal* expression. The much-ridiculed practice of the *ghazal* poet who reduces the slenderness of the beloved's waist to the point of invisibility is less ridiculous when one realizes that one standard identification of the beloved is God, of whose infinite beauty no conceivable comparison could possibly be too far-fetched an expression.[31] To which we must add that extremes of exaggeration are in any case acceptable to – even admired by – medieval listeners, where their modern counterparts cannot swallow them.

To sum up: we can begin to understand the metres of the *ghazal* if we analyse them in their own terms. If we remember that the *ghazal* is primarily composed to be recited before an audience, the disunity of content no longer seems strange to us; nor does the range of variation in pitch and tone of its successive couplets. The convention that the beloved is always referred to in the masculine form of words is at least understandable if we consider the wide range of 'beloveds' to which these words can refer, and the tendency in many languages to use a masculine form for concepts which cannot be limited to either men or women. Once we understand something of medieval purdah society, we can see that the tragic nature of *ghazal* love is not exaggerated, but a reasonably accurate reflection of the standard situation of love, where the lover did in real life generally love without any hope of fulfilment and where the beloved must generally – at least for a prolonged period – behave cruelly toward him. With this in mind we can more easily accept the expressions of self-pity and self-praise so common in the *ghazal*, recognizing that it is only our modern conventions which make such expressions seem objectionable.

All of which is not to say that this leaves nothing more to be explained. In every art form employed by another people of another age, living in another kind of society, there are bound to be features of which one can only say that they represent conventions to which we must simply accustom ourselves if we want to enjoy what another culture has to offer. Here it is helpful to think honestly about the extent to which conventions of one kind or another prescribe our own behaviour in every aspect of our own lives. Most of them are no more explicable in wholly rational terms than are the very different conventions of the *ghazal*.

This consideration should help us also to feel no great surprise that Urdu-speakers who admire their own traditional *ghazal* poetry are, in general, not able to help us far toward acquiring a comparable feeling toward it. What are problems to us are not problems to them, and people cannot solve a problem when they cannot see that it is there. And if there are aspects of their social and personal life about which they are unwilling to speak frankly, especially to people with a different social and cultural background, that too is fully understandable.

The *ghazal* occupies a position of quite key importance in Urdu literature as a whole. Not only does its influence permeate every other Urdu poetic form to an extent which neither Western scholars nor Urdu poets and critics have yet adequately realized. Its traditions are part and parcel of the whole outlook of most cultured members of the Urdu-speaking community. In the sustained, persistent, and patient search for the knowledge and understanding which alone can bring the power to appreciate it justly, we learn the need to bring a similar approach to all the other features of Urdu literature which seem at first sight odd, and about which one can all too hastily form the impression that they will not repay sympathetic study. There are other major forms, both in verse and prose, which still await such study.

The *Ghazal*'s Contemporary Appeal

I said at the beginning of this chapter that for those unfamiliar with the *ghazal* the task of understanding and appreciating it is a very difficult one – and that once this task is accomplished the rewards are great. It seems to me that the lover-hero of the *ghazal* can be a hero to us too. He is one in whom all the finest human potentialities have reached their full development, and who has the capacity to remain true to chosen ideals and to practise them in every aspect of life, no matter what the personal cost. All human societies have needed, and are long likely to need, such people, and poetry which sustains and inspires them will have the power to appeal as long as this need exists. It is true that some of the situations which the *ghazal* portrays – or, more often, of which it assumes a knowledge and understanding – are now quite unfamiliar to the modern reader in the West, and some of the lover-poet's reactions to these situations are correspondingly difficult to comprehend and assimilate. Even there, the sustained, imaginative effort to discover what they were all about, and in the course of this to understand and sympathize with the lover-poet's reaction to them, is one that is well worth making. The serious, sympathetic study of the poetry of another country and another age enlarges your range of understanding, not only of others, but of yourself, because in forcing you to pay careful attention to it it makes you more keenly aware of the fact that your own culture is only one of many, and not necessarily in every respect the best. Besides, the situations of love and life which the *ghazal* portrays are, in their essence, not so unknown to contemporary readers as a superficial study might suggest. In many modern societies the contexts of loving have changed, but the contexts of the world of the *ghazal*, though no longer universal or typical, are still to be found even in modern societies. In all those countries where racial tension prevails (and their number has greatly increased since the end of the Second World War) the black lover of a white beloved or the white lover of a black beloved is likely to experience all the hostility which *all* lovers experienced in the society that produced the *ghazal*, and millions who will never experience this hostility in the course of their own loves have, one hopes, the imaginative sympathy to identify with what such lovers must feel. The experience of unrequited love is still both universal and common. And even in modern society a man and a woman may fall so deeply in love that their love informs and guides their whole life, and yet live their lives physically apart because the fulfilment of their love for each other, which they would otherwise desire, would violate their obligations to others – husbands, wives, children – voluntarily entered into and voluntarily maintained to the end. To all such people and to all who have the humanity to identify with them, the *ghazal* still has a great deal to say.

In the wider areas of life this is perhaps even more generally true. We have seen that the *ghazal* poet's 'beloved' may be his God. In the now largely irreligious society of the West the force of this second identification is diminished if we express it simply in these words. In medieval society God was the source of all ideals in life, and God's will, and love of God, was the sanction which gave people the strength to remain true to these ideals. Today there are millions of people for whom such a religious sanction is not necessary, but whose ideals are as strongly and passionately believed in as religious ideals were in medieval society. In modern terms, therefore, the 'divine beloved' of the *ghazal* may be defined as those ideals in life to which the best and bravest of human beings dedicate themselves without counting the cost, and anyone who strives to be such a person can read the expression of this dedication in the symbols of the *ghazal* and can identify with its lover-hero and with the poet who speaks for him.

I said earlier that the *ghazal* concerns itself primarily with that area of human experience in which the 'lover', the self-sacrificing upholder of the highest ideals, is put to the supreme test, and sees how the rest of the world reacts to him. We have seen the categories, each personified in a stock character, into which the *ghazal* divides humanity when confronted with this situation. If you think of similar situations in recent history you will see how remarkably accurate the *ghazal* analysis is. For instance, the 'rival', the self-styled 'lover' whose real motive is mere self-interest, has a familiar modern counterpart in the politician who professes high ideals of service to 'the people' and sees this as no more than a means to attain his own selfish ends. Anyone who, in any society and any country in the world, takes a stand for principles which the establishment disapproves of will soon find how accurately the *ghazal* categories portray the most common reactions of his or her fellow-citizens. It soon becomes evident that few people are prepared for the sake of what they like to call an 'abstract principle' to do anything whatever that incurs even the mildest disapproval of those in authority over them. And when taking a stand for the principles they profess would mean putting their livelihood, or even their life, at risk, one knows very well what most people do. What was the attitude of most Germans during the Hitler years when the Jews were being exterminated? What was the attitude of most Americans when McCarthy and his lieutenants were slandering and persecuting those who upheld the principles set out in the Constitution of the USA and so found themselves accused of 'un-American activities'? Those small numbers of people who put their lives or their livelihoods at risk in those situations were acting as the lover-hero of the *ghazal* acts, and one hopes that both they and he command respect and admiration.

3. Mir – The Poet and the Man

I said in the last chapter that to understand and appreciate the *ghazal* is the most difficult task that confronts the modern Western student of Urdu literature, but it is the task which, once accomplished, brings the greatest reward. Certainly, to me, the *ghazal* is the crowning achievement of classical Urdu literature, and it is *ghazal* poetry that makes the strongest and deepest appeal to me.

The first of its greatest exponents was Mir, whose collected verse includes, along with verse in other forms, something like 1,500 *ghazals*. To me, he is still the greatest love poet in Urdu literature, and one of the great love poets of the world. But he faced in his own time, and his poetry still faces today, an attitude amongst many of those who formed his audience which prevented them from assessing his poetry at its true worth.

In the last chapter I raised the question: to what extent do a poet's *ghazals* represent his or her real experience and real outlook? In some extreme cases the answer seems to be, 'Not to any extent at all'. Love poetry of a sort can be written by people who have never been in love – either with a human beloved or with their God or with any high ideal in life. The rules of the *ghazal* both in regard to form and theme are so detailed, and its stock of traditional symbols and allusions so vast, that anyone who has grown up in Urdu-speaking society and has the technical competence can make a *ghazal* out of them. And Mir's difficulty arose from the fact that many in his audience assumed that *all* poets did just that, and nothing more. And when he claimed in his *ghazals*, as he frequently did, that he was *not* doing just that, and that his verses meant what they said, those claims too were all too often regarded as nothing more than the conventional expression of conventional themes.

Of course, it is impossible to prove conclusively that Mir's claim was a valid one. The ultimate test for the reader is whether or not for him or for her the poetry itself carries conviction that real, intense, sincere emotion is being expressed; and there may be sincere poets who cannot convince their readers of their sincerity, and insincere ones who come across as sincere. But for me, and for many thousands of others, the best of Mir's *ghazal* verses carry the absolute conviction of his sincerity. There is evidence besides the internal evidence of the *ghazals* themselves to sustain this conviction, and in this chapter I propose to present this evidence to you.[1]

Besides *ghazals* Mir wrote *masnavis* – short narrative poems in rhymed couplets – and a work in Persian prose *Zikr i Mir* (An Account of Mir), which is commonly described as his autobiography. In neither form is there any convention of saying what one has to say in any form that disguises the plain truth, and there is no reason to think that Mir is attempting any such disguise in what he writes in them. In two *masnavis* in particular he speaks in the first person, and in our *Three Mughal Poets* Khurshidul Islam and I assumed that he was speaking of his own experiences. It has since been pointed out to us[2] that writers may cast what they have to say in autobiographical form even where what they are writing is not strict autobiography; and that is of course true. True, but in my opinion not very significant, because Mir was clearly prepared to have his readers think that it *was* himself he was writing of and so to identify himself with the 'I' of his poems.

The first of the two *masnavis* is *Khvab o Khayal i Mir* (Mir's Fantasy). In it he describes how the cruel treatment with which he was punished for falling in love drove him mad, details the drastic measures, including starvation diet and copious blood-letting, employed to restore him to sanity, and tells of his eventual recovery; and the essentials of this incident in his life are supported by what he writes in *Zikr i Mir*. The second *masnavi* is *Mamlat i Ishq* (Transactions of Love – though in the case of this poem 'Stages of Love' would give a more accurate indication of its content). It tells of the inception, development, and tragic ending of his love for another woman.[3] It is significant that in neither poem does his mistress appear as the eternally cruel beloved of the *ghazal* drama – a point to which I shall return below. The outline of *Mamlat i Ishq*, told largely in his own words, is:

I would watch her whenever I was unobserved, but though my heart was full, I could not speak to her. Later we met discreetly when we could, and she was unfailingly kind and compassionate to me, though at times she would tease me too. For a long time things went no further than that, but in time we became more intimate, and she would let me hold her by the hand or touch her feet as I sat near her on the ground. I cannot describe her perfect beauty. She was as though cast in the mould of my desire, and her every limb was lovely. Her walk was incomparably graceful, and with all her beauty she was kind and loving too, and if she teased me, it was with such affection that it made me love her all the more. I would want to caress her, but she would only laugh, and would not let me. One day when she was eating betel leaf, I asked her to kiss me, and let me take the liquor of her mouth into my own; she laughed and refused at first, but later let me do as I wanted. Our love for each other increased, and I began to urge her to meet me where we should not have to fear any interruption. She too would speak of the same thing. But she kept delaying the day, and one day she said to me, 'No good can come of our love; how long can we go on pining for each other like this?' I was too consumed by love to see the truth of her words, but today I think of them and weep.

How can I describe what I suffered in separation from her? At nights I imagined her with me, but the days were unbearable. For years we did not see each other again. I was indifferent to the world, and to my wife and my children and my family. I would think with longing of the days when, in spite of all difficulties and dangers, I would sometimes come to her and sit silently by her. For her sake all my relatives and friends had set their faces against me and called me mad, and the meanest and most contemptible people had taunted me to my face. At last the grief of separation became more than either of us could bear. We met, and this time satisfied all the yearning of our hearts. We were together for several days, but there came a day when we again had to part. It was not her fault. Our fate was against us. She said, 'It is best that we should part for some time. In love there comes a stage when such things have to be faced. Do not think I am forsaking you, and do not grieve too much. As long as I live, you will be in my heart. I too grieve at this parting. But what can I do? My honour must be my first concern.' I could not speak in reply. I sat stunned and silent before her, trying to keep back the tears and speaking only if she spoke. After night fell, we parted, and I went from her lane as one who leaves behind him everything that is precious in the world.

I bear my sorrow alone. There is no one to whom I can tell my secret. Sometimes a message comes from her and I live again, but mostly nobody comes. How can I live parted from her like this? The memory of her is always with me – her loveliness, her tender love for me, her gentle speech, her grief at my distress, her longing to see me happy – and every memory brings the tears to my eyes. I long to be with her again, and without her I shall die.

It seems evident therefore that when Mir speaks in his *ghazals* of deep, passionate love for a woman he speaks of what he has himself experienced.

There is striking evidence too of the fundamental importance he attaches to love in every aspect of life. This is shown particularly clearly in *Zikr i Mir*. I have said that *Zikr i Mir* is generally referred to as his autobiography. It is difficult to know what else to call it, but it is not an autobiography in the sense in which we today understand the term, because Mir himself rarely comes into the foreground. In the bulk of it he tells the story of the decline of the Mughal Empire over the years 1748 to 1788, bringing in only an occasional reference to the way in which the course of events affected his own fortunes. But since this is the general character of the book it is all the more significant that a little more than the first third of it, covering only about ten years of a total span of sixty, is devoted almost entirely to stories of his father, of his father's young disciple Amanullah, whom Mir called 'uncle', and of their mystic associates; and it is abundantly clear that their teachings made a life-long impression upon him. They treated him as a child mature beyond his years, and he has vivid memories of the things they said to him or to others in his presence. Scholars dispute over the extent to which the incidents he relates can be regarded as reliable, but whether they are reliable or not, they testify to Mir's deep interest in mysticism and show what aspects of it most strongly appealed to him. Chief among these was the mystics' stress on the all-pervading force of love.

Above all it is what they had to say about love that he gives prominence to. He quotes his father's words to him, urging him to love and to learn that love is the supreme force in the universe. And years later he begins one of his *masnavis Shola e Ishq* (The Flame of Love) not with the lines in praise of God and the Prophet which convention prescribed, but with a hymn to love which virtually reproduces in Urdu verse these same words that his father had spoken to him. 'Love brought forth light out of the darkness,' it begins.

Without love God could not have made Himself manifest. Love alone drives on the work of the world: without it the world would cease to move, and the heavens to revolve. It is love that gave heat to the sun, love that scarred the heart of the moon. Love can set fire to water. It is love for the candle's flame that draws the moth to burn to death, and that same flame of love that melts the candle away. It is love that opens the delicate mouths of the rosebuds to blossom in a smile, love that moves the rose to unfold her beauty before the nightingale, and love for the rose that inspires the nightingale's sweet, lamenting song... It is love that sets man's heart aflame, that heart which, without love, is no better than a stone. It is love that inspires him to heroic deeds, love that makes him bow his neck gladly to receive the death blow from his beloved's sword, love that makes possible those things that, without love, man could not even conceive of. The whole firmament is filled with love, and earth and sky are brimming over with it.

The introduction to his own love story, *Mamlat i Ishq* (The Stages of Love) is on similar lines, and his own experience must have strengthened his conviction of the truth of his father's words.

I think, therefore, that Mir believed that the values one learns through the experience of love must guide one in every aspect of life, and that, to him, love for a woman, love for God, and love for a high ideal are three aspects of the working of a single spiritual force. And it is here that the *ghazal* theme of the cruel mistress, of whom so far as we know he had no experience in his own loves, stands him in good stead, for it affords him the means of expressing his belief that true love is absolutely unselfish, giving its all without demanding the slightest return, and proof not only against indifference but even against hatred. The true lover must be able, and *is* able, to 'love her that hates him'. In the mystic sense she is God – God who not only created all good, but all evil too, God who may afflict His true servant with life-long pain and suffering and yet whom His true servant loves with all his or her being.

In what one may call the quasi-mystic sense, the beloved may symbolize your country or your people, whom you labour all your life to serve, regardless of personal hardship, even though they never cease to reject you. Mir certainly felt himself to be in some sense in this position, as numbers of his verses testify. He speaks of being

مسافر ہی رہے اکثر وطن میں

a foreign traveller in my own land.[4]

as though he and his countrymen did not speak the same language:

رہی نگفتہ مرے دل میں داستاں میری

نہ اس دیار میں سمجھا کوئی زباں میری

How could I tell my tale in this strange land?
I speak a tongue they do not understand.[5]

Mir was firmly convinced that loyalty to God and His commands, which
entailed also loyalty to high ideals of personal conduct, brings upon you the
persecution of society no less certainly than loyalty to a human beloved; and
here it is important to be aware of the state of Mughal society in the age in which
Mir lived.

Mir was born in Agra, the one-time capital of the Mughal Empire, in 1722 or
1723 – fifteen years or so after the death of Aurangzeb, the last of the great
Mughal Emperors. The Empire had already declined from the zenith of its
power, but the decline had not yet become catastrophic. When he was about
sixteen he went to live in Delhi, a city which, in the words of T.G.Spear,[6] was
in those days 'a great and imperial city... with anything between one and two
million inhabitants... the largest and most renowned city, not only of India, but
of all the East, from Constantinople to Canton. Its court was brilliant, its
mosques and colleges numerous, and its literary and artistic fame as high as its
political renown.' Only a year later came the invasion of the Persian King Nadir
Shah, who completely defeated the Mughal armies, occupied Delhi, massacred
something like 20,000 of its citizens, and despoiled the city so ruthlessly that
after his return to Persia he was able to remit the revenue of his whole kingdom
for three years.

Mir lived in Delhi for twenty years, till 1760, years in which Nadir Shah's
Afghan successor, Ahmad Shah Abdali, invaded India three times – in 1748,
when he was turned back before he reached the capital, in 1757, when he
repeated Nadir Shah's occupation and looting of Delhi, so that when he returned
his cavalry marched on foot, loading their booty on their horses, while for
Abdali's goods alone 28,000 transport animals were needed [7] – and in 1760,
when, although he did not occupy Delhi himself, he allowed his soldiers to raid
and plunder it. Mir left the city in the same year, and did not return to it again
permanently until 1772. Then, for another ten years, he lived on there, in
conditions of great hardship, until in 1782 he migrated to Lucknow, the capital
of the great province of Avadh, where after nearly thirty years he died at the age
of 77 or 78.

During his long life he saw the rapid break-up of the Empire, and saw it for
many years from the capital, the point at which it could be seen most clearly.
He saw the provinces of the Empire fall away to become virtually independent

kingdoms. He saw the triumph of the Marathas to the South and their increasingly bold incursions into northern India until they made themselves the real masters of what was left of the Empire. He saw more plebeian movements of revolt gaining strength, like that of the Jats between Delhi and Agra and that of the Sikhs in the Panjab. He saw Delhi itself again and again attacked and looted by rival forces seeking the control of the Emperor, who alone could give constitutional sanction to their actions. He saw the Empire's own effective territory shrinking until it comprised no more than the region around Delhi itself, and increasing anarchy within that territory – a civil war that lasted for months, during which Old Delhi was plundered by the Jats, to determine who should be Chief Minister of the Empire; the victor in the struggle swearing on the Holy Quran to serve the Emperor loyally, and the next day throwing him into prison, later blinding him, and in the end murdering him. He saw soldiers, whose pay was anything up to three years in arrears, rioting in the streets, and peasants being submitted to artillery bombardment before they could be made to pay their taxes.

In all this turmoil every principle in which he believed was trampled under foot; for the men who dominated society and set the tone for everyone else the only value which had any meaning was self-interest asserted by treachery and violence. In short, the atmosphere was very much like that which is so vividly portrayed in Shakespeare's *Richard III*. A man who was your ally yesterday might be plotting your murder tomorrow, and ruthless, cold-blooded calculation decided everything.

This was not a congenial atmosphere for a man to whom the cardinal virtues were love and loyalty, and Mir, living at the centre of all this, and dependent like all the poets of his age on the patronage of the nobles, saw the disintegration of all moral values at close quarters. His reaction against it was bitter and intense. The uncertainties of the time often brought him long periods of distress and material hardship, and in this he finds at any rate one comfort. He writes:

گو توبہ سے زمانے کی جہاں میں مجھ کو

جاہ و ثروت کا میسر سر و ساماں نہ ہوا

شکر صد شکر کہ میں ذلّت و خواری کے سبب

کسی عنوان میں ہم چشمِ عزیزاں نہ ہوا

Although the fortunes of the age have not shown favour to me
So that the ways of wealth and grandeur could not be my ways
Praise be to God that I am poor and mean – for none can class me
With the great ones whom men delight to honour in these days.[8]

His *divans* (collections of *ghazals*) are full of verses lamenting the violation of
the old values.

عہد ہمارا تیرا ہے یہ جب میں گم ہے ہمر و وفا
اگلے زمانے میں تو یہی لوگوں کی رسم و عادت تھی

Ours is a dark age; men have lost all trace of love and loyalty.
In former days it was not so; these things were second nature then.[9]

کیا زمانہ نہ تھا وہ جو گزرا میر
ہم دگر لوگ چاہ کرتے تھے

What days were those! – the days that are no more,
The days when people loved their fellowmen.[10]

سو ملک پھرا لیکن پائی نہ وفا اک جا
جی کھا گئی ہے میرا اس جنس کی نایابی

Roaming from land to land I sought for loyalty.
Grief tears my heart; it is not to be found.[11]

And he says of an imaginary mistress, brought up in a society where these things
are the norm:

دوستی یاری الفت باہم عہد میں اس کے رسم نہیں
یہ جانیں ہیں مہر و وفا اک بات ہے گویا مدّت کی

Friendship, devotion, mutual regard –
All are outmoded fashions in her eyes.
She thinks that love and loyalty are things
One reads about in tales of days gone by.[12]

It is not difficult to see why Mir should have felt himself eternally at odds
with the society of his day – and not only with its powerful figures, but also with
all those around him who felt that high principles were all very well in their

way, but that a man has to make his way in the world and that in the practical business of life it is madness to bring high principles into it. To all this Mir replies, in effect, 'If your views are sanity, then give me madness every time'–and infuses into the conventional attacks on the *dunyadar*, the worldly-wise, an intensity of feeling which convinces us that for him at any rate, these attacks are not *merely* a convention. The wisdom, the 'good sense', of the worldly-wise is counterposed sometimes to the heart, whose impulses teach a much truer wisdom than the hard heads of 'practical' men, and sometimes to madness, portrayed with all its literal attributes, but symbolizing the conduct of a man so possessed by love (in all its senses) that he follows its dictates implicitly, regardless of what the world may think.

Just as madness is a symbol, so, I think, are wine, and revelry, and the idolatry of beauty. There is no evidence that Mir, so far as the externals of daily life were concerned, was in any marked way distinguishable from the average Muslim of his day; and in his poetry, wine and music and revelry, which banish the inhibitions of worldly wisdom and release the generous impulses in man's nature are, I think, simply the symbols of those impulses. The response to beauty, which is one aspect of the response to God, is symbolized by the worship of idols, a symbolism made easier by the standard metaphor (not unknown to modern English) of the idol in the sense of the adored mistress. All the same, the stress upon the essential oneness of the good Muslim and the good Hindu, is, I think, literally intended. Mir lived in an age when Muslim chauvinism – a Muslim sense of being separate from and superior to the Hindu majority – was on the increase. Many Muslims followed a trend already well in evidence in Akbar's time, and explained the decline of Mughal power as the end result of a long lapse from the true, strict principles of Islam, in which the pernicious influence of the Hindu environment had played a major part. Mir was quite definitely out of sympathy with this trend. The patron with whom he spent more years than any other and with whose conduct in public life he expresses the most satisfaction was the Hindu, Raja Nagar Mal. Where it was a common Muslim attitude to the Afghan Abdali to welcome him as the main hope for the restoration of pure Islamic government, Mir hated him as the invader and despoiler of his country, and expressed grim satisfaction when the turbulent Sikhs, for whom he felt no other sympathy, played such havoc with Abdali's army as it passed through the Panjab on its way back to Afghanistan.[13]

This attitude harmonizes well with the war against the *shaikh*, the self-satisfied pillar of orthodox Islam, which the *ghazal* convention wages. Once again one feels that Mir's verses on this theme represent much more than the mere observance of a convention. They have the same fresh vigour as the poems of his younger contemporary Robert Burns against the *shaikh's* spiritual kinsmen, the Holy Willies, and the 'unco guid' – the uncommonly good; and like Burns, range all the way from ridicule in which there is a sort of underlying pity, to invective of the most Rabelaisian kind.

Mir tried, according to his lights, to practise in his own life the values which he preached in his poetry. His autobiography, and many stories which others relate about him, amply illustrate his personal qualities. These stories have often been misinterpreted. From his own time onwards people have characterized him as a tactless, hypersensitive, and arrogant man. The first two charges may, I think, be conceded to be correct, though the environment in which he lived is perhaps more to blame than Mir himself. But the charge of arrogance seems to me in very large measure misplaced. The worldly-wise, the hard-headed realists, have always been ready to ascribe to arrogance the actions of a man who has too much self-respect and too much regard for principle to do as they do, and Mir's reputation has suffered a good deal at their hands. What they have called arrogance was, as I believe, a determination not to lie down under treatment which dishonoured and humiliated him, and – what is equally significant – a refusal to compromise his integrity as a poet. It was from the first motive that in 1772 he broke with a patron who had been his main support for the best part of fifteen years, though he was fifty years old at the time and had a wife and family to provide for, and though it brought him ten years of poverty and distress. Regard for the honour of his calling as a poet would not permit him, out of considerations of tact or the formal courtesies, to give a judgement on poetry which was not his true opinion. The best-known story in this connection is that of the 'two-and-three-quarters' poets.[14]

It is said that someone asked him whom he regarded as the poets of the age. 'First Sauda,' he replied. 'Next, your servant,' (that is, himself). Then, after a pause, 'And Dard is half a poet.' 'And Soz?' someone asked him. 'Oh, is he a poet too?' said Mir. 'Well, he is the *ustad* of Navvab Asaf ud Daula (the ruler of Avadh),' the man replied. 'Is that so?' said Mir. 'Well, make the total two-and-three-quarters then.' I think it would be quite wrong to regard this story as evidence of arrogance on Mir's part. In the first place, he and Sauda were generally regarded even at that time as being in a class of their own, while Dard was not quite of their level. As for Soz, we must note the grounds on which his claim is pressed. He is 'the *ustad* of Asaf ud Daula'. In other words he *must* be a great poet because he is the *ustad* of a great man. It is this characteristic but quite illogical assumption that provokes Mir's sarcastic reply. Finally it is worth noting that those who call Mir arrogant because he was pretty free with his strictures on his fellow poets, usually fail to notice that he was no less free with his praise of poetry which he thought good, even where it was the work of men who had not made a name for themselves.[15]

Both his self-respect as a man and his jealousy for the honour of poetry are perhaps involved in a story of the closing years of his life, when he had long been living in Lucknow. He had been invited there by the ruler of Avadh, Asaf ud Daula, who has just been mentioned, but some time after Asaf ud Daula's death his successor had discontinued his stipend, and he had for some time been living in poverty. One day a chance incident reminded the new Navvab of Mir's existence, and he sent a palace servant to him with a ceremonial robe and a present of one thousand rupees. Mir refused to take them, and told the servant to take them back to his master and tell him to give them in charity to some mosque. The Navvab was much taken aback, and tried again, sending the same presents, but this time by the hand of a young courtier-poet named Insha. Mir again refused them. Insha pressed him, urging him to accept, if not for his own sake, then for the sake of his wife and family, and adding that anyway one should not refuse a present from the ruling sovereign. Mir replied:

> He is king of his country and I am king of mine. If a complete stranger had behaved as he has, it would have been understandable, and I would have had no cause to complain. But he knows who I am and what my present situation is. All this time he has shown complete indifference towards me, and now he sends some menial with a robe for me. I would rather stay poor and hungry than submit myself to such insult.

It was only with the utmost difficulty that he was ultimately persuaded to change his mind.

Mir's life, then, testifies to the fact that his poetry is not 'just poetry' but the eloquent, sincere expression of his deepest feelings. His conviction that true poetry must be nothing less than this is evident in a story of his response to a young nobleman who approached him with a request to correct his verse. Mir told him:

> Young sir, you are a noble and the son of a noble. Practice horsemanship and archery and the handling of the lance. Poetry is a task for men whose hearts have been seared by the fire of love and pierced by the wounds of grief.[16]

He once said of his own verse:

مجھ کو شاعر نہ کہو میر کہ صاحب میں نے

درد و غم کتنے کئے جمع تو دیوان کیا

> Don't think me a mere poet – no, my verse
> Is made of pain and grief more than you know.[17]

and there is every reason to believe that this was so.

In short, when Mir in his best *ghazals* speaks as the lover – in all the wide range of senses which the word carries in the *ghazal* tradition – he speaks not in a role that he has assumed, but as himself. His poetry is that of a man who knew how to love with full commitment and who was ready to face all the hardships this entailed, alike in love for a woman and for those high ideals of conduct which reject with contempt the importance of social status and formal religious professions and unite all who share those ideals in a single community of people who contribute all that is most valuable to the life of humankind.

4. The *Ghazals* of Ghalib

Ghalib is by universal accord the greatest *ghazal* poet of the nineteenth century, and by equally universal accord his *ghazals* have something new and distinctive to say.

You may wonder how, within a form where themes and situations and imagery are prescribed in such detail, a poet *can* say anything new and distinctive. Well, firstly his style is distinctive – just as, to use a rough parallel, a man's handwriting is distinctive even if he writes the identical words that another man has written. And more important, the limitations of theme are not as severe as one might think. Firstly, the poet may present in a new light what I may call the stock characters of the *ghazal* – the lover, his mistress, his unworthy rivals for her love, and so on – or, in the sphere of religion and mysticism, he may again show in a new light man's relationship with God, his view of God's role in the universe, of the different prophets of Muslim tradition, and so on. Secondly, if themes of love (in both senses) predominate in the *ghazal*, they are not its only themes, and the *ghazals* of the great masters include verses on an almost unrestricted range of themes.

If I were to single out what seem to me to be the most characteristic, distinctive qualities which his Urdu poetry reveals, I would say that they are: firstly, a keen, unsentimental, detached observation of man and God and the universe; secondly, a strong sense of independence and self-respect; thirdly, a conviction of the originality, and of the value to mankind, of what he has to say and a determination to say it, upholding his beliefs to the end, no matter what other men may think of them (it is here above all perhaps that the *ghazal* tradition meets his needs most perfectly); fourthly, an ability to enjoy to the last drop everything that life brings, and yet to hold aloof, not to be trapped or enslaved by desire for the things he loves; and finally, a dry, irrepressible, unabashed humour which he is capable of bringing to the treatment of any theme, not excluding those on which he feels with the greatest seriousness and intensity. It is this last quality which has especially endeared him to successive generations of his readers.

Some of these qualities emerge clearly in his treatment of the conventional themes of love. The ambiguity or, as I would think it more accurate to call it, the universality of the 'beloved' serves the *ghazal* poet in good stead. His 'beloved' is someone, or some thing, to which his dedication is complete and unshakeable, but the precise identification varies from poet to poet. For Mir, Ghalib's greatest predecessor in this field, the identification with a woman already married to someone else is a valid one. Mir did love such a woman

deeply and constantly for years together, and suffered in consequence much of
the persecution which such a love incurred. Ghalib, almost equally certainly,
never experienced such love. He states his philosophy in a celebrated letter to
his friend Hatim Ali Beg Mihr in which he tries to persuade him to banish the
sorrow he felt at the recent death of a courtesan who had been his mistress:

Mirza Sahib, I don't like the way you're going on. I have lived sixty-five
years, and for fifty of them have seen all that this transient world of colour
and fragrance has to show. In the days of my lusty youth a man of perfect
wisdom counselled me, "Abstinence I do not approve: dissoluteness I do not
forbid. Eat, drink and be merry. But remember that the wise fly settles on the
sugar, and not on the honey." Well, I have always acted on his counsel. You
cannot mourn another's death unless you live yourself. And why all these
tears and lamentations? Give thanks to God for your freedom, and do not
grieve. And if you love your chains so much, then a Munna Jan is as good
as a Chunna Jan. When I think of Paradise and consider how if my sins are
forgiven me and I am installed in a palace with a houri, to live for ever in the
worthy woman's company, I am filled with dismay and fear brings my heart
into my mouth. How wearisome to find her always there! – a greater burden
than a man could bear. The same old palace, all of emerald made; the same
fruit-laden tree to cast its shade. And – God preserve her from all harm – the
same old houri on my arm! Come to your senses, brother, and get yourself
another.

Take a new woman each returning spring
For last year's almanac's a useless thing.[1]

The tone is of course humorous, and is adopted in a particular context which
it would take too long to go into here; but I think he is quite serious about the
philosophy of life which it expresses, and an entirely serious Persian letter
written many years earlier shows that it is one that he had formed quite early in
life.

Ghalib knew the joys of earthly love, and there are many verses which
express it:

نیند اُس کی ہے، دماغ اُس کا ہے راتیں اُس کی ہیں
تیری زلفیں جس کے بازو پر پریشاں ہوگئیں

Sleep is for him, pride is for him, the nights for him
Upon whose arm your tresses all dishevelled lay.

But he neither knew nor perhaps in practice believed in the kind of love for
a woman in which one devotes one's whole life and one's whole being
completely to her. He subscribes to the traditional view that the lot of the lover
– even if his love is not returned – is more enviable than that of any other man:

بیٹھا ہے جو کہ سایۂ دیوارِ یار میں
فرماں روائے کشورِ ہندوستان ہے

He who sits in the shade of his beloved's wall
Is lord and king of all the realm of Hindustan.

But if here we interpret 'beloved' in the more literal sense, it must be admitted that the beloved to whom it was applied might change from year to year. On the other hand, the verse can equally apply to a symbolic beloved, to a high ideal in life, and to the deep spiritual happiness which a man attains by serving it faithfully.

Given Ghalib's attitudes it is not surprising that in the conventional picture of human love, besides many verses distinctive in style rather than in content, there are many in which the rights of the *lover* are stressed as much as or more than the rights of this mistress, and in which the lover's self-respect is asserted. One of his *ghazals* begins:

ہر ایک بات پہ کہتے ہو تم کہ "تو کیا ہے؟"
تمہیں کہو کہ یہ اندازِ گفتگو کیا ہے؟

To every word that I utter you answer, 'What are you?'
You tell me, is *this* the way, then, I should be spoken to?

And another begins with a rejoinder to her taunt that what he suffers from is not love, but madness:

عشق مجھ کو نہیں وحشت ہی سہی
میری وحشت تری شہرت ہی سہی

'It is not love, but madness'? Be it so.
My madness is your reputation though.

– that is, it is my mad love for you that makes *you* famous.

The lover traditionally accepts all that fate has to inflict upon him, and is proud to do so for the sake of his love. Ghalib sometimes takes a different view, and one feels that it is not in any very respectful tone that he addresses his 'friend', as the Urdu *ghazal* calls the beloved (even though the friendly feelings are generally only on the lover's side), when he says:

یہ فتنہ آدمی کی خانہ دیرانی کو کیا کم ہے؟
ہوئے تم دوست جس کے، دشمن اُس کا آسماں کیوں ہو؟

A lover needs no more than this to work his ruin utterly.
You are his friend. What need is there for fate to be his enemy?

and, in the very next verse of the same *ghazal*, protests against the harsh treatment designed, as she alleges, to test him:

یہی ہے آزمانا، تو ستانا کس کو کہتے ہیں؟
عدو کے ہو لئے جب تم، تو میرا امتحان کیوں ہو؟

If this is testing, can you tell me, what would persecution be?
It was to *him* you gave your heart; what do you want with testing *me*?

It would not, I think, be true to say that no poet before Ghalib ever spoke of, or to, his beloved in this way, but it is certainly true that in Ghalib this bold, mocking tone occurs a good deal more frequently than in his predecessors.

But if these verses are especially characteristic of Ghalib, there are plenty more that are closer to the main tradition in their handling of the themes of earthly love. To those who have, so to speak, grown up in the company of the *ghazal* I think that perhaps these present no problem. To us in the West, they do. We have seen that Ghalib was not the man to bind himself in the bonds of a single love. Why then does he so often speak as though he were? If one takes the whole range of these verses, I think the answer is threefold. Firstly, some are there to show that he too can handle these themes just as well as the great masters of the past; and he does indeed show this. Secondly, in some of them he is creating in fantasy the beloved which real life denied him, and pouring out to her all the intensity of feeling which no real woman in his life ever inspired in him. And, stated in these terms, his situation is not an uncommon one in the history of the *ghazal*. I have argued elsewhere that in medieval society the ghazal often represented, for poet and audience alike, the release in fantasy of emotion which could not, without drastic consequences, have been released in real life.[2] In the typical case it is a fear (a very understandable fear) of the social consequences that holds the poet back from the forbidden joys of love: in Ghalib's case it was perhaps rather that no woman ever evoked in him the intense, all-consuming devotion that he would have wished to experience. In a letter written perhaps only a year or two before his death he looks back on his life and quotes a verse of the Persian poet Anwari as describing his own position:[3]

اے دریغانیست ممدوحے سزاوارِ مدیح

وے دریغانیست معشوقے سزاوارِ غزل

Alas! there is no patron who deserves my praise.
Alas! there is no mistress who inspires my verse.

It is perhaps not too fanciful to read into this something of the situation I have
described.

But there is a third explanation which, valid though I think the other two are,
has, I feel sure, a much wider relevance. This has to do with what I described
earlier as the universality of the *ghazal*'s symbolism. If one sketches the
character of the lover/hero of the *ghazal*, first with the context of literal earthly
love in mind, and then in more generalized terms, one can see its striking
relevance to Ghalib's character and personality, and to his expression of what
he feels in terms of the *ghazal* tradition. The lover is a man whom the experience
of an all-consuming love has completely transformed. Few men in the society
in which he lives have ever undergone such an experience, and to one who has
not undergone it, it is something that thought and emotion alike can hardly even
begin to comprehend. Yet it is this experience which alone gives meaning to the
lover's life. All other values, all other standards of conduct, are either discarded
or are absorbed into, and given new meaning by, the way of life which is learnt
from love, and which love alone can teach. The lover thus lives out among his
fellow men a life dedicated to, and directed by, ideals which even the most
sensitive and sympathetic among them cannot comprehend; and that great
majority which is neither particularly sensitive nor particularly sympathetic,
because it cannot comprehend his values, shuns him and fears him; and because
it fears him, hates him; and because it hates him, persecutes him. If one
condenses this description and expresses it in more general terms one can say
that the hero of the *ghazal*, and the *ghazal* poet casting himself in that role, is a
man to whom all the things that are most precious in life are the product of a
unique, nearly incommunicable experience which is to him all-important, but
which isolates him from his fellows and condemns him to live his life among
men who cannot understand him, let alone appreciate him, and who cannot
really accept him as one of their own community. But if this is true, any man
who is a poet and who feels himself to be in this position, can express what he
feels by using the *ghazal*'s portrayal of the situations of the lover as the symbols
of his own experience. Ghalib, both as a poet and as a man, felt himself to be in
this position, and used the *ghazal* in this way. His great poetic forebear Mir,
whose diction was often of a crystal simplicity, described himself in metaphor
as 'speaking a language no one understood'.[4] Of a great part of his own verse,
and more especially of the Persian work which he so prized, Ghalib could say
the same even in a literal sense. And in the metaphorical sense it was true even
of his Urdu, for in the best of his Urdu there is only a small proportion of which

audience's problem, not Ghalib's

it could be argued that it was the obscurity of his style that baffled his audience; for the most part it was the poverty of their emotional and intellectual experience that denied to the verse into which he distilled the essence of himself the appreciation which he justly felt to be its due. Writing to his friend Alai in his sixty-eighth year he says: '... I share your inauspicious stars, and feel your pain. I am a man devoted to one art. Yet by my faith I swear to you, my verse and prose has not won the praise it merited. *I* wrote it, and I alone appreciated it.'[5]

As a man, too, he often felt that he stood alone. He felt it the more keenly when he reflected on the reason for his position, for he was forced to conclude that he put himself in this position because he lived by the standards which all his fellows professed, but which he was almost alone in practising. He had seen the practical value of their professions in 1847, when he was imprisoned and when, of all of his friends in and around Delhi, only Shefta stood by him and fulfilled the obligations of friendship towards him. Nearly fourteen years later he still held to the same position, and, just as the lover accepts that steadfastness in love necessarily makes him the target of persecution, so does Ghalib accept that steadfastness in observing a high standard of personal conduct necessarily brings misfortunes in its train. He writes to his friend Shafaq in 1861: 'You are a prey to grief and sorrow, but...to be the target of the world's afflictions is proof of an inherent nobility – proof clear, and argument conclusive.'[6] This was a judgement he was to repeat in the words of one of his Persian verses little more than a year before his death, when he had to witness the spectacle of respectable gentlemen who had been on visiting terms with him taking the stand in court and testifying against his character in the most insulting and humiliating terms.[7]

بہ ہر چہ در نگری جز بجنس مائل نیست

عیارِ بے کسئ من شرافتِ نسبی است

Like draws to like, and all men draw to others of like quality
The measure of my friendlessness is my inborn nobility.

When therefore Ghalib depicts himself in his *ghazals* as the true lover of a beautiful woman, gladly suffering all her cruelties, what he is often doing is asserting in traditional symbolism his unshakeable conviction of the soundness of his values and/or of the high quality of his poetry, and declaring that so long as he has breath he will continue to affirm them:

لکھتے رہے جنوں کی حکایاتِ خوں چکاں

ہر چند اس میں ہاتھ ہمارے قلم ہوئے

I filled the blood-stained pages with the story of my love
And went on writing, even though my hands were smitten off.

Interpreted in this sense, many of the verses that on first reading seem to be depictions of love of man for woman are instead (or, perhaps, as well) expressions of emotions and belief which fall within the traditional category of mystic love of God but which, I have suggested, a modern audience understands most readily as dedication to ideals which are not necessarily religious.

Where Ghalib writes more explicitly in the mystic tradition his verses show the same sort of range as those which depict the situations of earthly love. For example, there are verses expressing the same bold, almost impudent attitude to God – his Divine Beloved – as some of those in which he addresses his human mistress. He demands from God treatment consistent with his self-respect. He tells Him:

بندگی میں بھی وہ آزادہ و خود بیں ہیں کہ ہم
اُلٹے پھر آئے در کعبہ اگر وا نہ ہوا

I serve You: yet my independent self-respect is such
I shall at once turn back if I should find the Ka'ba closed.

And in numbers of verses he makes it clear that he does not always receive such treatment. According to Muslim belief, man's good and evil deeds are written down by recording angels, and it is on their written testimony that his fate is decided on the Day of Judgement. What sort of justice is that? asks Ghalib. You take the evidence for the prosecution, but what about the witnesses for the defence?:

پکڑے جاتے ہیں فرشتوں کے لکھے پر ناحق
آدمی کوئی ہمارا دمِ تحریر بھی تھا

The angels write, and we are seized. Where is the justice there?
We too had someone present when they wrote their record down.

Here, as often, he speaks in some sense as the champion of humankind as a whole. Similarly he does so when, like other poets before him, he accuses God not only of injustice but of simple inconsistency in His treatment of mankind. He refers to the story of how when God created Adam He commanded the angels to bow down before him. All did so except Iblis – and Iblis was punished by eternal banishment from Heaven. If this, then, was the status that God intended for man, how is it that God himself has not continued to uphold it?

ہیں آج کیوں ذلیل؟ کہ کل تک نہ تھی پسند
گستاخیٔ فرشتہ ہماری جناب میں

Today we are abased. Why so? Till yesterday You would not brook
The insolence the angel showed towards our majesty.

Elsewhere Ghalib, being Ghalib, speaks not for humankind at large, but
specifically for himself in his relationship with God. Here am I, he says in effect,
a great poet, and a man of unique understanding, and there are You passing me
by and revealing Your secrets to men who cannot sustain them!

رگرنی تھی ہم پہ برقِ تجلّی، نہ طور پر
دیتے ہیں بادہ، ظرفِ قدح خوار دیکھ کر

You should have let your radiance fall on me, not on the Mount of Tur
One pours the wine having regard to what the drinker can contain.

The reference is to the story which appears in Christian guise as that of Moses
and the burning bush. The Mount of Tur is the place where God revealed his
radiance to Musa – the Muslim name to which our 'Moses' corresponds.
Ghalib's lines suggest two comparisons. The first is between himself and the
mountain – the huge, strong mountain, which for all its strength cannot compete
with man – man whose apparent frailty is more than counterbalanced by an
awareness and a sensitivity which enables him to accept from God the heavy
burden of a trust which even the mountains could not sustain.[8] Secondly, the
verse suggests a contrast between Ghalib and Musa. Musa's response to God's
radiance was to swoon before it; Ghalib would have had the strength to gaze
upon it.

He certainly does not accept either the earlier prophets or the outstanding
men of his own day as men who know all that a man needs to know, men in
whose guidance he can implicitly trust. Thus he says of Khizar, that somewhat
mysterious figure in Muslim legend who found and drank the water of eternal
life, who roams the desert places and comes to true Muslims who have lost their
way and guides them on to the right path, and who on one occasion explained
the mysterious working of God's benevolence to a perplexed Musa:

لازم نہیں کہ حضرؔ کی ہم پیروی کریں
جانا کہ اک بزرگ ہمیں ہم سفر ملے

I am not bound to take the path that Khizar indicates.
I'll think the old man comes to bear me company on my way.

Or, rather less politely, he hints that Khizar is in any case not above some
rather sharp practice. Legend has it that he guided Sikandar (Alexander the

Great) to look for the water of eternal life and that, in somewhat obscure circumstances, Khizar got it and drank it while Sikandar did not:

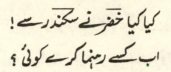

You know how Khizar treated Alexander.
How then can one make anyone one's guide?

And he states it as his own principle:

چلتا ہوں تھوڑی دور ہر اک تیز رو کے ساتھ
پہچانتا نہیں ہوں ابھی راہبر کو میں

I go some way with every man I see advancing swiftly.
So far I see no man whom I can take to be my guide.

One is reminded of what he once wrote in a letter to his friend Tufta: 'Don't think that everything men wrote in former ages is correct. There were fools born in those days too.'[9]

But if he sees himself as unique among men, he fully accepts, in line with the whole tradition of the *ghazal*, his oneness with his fellow men, the value of man *as* man, regardless of his formal religious and other allegiances. We have seen one aspect of this belief in his assertion of the rights of man in his relationship with God. He asserts the same values in relationships between man and man. And here he is not simply following a poetic convention. He was a man who had a wide circle of friends in all communities – Muslim, Hindu and British – and he rejected all narrow communal and national prejudices in his dealings with them. In one of his letters to his friend Tufta he wrote: 'My gracious friend, I hold all mankind to be my kin, and look upon all men – Muslim, Hindu, Christian – as my brothers, no matter what others may think.'[10] His verses express this attitude. One of them links it with the central tenet of Muslim belief – belief in the absolute oneness of God:

ہم موحّد ہیں ہمارا کیش ہے ترکِ رسوم
ملّتیں جب مٹ گئیں، اجزائے ایماں ہو گئیں

My creed is oneness, my belief abandonment of rituals;
Let all communities dissolve and constitute a single faith.

But like his predecessors he knows how hard it is for men to hold consistently to the principles of humanism, and he expresses this in paradox:

بس کہ دشوار ہے ہر کام کا آساں ہونا

آدمی کو بھی میسر نہیں انساں ہونا

How difficult an easy task can prove to be!
Even a man does not attain humanity.

Armed with this sort of philosophical outlook he surveys the whole human drama and the universe in which it is played. He recognizes how limited is the scope that the universe offers, both for joy pure and simple, and for that more complex joy which is inextricably linked with sorrow and sacrifice. And by the same token he recognizes that a man should live intensely, treasuring all that life can bring – not only its pleasures, but its suffering too. Poor Khizar again comes in for a rebuke in this context:

وہ زندہ ہم ہیں کہ ہیں روشناس خلق، اے خضر

نہ تم کہ چور بنے عمرِ جاوداں کے لئے

Khizar, *we* are alive who know the busy world of men
Not you, who slunk away unseen to steal eternal life.

Ghalib states his own attitude in two successive verses of a *ghazal*, deliberately parallel in their structure, in which he speaks in turn of the cruelty of fair women and the transience of spring, and stresses that without in any way blinding himself to these realities, it is to their beauty that he surrenders himself:

نہیں نگار کو الفت ، نہو، نگار تو ہے

روانئ روش و مستئ ادا کہئے

نہیں بہار کو فرصت، نہو، بہار تو ہے

طراوتِ چمن و خوبئ ہوا کہئے

The fair are cruel. What of it? They are fair.
Sing of their grace, their swaying symmetry.

Spring will not last. What of it? It is spring.
Sing of its breezes, of its greenery.

Or, in a more general statement:

دِلا، یہ دردِ والم بھی تو مغتنم ہے، کہ آخر
نہ گریۂ سحری ہے، نہ آہِ نیم شبی ہے

My heart, this grief and sorrow too is precious; for the day will come
You will not heave the midnight sigh nor shed your tears at early morn.

Linked with this view of life is a strong feeling for the value of the here and
now, and a marked scepticism about even the allegedly certain benefits still to
come. It is not that Ghalib lives only for the moment, heedless of the future; to
describe his outlook thus would be to cheapen it and do him less than justice. It
is rather that he seeks to live every moment to the full, prepared to face what is
still to come, but careful to make no optimistic assumptions about it. Verses in
which he expresses this sort of feeling even about life after death – usually in a
humorous tone – are strikingly frequent. He *knows* the joys that he has tested;
as a Muslim he believes in the coming joys of Paradise; and yet...after all he has
not proved them by experience. Best not assume too much. But anyway, leaving
aside the question of whether or not they will prove to be hereafter all that is
claimed for them, they are pleasing fancies here and now, and even at this rating
they have their value:

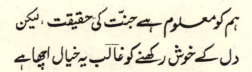

I know the truth, but, be that what it will,
The thought of Paradise beguiles me still.

The true Muslim is forbidden to drink wine here on earth, but in Paradise God
will give him to drink his fill of the wine of purity. Well, Ghalib has broken the
prohibition, and has verified here and now that wine is good to drink. So this, at
least, is one of the joys of Paradise that he has already proved. In fact, come to
think of it, it is perhaps the *only* joy of Paradise that he has proved; and he says:

وہ چیز، جس کے لئے ہم کو ہو بہشت عزیز
سوائے بادۂ گلفامِ مُشکبو کیا ہے؟

For what else should I value Paradise
If not the rose-red wine, fragrant with musk?

For the rest, he *hopes* that the joys he will know there will match the joys he has already known here in this present world. He tells his mistress:

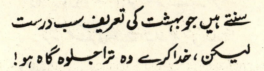

All that they say of Paradise is true, and yet –
God grant it be illumined by *your* radiance.

Space does not here permit more than the bare assertion, but in my view the vicissitudes of the historical period in which he lived, the traditions of his immediate ancestors, and the environment in which he passed his boyhood were all forces which led Ghalib to conclude early in life that he must 'settle on the sugar, and not on the honey' and to cultivate the attitudes that these verses express. It is very characteristic of him that, in life and in poetry alike, he shields himself against 'the slings and arrows of outrageous fortune' with an irrepressible, unquenchable humour, and with an ability to get outside himself and look at himself even in the most painful situations with a dry, ironical detachment. This is one of his most appealing qualities, and who can help warming to him when he tells his mistress who spurns his love, even though she knows that he demands nothing of her:

مَیں نے مانا کہ کچھ نہیں غالب

مُفت ہاتھ آئے، تو بُرا کیا ہے؟

I grant it you, my dear, Ghalib is nothing.
But if you get him free then what's the harm?

Part 2
Literature in Reaction to British Rule (1857-1922)

5. The Raj and the Muslim Response

The period in which 'Urdu literature' is almost synonymous with 'Urdu classical poetry' extends roughly from the first decades of the eighteenth century to the middle of the nineteenth, though, as we shall see, the *ghazal* has continued as an important part of the literature up to the present day.

After the revolt of 1857-59 a tremendous change took place, and in the second half of the nineteenth century the impact of British rule and of British Victorian values was so great that the whole character of Urdu literature was changed by it. In order to understand adequately the literature of this period, it is first necessary to know something of how these dramatic changes affected the Muslims of North India, and of the different ways in which they responded to the situation in which they found themselves.

The defeat of the great revolt made it impossible for the old outlook of the Muslim elite to continue unchallenged. This did not immediately become evident. In the early days of the revolt it must have seemed to many that the hopes, which they had never ceased to cherish, that their former power and influence would one day be restored were now at last about to be realized. The revolt broke out with Delhi as its centre, but with a sweep that extended throughout the Urdu – Hindi-speaking area from Delhi to the borders of Bengal. Its initial successes lasted several months; the rebel forces held Delhi from May to September, and the Mughal Emperor, hitherto for many years a mere pensioner of the British, was compelled to put himself at its head; and though the British retook Delhi in September 1857 and increasingly re-established their control during 1858, it was not until 1859 that the revolt could be regarded as finally crushed. But crushed it was, and that too with a ruthlessness that was traumatic in its effects; and thereafter the British impact fell with shattering force.

The completeness of the British victory showed unmistakably, to friends and enemies alike, that the old order was gone for ever and that its survivors must either come to terms with the new order or perish. Reactions among the old Mughal elite were necessarily drastic. Its role had not been as simple as the modern description of the revolt as 'the War of Independence' might suggest. Some sections of them had, unlike most of their fellow Muslims, been admirers of the British, and had supported them throughout. Much larger numbers had not indeed admired the British, but had been well enough aware of British strength to consider revolt against them doomed to failure; and these had done their best to keep clear, taking sides only if and when pressure of circumstances made it almost impossible to do otherwise. And only a few had wholeheartedly identified themselves with the revolt. Moreover, the struggle was not a national struggle in the sense which modern European history, and contemporary Asian, African and Latin American history, have given to the words – not, in other words, a struggle in which a new, coherent, almost mystic sense of a common nationality welded and inspired the forces of revolt, and in which those who opposed it were regarded as traitors to their people. One can speculate (if one likes speculating) on what would in fact have happened had the revolt succeeded, but there is no doubt that it consciously aimed at the restoration of the old Mughal Empire, that is, of a feudal type of society ruled by its traditional elite. That elite naturally determined its course of action in the revolt by a calculation of its own interests, and showed a sense of solidarity which continued before, during and after the revolt, regardless of the differing roles which its members played in it. The more plebeian element, though well aware of the lukewarmness of its upper-crust allies, regarded the traditional elite as its natural superiors, and the obvious rulers in the regime which would have replaced the defeated British power. The revolt therefore did not produce a great gulf within the Muslim community comparable to that, say, which in 1940-45 France divided those who collaborated with the Germans from those who led the resistance to them. The common aims and assumptions of all of its members always had been, and were long to remain, more important than the differences over strategies and tactics which had divided them and which had prescribed different courses of action during the revolt. There were no bitter mutual recriminations after the final, decisive defeat. The aims of the community remained the same – the regeneration of Islam, and the recovery of an elite position in the subcontinent.

There were, nonetheless, sharp differences of opinion about how best to pursue these aims. There were those who remained obdurately, though now for the most part silently, hostile to the British and all their ways. They had emerged from the struggle with heads, so to speak, bloody but unbowed. They recognized – as who could fail to recognize? – that British power was firm and unassailable for many, many years to come, and drew the conclusion that for the present the task was to abandon a hopeless political contest, to cherish the true spirit of Islam, to educate in that spirit all the members of the Muslim community who sought such education, and so keep their spiritual powder dry for some future day when the worldly prospects of Indian Islam would again improve and a return to the political field of battle would be practicable and desirable. The great centre for Muslims of this school was the theological seminary, which still flourishes, at Deoband, in north-western Uttar Pradesh.

There were others who saw the only hope for preserving whatever could be preserved of the privileges and influence of the old guard in a policy of 'If you can't beat them, join them.' The outstanding advocate of this policy was Sayyid Ahmad Khan (1817-1898), later to become *Sir* Sayyid Ahmad Khan, and now generally known simply as 'Sir Sayyid' both to Indian and to Pakistani Muslims. He came from an old aristocratic family, which had been close both to the Mughal court and to influential British figures long before the 1857 revolt. He had himself entered British service and during the revolt had, with considerable courage, stood unswervingly on the British side, regarding the uprising as an act of folly for which his community would have to pay dearly.

A man of immense energy and determination, he took stock of the situation after the defeat and evolved the policies which for the remaining forty years of his life he pursued consistently. The logic of his position could be stated like this: Muslim ascendancy was gone for ever, and only in one way could the traditional Muslim elite hope to restore its fortunes: by complete identification with the aims and outlook of the new, unchallengeable British rulers of India – an identification which would make it, in effect, the junior partner in a ruling British – Muslim alliance. This was to be achieved first by dissociation from all political activity not approved by the British; second, by education to implant the values of Victorian England in the minds of the educated, articulate sections of the Muslim community; and third, by a reinterpretation of Islam along modern lines.

Having determined what he thought was the proper aim for his community, Sir Sayyid commenced with an all-pervading zeal to remould his fellow-Muslims' thought along the lines most likely to help in achieving that aim. He argued against every traditional Muslim belief, idea and prejudice which stood as an obstacle in the way of reconciliation and harmony between the Muslims and their new British rulers. Islam correctly interpreted, he argued, led directly to the modern outlook of which, by the accidents of history, the British were now the spokesmen. There was, and could be, no contradiction between the teachings of the Quran and the teachings of modern science. There was a real and natural identity of interests between the British and the Muslims, and once misunderstandings on both sides were removed, this natural identity of interest would assert itself.

Sir Sayyid was often quite unscrupulous in his arguments, suppressing things that were inconvenient to his case and highlighting – even inventing – things that supported it. Thus, in a speech of 1884, he not only declared that the Muslims prayed that British rule in India might last for ever, but added unblushingly that the Muslims had always been on the British side and in fact had helped them to establish their rule. No matter was too small for his attention. He argued that Islam permitted Muslims to dine with the British, that the British practice of killing a chicken by wringing its neck was permitted by Islam, and that the unbecoming British habit of urinating from a standing position was not forbidden by the Muslim religion.

Sir Sayyid's movement came to be called the Aligarh movement from the college at Aligarh (now the Aligarh Muslim University) which he and his co-workers founded to be the centre and propagandist of what was called the New Light, and by the 1880s their zeal had established the 'Aligarh' policy as the dominant trend in the Muslim community – and in Urdu literature. Almost all the significant prose literature of the period was the work of Sir Sayyid himself and of his supporters and sympathizers, and it was voluminous, ranging over almost every field of writing and particularly effective in the prose narratives of Sarshar and Nazir Ahmad.

To a lesser but still significant extent the Aligarh movement affected Urdu poetry too. It did not at all approve of the subversive sentiments of the *ghazal*, and tried to dislodge it from its dominant position, to modify its traditional content so as to bring it into closer accord with Aligarh values, and to compel it to make room for a completely new kind of poetry which would directly express the thought and emotion appropriate to the new era. In this last aim it succeeded, but the traditional *ghazal* was (and is to this day) a formidable adversary to take on, and efforts to reform it made little headway.

Towards the end of the nineteenth century reaction against the Aligarh movement began to gather force, expressed above all in the verse of Akbar Ilahabadi (1846-1921). Akbar was not opposed to everything that Sir Sayyid and his supporters stood for. He saw, for example, the need for Muslims to embrace the opportunities to acquire a modern education and to use their new accomplishments to improve their material condition. But he did not accept the view propagated by Sir Sayyid, that British interests and Muslim interests were identical, and that Muslims should make themselves into brown Englishmen in everything except religion. He saw that the British were concerned with their own interests and nobody else's, and that English education was, for them, mainly a means of producing the supply of junior administrative clerks which they needed to govern the country. He saw that the new education could produce, and indeed was beginning to produce, a servile breed of people who blindly imitated their British masters' ways, took an absurd pride in adopting them, and looked upon their own traditional culture as old fashioned and obsolete. Akbar's verse is a sustained, witty polemic against these undesirable things; and though Akbar would not have agreed with the Aligarh ideologists' censure of the traditional *ghazal*, and though he himself wrote *ghazals* of merit, the polemic which preoccupied him demanded other forms in which to find adequate expression. Thus Akbar's popularity itself contributed something to the decline of the *ghazal's* importance. The traditional *ghazal* was left largely to poets who insulated themselves from modern movements by taking refuge in princely domains like Rampur and Hyderabad, where the old order was permitted to survive in return for its feudal rulers' loyalty to the British power. Understandably, these poets had little new to say. The best of them was Dagh (1831-1905) and his main distinctive qualities are his command of language and his frankness in describing sexual love.

By the turn of the century dissatisfaction with Sir Sayyid's policy was quite rapidly growing, and early in the twentieth century events occurred which by the end of the second decade brought the Muslim community into head-on collision with its British rulers. The new and powerful emotions that now arose in Muslim breasts found their fullest and most effective expression in the poetry of Iqbal (1877-1938). It is a remarkable and significant fact that the events which above all gave rise to this great change in Muslim opinion took place in countries hundreds of miles distant from India. South Asian Muslims have always had a romantic attachment to the original homeland of Islam in which they feel that the main roots of their culture lie, and in the years after their dominance in South Asia had been lost for ever – or if not for ever, for many, many years to come – they had derived some consolation from the fact that elsewhere Muslim dominance was still a fact, and that the Ottoman Empire still extended over an area stretching far beyond the boundaries of Turkey, the homeland of its rulers, into Europe, along the North African coast, and over the Arab lands of the Middle East. But the Ottoman Empire had long been under pressure from its non-Muslim enemies, attacked from within by its non-Muslim Greek and Bulgarian subjects, and from without by aggressive expanding Western imperialist powers, of whom the British rulers of India were one. Italian aggression against Libya in 1911, French aggression against Morocco in 1912, and the Balkan war of the same year, which ended Ottoman rule over all but a small part of the European mainland, all aroused indignation and sorrow in the hearts of the Muslims of India. When the First World War broke out in 1914 and Turkey entered it on the German side, Muslim feeling began to mount steadily higher, reaching a climax when Kemal Ataturk successfully resisted the Allied attempts to carve up his country. But the picture which Indian Muslims formed was an increasingly romantic and increasingly unrealistic one. For centuries now none of them had seriously believed that there was, or any more could be, a caliph of the whole Islamic world. But now in their Islamic fervour they conceived of the Ottoman Empire as a great, happy band of Islamic brothers, ruled over by their caliph, who was at once the ruler of a great empire and the spiritual head of the whole Islamic community. Kemal was his holy warrior, defending the Islamic community against the infidel. The Arabs who (manipulated, it is true, by the British and the French) had thrown off their allegiance to the Ottoman Empire, were in Indian Muslim eyes, shameful traitors to the community of Islam. It was this concept that now rallied the Muslims on an unprecedented scale to come out in open opposition to their British rulers.

The rise of the Khilafat (caliphate) Movement – that is, the movement in defence of the caliphate – took place at a time when all India was angry and indignant. The British, when they needed Indian support for their war, had given Indian leaders to understand that in return for such support they would, when the war was over, concede many of India's national demands; the support was given and the war was won, but when Indians now asked that British promises be kept, the British response was one of savage repression. Gandhi, at that time a relative newcomer on the Indian political scene, launched the first real mass non-cooperation movement to enforce Indian demands, and had the shrewdness to lead his predominantly Hindu mass following into an alliance with the already powerful Khilafat Movement, and a wave of enthusiasm for Hindu–Muslim unity swept the country.

The spirit of those times enabled the *ghazal* to recover much of its earlier importance and to produce *ghazal* poets of much greater merit than Dagh. The *ghazal* idiom is not one in which one can expect to find much direct reflection of specific political movements, but the relevance of the *ghazal* tradition to the kind of situation I have outlined is obvious. Its mood of revolt against the pillars of the established order (now identified with the British and their Indian supporters) and its stress on the oneness of all true lovers of God and the right – Muslim, Hindu and others – regardless of the names by which they know Him and the modes in which they worship Him, clearly struck a chord in the contemporary Muslim consciousness. This is the background of the poetry of

Hasrat Mohani, one of the best *ghazal* poets of this century. His name would certainly be listed as one of the worthwhile poets of the whole two-and-a-half centuries of the Urdu *ghazal's* history. It is significant that Muhammad Ali, perhaps the most popular of all the Muslim leaders in the Khilafat days, was also a *ghazal* poet, and that the bulk of his output belongs to this period. As poetry it is undistinguished, but for those who would understand the ideologies which inspired the Muslim movements of the period it is a document of some importance.

Ghazals also form a significant part of the work of Iqbal, and, what is equally important, concepts derived from the *ghazal* tradition inform the whole of his work to an extent unsuspected by some of the modern Iqbal scholars who have studied his work without a substantial knowledge of the *ghazal*. (For example, Iqbal's concept of *ishq* – love – comes straight from the *ghazal*, though he adds something of his own content to it.)

The Khilafat Movement, and the unprecedented unity between Hindus and Muslims which accompanied it, did not last. Both came to a sudden end in 1922. In February, Gandhi called off the non-cooperation movement when it was reaching its height; later in the same year Kemal first deprived the emperor caliph of his political functions and, two years later, abolished the caliphate altogether. Muslim leaders felt betrayed both by Gandhi and by Kemal, and they and their followers had ultimately to recognize that they had been sacrificing themselves in defence of an institution and an empire that had practically ceased to exist anywhere except in their own imagination. They had, as best they could, to come to terms with the true picture. They had to recognize that the Arabs had not been 'traitors to Islam' but people fighting for freedom from Turkish rule just as Indian Muslims were fighting for freedom from British rule; that Kemal was not in the least concerned to preserve the Ottoman Empire; that he had no desire to maintain Turkish rule over non-Turkish lands, and that he was fighting for a new Turkey in which secular norms would prevail, and medieval institutions, including the caliphate, would be abolished.

The year 1922 marked the beginning of a new and very different period. This will provide the subject matter for the last section of this book.

6. The Development of the Modern Novel

Early Narrative Fiction

The earliest narrative fiction in Urdu appeared in verse rather than in prose, in the *masnavi* form. Broadly speaking, these *masnavis* are of two kinds, and love is the theme of both. The first kind, which developed earlier than the second, comprises relatively short poems (one may describe them as being of short-story length) which describe in directly realistic terms the tragic stories of lovers — tragic, because in the society of the day love necessarily *was* a tragedy. Some of these poems are presented as accounts of the poet's own experiences. Those of Mir (?1722/3-1810), the great master of the lyric, are among the earliest and best in this class, while those of Shauq (d. 1871), written probably between 1846 and 1862,[1] are the last of real merit. In a society where that most drastic form of segregation of the sexes, the purdah system, is still widely prevalent, and where love is therefore by definition scandalous, orthodox opinion still frowns upon poems of this kind, and they are consequently less widely known and appreciated than they deserve to be. The best of them are fine and moving poems, and European taste would appreciate them as such. The other kind of *masnavi* is a much longer poem and tells the story of how young lovers, separated from each other by the magic powers of *jinns* and *peris,* are ultimately reunited to live happily ever after. By general consent the best of these is Mir Hasan's *Sihr ul Bayan* (The Enchanting Story), completed in 1785.[2] Its great popularity, which still continues, is well deserved, for within the conventional form Mir Hasan has written an essentially realistic poem in which the experiences of love are beautifully portrayed. It is worth noting in passing that his planning and construction of the story are outstandingly good; this stands in striking contrast to much of Urdu narrative prose fiction, where even to the present day faults of construction are particularly noticeable.

In prose, Urdu had to struggle much longer to supersede Persian. Up to the end of the eighteenth century no prose work written in Urdu would have been classed as a work of literature, and not until the late 1860s could an Urdu prose which really is quite distinctively Urdu establish itself as the norm. It is a striking indication of the long supremacy of Persian that it continued, even under the British, to be the language of administration; thus it was only in 1837 that Urdu took its place in the law courts of those areas of present-day Uttar Pradesh, Bihar, and Madhya Pradesh that were then under British rule.[3] Nevertheless, one can say that Urdu began, in effect, to contest its monopoly from about 1800, when works of narrative prose fiction made their appearance, consciously and deliberately written in the spoken idiom of educated native speakers of Urdu. The qualification 'in effect' is necessary because those who made the innovation did not do so with the conscious aim of ousting Persian as the normal medium of literary expression in prose, but for more temporary and mundane motives. By an accident of history the British authorities were closely involved in this. Shaista Akhtar Banu Suhrawardy, in her book *The Development of the Urdu Novel and Short Story* (London, 1945) has described how.[4]

> In order to enable the employees of the East India Company to learn the vernaculars, the Fort William College, Calcutta, was founded in 1800, and Dr John Gilchrist placed at the head of it.... He travelled in the regions where the choicest Urdu was spoken, and from Delhi, Lucknow, Cawnpore and Agra he collected a band of men who were masters of Urdu idiom. He set them to translate[5] into Urdu prose stories from Persian and Sanskrit. As the object was to get as quickly as possible books which could be used as textbooks for teaching young Englishmen Urdu, he had them written in easy flowing prose....

The best of these productions is generally held to be Mir Amman's *Bagh o Bahar* (Garden and Spring) which was written in 1801.[6] It is a story–or rather, five stories set within a single frame-story – very much in the style made familiar to the English reader by the *Arabian Nights*. Those who wish to acquaint themselves with it can do so through the rather literal, but quite readable translation of Duncan Forbes, published in London in 1862.[7] Nearly all the Fort William productions are stories of this kind.

It is significant that though these books were primarily intended as texts for English students, they did in the course of time reach a wider public. The process by which this happened has not been investigated as it deserves to be. The fact that Fort William College had a press which printed and published these works was doubtless an important factor. Nevertheless, judging by the India Office Library Catalogue of Hindustani (Urdu) Books, *Bagh o Bahar* seems to have taken nearly thirty years to acquire sufficient popularity in the real homeland of Urdu – the Delhi–Uttar Pradesh area – to warrant publication there.[8] The reception accorded to these Fort William works was by no means one of unmixed enthusiasm, and in Lucknow in particular they were the target of much ridicule – not on account of their subject-matter, but because of the language in which they were written. Every gentleman of taste, asserted the Lucknow critics, knew that this was not the way to write literary prose; and to show how it should be done they pointed to Rajab Ali Beg Sarur's *Fasana i Ajaib* (A Tale of Wonders).[9] It is not known when Sarur wrote this book, but according to his own statement it attracted little attention when it first appeared, and it was not until many years later that its popularity suddenly began to grow rapidly, and to such an extent that it was decided to print it. (This, it can be established, was between 1838 and 1842.) Sarur himself tells us that his literary ambitions first led him to attempt writing in Arabic and Persian, and only when he was regretfully forced to conclude that he would never excel in either of these languages did he turn to Urdu. It is clear that he consoled himself by making his

Urdu prose as close as he possibly could to the ornate Persian prose style then in fashion. *Fasana i Ajaib* is written in rhythmical, often rhyming, prose. The closest parallel to his prose in English literature is perhaps Lyly's *Euphues,* but a closer parallel still is provided by those passages of rhyming prose in the *Arabian Nights* which Burton was at such pains to imitate in his translation, and which he has done perhaps as well as it can be done in English.

This then was the style which for decades together contested with that of Mir Amman for acceptance as the norm, and the volume of support which it could command is amply attested by the number of editions of the book which continued to appear.[10]

Obviously this contest is of great importance in the history of the prose narrative in Urdu, but the accounts of it occupy what is, in my view, a disproportionate place in the histories of Urdu literature. For the main form of Urdu prose narrative before the modern period is neither that of Mir Amman nor that of Sarur, but that of what in Urdu is called the *dastan.* (Indeed, Sarur's book itself is only a special kind of *dastan.*) The word, which comes into Urdu from Persian, means simply 'story' or 'tale', but it is used primarily of enormous cycles of medieval romance, closely comparable to those of medieval Europe which Cervantes parodied in *Don Quixote.* The most famous is that which relates the exploits of the legendary champion of Islam, Amir Hamza,[11] the uncle of the Prophet, who, like the Christian knight of medieval European romance, rides through the pages of the tale fighting for the true faith against unbelievers, witches and sorcerers, and emerging triumphant over seemingly insuperable difficulties. Most popular in India was one part of this enormous cycle entitled *Tilism i Hoshruba* ('the enchantment which steals away one's senses') which itself comprises seven tall, bulky volumes, totalling more than 7,500 pages. (The totals for the complete *Tale of Amir Hamza* are 18 volumes and nearly 16,500 pages.) The stories on which the *dastan* is based seem almost certainly traditional in origin and go back several centuries. One Indian tradition was that the *Tale of Amir Hamza* was written in Persian by Faizi,[12] the great courtier of the Mughal Emperor Akbar (1556-1605), while some add that its purpose was to divert the Emperor's attention from the great Hindu epic, the *Mahabharata.*[13] But there is no evidence that this tradition is correct. As to content, the stories are almost certainly much older, while as to form, the most reliable writer on the subject[14] argues convincingly that the *dastan* assumed its present shape in the second half of the eighteenth century. The *dastans* were originally recited at the courts of the nobles, but also before more plebeian audiences, in very much the same way as their Arabic counterparts were once recited in Egypt. In fact the chapters headed 'Public Recitations of Romances' in E.W. Lane's classic *Manners and Customs of the Modern Egyptians,* first published in 1836, will serve also as a generally accurate description of the way the Urdu *dastans* were recited in India.[15] (The rhythmical prose, with its rhyming phrases, surely owes much of its origin to this tradition of recitation.) The *dastans* had been widely popular as oral literature long before the present version – or more accurately, the most substantial of the present versions – was written down, at the instance of Newal Kishore, the founder of a press which

still exists in Lucknow and has performed inestimable services to Urdu literature. The present versions are in part the work of two of the most famous
dastan-reciters of old Lucknow, Mir Muhammad Husain Jah and Ahmad Husain
Qamar. In publishing them Newal Kishore stated that they were translated from
Persian originals, but this is somewhat too large a claim. Persian versions of
some parts of the story do indeed exist, but there is no known Persian original
for the greater part of the work, and in at least one instance the 'translator'
himself notes that he has departed from the Persian version he has before him
because it does not accord with the story in the tradition with which he is
familiar. An inquiry recently made on this point to the successor of the Newal
Kishore Press brought the reply that 'No trace of Persian originals (of the
dastans in their present form) can be found. The truth is that there certainly were
one or two books on which they were based, but the *dastan*-reciters employed
by the Press used to come every day and recite the stories, and the scribes would
write them down.... And this is how they came into existence.' There is no reason
to doubt that the facts are substantially as here stated.[16]

The *dastans* are therefore, in the main, original Urdu works, and even so brief
an account of them makes it clear that the importance of Sarur's *Fasana i Ajaib*
should not be exaggerated. In both language and content it is entirely within the
dastan tradition, and the most that can be claimed for it, considered as a step
towards the development of the modern novel, is that its material is presented
within the compass of a single short volume.

The *dastans* can quite justly be called propagandist literature of a highly
tendentious kind. Everything is in black and white – the virtuous are all virtue
and the vicious all vice. It follows that there are no three-dimensional characters,
and very little realism of any kind. Neither is there anything that can really be
called a plot, nothing but a succession of episodes following one upon another
in endless profusion. It is noteworthy that the *dastans* flowered in the second
half of the eighteenth century, when the Mughal Empire was in headlong decline
and where every principle of conduct in the medieval code was everywhere and
every day being violated. Men who knew no other code, including those who
were daily offending against it, could escape from the sordid reality around them
into the world of the *dastans* where everything was splendidly simple and where
the true Muslim warrior not only behaved unfailingly as a true Muslim should,
but by doing so achieved the most eminently satisfactory results. Moreover, the
authors of the *dastans* had made provision for pleasing changes of diet. In the
Tale of Amir Hamza the hero is accompanied and supported in his exploits by
his trusty friend Amar Ayyar – Amar the Artful, who possesses magic powers
and uses them to reinforce Amir Hamza's valour. He does this mainly through
the use of his magic bag Zanbil into which he can cause almost anything to
disappear and out of which he can cause almost anything to emerge. Very often
he uses his magic to make his enemies look ridiculous, and his function in the
tale is thus, to a large extent, to give comic relief from the prevailing atmosphere
of high seriousness. Relief of another kind is provided by episodes with a love
interest, in which the Islamic warriors' amorous adventures are related, often in
circumstantial and titillating detail. (Their conduct in these scenes is not quite

perhaps that which strict adherence to Islam would permit; but everyone seems to have been too absorbed to notice this.) Thus the *dastans* provided a rich banquet of good and varied fare.

The Transition To The Novel

Ratan Nath Sarshar (1846-1902)

The elements of the modern novel come into Urdu literature piecemeal, and the development is most clearly seen if one follows a logical, rather than a strictly chronological, order, beginning with the work which is closest to the *dastan*, namely, Ratan Nath Sarshar's[17] *Fasana i Azad* (*The Tale of Azad*). Sarshar himself was at pains to emphasize that *Fasana i Azad* was something quite new in Urdu fiction, and, as we shall see, there are good grounds for his claim. But for all that, its points of resemblance to the *dastan* are striking. The most obvious resemblance is in sheer length; its four larger-than-A4 size volumes contain about 3,000 pages in all, with two columns of print to the page. (A rough word count gives a total of two-and-a-quarter million as against about 700,000 words for the Maudes' English translation of Tolstoy's *War and Peace*.) But this is only the first resemblance of many. Azad, its hero, is a typical, two-dimensional *dastan* hero – handsome, brave, intelligent, talented, a great lover (though at the same time, of course, purity itself), and a great champion of the right. There is the same absence of plot, the same endless succession of loosely connected episodes, the same pattern of innumerable difficulties triumphantly surmounted, and the same black and white tendentiousness. Just as Amir Hamza has his faithful companion Amar the Artful, so does Azad have *his* faithful companion Khoji, and Khoji's main function is, like Amar's, to provide comic relief. Finally there is a marked resemblance even in style and language, for Sarshar is almost as fond of rhyming prose as the *dastan* writers were. Thus is would not be hard to defend the statement that *Fasana i Azad* is in the direct line of descent from the *dastan*.

Nevertheless, in *Fasana i Azad* the *dastan* form is adapted to what is in one major respect a new content. Azad is the champion of the New Light against the Old, the champion of modernism (which, in this context, means the values and outlook of Victorian England) against every form of medievalism. Very conveniently, historical circumstances enabled him to be at the same time the champion of Islam, in true *dastan* tradition; for the framework story tells how Azad falls in love with a beautiful, pure, and above all *educated* lady named Husn Ara ('Beauty-adorning') and is commanded by her to go off to the Crimean War and fight alongside the British and his fellow-Muslims, the Turks, in their struggle with the Russians. He does so, and returning victorious after countless adventures, wins Husn Ara's hand. (Had Sarshar been writing a few decades later, when the expansion of the European powers brought them into conflict with the Muslim states in the Near and Middle East, he would have been denied this happy chance of combining his hero's new role with the old. But in fairness to him it must be added that when at the end of the last volume the British authorities in India ask Azad's help in their war against Muslim Afghanistan, he gives it without hesitation. It is the fight for modernity which is his real mission.) Another major difference from the *dastans* is that *Fasana i Azad* is virtually free of supernatural incident, and its setting is in the contemporary world. In the earlier part the scene is laid in nineteenth-century Lucknow, which is vividly and realistically described.

Thus there is a certain parallel between *Fasana i Azad* and *Don Quixote*, and we know that *Don Quixote* did in fact directly influence Sarshar.[18] His later book *Khudai Faujdar* (The Godly Warrior) *is Don Quixote*, though considerably abridged and freely adapted. In *Fasana i Azad* itself, the character of Khoji, Azad's ignorant, uncultured, cowardly, blustering, but faithful friend, owes at least as much to Sancho Panza as it does to Amar the Artful. But in other respects Sarshar's characters are, of course, the reverse of Cervantes'. Whereas Don Quixote is the deluded champion of the old, Azad is the clear-thinking, self-confident champion of the new. Whereas Sancho Panza is, in one of his aspects, the expression of down-to-earth common sense, Khoji is, especially in the earlier part of the book, little more than a buffoon, the personification of everything ridiculous and outmoded in the traditional Indian way of life. True, as the story progresses he becomes a more complex figure, embodying also, especially in his complete loyalty to Azad, much that was admirable in the old order; and here there is a certain parallel between him and Don Quixote. Other differences between the two writers go deeper. Sarshar has nothing of Cervantes' mature wisdom, or of his intellectual and artistic power. His modernism is of the most crude and uncritical kind. The values and the way of life of Victorian England are to him the last word in human wisdom, and all that is 'old-fashioned' in Indian life (with the one significant exception of the purdah system) is condemned in an equally wholesale way. Once again one is reminded of the *dastans*, where good is unalloyed good and evil unalloyed evil, and the struggle between them free of all possible ambiguity. But to say no more on this point would be to do Sarshar an injustice. In his crude extremism Sarshar is the child of his age. In the 1870s the cultural conflict in Muslim India as a whole was all around him being fought out in just these extreme terms. These were the years in which Sir Sayyid Ahmad Khan was bringing about those radical changes in the outlook of the Muslim upper classes which for better or worse (for better *and* worse would perhaps be more accurate) were to determine their course of action for a century to come. Sir Sayyid was perfectly clear about what he was attempting. It was his aim, he said, 'to produce a class of persons, Muslim in religion, Indian in blood and colour, but English in taste, in opinions and in intellect.'[19] (The words, except for 'Muslim in religion', are taken bodily from that most extreme manifesto of British cultural policy in India, Macaulay's Minute on Education of 1835.)[20] And he made equally clear to his compatriots how far he thought they would have to travel to reach this desirable goal. In a letter from London dated 15 October, 1869, he wrote: 'The natives of India, high and low...educated and illiterate, when contrasted with the English in education, manners, and uprightness, are as like them as a dirty animal is to an able and handsome man.'

(It should be stressed that this is not an opinion confidentially expressed in a private letter; the letter was intended for publication in India and was duly published there.)[21] Not surprisingly, the opponents of the New Light were driven by this kind of thing to a similar extremism and championed the cause of everything traditional simply because it *was* traditional. In any true appreciation of *Fasana i Azad* all this has to be borne in mind. Not only is Sarshar's own attitude fully typical; his characters too, with their wholesale acceptance or wholesale rejection of the New Light, are portrayed with a greater realism than the present-day reader might at first sight think.

Two extracts will serve to illustrate both the weakness and the strength of Sarshar's work. At one point in the story[22] Azad runs into an old friend who asks him, quite out of the blue, whether he thinks the Europeans and the Bengalis more advanced than the people of Lucknow. Azad says that undoubtedly they are, but his friend demands proof, which Azad promises to give him. Next day as soon as it is light they set off together, and walk until they have left the city proper behind them and reached the cantonment. There they see from the road a fine bungalow standing in well-kept grounds, and inside it, an English gentleman and his wife taking their breakfast. Sarshar's description is interesting. The English gentleman is barely mentioned, but the lady is accorded the full *dastan* treatment, rhyming prose and all (which, however, I have not attempted to reproduce in my translation).

There in a fine room was a Sahib seated on a chair, and near him an idol [the standard metaphor for a beautiful woman] with a face like a houri of Paradise – her body as delicate, and her cheeks as red, as a rose – gracing a more delicate chair. Here face was radiant, her black dress was of costly silk, and her perfume so fragrant that gusts of its were wafted to the road outside and permeated all one's senses. Both were conversing sweetly together and making short work of [the expression in the original is equally colloquial] some mutton chops. Azad's friend was lost in admiration and delight.

In other words, the sight of a nondescript Englishman and a highly perfumed Englishwoman eating mutton chops at about seven in the morning[23] is enough to prove the superiority of the English way of life! The narrative continues:

They pressed on. Five young Bengalis were coming towards them in a carriage – one a barrister, one a civil servant, two MAs and one BA. [Azad seems to have detected these details at sight.] Azad knew one of them, and greeted him. He got down and offered Azad a cigar. Inquiry revealed that all the other four came of a poor family, but friends of their learned father had raised the money to send them to England to be educated; and now they held important positions....

And so on and so forth.

This kind of thing is so crude as to be laughable. Yet side by side with it one finds pieces of excellent descriptive and realistic writing. In the first volume,[24] where Azad has not yet gone off to the war, he and Khoji go on a railway journey from Lucknow. They reach the station in good time, and Azad finds the refreshment room and goes in. Sarshar continues: 'He was delighted with what he saw: everything was spotlessly clean and in its proper place. From one end of the room to the other were tables with chairs arranged round them, and glasses set out upon them. Lamps were burning brightly on all sides. Azad sat down. "Bring me something to eat," he said. "But, mind you, no wine, and nothing with pork in it."....' The waiter, spick and span in his clean uniform, and with a turban on his head, brought him all manner of English dishes [*sic*] which he served from costly plates of the most expensive kind. Azad plied his knife and fork with a will, and finished off with lemonade and soda-water. When he came out, there was Khoji, his bedding unrolled on the platform, eating parathas and kababs.

'You look as though you're doing all right,' said Azad, 'the way you're scoffing those kababs.'

'That's right,' said Khoji, 'some of us like kababs and some of us like wine.'

'What do you mean, "Some of us like wine"? Do you think I've been drinking wine? I never touch the stuff. I'll swear on the Quran I haven't touched a drop. You might as well accuse me of eating pork.'

Khoji smiled. 'Right!' he said. 'You wouldn't let *that* chance slip. "You might as well say I've been eating pork!" he says. Well said! You have to think these things forbidden or repulsive to keep off them. But both are allowed to you. You think it's a great thing to have them. Well done, my friend! Today you've really shown your paces!'

'Have you finished? Or do you want to go on abusing me? I tell you, you can put me on oath. I've not so much as put my hand to wine; I've not even looked at pork.'

'You put that well. All right, you haven't put your hand to wine. But it went down you throat, I'll be bound. And anyway, who takes any notice of *your* oaths? An oath means nothing to you. *I* can't make out to this day what your religion is....Oh well, we shall all get the reward of our deeds. Why should I worry about it?'

'You're not going to admit you're wrong, are you?'

'Why should I? Didn't I see you with my own eyes using a knife and fork?'

'Well? Do you think you drink wine with a knife and fork?'

'How do *I* know how you drink wine? Better ask one of your drunken friends about that. But I'm sorry you're so far gone. What a pity! What a shame!'

'Do just one thing for me: just go into the refreshment room and see for yourself.'

'What, *me*? Me, a true Muslim, go into a refreshment room? God forbid! God save us! I leave that to you, and welcome. *Me? Go into a refreshment room? May God protect me!*'

Azad left Khoji to his kababs and strolled along the platform. A gentleman with a beard a yard long accosted him, 'Well, sir, may I know your name?'

'Azad.'

'Azad.' He smiled. 'Yes, indeed. The name suits you. Freedom and free-thinking [Azad means free, but its senses range from liberty to licence and 'free-thinking'] are written all over you. And your religion?'

Azad quoted a Persian verse and then replied, 'Respected sir, your humble servant is a Muslim. Islam is my faith, and I observe the Shariat [Muslim religious law]. And *your* name, Maulvi Sahib?'

'Never mind *my* name. Allow me to express my sorrow.'

'Please do. Burst into tears if you like. But remember that Muharram [the month when the martyrdom of Husain, the grandson of the Prophet, is mourned] isn't far off. You'll be able to weep then to your heart's content. Why so impatient?'

'You say you are a Muslim and observe the Shariat, and yet you go into a restaurant and drink wine. God have mercy on us! My good man, do you never think of Judgement Day?'

'Respected sir, what can I say? I have no more to say to you. God save us!'

'Pardon me if I am rude; but think of yourself when you say "God save us!" Well, you have done Satan's work, but praise God that your better self reproaches you.'

'Maulana, I swear by God I took only food in the restaurant, and that too only what Islam permits. Be fair! What is wrong with that? After all, in Istambul everybody – including the most eminent doctors of Islam – dine with Christians. Why on earth is it that in India Muslims think it a sin?'

'Listen; I'll explain it all to you. To eat in a restaurant is not creditable to a Muslim. If you'd spread your mat and had the same food brought out to you, that would have been all right. That too would have been open to objection, but not to the same extent. Then again, you may swear as many oaths as you like, with the Quran raised in your hand, but no one will *believe* that you didn't have pork and wine. If you trade in coals your hands will get black. And don't talk to me about Istambul. The Shah of Persia drinks wine and orders the most expensive brandy. But does that make wine-drinking permissible? Let the Turks eat with Christians as much as they like. That doesn't mean that *we* should. It's against our traditions to do so. Have you got to live in Istambul? Or have you got to live here in India? When you're *in* Istambul, do as they do. But are we talking about Istambul or are we talking about India? After all, there's no lack of food outside the restaurant – kababs, parathas, biscuits, everything. So what was to be gained by going there? Why make yourself conspicuous and get yourself laughed at for nothing?'

'My dear sir. First, the food in there is fine and tasty. Secondly, the place is spotlessly clean. Then you can sit and *enjoy* the food. There's a man to pull the fan. The fan is clean. The plates are clean. The tables are clean. There are four waiters standing ready to serve you. Can I get all that outside? God save us!'

'The food may be fine according to *your* taste. As for the fan, out here you can pay a pice [about a farthing] and get yourself fanned for an hour at a time. And what do you want with cleanliness when you are travelling? Besides, it's not as though things out here are filthy dirty. If *you're* over-particular, that's quite another matter. Anyway, it's your business and you can get on with it. But youngsters should listen to what their elders tell them. I've told you. But you must do as you like.'

Azad thought to himself, 'I shan't do such a stupid thing again. It's up to me whether I eat in a restaurant or not, but I don't have to advertise the fact. From now on I'll be more discreet.'

'Well,' said Khoji, '*now* what about it? You thought you could make a fool of *me*; but now the Maulvi Sahib has told you off. I bet you won't go again in a hurry!'

It is clear that we are here dealing with modern realistic writing of considerable talent, which owes little or nothing to the *dastan* tradition; and because such writing in not rare in *Fasana i Azad,* it is, despite its obvious links with the *dastan,* at the same time a work which brought permanently into Urdu literature some of the major elements of the modern novel.

Nazir Ahmad (1836-1912)

Sarshar continued to write prose fiction for nearly twenty years after *Fasana i Azad* appeared, but none of his subsequent works shows any very great advance upon the best in what he had already achieved, and a rapid and very marked decline soon sets in. To see the advance towards the modern novel carried further, one has to turn to his older contemporary, Nazir Ahmad.

Nazir Ahmad was ten years older than Sarshar, and the first of the series of tales which he wrote between 1869 and 1892[25] pre-dates *Fasana i Azad* by some years. (Nazir Ahmad's first tale, *Mirat ul Arus, [The Bride's Mirror],* was written in 1869. The first instalment of *Fasana i Azad* – it appeared initially as a serial – came out in 1878, and the last in 1879. It was issued in book form in the following year.) But whereas Sarshar's power as a writer soon wanes, Nazir Ahmad's continues strong throughout at any rate the greater part of his literary life. He was a man of much more vigorous intellect than Sarshar, with a stronger character and a keener sense of realism, and these qualities are reflected in his writings. They have led most modern Urdu critics to regard him as a novelist, and to judge him accordingly. From this standpoint they have either praised him extravagantly or else belittled his achievement – with the majority taking the latter course. But to judge him as a novelist is in itself to do him a serious injustice, and one which is all the less excusable because he himself to the end of his days never made any claim to be one. He wrote to instruct, and he chose a fictional form because in that way he could make his instruction more palatable. That he makes no larger claim than this is clear from a preface written in the year of his death to a little text-book on writing the Urdu script. There he tells us: 'I began writing books at the time when my own children were of an age to start their schooling. I had my own experience both of learning and teaching, and as an employee in the Education Department had also had the occasion to supervise teaching. I knew in every detail all the defects of the educational methods and of the books in use. "Once you have seen the fly in your drink, you cannot swallow it" – and so I began to write books on my own account and to teach from them. This was the motive which first impelled me to write.'[26] This is entirely in keeping with what he had written more than forty years earlier, explaining how his first book, *Mirat ul Arus,* came to be written.[27] Its quite unexpectedly large measure of success[28] encouraged him to write other tales, planned now for a larger audience, but with similar aims in view.

An outline account of *Mirat ul Arus*, which is available in an English translation by G.E. Ward (London, Henry Frowde, 1903) illustrates well enough the method of all of them. The aim of the book is to show the young Muslim girl what qualities she must cultivate if she is to meet successfully the problems she will face when she is married. In this case the lesson is taught by a story in two parts – the first a cautionary tale of a girl named Akbari, and the second (which Nazir Ahmad in fact wrote some eighteen months after his daughter had finished with Akbari and was clamouring for more)[29] the story of her model sister Asghari. Akbari has always been spoilt, and the result is that when she is married and goes to her new home (which meant, as in most cases it still means, the home of her husband's parents) she cannot stand the trials to which every new wife is subjected and has a very miserable time of it. The passage in which Nazir Ahmad concludes his account of Akbari's misadventures and turns to Asghari sets the tone of the book.[30]

> Now listen to the story of Asghari. This girl was to her family what a rose in full bloom is to a garden, or the eye to a human body. Every kind of acquired excellence, every kind of natural intelligence was hers. Good sense, self-restraint, modesty, consideration for others – all these qualities God had bestowed upon her. From her childhood she had a distaste for romping and jesting and ill-natured jokes.* She loved reading, or doing the work of the house. No one had ever seen her chattering rubbish, or quarrelling with anybody. All the women of the *muhalla* loved her as they did their own daughters. Blessed indeed was the fate of those parents who owned Asghari for a daughter! And happy was the lot of that family into which Asghari was now to be admitted as a bride![31]

Asghari is married at the age of thirteen, and the first period of her life in her new home is well described.[32]

> In the earlier days of her wedded life Asghari did feel very ill at ease, as was only natural after suddenly quitting her mother's house to live among entire strangers. She had become inured to a life of constant activity and supervision; she could not bear to be without employment for a quarter of an hour. And now she was condemned to sit demurely, confined to one room, with nothing going on, for months together. The liberty which she enjoyed in her parents' home was no longer hers. As soon as she arrived in her mother-in-law's house, everyone was intent on watching her, and scrutinizing her every action. One scans her features; another appraises the length of her hair; another guesses her height; another examines her jewels: and another takes stock of her clothes. If she eats anything, each morsel is observed. What sized bit did she take? How wide did she open her mouth? How did she masticate it? And how did she gulp it down? If she rises from

---

*'Ill-natured jokes' is a stronger phrase than the original Urdu warrants: 'teasing' would be a nearer equivalent.

her seat, they look to see how she robes herself in her mantle, how she holds up her skirts. And if she sleeps, they count the hours; what time did she go to sleep? When did she get up? In short, every phase of her deportment was under observation.

All this was terribly distressing to poor Asghari; but since she was endowed with common sense and a good education, she emerged with credit even from this ordeal, and her manners in general were approved of by her husband's relations.

From this good beginning Asghari proceeds by unfailing tact, a proper humility before her elders, constant hard work, and sheer cold-blooded calculation and intrigue, not only in triumphing over all her difficulties, but also in establishing herself as the real ruler of the household.

Mirat ul Arus was followed by *Banat un Nash* (literally 'Daughters of the Bier' – one of the names given in Urdu to the constellation of the Plough) which is a sequel to it.[33] It consists mainly of an account of a school set up by Asghari for the girls of the *muhalla,* and details at length the lessons on history, geography and elementary science which she taught in it. A third book, *Taubat un Nasuh,* was written to counter indifference to religion, and others to show the evils of polygamy, to ridicule the practice advocated in some advanced modernist circles of adopting English dress and furniture and manners, to argue (rather cautiously) for widow re-marriage, and to expound the application of Islam to modern problems.[34] The didactic aim is well to the fore in all of them, and was intended to be.

Of these tales *Taubat un Nasuh* (The Repentance of Nasuh) has won more popularity than the others, mainly, perhaps, because its message, unlike that of some of the other tales, is one which the orthodox can approve without reservation, and because, while the others deal each with a relatively restricted, though important, theme, this ranges more widely and seeks to inculcate the importance of religion to the whole conduct of life. But on purely literary grounds too it fully deserves its reputation.

The book begins with an account of a cholera epidemic in Delhi. After three other members of his household (including his father) have died Nasuh himself succumbs. He thinks that his last days have come, but the doctor gives him a powerful medicine which saves him. He falls asleep, and has a vivid dream of a court room in which God as judge is judging people being brought before him. Nasuh is astonished to see his father among those in custody awaiting trial, because his father had been a popular and much respected man. His father shows him the record of his deeds, which includes a long chargesheet, each charge supported not by reference to the Indian Penal Code, but by reference to verses of the Quran.

Nasuh awakes, full of regret at his own laxness in religion and his failure to instruct his family properly and bring them up in religious ways. He begins to observe all his religious duties, and radically changes his behaviour towards his family. His household had always lived in awe of him and his quick temper, but now there is no trace of this in his behaviour.

He sends for his wife, Fahmida, a woman who has received some education 'because by that time', Nazir Ahmad innocently tells us, '*Mirat ul Arus* had been widely read, and in many families people had begun to act on its advice.' Nasuh tells Fahmida of his dream and of his change of heart. She is much impressed, and he discusses with her what is to be done and enlists her willing help.

The rest of the book describes Nasuh's efforts to bring home to his children the importance of their religious duties. The younger ones – the six-year-old Hamida and her brothers Salim (10) and Alim (14-15) – respond readily, but the two elder ones, Naima and her brother Kalim, both of whom are grown up and married, are far from ready to reform their ways. The first storm bursts when Naima and her mother have a violent quarrel. Naima had been married two years ago, and after living for two years at constant loggerheads with her husband's family has come back to her mother's house, bringing her five-month-old baby boy with her. The quarrel breaks out because Hamida, who has had the baby in her lap, puts him down to say her prayers. The baby begins to cry, and Naima hits Hamida while she is saying her prayers, and scolds her. She (Naima) then beings to speak disrespectfully of her mother's new-found religiousness, and speaks so blasphemously that Fahmida gets very angry, and slaps her, where-upon Naima raises such an uproar that the neighbours are alarmed. She sulks, refuses to eat and drink, neglects her child all day, and will not let anyone come near her.

Meanwhile Nasuh sends for Kalim. But Kalim flatly refuses to respond to his father's summons, despite all the urgings of Alim and his mother. The contest between father and son, in which neither will yield an inch to the other, now becomes the main theme of the book, occupying four of its eleven chapters. In the end Kalim leaves home, enlists in the armed police in a small princely state and in a skirmish loses a leg. He is brought back to Delhi, but after being reconciled with his father, dies of his wounds.

If Nazir Ahmad was not, and never claimed to be, a novelist, it is not difficult to see why he came to be regarded as one. His stories without doubt embody some of the major elements of the modern novel, and these are not only more prominent in his works than in Sarshar's, but show, in general, more talented writing. His mastery of dialogue is outstanding. Every character *speaks* in character as well as acting in character. Indeed, it is mainly through dialogue that the characters are allowed to establish themselves. In chapter 8 of *Taubat un Nasuh,* which describes the efforts of Alim, and then of Fahmida, to persuade Kalim to go to his father, what happens is conveyed almost entirely through dialogue. In the edition which I have before me as I write, this chapter occupies 30 pages, with 19 lines to the page. Only once is the dialogue interrupted by linking passages of more than a few lines, and this is where Alim, having failed to make any impression on Kalim, runs in desperation to his mother and asks *her* to talk to him. He finds her in a state of acute distress at her quarrel with her daughter and full of anxiety about what it may lead to, and Nazir Ahmad vividly and movingly describes her unhappiness and her reluctance to take up this fresh burden. All this is done in two-and-a-half pages, and dialogue is then resumed.

Not only do the characters reveal themselves in the way they speak and act:

they come alive and, so to speak, assume an independent life of their own. So that in all his tales one sees again and again characters created to typify this or that idea developing according to their own logic, and with results that their creator never intended. An extract from Chapter 8 will illustrate these points. Kalim has always maintained that his father had been given the wrong medical treatment, that this had resulted in the balance of his mind being disturbed, and that it would therefore be pointless to go and listen to what he had to say. Alim, after some discussion, shifts him to the extent that he says that he would probably be able to form a more accurate estimate of his father's state of mind if he talked to his mother. At this Salim says, 'Mummy is very cross today'. (Nazir Ahmad sets out his dialogue in a way which English readers do not expect to see in a narrative, but as it is set out in the printed text of a play. I remember how absurdly disconcerted I was by this perfectly reasonable device when I first encountered it.)

Salim: Mummy is very cross today.
Kalim: Why?
Salim: Don't you know? She and Naima have had a great quarrel.
Kalim: What about?
Salim: Naima handed the baby to Hamida while she went to wash her hands and face. Hamida put him down to say her prayers. Naima pushed her while she was praying and she fell and hurt her nose on a nail in the floor. It bled a lot. That's what started it. Naima several times said bad things about praying. Mummy kept telling her not to, but she took no notice, and in the end Mummy slapped her.
Kalim: Truly?
Salim: Go and see for yourself. She's lying there in the little room crying. She hasn't had anything to eat since morning.
Alim: It's true. There must have been a quarrel about something. When I went to see Daddy, and on the way back, I saw how quiet everyone was, I could tell there must be some reason for it.
Kalim: Has everyone in the house gone mad? They've started Holy War already. Just see. Hamida is saying her prayers – and, just think of it, Naima, poor woman makes some trifling remark and gets slapped for it.
Alim: I don't think there's anything in all that to be surprised at. What's so remarkable about Hamida saying her prayers? [These days] she talks like a grown up.
Kalim: And if she talks like a grown up does it follow that she should be saying her prayers like a grown up too? At her age she ought to be playing with her dolls and her pots and pans, not practising meditation and ascetic exercises.
Alim: Is saying her prayers something too difficult for her to understand?
Kalim: If you beat her until she 'understands' she'll probably say she understands Sadra and Shams Bazga. [Exceptionally difficult Arabic authors.]
Alim: But no one has beaten her.

Kalim: Beating one is as good as beating all. When Mummy slaps Naima, any of us can be humiliated. A grown woman, married, and mother of a child – is that the way a religious lady of good family should behave towards her?

> Unfit to enter either mosque or temple–
> Such faith is something to be marvelled at!

Good riddance to the kind of religion that makes you take leave of your senses and forget what religion and worldly usage alike demand of you. Naima's in-laws are bound to hear of it. What will they say? Anyone with a sense of self respect would drown herself; anyone with a sense of shame wouldn't show her face to the family. And you still tell me I ought to go to Daddy! If I suffer the same thing at *his* kind hands then

> I am a man whose head will roll
> In dust and blood

[i.e. will never submit to such treatment, come what may – the original is a line of Persian verse.] I don't think Naima will survive such treatment...
Alim: I too am surprised at what's happened. But until I hear Mummy's account of it I can't say whether she did right or not.
Kalim: If it happened to you and you'd suspended judgement about whether it was right or not I'd have known you for a truly virtuous and dutiful son.

> Those who have felt it know what it is like
> What do those know who haven't felt the pain?

All the speakers in his dialogue speak in character. We know that Kalim sees himself as a promising young poet, and such a person would intersperse his speech with quotations from Urdu and Persian verse in just the way he does. But more than that you feel increasingly as you read it, 'Well, Nasuh and Fahmida may have right on their side, but that doesn't mean that every single thing they do is justified, and Kalim's thoughts on the matter are certainly not to be dismissed out of hand.' You sympathize even with Naima, and with the sense of shock and outrage she must have felt, and when Nazir Ahmad later portrays Fahmida's own distress in the aftermath of the quarrel you feel, 'Yes, she *should* feel like that.' All of which enhances the realism of the book – and at the same time blurs its didactic message. In short, here as often, Nazir Ahmad the realist takes over the reins from Nazir Ahmad the moralist – and to the great enhancement of the literary value of his work.

For the benefit of modern English-speaking readers it should be said that they are likely to react more favourably to Kalim and Naima than Nazir Ahmad intended and than his Urdu readers would. Kalim is emphatic that a grown-up son is under no obligation to accept his father's views or defer to his wishes, and modern English-speaking readers would tend to agree. Naima could not get on with her in-laws when she lived with them, and modern English-speaking readers might well feel that this may be regrettable but is not particularly reprehensible. To Urdu readers on the other hand both Kalim's and Naima's attitudes would have been (and more than a century later would still be) quite unacceptable. Even so, these readers too would not feel that Kalim and Naima are the wholly unsympathetic characters that Nazir Ahmad would have made .hem if he had kept his didactic aim more resolutely in mind.

It would be unjust to Nazir Ahmad to conclude even so brief an account without saying something about his prose style. As might be expected, the content of Nazir Ahmed's writing owes nothing to the *dastan* and its world of fantasy, and his prose style reflects that fact. For the most part he writes in the vigorous near-colloquial which the Fort William writers had pioneered seventy years earlier; but it acquires in his hands an ease and flexibility which they in their day had not yet been able to impart to it. His excellence as a writer of Urdu prose has in my view always been much underrated. His great contemporaries Hali and Sir Sayyid Ahmad Khan are simply not in the same class. Sarshar has an impressive command of racy Lucknow colloquial, but this language is too light-weight to sustain serious themes. And Sharar (of whom more below) is fluent but pedestrian. Nazir Ahmad has an astounding range of vocabulary and a sureness of touch which enables him to write effortlessly and appropriately on every theme, and which makes one feel that he is never at a loss for suitable words. I have said that his language is for the most part that of vigorous, near-colloquial speech (because this is what his themes generally demand). But this does not indicate any lack of command over the formal, elaborate style which the older literary canons prescribed. Where he thinks it appropriate to employ this style he does so with much of the same power as Ghalib did in his Persian prose, a power which puts Sarshar to shame. In Sarshar the fondness for rhyming prose and for standard descriptions in vague superlatives is still very much in evidence, and where it intrudes, as it often does, even in the depiction of the everyday contemporary scene, it seems irritatingly out of place. In Nazir Ahmad, all and more of Sarshar's technical skill is used to great effect, and his range of descriptive power and ability to evoke atmosphere is something which Sarshar cannot match. His description of the cholera epidemic in Delhi,[35] or of a scene in the 'Mutiny' of 1857 where Ibn ul Vaqt (the main character of the story in question), returning to his home at sunset, comes upon the corpses of some of the English shot by the rebels,[36] or of his character Nasuh's dream of the Day of Judgement,[37] a dream so vivid that it marks the turning point in his life – all these are magnificent pieces of writing and make a most powerful impact.

Such passages defy effective translation into English, for their power derives from a skilful use of a range of literary devices for the most part unfamiliar and unappealing to contemporary English-speaking readers. To people of my generation the nearest parallel is the solemn and sonorous prose of, for example, the general confession in the Book of Common Prayer or such passages as that on faith, hope and love in the Bible. Strongly marked rhythms, alliteration, and the multiplication of near synonyms ('erred and strayed', 'devices and desires') are features of such passages, and Nazir Ahmad's prose shows these features too. But it also shows many more – self-consciously poetic diction, hyperbole, play upon words, rhyming phrases, and successive, parallel statements of a single theme expressed first in splendid language abounding in Arabic and

Persian loan words and then in the homely language of indigenous colloquial speech. The contemporary English-speaking reader would be disconcerted to come upon passages in this sort of style in a modern novel of family life – which is what *Taubat un Nasuh* is. But Nazir Ahmad's readers, people whose first acquaintance with the written word was made through the poetical prose of the Quran, people in whom the love of poetry and an appreciation of just such literary devices was universal, would have enjoyed reading such prose as much as he must have enjoyed writing it. In the scene in *Ibn ul Vaqt,* Chapter 2, where Ibn ul Vaqt, accompanied by his servants and subordinates, is returning home in the evening and comes upon the corpses of Englishmen killed by the rebels of 1857, the sun is setting and the corpses are lying in the shadow of a wall. Nazir Ahmad writes, 'There was the sun, wrapped in the bloodstained shroud of the sunset, ready to be lowered into its grave in the west. And here were these shroudless corpses, wrapped in the black, mourning shroud of the shadow of the walls.' Not the straightforward prose of narrative, but on the Urdu reader the simultaneously stressed likeness and unlikeness of the setting sun to the dead bodies, and the paradox of 'unshrouded' corpses 'shrouded' in dark shadow would make a great impact, and would not be felt to be in the least far-fetched; and this is but one example of the way in which Nazir Ahmad used such devices not for their own sake but in a way completely relevant to his essential purpose.

For all these reasons I can never read Nazir Ahmad without being tempted to the no doubt futile, but nonetheless attractive speculation of what Nazir Ahmad might have done if he had chosen to write novels rather than improving tales.

Abdul Halim Sharar (1860-1926)

Both Sarshar and Nazir Ahmad had already produced their best work when a new writer appeared on the scene, bringing with him fresh themes to diversify the growing stream of prose narrative fiction. This was Abdul Halim Sharar, the pioneer of the historical romance in Urdu. It is in this role that we shall consider him here; but it should be remarked in passing that the historical romance was not his only significant contribution to Urdu literature. He was a strong supporter of Sir Sayyid Ahmad Khan's ideas, and his prolific writings, which include essays, popular history, and novels on contemporary social themes as historical romances, were all intended in one way or another to serve the cause of the New Light. In one striking respect his ideas were more advanced than Sir Sayyid's, for he was a staunch and outspoken opponent of purdah, and one of his novels is designed to show the disastrous effects which the purdah system could produce.[38] The day will perhaps come when he will be most valued for his essays, and particularly for the whole series of essays which, taken together, paint a vivid portrait of old Lucknow before the British annexation of 1856. (An English translation of these was published in 1975.)[39] But from his own time to the present day it has been his historical romances which have made the strongest appeal to Urdu speakers. His best known words in this genre appeared between 1887 and 1907,[40] and won immediate acclaim. Stated in the broadest terms, they all have a single theme – the portrayal of the glorious past of Islam and of the great superiority of Islamic civilization in its heyday over that of contemporary non-Muslim (especially Christian) powers. His method may be illustrated by a study of *Flora Florinda* which is generally agreed to be one of the best of his books. It was first published serially, from 1893, and appeared in book form in 1899. The story of *Flora Florinda* is set in Spain in the third century of the Muslim era (ninth century AD) when Muslim power in Spain was at its zenith. At the time when the story opens, Flora, the heroine, is about eighteen years old. She is the daughter of a Muslim father and a Christian mother and has an elder brother Ziyad. The father had done his best to convert his wife to Islam, but without success. She had never used the Muslim name Zahra which he had given their daughter, but always called her Flora, and in the end the whole family called her by this name. Moreover she had secretly brought Flora up as a Christian, assisted in this, especially after her husband's death, by the organized, secret activities of the Christian Church. The mother too is now dead, but the Christians' secret contacts with Flora have not ceased, and her brother Ziyad, who has all the time been unaware of what was going on, now gets wind of the true situation and like a good Muslim takes steps to correct it. Flora is cut off from all Christian contacts by his command that only visitors who are personally known to him may come to the house. This presents the Christians with a difficult problem, and the Patriarch of the Christian community in Spain personally draws up plans for dealing with it. A nun, Florinda, is sent in the guise of a young Muslim widow to occupy a house in the locality where Flora and her brother live. She is to cultivate their acquaintance, win their confidence, and when opportunity offers, get Flora away to the great cathedral at Cordova, where further arrangements will be made. This she succeeds in doing. Just as the whole Christian Church had been involved in the attempt to get Flora away, so is the whole Muslim machinery of state brought into action to recover her. But no trace of her can be found, and in the end Ziyad disguises himself as a Christian monk and goes out in search of her.

Meanwhile the Patriarch, Florinda and Flora are in hiding in a village in the Pyrenees, and Princess (*sic*) Helen, daughter of Alfonso, Duke (*sic*) of San Sebastian, is soon after sent for to keep her company. She becomes deeply attached to Flora, whose beauty now attracts the unwelcome attentions of the Patriarch. Flora determines to take refuge in a convent, thinking that there she will be safe. Helen and Florinda both try to dissuade her – Helen because she does not want to lose Flora's companionship, and Florinda because she too has grown fond of Flora and as a nun she knows that once in a convent, far from being safe from the Patriarch's attentions, Flora will be compelled as a religious duty to submit to them. Her vows of secrecy forbid her to reveal this to anyone, but after Flora's departure for the convent, in her emotional distress she tells Helen. Helen reacts with anger and contempt both for Florinda and the Patriarch and for nuns and priests in general, and stays on alone in the village when they have gone – Florinda to stay for a while in the same convent as Flora. Some days later a young monk (Ziyad) appears, having traced the fugitives to the village. He and Helen fall in love; he reveals his true identity to her, and she persuades him to take her along with him in his search for Flora.

Flora, now a nun, is raped by the Patriarch and becomes pregnant. Helen marries Ziyad, and though he makes not the slightest attempt to convert her, she of her own accord grows steadily more sympathetic to Islam. Ultimately, after several months they succeed in tracing Flora, Florinda and the Patriarch to the convent where, for the moment, all three of them are. The place is surrounded by Muslim forces and thoroughly searched, but without success; for only an hour or so earlier, dramatic events had taken place there.

Flora, now seven to eight months pregnant, had been summoned at night by the Patriarch to the comfortable outlying room at the nunnery set aside for the satisfaction of the carnal lusts of the monks, priests and dignitaries of the Church; she had submitted to him with apparent complaisance and then, when he was sunk in sleep, attacked him with a knife she had concealed in her robes, and taking advantage of the uproar resulting from his discovery, had escaped leaving him for dead. The Patriarch had been removed to the home of a poor Christian layman, where he could be tended without fear of discovery until he should recover.

Flora flees blindly from the city and ultimately finds herself in a cave. By a remarkable coincidence this turns out to be the very cave in which Ziyad, on assuming Christian dress, had left his clothes and his sword. Flora recognizes them, and assuming for some reason that he has been killed by the Christians, determines there and then to disguise herself in his clothes, to discover his murderers and to revenge his death with his own sword. Without informing us how a girl in such an advanced state of pregnancy achieves this remarkable feat, Sharar assures us that in Ziyad's clothes she is taken for a strikingly handsome young Muslim man, and in this guise she is taken into the service of a Muslim traveller named Abu Muslim, and eventually reaches the outskirts of Cordova in his company. Here she takes leave of him, and again assuming Christian dress, takes a house in an obscure quarter and settles down to wait until an opportunity for revenge should offer itself.

We are now in the 30th and final chapter, and Sharar having written 340 pages[41] seems all of a sudden to feel that all this has gone on long enough and it is time to end. In no more than 13 pages, therefore, he resolves all his outstanding problems, and the story comes to an end in a welter of blood, tears, improbabilities and striking coincidences which take the reader's breath away. Flora realizes that the birth of her child cannot now be far off, and that her condition is so obvious that only by the utmost care can she continue to make her male disguise plausible. For the next few days, therefore, she goes out as little as possible, and that too only after nightfall. One evening as she returns from the bazaar she is approached by a Christian priest who even at close quarters notices nothing to suggest that she is anything but the young man she wishes to be taken for, and asks if he can be of service, for he has observed that 'he' is a newcomer and is alone. Flora (to the reader's astonishment) says she would be obliged if he would occasionally visit her, and gratefully accepts his suggestion that he should call in every morning as he returns home from church. He pays his first call the next morning and sits talking to Flora at length without any untoward suspicion arising. (The problem of concealing her pregnancy seems to have disappeared.) From the conversation she learns that the Patriarch, whom she had left for dead, has recovered, that he is in hiding in Cordova, that her visitor knows his whereabouts and has been to see him several times, and finally that he is willing to grant Flora's wish that he should take her to see him; and he goes to get the Patriarch's formal consent to this, saying that he will then be able to take her to him that very evening. Flora rejoices at this unexpected opportunity of taking her revenge on him and decides to do this first and pursue Ziyad's murderers afterwards if she survives to do so. Between her visitor's departure and his return the same evening Sharar conveniently arranges for Flora to be delivered of her baby and make herself presentable for her interview with the Patriarch. She realizes that to conceal the child as she takes it along with her will be 'a little difficult' – which the reader may feel to be a considerable understatement – but this too is managed. She puts the child in a sort of bag improvised from a sheet and carries this on her arm, puts on a flowing robe which conceals the bag, and accompanies her guide to the Patriarch's hiding place. All this while the child makes no sound. At length she is conducted to a small room where the Patriarch awaits her. She bows before him, and at the same time lays the child on the ground and draws the sword (which she has also concealed under her flowing robe); with this she half-severs his neck, and then plunges it into his breast, calling upon him as he dies (and, as we shall see, he is allowed more than enough time for this) to see to the fruit of his evil-doing lying on the ground at his feet. The Patriarch now recognizes her, and calls on someone to revenge him on her while he still lives to see it. At this a door opens and a man springs upon her and stabs her in the side. She falls dying to the ground, and she and her assailant then recognize each other. He is Abu Muslim, the man in whose employment she had come to Cordova. She is asking how he, a Muslim, comes to be where he is when three others burst into the room. These are none other than Ziyad, Helen and Florinda. (Ziyad had by a lucky chance caught Florinda and a monk red-handed in a plot to murder Helen: he had killed the monk on the spot, and Florinda had later been compelled on pain of death to guide Ziyad and Helen to the Patriarch's hiding-place.) Ziyad asks the dying girl who she is, and she tells him she is Flora. At this Helen runs to her and embraces her. Flora calls her by name and Abu Muslim no sooner hears it than he turns his wrathful gaze upon her and leaps upon her with dagger drawn; but Ziyad intervenes in time, and strikes his head off with his sword at the same moment as Helen recognizes him as her father. The Patriarch now calls out in a feeble voice telling Ziyad to kill Florinda, but he refuses to sully his sword with her blood. But the priest who had guided Flora here, and has been standing in astonishment all this time, now picks up Abu Muslim's dagger and buries it in Florinda's breast. The Patriarch urges him to kill Flora and Helen too, but dies as he speaks the words, and Ziyad seizes the man, wrests the dagger from him, and binds him fast. Flora now has time to give Helen a concise account of all that had befallen her since they parted in the Pyrenees, and having done so, turns to her brother, declares herself a convinced Muslim and asks his forgiveness. Ziyad is now weeping uncontrollably, and Helen, in the double grief of

Flora's and her father's loss, is in even greater distress. But she takes Flora's baby in her arms and weeping copiously, promises, despite Ziyad's initial objection, to bring it up as her own son. At this Flora bursts into tears and in the same moment dies. Ziyad and Helen continue weeping for a long time; then Ziyad asks her forgiveness for killing her father. She recognizes that he could hardly have done otherwise, and forgives him readily. We are now on the last page of the book. Helen goes on to say that now her father is dead there is no longer any reason why she should not openly embrace Islam, and she thereupon does so. And so all ends satisfactorily.

It hardly needs saying that a tale of this kind takes us right back to the world of the *dastan,* although Sharar himself boldly calls his book a '*naval*' (novel). The opening sentence of *Flora Florinda* reads, 'Our interesting novel begins about the year AH 230' (about AD 845). There are indeed significant differences. It does not exceed the length which the use of the word 'novel' would lead one to expect, and the narrative is well-constructed (albeit full of improbabilities), moves at rapid pace and is, in general, written in simple but vigorous Urdu. Its dialogue too, where the themes are those of everyday occurrences, is natural and convincing. Yet the overall atmosphere is unmistakably that of the *dastan.* There is the same evocation of the heroic age of Islam, the same battle of unalloyed virtue against unalloyed vice, the same dependence on exciting episodes following one upon another to maintain the reader's interest, and the same spicing of the story with erotic detail. Faiz Ahmad Faiz, in an excellent article on Sharar, writes of him,[42] 'It is rather a harsh thing to say, but all the same it must be said that when in his moral and religious zeal he depicts the evils of the churches and the monasteries...his writing borders on the pornographic.' This judgement is fully justified. Sexual lust, allied with religious fanaticism, is portrayed as the dominant motive of the Christian characters. Sharar sets the tone on page 10, where Christians first make their appearance. A small number of monks and nuns are depicted as they assemble at a desolate spot in the mountains outside Toledo. Sharar writes, 'But it is impossible to tell why they have come here in this way, and with what object they have assembled in this desolate and awe-inspiring place.' He goes on, quite gratuitously,

> Incidents arising from the carnal desires and illicit lusts of nuns and priests are so well-known throughout the country that everyone will at first surmise that they have come here to this wild and lonely place to give full vent to their uncontrolled desires and allow full freedom to their lusts. But no, that is not the case.

Similarly, Ziyad, in his first serious talk with Flora warning her of the dangers of too tolerant an attitude towards Christians, tells her,[43]

> Their monks who pretend to have abandoned the world, are the worldliest of men – in fact, they worship worldly things and more than anyone else in the world they are the slaves of their own desires. In the same measure nuns, who are dedicated to the Church to live out their lives as virgins, are almost without exception addicted in the highest degree to fornication. And the

association of these lustful monks and abandoned nuns has resulted in a situation where the church has generally become a place of fornication. Thousands of abortions are carried out, and thousands of babies are secretly buried alive in the precincts of the church.

And such immorality is not confined to the monks and nuns; the institution of confession spreads it amongst the laity as well. We are told in a footnote (in Chapter 18):

> In the Roman Catholic religion it is obligatory for every man and woman once a week to go before the priest and confess all his or her sins of the week, and to ask forgiveness. On these occasions the priests receive the right to ask respectable women all manner of shameless questions, and to express freely to them their lustful desires. This is what is called confession. In former days, under the cloak of this confession, priests have depraved thousands of chaste women – not to speak of the fact that, since the priests become fully acquainted with all the women's secrets, they can bring such pressure to bear on respectable women that, from fear that their secrets may be revealed, they are in no position to refuse any of the priest's desires.

Examples could be multiplied. More characteristic still of the *dastan*-like atmosphere is the whole chapter in which Florinda step by step arouses Ziyad's passion until he escapes the sin of fornication by a hair's breadth, saved by his strong devotion to Islam, but constrained by the violence of his feelings to press Florinda to marry him without delay.

The only Christian character portrayed from the start with any sympathy is that of Princess Helen, and here the fervour with which Sharar describes her beauty as good as tells us at once that she is destined to become a Muslim – which, as we have seen, she ultimately does on the very last page of the book. Sharar makes full use of her as his most effective propagandist for Islam. At one point she interrupts Florinda to tell her forcefully:[44]

> It was you people who had impressed the idea upon me that the Muslims are cruel and bigoted. But since I came here it has become crystal clear to me that it is you nuns and monks that go around slandering them and fanning the flames of prejudice against them. In fact they are people who prize justice, and there is no trace of deceit or hypocrisy in them. They respect and honour any man who lives a sincere and honest life, no matter what his religion may be. My own example is there to prove it.

It is indeed; but readers will recall another example which leads perhaps to a less flattering conclusion. In Chapter 2, Ziyad is explaining his family history in a gathering adorned by numbers of the most distinguished and admirable figures of Muslim Spain. He tells how his mother had from the outset secretly brought Flora up as a Christian, and how in spite of all his efforts to cut her off from all contact with Christians he is only too bitterly aware that he has not been able to bring about a change of heart. He turns to his host – the most holy and most distinguished Muslim in Cordova – and asks him what he should do. His host replies:[45] 'You should make it clear to Flora that if she adopts the Christian religion she will be put to death; for in Islam the penalty for apostasy is death. Probably this threat will be effective.' The non-Muslim reader and, indeed, one hopes many Muslim readers too, will be bound to conclude that a man who can give such advice may have many virtues, but that tolerance is not among them; for leaving aside the question of whether tolerance and the death penalty for apostasy can go together, to regard as an apostate a girl who from earliest childhood has been taught Christian doctrines by her mother is, to say the least of it, going rather far. But Sharar was writing for an audience which took such things in its stride.

As in the *dastans*, the love-interest is as strongly in evidence in the Muslim camp as in that of its adversaries – though here, of course, nothing in the least reprehensible occurs. The portrayal is again in *dastan* terms – terms which, incidentally, are common to the *dastan* and the *ghazal*, the traditional Urdu lyric. Love at first sight, or nearly at first sight, expresses itself in an immediate, complete, and absolute devotion to the beloved, and in a declaration of willingness to sacrifice even life itself in her cause. And here both the depiction of the lover's feelings and the dialogue between lover and beloved are completely stylized in marked contrast to the dialogue elsewhere. Sharar is clearly aware of the appeal which such scenes made to his audience, for they recur throughout the book, and often in contexts where they are of little or no relevance to the development of the story.[46] It is commonly said that another feature which Sharar's tales share with the *dastan* is his interruption of the narrative to display his skill in depicting the scenes in which the action is set. But in *Flora Florinda* at any rate this is not much in evidence.

Sharar's tales have played an ambiguous role from the time they made their first appearance right up to the present day. The popularity which he won is, I think, largely explained by the same sort of combination of historical circumstances that favoured Sarshar. The apostles of the New Light had found that one effective way of appealing to their fellow-Muslims was to remind them of their glorious past – the argument being that the civilization of Islam had once been far in advance of the Christian world, and that the Muslims therefore had it in them to emulate, and even overtake, the advanced nations of the West. Sharar himself belonged to this school of thought. But by the end of the nineteenth century the argument had tended to boomerang. The recollection of the glorious past of Islam was used to justify the argument that Muslims had nothing of importance to learn from the British and that the awe and respect with which the New Light regarded them was entirely misplaced. Sharar's books must, I think, have appealed to both audiences. Faiz, in the article already quoted, writes,[47]

Sharar's age is...an age when the Muslims had just awoken to a consciousness of their decline. These romantic tales in the first place helped them to forget the bitterness of everyday life. Secondly, the recital of past conquest partly inspired them with self-respect and partly with emotional solace, with the thought that even if *they* were not heroes at least their forefathers had been.

And thirdly the description of the vices of other peoples provided them with a way of taking mental revenge for their present subjection....This is why Sharar's novels are so popular....Sharar is not a novelist, but a teller of tales, and one of considerable skill....In general, all children and a good many among the young and not so young expect nothing more of a story-writer, and Sharar is till the novelist most popular with these young and not-so-young children.

The First True Novel: Rusva's *Umrao Jan Ada*

If Sharar's work, as compared with Nazir Ahmad's and even with Sarshar's, represents in some measure a reversion to the *dastan*, his contemporary Mirza Muhammad Hadi Rusva (1858-1931) took the next major step forward, and that too a step of such significance that one can truly say of his greatest work *Umrao Jan Ada* (1899) that with it a real novel, in the internationally accepted modern sense of the term, at last makes its appearance in Urdu literature. In the preface to another book[48] he sets out his views on the writing of fiction, criticizing in passing both Nazir Ahmad and Sharar, although without actually naming either. On Nazir Ahmad he expresses himself quite mildly:

> It is the practice of some contemporary writers to frame a plot in order to prove a particular point and then fill in the details accordingly. I make no objection against them, but I shall not be at fault if I simply say that my method is the opposite of theirs. I aim simply at a faithful portrayal of actual happenings and am not concerned with recording the conclusions to be drawn from them.

On Sharar his tone is more sarcastic; after saying that he (Rusva) writes of what he knows, he goes on:

> I have not the inventive power to portray events that happened thousands of years ago, and moreover I consider it a fault to produce a picture which tallies neither with present-day conditions nor with those of the past – which, if you study the matter carefully, is what usually happens. Great ability and much labour is required to write a historical novel, and I have neither the ability nor the leisure to do it.

He gives his own view of fiction at some length, saying that the fiction-writer is a kind of historian, and in a way his fiction is of greater value than histories are, because historians write the history of individuals (*sic*) and cannot give an overall picture of reality. The novelist generally gives a picture of what he has seen in his own time – that is, the novelist who makes Nature his teacher; for this is what a novelist should do. Aristotle well said that poetry is the imitation of Nature.

Understanding these things, [Rusva continues] I have made it a principle in my own writing to record in my novels those things which I have myself seen, and which have made an impression upon me, believing that these things will make an impression on others also.

He goes on to apologize, perhaps with his tongue in his cheek, for the fact that 'the scene of most of my novels is my birthplace, Lucknow', but excuses himself on the ground that this is the only place that he knows well – after which follows the hit at Sharar already quoted. Elsewhere[49] he reinforces his earlier point: 'My novels should be regarded as a history of our times, and I hope it will be found a useful one.'

In *Umrao Jan Ada* he showed that he could not only enunciate these principles but also apply them in practice (though at the same time it must be said that his other novels fall short of the standards he set himself). The book is the life-story of a Lucknow courtesan, whose name forms the title of the novel, and the story covers, roughly, the years 1840-70 – that is the decades spanning the great watershed of the 'Indian Mutiny' of 1857. In those years courtesans of Umrao Jan's class – beautiful women, who besides being expert singers and dancers were also highly educated in the traditional culture of their day and were quite often poets, as Umrao Jan herself was – played a role in Lucknow society closely comparable to that of the *hetaerae* in ancient Athens, and through her experiences one really does see something of the social and cultural history of the times. The story is beautifully told and extraordinarily well constructed. Not only are the characterization and the dialogue excellent; the story has a proper plot, and real development, with 'a beginning, a middle, and an end'. Rusva begins with an account of how it came to be written. He had a friend from Delhi, who was very fond of Lucknow and frequently came to stay there for long periods. On these occasions he would rent a small house, and would often invite his friends there to spend the evening with him. The room where they used to sit together, talking and reciting their verses to one another, was separated by only a thin partition wall from the house next door. In it was a sort of hatch, the shutters of which were, however, always kept closed. They had been given to understand that the occupant of the house on the other side of the wall was an elderly courtesan, but had often noticed how quiet and unobtrusive a neighbour she was. One evening the host arranged a small informal *mushaira*, that is a gathering at which the guests, turn by turn, recite their verses. (This is still a popular institution with educated Urdu-speakers, amongst whom almost every other person seems to be a poet.) On these occasions the expression of appreciation is loud and uninhibited, and on this particular evening Rusva has just recited a verse when the company is surprised to hear an exclamation of approval coming from the other side of the partition wall. The host smiles and calls out, 'Come in and join us. It's not proper to call out from there.' But there is no reply. A few minutes later a maidservant appears and asks, 'Which of you is Mirza Rusva?' Rusva identifies himself, and the maid says that her mistress is asking to see him. The other guests are quick to note that the lady next door knows Rusva well enough to recognize him from the sound of his voice,[50] and there is some chaffing at his expense. He excuses himself, goes out with the maidservant, and is taken in to see her mistress, whom he at once recognizes as Umrao

Jan. Knowing her accomplishments as a poet, he urges her to return with him and take part in the *mushaira,* and after some demur, she does so. Her verses are much appreciated, and after that evening she frequently visits the house to take part in gatherings of this kind. One evening she and Rusva are talking with their host after the other guests have gone, and they tell her how interesting it would be if she would relate to them the story of her life. Rusva is particularly persistent; and in the end she agrees to do as they ask. The rest of the book is an account of the successive meetings with Rusva in which she tells him her story. After each occasion, unbeknown to her, Rusva writes it all down, including the occasional exchanges between them with which her narrative is interrupted – a device which very effectively enhances the illusion of reality.

She begins with her childhood recollections, until at the age of seven she is kidnapped by a sworn enemy of her father and taken to Lucknow to be sold into a brothel, and then recounts all her changing fortunes during thirty years until she retires quietly to spend her old age alone in the house she now occupies. When her story is complete Rusva hands her his manuscript and asks her to read it through and correct any mistakes he may have made. She later describes to him her reaction.[51]

Mirza Rusva Sahib, when you first handed me the manuscript of my life-story and asked me to revise it, I was so angry that I felt like tearing it into little pieces. I kept thinking to myself, 'Have I not suffered enough shame in my own lifetime that now my story should be written down, so that people will read it and curse me even after I am dead?' But my own dilatory nature, and a regard for the labour you had spent on it, restrained me.

Last night at about twelve o'clock I was dropping off to sleep when suddenly I felt wide awake. As usual, I was alone in the room. The servants were all asleep downstairs. The lamp was burning at the head of the bed. For a long time I kept tossing and turning, trying to get to sleep; but sleep would not come, and it the end I got up and made myself a *pan* and called the maidservant to come and get the hookah ready. I lay down again on the bed and began to smoke. I thought I might read a story. There were plenty of books on the shelves at the head of the bed, and one by one I picked them up and turned the pages. But I had read them all before several times, and could not arouse any interest in any of them. Then my hand fell upon your manuscript. I again felt deeply agitated, and, I tell you truly, I had quite made up my mind to tear it up when it seemed as though some unseen voice said to me, 'Very well, Umrao. Suppose you tear it up, throw it away, burn it. What difference will it make? The recording angels of God – a just and mighty God – have by His command written down in every detail a clear account of all the deeds of your life. And who can destroy *that* record?' I felt myself trembling in every limb, so that the manuscript nearly fell from my hand, but I managed to rally myself. Now all idea of destroying it had left me, and I wanted to put it down again and leave it as it was. But as though without my own volition, I began to read. I read the first page and turned over, and before I had finished the next half-dozen lines I was seized with so consuming an interest in my story that the more I read the more I wanted to. No other tale had ever engrossed me so completely. When you read stories the thought is always with you that all this is invented, and did not really happen; and this thought lessens the pleasure you feel. But your whole narrative was made up of things which I myself had experienced, and it was as though they were all returning to pass before my eyes. Every experience seemed as real to me as it had been at the time, and I felt more vividly than words can describe all the emotions which it had aroused in me. If anyone could have seen me then, he would have thought me mad. Sometimes I would burst out laughing; at other times the tears would overflow and drop on to the page. You had asked me to make corrections as I read, but I was too absorbed even to think of it. I read on and on until daybreak. Then I performed my ablutions, said the morning prayers, and slept for a while. I woke again at about eight o'clock, washed my hands and face, and again began to read. By sunset I had finished the whole manuscript.

The book concludes with the account of a final session together in which Umrao tells Rusva her own reflections on the experience of her life.

We are not left in any doubt that Rusva's deepest sympathies are with Umrao Jan, whom he sees as the victim of others' sins against her; and a striking passage in the novel shows how passionately he feels about such things. He tells her,[52] Wise men have divided sins into two kinds. The first are those which affect only the sinner, and the second those whose effect extends to others. In my humble opinion the first are minor sins and the second are major sins (although others may think otherwise); and sins that affect others can be forgiven only by those whom they have harmed. You know what Hafiz[53] says: Drink wine; burn the Quran; set fire to the Kaba, and dwell in the house of idols: but do not harm your fellow men! Remember this, Umrao Jan: to harm one's fellow men is the worst of sins. This is a sin for which there is no forgiveness, and if there is then, God preserve me, His godhead is in vain.

Characteristically, the words are spoken in a context where they do not apply directly to Umrao Jan. (Whenever Rusva talks to her about herself it is always in a half-serious, half-bantering tone.) But their application to her own case is clear. Yet Rusva's approach to her is entirely unsentimental, and he can speak to her with a bluntness which is almost cruel. At one point in the story Umrao is living in hiding at the house of a lawyer, who is defending her in a long-drawn-out lawsuit. One day when he is away, his wife, feeling the need of someone to talk to, comes across to the outhouse where she has her quarters and invites her into the house. While they are talking quite amicably together, an old woman comes in. She completely ignores Umrao, but speaks contemptuously about her to the wife, and when she remonstrates with her a heated quarrel develops, which ends in the wife beating the old woman with her slipper. By this time the wife's mother-in-law and her old maidservant have appeared on the scene, and these two, who also treat Umrao as though she were not there, proceed to discuss the rights and wrongs of the wife's conduct. As a result the old woman is ordered out, but they agree that in the first place it was the wife who was at fault. Umrao, seeing that she is not wanted, returns to her own room. As she relates the incident to Rusva she expresses the anger which after the lapse of all these years she still feels at the contempt with which she had been treated. Rusva cuts her short and tells her bluntly that in his opinion the old women had been quite right to behave as they did, that the wife was indeed to blame, and that if *his* wife should ever do such a thing he would send her packing back to her parents and not allow her to set foot in his home again for six months. Umrao demands to know why, and Rusva replies:[54]

> I will tell you why. There are three kinds of women – good women, depraved women and prostitutes. And depraved women are of two kinds – those who keep their depravity secret, and those who openly lead a wicked and immoral life. Haven't you the sense to see that only women whose character is unstained can associate with good women? Think of their position. Poor women, they spend their whole lives imprisoned within their own four walls, and have troubles without end to endure. When times are good anyone will stand by a man, but these stand by him in good times and bad alike. While their husbands are young and have plenty of money, it is usually other women who get the benefit of it. But when they grow old and have nothing, no one else so much as asks after them; and it is the wives who go through all manner of distress, and trust in fate to revenge them on the others. Don't you think they are right to pride themselves on all this? And it is this pride which makes them look upon immoral women with utter loathing and abhorrence. God will forgive a sinner who repents, but these women will never forgive her. And there is another thing. You often find that no matter how beautiful his wife may be, or how admirable her character, or how adequate in all her duties, her fool of a husband will get an infatuation for prostitutes who cannot so much as compare with her on any score, and will desert his wife, sometimes temporarily, and sometimes for life. That is why they get the idea – or rather the conviction – that prostitutes practise witchcraft which dulls their husbands' senses. And that too, in a way, testifies to their goodness; because even in these circumstances it is not their husbands that they blame, but the immoral women who lead them astray. And what greater proof of their loyalty could there be than that?

Umrao's own attitude towards herself is equally unsentimental. She tells Rusva at the end of her story that a woman like herself who has been a courtesan is deluding herself if she thinks that marriage or love or security, or indeed any relationship which demands of others that they love and trust her, is possible for her. She must live her own life and rely on no one but herself to see her through. She obviously regrets that this should be so, and says she now shares the deep admiration and respect for purdah women which Rusva had expressed earlier, and wishes that their lot could have been hers (though she adds, with characteristic realism, that the suffocating atmosphere of purdah would now be unbearable to her). But all this is said in a dry, matter-of-fact way, and with a complete absence of any maudlin self-pity.

It is unfortunate that the only English translation of the great novel is that of Khushwant Singh and M.A. Husaini, published in India in 1961.[55] The translators have failed to do justice to the original, and so have given a very inadequate impression of its true worth.

Subsequent Developments

Umrao Jan Ada has remained in many respects an isolated achievement. Even Rusva himself never wrote anything to compare with it. His other two major novels are more closely comparable with Nazir Ahmad's tales than with his own masterpiece. They deal with two contrasted themes. In one[56] the central character is a member of the old decadent Lucknow aristocracy whose complacent persistence in an outmoded way of life brings him to inevitable ruin. In the other[57] the hero is also a man of aristocratic family, but one who is thrown entirely upon his own resources early in his life and makes his way in the world through sheer hard work and determination to adapt himself to the new conditions around him. The moral is in both cases made as crystal clear as in anything that Nazir Ahmad ever wrote.

The strong moral didactic trend continues in Urdu prose narrative to the present day. The propaganda for Western ways began to be met early in the twentieth century by counter-propaganda for the traditional Islamic way of life which stressed the danger to religion and morals which the Western outlook brought in its train. (Very little writing of this kind – and there is a good deal of it – reaches any worthwhile standard.) In the twenties, themes of nationalism and Gandhism appear, especially in the work of Prem Chand (1880-1936); and from the thirties, socialist and communist trends emerge strongly, to continue up to the present day. The development of prose narrative in the twentieth century has been not so much towards a greater realism as towards an extension of the range of themes.

Some of the factors that hold back the development of the novel are undoubtedly economic. Urdu writers work in a community where the standard of living is low and the percentage of illiteracy is still very high. A collection of short stories by a popular writer with an already established reputation will rarely be published in an edition of more than 1,000 copies, and at a price which puts it beyond the reach of very many would-be readers. No Urdu writer can depend solely on writing for a livelihood, and few can devote even a substantial part of their time to it. (This is one of the reasons why the short story has flourished more than the novel.) Another factor is that of cultural tradition. Poetry still enjoys a higher prestige than prose literature, and people who feel that they have creative talent tend to apply it accordingly. Nevertheless, the achievement in the field of prose narrative is substantial enough, and forms a firm basis on which present and future writers will continue to build.

7. Nazir Ahmad and the Aligarh Movement

Nazir Ahmad, as the previous chapter makes clear, was one of the founders of the modern Urdu novel, and this is his main importance in the history of Urdu literature. But his importance is by no means confined to this. The remarkable qualities, both as a man and as a writer, which his tales reveal, and which are still very generally undervalued, show themselves also in other important areas of his life and work. He was an outstandingly able translator, a sound practical educationist, the greatest orator the Aligarh movement produced, and a powerful and original religious thinker. In this chapter I aim to give an account of some of these achievements, set within the framework of the story of his life.[1]

Early Life (1830-1857)

Nazir Ahmad was born in 1830 in a small town, Rehar, in Nagina Tahsil, District Bijnor,[2] in Rohilkhand, the western part of what is now the Indian state of Uttar Pradesh. His father was descended from a *khalifa* (authorized successor) of the great 16th century Muslim thinker and *pir*, Shaikh Abdul Quddus Gangohi. The family was poor, but respected for its traditions of learning, and Nazir Ahmad's father earned his living by teaching. It was from him that, up to the age of nine, Nazir Ahmad learned Persian and Arabic.

From 1839 to 1842 he and his elder brother were sent to live with a wealthy and influential disciple of Nazir Ahmad's paternal grandfather, named Nasrullah Khan Khurjavi (that is, of Khurja, a small country town some twenty-five miles north of Aligarh). This man was one of the few remarkable men of his time who both knew the old traditional learning intimately and had risen to quite high positions in the service of the British. At the time Nazir Ahmad and his brother were put into his care he was Deputy Collector in Bijnor. He knew not only Arabic and Persian but also Pashto and Turkish, and was the author of a number of short treatises and of a history of the Deccan, written in Persian. At one stage in his life he was responsible for one of the six administrative areas into which the princely state of Hyderabad was divided, and by a historical coincidence Nazir Ahmad later in life occupied the same post. Nazir Ahmad stayed with him until 1842, when other preoccupations prevented Nasrullah Khan from continuing to take care of his education.

In 1842, on Nasrullah Khan's advice, Nazir Ahmad's father took him and his elder brother to Delhi, where he put them in the care of Maulvi Abdul Khaliq (whom he already knew) in the Aurangabadi Mosque in the quarter of Delhi known as Panjabi Katra. (This Mosque stood on the exact site of the present Delhi railway station. The Mosque and the whole quarter in which it stood were demolished by the British after the great revolt of 1857.) He studied in the Mosque until January 1846, when he and his brother were admitted as students, on a grant, to Delhi College, the remarkable institution, founded by the British, in which many of the later achievements of the Aligarh Movement were foreshadowed. He studied here until the end of 1853.

It was during this period that he met the girl who later became his wife. Maulvi Abdul Khaliq's elder son was Abdul Qadir and Nazir Ahmad was a frequent visitor at his house where, as the descendant of a *khalifa* in the line of spiritual succession of Shaikh Abdul Quddus Gangohi and as a specially bright student of Persian and Arabic, he was accepted on terms of considerable familiarity. At this time he was no more than 14 or 15 years old, but in intellectual development he was in advance of his years. The girl with whom he formed an attachment was Abdul Qadir's eldest daughter, who, as such, played a responsible part in the running of the house. Nazir Ahmad offered to help her grind the spices, and we may assume that the offer was made on the calculation that this would give him the opportunity to be in her company and talk with her. In the course of time the relationship developed into one of love. When after January 1846 he entered Delhi College he continued to visit Abdul Qadir's home, and eventually his love for the girl gave him the courage to ask that he should be married to her. Nazir Ahmad never avowed this openly; he preferred to give the impression that his was a respectably arranged marriage and presented it as a coincidence that the girl for whom he had ground spices later became his wife, but in a letter to his son written about 1875-76 he urges him to arrange his own marriage and goes on to say that this is what he himself had done.[3]

There is strong evidence that in the same period, under the influence of Master Ramachandra, one of the most notable figures associated with Delhi College and himself a convert, he accepted the doctrines of Christianity, and that only the strong pressure of his fellow Muslims prevented him declaring himself a Christian. (A period of fundamental religious questioning continued until 1864.)

Early in 1854 he was offered a posting in the Education Department to Bareilly, but got his elder brother accepted in his place (probably because, having upset his family by his marriage, he did not want to be so near home) and himself went to a posting in District Gujarat in the Panjab where Richard Temple[4] was at that time in charge of education. He disliked this job and did his utmost to get away from it. Early in 1856 he received simultaneously two offers of employment, one of a post as teacher of Arabic in Ajmer College and the second as a Deputy Inspector of Schools in Kanpur. He took the Deputy Inspectorship, but this job, too, proved uncongenial and he gave it up at the beginning of 1857. It is said that he resigned because one of his British superiors objected to his chewing *pan*.

Throughout the revolt of 1857 he was in Delhi and experienced both the rule of the rebel sepoys and the subsequent hardships inflicted by the British when they retook the city in September. Members of his wife's family saved the life of a British woman during these days (Nazir Ahmad, and still more his biographers, have exaggerated his own role in this) and were duly rewarded by the British.

Translations, School Books, And The First Three 'Novels' (1857-77)

At the end of 1857 he was appointed to a Deputy Inspectorship in Allahabad. He lodged there with one Abdullah Khan, who strongly urged him to learn English. Nazir Ahmad took his advice, took six months' leave, and used it to acquire a serviceable working knowledge of English. Shortly afterwards he was introduced to Sir William Muir, Lieutenant-Governor of the North West Provinces (the western part of what later became the Indian state of Uttar Pradesh – U.P.), and henceforth an important influence in promoting Nazir Ahmad's advancement, and in 1859-60 began work on translating the Income Tax Law into Urdu. Other translations followed, including his most famous translation from English, that of the Indian Penal Code. Nazir Ahmad was at first not associated with this project, but after he became involved in it he quickly assumed the role of the main translator and was recognized as such, being ultimately entrusted with the revision of the whole work and then being sent to Lucknow to see it through the press. This work was finished in 1861. Largely as a result of it he was recommended for the post of Deputy Collector, but since there was no immediate vacancy he accepted appointment as *tahsildar* of Salimpur in District Kanpur. Here he continued his work as a translator, in 1863 translating some of Aesop's fables into Urdu and publishing a translation of an English official's account of his experiences during the 1857 revolt under the tile of *Musaib i Ghadar* (The Tribulations of the Mutiny). This work was undertaken at the instance of a Hindu superior, described by some as a very bigoted Hindu. Nazir Ahmad apparently felt it necessary to undertake the work, but he seems, at any rate in later years, to have wished that he had not, and he never spoke or wrote of the fact that he had done this work.

In 1863 he was made Deputy Collector (hence the common reference to him as 'Deputy Nazir Ahmad') and between 1863 and 1872 served in Kanpur, Gorakhpur (where he made a thorough study of the Bible), and Orai (District Jalaun). In 1872 he was posted to Azamgarh, and served there until 1877. In the years from 1854 to 1864 his overriding aim in life was to rise to a high position in government service. With his promotion to Deputy Collector in 1863 he had achieved this aim. His biographer, Iftikhar Ahmad Siddiqi, adds, rather coyly, that this was a period in which 'it is said that he was fond of dancing and singing', adding, on what evidence we are not told, that 'this youthful enthusiasm, however, was unstained by the dirt of lust'.[5]

Round about 1865 or 1866 he had begun writing textbooks for schools. In 1868 the government announced the institution of prizes for books judged suitable for use in the Education Department and Nazir Ahmad's first tale, *Mirat ul Arus,*[6] was written in 1869 in the hope of winning one. His own account is that he had written it for his children, without thought of publication, and that it was only its chance discovery by Kempson, then Director of Public Instruction for the province, which led to its being submitted for the award of a prize. Iftikhar Ahmad Siddiqi has convincingly shown that this story is false, remarking in passing that this is only one of a number of 'invented stories'. He adds,

> The responsibility for these invented stories lies with Nazir Ahmad himself, who, in his zest for the telling of tales, was accustomed to adding drama to the events of his life. And wherever he fell short, his biographers supplied the deficiencies.[7]

Nazir Ahmad won the prize he had hoped for in 1870, and in 1872 he wrote a sequel, *Banat un Nash,* for which he also won a prize. By this time he had already begun to write a series of short educational books. *Muntakhab ul Hikayat* ('A selection of stories' – a collection of moral tales, many of them based upon Aesop) was probably written in 1870-71, *Cand Pand* (roughly 'Some Good Counsel', but in fact in the main a short compendium of general knowledge) in 1871-72 (when he was also writing *Banat un Nash*) and *Mubadi ul Hikmat* (on logic) in 1871. A pamphlet on Arabic grammar was also probably written in 1871, though it was not printed until 1877. In 1872 he translated a book on the law of evidence, and in the same year translated the English version of a book originally written in French by A. Guillemin and entitled in English translation *The Heavens*. (The English translation was by Le Poer Wynn, an Englishman who was then serving as his superior in the British administration.) A year or two later (Iftikhar Ahmad Siddiqi thinks between 1874 and 1877) he wrote four booklets, of which the last is *Rasm ul Khat*, a small book to teach the Urdu script,[8] and in 1874 he wrote *Taubat un Nasuh*.[9]

Service In Hyderabad State (1877-1884)

In February 1877 he was offered a job in the largest princely state in India, the Nizam's Dominions of Hyderabad. Muhsin ul Mulk offered him this job on the recommendation of Sir Sayyid. He was offered a salary of Rs 800 a month, rising to Rs 1,000 a month – a sum which, having regard to the much greater value of the rupee at that time, would have ensured him considerable affluence. He demanded Rs 1,200 a month and an undertaking that his service in the British administration would be counted towards his pension, and these demands were accepted. He therefore took two years' leave from his employment in British India and accepted the appointment. He left Azamgarh and reached Hyderabad on 27 April 1877. He worked in two districts of that region of the state known as Telengana. He had to write his reports in Persian, and his command of the language was much appreciated. In July 1877 he was posted to Patancheru on a five-year posting. In this post he had to spend a lot of time on tour. In 1879 when his leave was due to expire he said that he was anxious about the future of his family. The Hyderabad authorities thereupon gave employment to his son and two other relatives, whereupon Nazir Ahmad resigned from British service and sent for his family to join him in Hyderabad. In 1883 he was given further promotion and his salary was raised to Rs 1,700. At the end of February 1884 he suddenly resigned his position and left for Delhi, a victim to political manoeuvrings which more or less forced him to make this decision. During his stay in Hyderabad he wrote almost nothing except a few booklets for the education of the young ruler of the state, but he was thinking strenuously about the problems of the Muslim community in India and spending a lot of time in study. He is said to have learned Telugu during this period, and in 1877, within six months and seventeen days, learned the Quran by heart and so became a Hafiz.

Later 'Novels', Letters, And Lectures (1884-1905)

After leaving Hyderabad he spent the rest of his life in Delhi. When he reached Delhi he at once started writing again. In 1885 he wrote *Muhsinat: Fasana i Mubtala*, though it was not published until 1887. In 1887 his son Bashir, in collaboration with one of Nazir Ahmad's friends, published a collection of over one hundred of his letters under the title *Mau'iza i Hasna*. All but a few are addressed to Bashir, and are remarkable for the freedom and assumption of rough equality wit' which he addresses him. In 1888 he published *Ibn ul Vaqt*.

In the same year (1888) he made his first speeches on public platforms, when his talent for oratory emerged 'like a *jinn* escaping from a bottle', as Iftikhar Ahmad Siddiqi puts it.[10] He proved to be an extremely forceful and popular speaker and from 1888 to 1905 he lectured regularly for the Muhammadan Education Conference, the *Anjuman i Himayat i Islam* ('Society for the Support of Islam') and the Delhi Tibbiya College. He shared Sir Sayyid's hostility to the Indian National Congress, founded in 1885. In 1888 a meeting aimed at winning Muslim support for the Congress was held in Delhi Town Hall. To counteract this, a meeting, also in Delhi Town Hall, was held shortly afterwards under official auspices. It was presided over by a member of the former Mughal royal family, Mirza Muhammad Sulaiman Shah, and Nazir Ahmad was the main speaker. He spoke for an hour and a half, and so great was the impact of his speech that Sir Sayyid at once approached him to speak at the next session of the Muhammadan Educational Conference, the Delhi *Madrassa i Tibbiya* (Muslim College), and the (Panjab) *Anjuman i Himayat i Islam*. The largest published collections of his lectures comprise forty-four.

Both Sir Sayyid and Muhsin ul Mulk were full of praise for his power as a speaker, and his popularity may be judged from the words which Muhsin ul Mulk spoke of him in his presidential address to the final session of the Muhammadan Educational Conference at Aligarh on 29 December (Iftikhar Ahmad Siddiqi does not give the year):

Today, after two days (at the Conference) people were tired. And it was raining. I was thinking to myself that probably I myself would be one of the first to arrive for the session; but, gentlemen, believe me when I say that the moment I reached the door I was astonished at what I saw – a sight such as I have never seen before. I saw that in their eagerness to hear (him) such a throng of people had assembled that had I not been president I doubt whether I should have been able to get into the hall and find a seat. Not to speak of the chairs, benches, galleries, there was no room to stand anywhere – or rather 'no room to put a sesamum seed'.[11]

Many factors contributed to the impact he made. His impressive personality and bearing, his striking (and often unusual) appearance, his dress, the timing of his entry and exit, his resonant, powerful voice and a spell-binding delivery in which a mastery of language and of every rhetorical and literary device was spiced with wit, humour, personal anecdote (in which there was a strong element of self-display and self-praise), apt quotation from Urdu, Persian and Arabic verse and from the Quran and Hadis, and the use of impressive-sounding (and often unnecessary) English words and phrases. He regarded no one as too exalted to be the target of his humour and ridicule, but he was forthright not only in criticism but in generous, open-hearted praise, and he was not afraid to direct his mockery against himself. His humour was often distinctly vulgar in its tone and would on occasion have been in some measure offensive to many members of his audience.

It was these qualities that gave him an appeal which Sir Sayyid and Muhsin ul Mulk could never rival, excellent, powerful speakers though they were. Muhsin ul Mulk's speeches were models of scholarly analysis and of coherent, reasoned argument, but people preferred the long, wide-ranging, vigorous, varied speeches of Nazir Ahmad. It is important to note that the element of reasoned argument was not lacking in them. He said of himself:

I have one great fault. I start upon a theme, and as I go on speaking I stray far from the point. But sit there patiently! I know what themes I have left unfinished, and God willing, I shall complete them all and connect them one to the other.[12]

This he would always do. His lectures, in regard to their content, exemplify a modern school of thought, but their style continues the traditions of the old preachers and orators.

Nazir Ahmad's career as a speaker extended over seventeen years. His last lecture was delivered to the *Anjuman i Himayat i Islam* in 1905, when he gave up speaking for the Muhammadan Educational Conference because of a serious disagreement with Muhsin ul Mulk. During these years he had completed his series of 'novels'. *Ayyama* was published in 1891, and his last tale, *Ruya i Sadiqa*, was published in 1892, and now he started his directly religious writings.

Religious Writings (1893-1910)

From 1893 to 1910 he concentrated wholly on religious writings. In 1896 his translation of the Quran appeared. In 1906 he published *Al Huquq o al Faraiz* (Rights and Duties), a comprehensive guide to the conduct of life compiled by collecting and arranging in systematic order passages from the Quran and Hadis. In 1908 *Al Ijtihad* was published – *ijtihad* is the process whereby a Muslim who finds insufficient guidance for his conduct in the Quran, the Hadis and the consensus of Muslim thinkers, exercises his own powers of judgement to form conclusions. And in 1909 his most controversial book *Ummahat ul Ummat* (Mothers of the [Muslim] community) was published – an account of the wives of the Prophet. His earlier writings had already incurred some disapproval from leading Muslim divines, who held (with some justification) that his translation of the Quran incorporated here and there words which expressed a particular interpretation not warranted by the text. But stronger objections were raised because Nazir Ahmad's language was not sufficiently reverential, and the style of *Ummahat ul Ummat* provoked such a storm that he felt obliged to collect all copies of the book and hand them over to be burnt. Thereafter Iftikhar Ahmad Siddiqi says that he had no heart to write any more, but in 1909 his collected poems under the title of *Nazm i Benazir* (Verse without Parallel) were published, and in 1910 the first parts of an uncompleted work called *Matalib ul Quran* (Meanings of the Quran) appeared.

He suffered a stroke on 27 April 1912, and on 3 May he died.

In my opinion Nazir Ahmad's religious writings need to be studied more thoroughly than they have been, and with much greater respect. If his bluntness has caused offence, this speaks much more eloquently of the deficiencies in those who have felt offended than of any shortcoming in him. Both the knowledge and the seriousness which he brought to his task are beyond question, and so too is his complete and sincere commitment to the precepts of Islam as he understood them. His bluntness reflects this, and is fully justified. At the end of his preface to *Al Huquq o al Faraiz*, after explaining what he has done, he concludes:

> In short (this book) is a comprehensive guide to action, with instruction and guidance for all the situations that people confront in life. Every Muslim who professes to *be* a Muslim and who can read and understand Urdu should have a copy; at any rate every Muslim family should have a copy, and now don't say 'Nobody told us [what to do]'. If you do say that, who will listen to you?

That is a statement of great vigour, but it is one which no reader who is seriously concerned with seeking guiding Islamic principles for the conduct of life has any right to resent. If he treats the wives of the Prophet as human beings with human virtues and human frailties and writes accordingly, that is a far sounder and more truly religious attitude than that of those who believe that they were angels in human form. I have not studied his religious writings extensively, but what I have read is enough to give me a picture strongly favourable to Nazir Ahmad and sharply critical of his critics.[13] From Iftikhar Ahmad Siddiqi's account a clear picture of him emerges as one of the few great figures in Urdu literature who has had the courage to express a cordial, open, and fully justified contempt for those self-styled pillars of the Muslim community whose time and energy is spent (today as in Nazir Ahmad's time) in proving that every Muslim whose interpretation of Islam differs in the slightest degree from theirs is either a renegade or an infidel. Iftikhar Ahmad Siddiqi quotes him as saying,

> If you look into their position you will find that you can learn two lessons from the maulvis – first hypocrisy, and second idleness. How can a community prosper when people like these are its leaders and counsellors?[14]

and considers that 'Nazir Ahmad's bitter tone and colourful style alienated the maulvis quite unnecessarily'.[15]

On the contrary, open, vigorous opposition to Muslim divines of this kind was in Nazir Ahmad's day and remains today a paramount duty of every sincere Muslim who sees the need to restore Islam to the position of respect in the eyes of the world that it once commanded and to enhance that respect further.

Nazir Ahmad, for reasons which I can understand but in no way share, was bitterly and contemptuously hostile to the *ghazal*. But, ironically, it is one of the fundamental values of the *ghazal* that he upholds in his essay on man as the *khalifa*, or vicegerent of God. The essay is worth summarizing at length.[16]

He begins by saying that God, for reasons which He alone knows, created the universe and established the laws which govern it. Then, for reasons which He alone knows, he decided to create man and to make him His *khalifa* – that is, His representative or 'vicegerent' on earth, giving him the role of his assistant and endowing him with certain limited powers of independent action.

In order to exercise his powers most effectively he needs to understand the laws of the universe and is in a sense at one and the same time both subject to these laws and in control of their operation, like the rider of a horse who is enabled to reach his destination only by the power of the horse but nevertheless controls and directs that power.

He lays stress upon the fact that the role of vicegerency was conferred by God on every man 'without distinction of country or religious community. It is in his capacity as man that he is the vicegerent of God.' It is, of course, true that some are more capable of exercising their powers to the full than others are, but the key difference between man and man is that which is created by the degree of his knowledge of the laws of the universe. 'Hindus, Muslims, Christians, Jews, idolaters – any man, no matter where he lives, what his colour, what his constitution and what his beliefs – is the vicegerent of God.'

He goes on to discuss why it is that the Muslims have fallen so low and answers that it is because they have not understood what it means to be the vicegerent of God, have not grasped what God's objective was in creating mankind, have not estimated their worth truly, and have not been assiduous in discovering the laws of the universe. This last point is the key one in Nazir Ahmad's view, and he therefore stresses that it is everyone's duty to be tireless in the pursuit of knowledge, and that, too, not the traditional knowledge which he describes as 'nothing but verbosity and intellectual hypotheses'. but the new education which the English are spreading.

He concludes by saying that, as the verse of the Quran says, 'There is no created thing which does not praise Him', that all created things worship their Creator, and that their worship consists in their performing the functions for which God created them. Thus the sun's worship consists in giving warmth and light to the earth. The earth's worship is to produce food for those who dwell upon the earth. And men and women worship by fulfilling the duties that have been entrusted to them as God's vicegerents, that is, in constantly increasing their knowledge of the laws of the universe so that they may make the maximum use of them to enlarge their powers. He concludes his article with two quotations. The first is from the Quran and says, 'Without doubt the most god-fearing among His servants are the learned.' The second is from the Hadis and says, 'Without doubt the acquiring of knowledge is the duty of every Muslim man and every Muslim woman.'

A writer who has thought so deeply and rigorously on so key a concept is clearly one who will repay closer and more sympathetic study than he has yet received.

8. Changing Attitudes to Poetry: Azad and Hali

The main contribution of the 'Aligarh' period to Urdu literature was made in prose, and more particularly in prose narrative fiction, but the Aligarh outlook also exercised a significant influence on attitudes to Urdu poetry, expressed mainly in two books which between them laid the foundation of modern literary criticism in Urdu. These were Muhammad Husain Azad's *Ab i Hayat* (The Water of Life), first published in 1880, and Altaf Husain Hali's *Sher o Shairi* (Poetry and Poetics), published in 1893.

Azad was not closely associated with the Aligarh movement, but he was in general agreement with the Aligarh line of support for British rule and readiness to learn from contemporary British values. This outlook is expressed in *Ab i Hayat* in the fact that for the first time it presents Urdu poetry against some sort of historical background and gives critical assessments of the poets in something approaching a modern style.

Up to that time the main written sources of information about the Urdu poets had been the *tazkiras*. In general, these can be described as brief biographical dictionaries of the poets. Each entry would give, for example, the poet's name, his *takhallus* (pen-name), the city of his birth, his patrons, the date of his death, a description of the quality of his poetry, couched in rather conventional terms, and one or two specimen couplets from his *ghazals*.

It is generally said of them that this is just about all that they provide, that their major deficiencies are that they give no assessment of the poet's character and distinctive qualities, that their assessment of the poetry is more conventional than critical, that they show quite inadequate regard to historical accuracy, and that they have no sense of historical development or periodization.

A recent survey[1] of the *tazkira* literature, however, shows that these criticisms are too sweeping. The picture that emerges warrants the conclusion that you can take each of these criticisms one by one and in every case cite one, two or more *tazkiras* to which it applies, but there is perhaps none to which *all* apply; and, conversely, in one *tazkira* or another you can find something at least of *all* the qualities in which *tazkiras* in general are said to be deficient.

Ab i Hayat therefore represents less of an advance upon the *tazkira* literature than has generally been claimed. All the same it does take up and develop fully the good features of the *tazkira* literature, and adds substantially to the materials derived from it.

Its most striking feature is its periodization of Urdu poetry. Azad establishes five periods. He introduces each with a general characterization, generally couched in terms of poetic metaphor, and in most cases concludes with a similarly general survey. The bulk of the intervening material consists of accounts, turn by turn, of the major, and some not so major, poets of the period in question, beginning in each case with a fairly brief sketch of the events of the poet's life, and continuing at much greater length with a series of vivid anecdotes about him which bring out very well the character and outlook which find expression in the poetry. The account concludes with a selection from the poet's verse – generally only from his *ghazals*, but sometimes from other forms as well.

This overall pattern is, in general, a very satisfactory one, even though Azad's criteria for periodization are not. For him there are two – simple chronology, and changes in the language that the poets use. The distinct features of the different historical periods to which the poets belong are not explicitly brought out.

With Urdu speakers, Azad has a high reputation as a prose stylist. In my opinion his best prose is that in which he tells his anecdotes of the poets. These show both an eye for vivid details and a mastery of dialogue. Urdu speakers attach more importance to the more self-conscious passages, especially to the sustained metaphors of the opening and closing passages of each main section of *Ab i Hayat*. These are characterized not only by this quality of sustained metaphor but also by a fondness for *riyayat i lafzi* – play upon words – which is, in general, effectively used. Even where there is no particular point to be made it, it is often quite pleasing, as for example where he calls himself *banda i Azad*, 'your humble servant Azad', but where the words, at another level, mean the contradiction in terms 'free slave'. Typical passages in which he used *riyayat i lafzi* to good effect occur in his account of Atish, both at the point where he first speaks of his excellence as a poet, and later where he speaks of his death. These two passages are:

مصحفی کے شاگرد تھے ۔ اور حق یہ ہے کہ اُن کی آتش بیانی نے اُستاد کے نام کو روشن کیا ۔ بلکہ کلام کی گرمی اور چمک دمک نے اُستاد شاگرد کے کلام میں اندھیرے اُجالے کا امتیاز دکھایا ۔

یکایک ایسا موت کا جھوکا آیا کہ شعلہ کی طرح بجھ کر رہ گئے ۔ آتش کے گھر میں راکھ کے ڈھیر کے سوا اور کیا ہونا تھا؟

Only a rather literal translation can bring out the word play. Atish means 'flame', and the passages use metaphors of related concepts – light, radiance, heat, brightness, light and darkness, and ashes. I italicize these in the translation.

The first passage says:

He was the pupil of Mushafi, and the truth is that the *fire* of his expression gave *lustre* to the name of his master – indeed, the *heat* and *flash* of his poetry contrasted the verse of the master and the pupil as *light* and contrasts with *darkness*.

The second speaks of Atish's sudden death in poverty:

The sudden onslaught of death *extinguished* him as a gust of wind extinguishes a *flame*. And in the home of Atish (*fire*) what would be left but a heap of *ashes*?

All this he does without any apparent straining for effect. Another example is in his reference to *rekhti* (a rather curious genre of poetry in which the male poet speaks in the role of a woman), where he says, comparing Rangin and Insha:

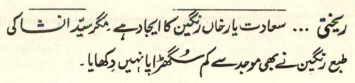

That is,

Actually *rekhti* is Rangin's invention, but Insha showed even greater *sughrapa* in it.

Sughrapa is the quality of being a neat and competent housewife, and its aptness in speaking of *rehkti* is obvious.

There was a time when critics belittled the value of Azad's work. In *Three Mughal Poets*[2] Khurshidul Islam and I wrote of this:

Many modern critics are inclined to dismiss Azad's stories as mere gossip, and therefore of no account. In our opinion this is too sweeping an attitude. At the time when Azad wrote he had access to written and oral sources which we no longer possess today, some deriving from the accounts of men who had personally known the poets of whom he wrote. Where his anecdotes do not conflict with more reliable evidence and are consistent with the picture which emerges from a study of the poet's own work, there is no reason to reject them absolutely, even though means of positive substantiation may be lacking and points of detail, on occasion, demonstrably false. At the very lowest assessment Azad's anecdotes are of value in showing the sort of impression their personalities made on their contemporaries.

Hali, unlike Azad, was deeply involved in the Aligarh movement, and fully committed to its political, social and cultural objectives. Before the movement had got under way he had already achieved some reputation as a *ghazal* poet, but he quickly became a fervent supporter of Sir Sayyid (whose biography he wrote) and put his poetic and critical skills at the service of the new movement. He did this in two ways: firstly by producing something quite new in Urdu verse (above all in his famous *musaddas*, to which I shall return later), and secondly by critically reviewing in *Sher o Shairi* the whole stock of classical poetry.

His attitudes – for one cannot speak of a single attitude – towards classical poetry are interesting. At his most unambiguous, he is at one with that other pillar of the Aligarh movement, Nazir Ahmad. Both men knew classical Persian and Urdu poetry well – and both roundly condemned it is as not only worthless but depraved and depraving. Nazir Ahmad on the very first page of his tale *Muhsinat: fasana i Mubtala* says:

همارے يہاں كی شاعری ميں عشق بازی اور بے تہذيبی كے سوا ہے كيا؟

What *is* there in our poetry except love-making and lack of refinement?

and he clearly regards addiction to poetry as one of the causes of the ruin of both Mubtala (the main character in *Muhsinat*) and Kalim, in *Taubat un Nasuh*. His view is not based on ignorance. His portrayal of Kalim, whose dialogue abounds in quotation from Urdu and Persian verse, is more than adequate evidence of this.

He has Nasuh explain to his wife Fahmida:

Poetry is not in itself bad; in fact if one defines it as mastery of language it deserves praise. But it has become the general rule to use that mastery as a vehicle for evil and indecent ideas; and that is why people who know the world regard it as a vice and a sin. Where its theme is satire, it comes in the category of slander; exaggerated praise is lying and falsehood. Impure thought of love and sexuality provide all its themes, and these are an offence against the law of Islam; and mocking at religion and ridicule of religious men is the equivalent of sinfulness and unbelief.

He goes on to attack the *Gulistan*, perhaps the most famous prose work in the whole of classical Persian literature. It was written by the great thirteenth century poet and prose writer Sadi, and has traditionally always been the first text that students of Persian read. But Nasuh (like Nazir Ahmad) is not the man to feel in the least inhibited by the fame of the book and the great reverence in which its author has traditionally been held. He asks Fahmida:

"Don't you remember when you were studying the Gulistan?"
'Of course I do,' she replies, 'I began it the day after Hamida was weaned.'
'And do you remember how before I set you a passage to read I would first delete line after line with black ink and sometimes paste plain paper over whole pages so as to hide them from you?'
'I certainly do. You must have done that to at least a quarter of the whole book.'
'It was only because it was you that I cut out so little as a quarter. If it had been another woman or a girl, I would have treated half of it in the same way. Those parts were all indecent.'
'Really? I thought you had cut them out because you thought they would be too difficult for me.'

'No, I couldn't have faced you with all that obscene and indecent stuff; and that is a book which aims to teach morality, the work of a writer whose name hardly any Muslim will speak without adding 'God's mercy be upon him' and regarding him as one of God's saints....'[3]

Hali, in his *musaddas*, is even more virulent than Nazir Ahmad:

That foul collection of verses and odes, which stinks worse than a cesspool, which has an impact in the world no less than an earthquake, and which makes the angels in heaven feel shame at it, has been the ruin of learning and religion. Such is the role among our arts and sciences of the art of literature.

If there is any punishment for the composing of depraved verse, if the telling of vain lies is impermissible, then that court in which God is judge, and in which retribution of good and bad deeds is decreed, will release all other sinners and fill hell with our poets.

In his *Sher o Shairi*, a comprehensive survey and critique of the whole range of Urdu poetry, he is more careful, particularly in his critique of the *ghazal*, which is perhaps the most significant part of the book. The way in which he approaches it is striking. He acknowledges that the popularity of the *ghazal* is unrivalled, with literate and illiterate. With young and old alike, and that its influence is enormous. He recognizes that this popularity is based upon its preoccupation with the themes of love, and that without this its allure cannot be maintained. Unless its foundations continue to rest on themes of love, he says, the *ghazal* can no more prosper and maintain its popularity than wine can intoxicate after it has turned to vinegar.

But this situation presents him with a formidable problem. He recognizes, with a refreshing bluntness which is to this day exceptional, that the human beloved of the *ghazal* can only be either a woman who is already betrothed or married, or a courtesan, or a boy; and he is at pains to point out that in a community that observes purdah, to write of your love for another's betrothed or another's wife, or for a courtesan, is to advertise your lack of moral fibre. Though he has insisted throughout the book that poetry must be 'simple, full of passion, and founded upon reality' (*sada, josh se bhara hua, aur asliyat par mabni*), such illicit love is an aspect of reality which he does not want portrayed, because he shares the disapproval of it which the social and religious establishment feels. The way he argues himself out of this dilemma is to stress (unnecessarily) that love has many manifestations. There is the love between man and God, between children and parents, between husband and wife, between king and subject, master and servant, friend and friend, man and animal, man and home, birthplace, country, community (= *qaum*), family, and so on. (This stress is unnecessary because, as he himself points out, the *ghazal* concept of love has always embraced all these things.) He hopes he can persuade *ghazal* poets, if not to stop falling in love with other people's fiancées and wives and courtesans and boys, at any rate to conceal this and to write of love only in terms which can apply equally to all the kinds of love he has listed. It is not surprising that this appeal to, so to speak, draw the teeth of the ghazal did not meet with a very enthusiastic response even in his own time and has been generally ignored ever since. Perhaps people have felt that his recipe was itself one which would turn the *ghazal's* wine into vinegar.

There is some reason to think that, here as in other fields, Hali felt himself torn between conflicting ideas. His best prose work is *Yadgar i Ghalib* (A Memoir of Ghalib) in which his love and respect for Ghalib is evident throughout. It is clearly because he loved Ghalib that he wanted to write about him and could not resist this desire. But his ideology told him that the object of biography is to hold up improving examples which readers would be encouraged to emulate. He knew that Ghalib didn't really fit this bill, and so he had to find some equally respectable justification for writing about him. One can only smile at the justification he found.

> Ghalib's life is not entirely devoid of those lessons which a biography ought to teach us. But even if we disregard these lessons it is still important that people of a society despondent and dead at heart should be told the story of a life which – even if there had been nothing to learn from it – is full of a kind of vivaciousness and joy.[4]

Similarly with the *ghazal*. He valued his own *ghazals*, and it is interesting to note that he wrote *Sher o Shairi* as a *muqaddima* (introductory essay) to his collected *ghazals*. Yet the best of the *ghazals* do not exemplify, or at any rate do not consistently exemplify, the principles which his introductory essay lays down. One feels that at some points in his essay he wrote what he wished he thought rather than what, deep down, he actually did think.

Hali's prose style only very rarely rises to any appreciable heights. He is honest and earnest but uninspired, and his pedestrian and often convoluted prose reflects these qualities. Only on the rare occasions when he feels strong emotion (usually of remorse or regret) does his prose come to life, as when he concludes his long, painstaking (and sometimes painful) survey of Urdu poetry with these words:

> And here I conclude my essay. To expect that our old poets, steeped in the traditions of the old poetry, would deign to pay any attention to it, or to think it worthy of any attention, would be pointless; and it would be absurd to think that everything I have written in it must command acceptance. But I hope that my young fellow countrymen who have a taste for poetry and can read the signs of the times may read it and at least acknowledge that Urdu poetry in its present state stands in need of reform and improvement. I have set out in this essay my humble opinions on the reform of poetry; even if they do not accept a single one of these and yet my essay gives currency in our country to the thought that poetry does indeed need reforming, I will consider that I have been completely successful, because the first step on the ladder to progress is the awareness of one's decline...
>
> I am only human, and if I have written anything that gives offence to any of my fellow countrymen, then in all humility and with all respect I ask their forgiveness. Since this essay is, as far as I am aware, the first of its kind in

Urdu, it is possible that along with its merits (if it has any) there will be faults... Although God has given us the principle 'Good qualities cancel bad ones', man has established the principle. 'Bad qualities cancel good ones'. So I should not entertain the hope that along with the mistakes in the essay its good points too will be spoken of. But if people will content themselves with pointing out the mistakes and not take pains to present the good points in the guise of mistakes, even then I will think myself extremely fortunate.

I said earlier that in the field of poetry Hali served the aims of the Aligarh movement in two ways – firstly by contributing something quite new in Urdu verse and secondly by writing a critique of classical poetry. The new contribution (which preceded the critique) is represented above all by his long poem *Madd o Jazr i Islam* (literally, 'The Flow and Ebb of Islam') first published in 1879. It was written in the *musaddas* form (six-line stanzas rhyming AAAABB, CCCCDD, and so on) and is commonly known simply as *Hali's Musaddas*. In it he tries to rouse the Indian Muslims to an awareness of their degradation, celebrates the cultural and scientific achievements of Muslims of former times, and calls upon his contemporaries to draw inspiration from the past to once more make their mark in world history. The popularity of this poem was immense, and Sir Sayyid's own assessment of it a very high one. He wrote of it:

Yes, it was I who urged you to write it, and I rank this so high among my stock of good deeds that when (on Judgement Day) God will ask me, 'What have you brought here?' I will say, 'I have brought the *Musaddas* which I got Hali to write: nothing more.[5]

Abdul Haq (often described as the *baba i Urdu* – grand old man of Urdu of the present century) vividly described the impact that the poem continued to make years after it was written. He heard it recited at a function held to celebrate his cousin's circumcision, and writes:

It was morning. A huge marquee had been erected on the open ground and not only was it packed: the crowd extended far beyond it. Most of the people present were villagers – from his own village and from villages nearby. Now a courtesan stood up – she had been sent for from Lahore; she cast an eye over the people assembled and all at once began to sing Hali's Musaddas... All the while she was singing there was dead silence. Some of the audience were swaying to the rhythm, and some were in tears. I can still see the scene, and her singing still rings in my ears.

Shaikh Muhammad Ikram, who quotes this passage in his book *Mauj i Kausar*[6] (a history of Muslim movements in nineteenth century India), comments, quite rightly, that in the twentieth century its popularity has declined. In my view it is now less highly regarded than it ought to be. It does not maintain a uniformly high level of excellence, but the opening verses, in which he expresses a deep and bitter sense of the deplorable and yet complacent backwardness of his contemporaries, and those in which he describes the revolution in social life which Muhammad brought to Arabia, are moving poetry of great power.

Little else in 'Aligarh' verse survives that can be classed as a really valuable contribution to Urdu literature. Nevertheless, both Azad and Hali were significant influences on Urdu literary taste in their own day, and their influence has left a permanent mark. Azad encouraged Urdu speakers to assess their poetic heritage by new standards and at the same time to cherish it, while Hali, for all his excesses, challenged them to take a clear, hard look at it, to be more discriminating in their judgement of it, and to open their minds to the need for new forms in which they could express more freely and precisely a response to the demands of a new age.

9. The Satirical Verse of Akbar Ilhabadi

Ralph Russell and Khurshidul Islam

Akbar Ilhabadi – Akbar of Allahabad – has been the victim of much injustice
at the hands of scholars, both in the West and in the Indo-Pakistan subcontinent
that was his homeland. The reason is a simple one. Akbar's fame is based – and
quite properly based – upon his humorous verse; and scholars tend to be rather
solemn people who may enjoy reading humorous verse in the brief periods of
recreation which they allow themselves, but to whom the thought simply does
not occur that a man may express in humorous verse ideas just as significant,
and basically just as serious, as, let us say, a man who writes a voluminous
commentary on holy writ. Akbar was such a poet. Indeed in one of his verses
he tells us as much:[1]

شاہدِ معنی نے اوڑھا ہے ظرافت کا لحاف   سردِ موسم تھا ہوا ئیں چل رہی تھیں برف بار

Which may be translated:

> It was the winter: icy winds were blowing cold;
> My meaning's beauty wrapped itself in humour's cloak.

What he thought of as the 'icy winds' of winter will become clear in the course
of this article.

Akbar was born in 1846, and lived till 1921. He made his name as a poet at
a time when the Aligarh movement of Sir Sayyid and his supporters was
established as the major trend among the Muslims of the age. But Akbar's view
of British rule was very different from that which Sir Sayyid held. Both men
were agreed that British power was supreme and, for the foreseeable future,
unshakeable. But where Sir Sayyid saw in this the creation of conditions in
which a natural identity of British and Muslim interests would assert itself, the
guarantee of progress, and the hope of ever closer association between ruler and
ruled, Akbar ridiculed the idea. In more than one verse he quotes with approval
the homely Indian peasant equivalent of the sentiment that 'might is right' – 'he
who wields the big stick owns the buffalo' – with its implication not only that
the British ruled because no one else was strong enough to challenge them, but
also that they ruled in their own interest, and not with any nobler aim in mind.

To Sir Sayyid's talk of 'progress' and 'association' he replies bluntly:[2]

کیسی ترقی کیسا میل   ہم سے سن لو اس کا کھیل

جس کی لاٹھی اس کی بھینس   فعلٌ فعلٌ فعلٌ فعل

(The last line is meaningless, and simply exemplifies the beat of the metre.)
I translate the verse:

> What do you mean? 'Progress', 'Association' –
> Listen to me, *I*'ll tell you how it's done.
> '*He* owns the buffalo who wields the cudgel.'
> Ti-tum ti-tum ti-tum ti-tum ti-tum.

– 'ti-tum ti-tum ti-tum ti-tum ti-tum' – or, in other words, if you want another
line to complete the piece, you can have one – but really once you have said '*He*
owns the buffalo who wields the cudgel', there's nothing more to *be* said.

Akbar doesn't want to varnish reality in any way. The British rule India
because they have the *power* to do so, and not for any other reason, and that is
no reason for an Indian to rejoice, and still less for an Indian Muslim to rejoice.
He doesn't forget, and doesn't *want* to forget, what the establishment of
unchallengeable British power has meant to his country, and what are the
penalties of defeat:[3]

جو گزرو گے ادھر سے میرا اُجڑا گاؤں دیکھو گے   شکستہ ایک مسجد ہے بغل میں گورا بارک ہے

> If you should pass that way you'll see my ravaged village:
> A Tommies' barracks standing by a ruined mosque

– the Tommies' barracks the symbol of British power, and the ruined mosque
the symbol of Muslim defeat.

The themes of the all-pervading power of the British and of the irreversible
changes they have wrought occur again and again in his verse. A whole poem of
nine couplets has the recurring rhyme *un ke hath men* – 'in their hand' or 'in their
grasp, in their control'. A rather literal, and slightly abridged, translation of some
of its lines[4] will give some idea of the recurring, heavy force of this refrain.

ملک ان کا رزقِ کی تقسیم اُن کے ہاتھ میں   تختِ کے قابض وہی دیہیم ان کے ہاتھ میں

آ گیا تارِ امید و بیم اُن کے ہاتھ میں   . . . .

سب کی ہے تذلیل اور تعظیم اُن کے ہاتھ میں   . . . .

قوم ان کے ہاتھ میں تسلیم اُن کے ہاتھ میں   . . . .

ایک دن دیکھیں گے ہفت اقلیم ان کے ہاتھ میں   مغرب الٰہی ہی رہا اور ہے اگر مشرق یہی

They hold the throne in their hand. The whole realm is in their hand. The country, the apportioning of men's livelihood, is in their hand....The springs of hope and of fear are in their hand....In their hand is the power to decide who shall be humbled and who exalted....Our people is in their hand, education is in their hand....If the West continues to be what it is, and the East what *it* is, we shall see the day when the whole world is in their hand.

Another complete poem expresses the sense of living in a new world, in which everything has changed.[5]

وہ مطرب اور وہ سازو وہ گانا بدل گیا   نیندیں بدل گئیں وہ فسانہ بدل گیا

رنگِ فروغِ بہار کی زینت ہوئی نئی   گلشن میں بلبلوں کا ترانہ بدل گیا

فطرت کے ہر اثر میں ہوا ایک انقلاب   پانی فلک پہ کھیت میں دانہ بدل گیا

The minstrel, and the music, and the melody have all changed. Our very sleep has changed; the tale we used to hear is no longer told. Spring comes with new adornments; the nightingales in the garden sing a different song. Nature's every effect has undergone a revolution. Another kind of rain falls from the sky; another kind of grain grows in the fields.

What, in more concrete terms, these changes are, he will tell us in other poems. The British themselves, he notes sardonically, tend to be reticent about them. He reflects bitterly how often the British accuse the Muslims (and the accusation is still a familiar one in the West) of having spread their religion by the sword. Even if that were true, Akbar tells them, the force *we* used cannot compare with the force you have used. And if we spread Islam, we brought to our subjects a faith which inspired those who embraced it with a new dignity and a new purpose in life. And what have *you* brought *your* subjects?

یہی فرماتے رہے تیغ سے پھیلا اسلام

یہ نہ ارشاد ہوا توپ سے کیا پھیلا ہے

You never ceased proclaiming that Islam spread by the sword:
You have not deigned to tell us what it is the gun has spread.[6]

Akbar has no inhibitions about saying 'what it is the gun has spread'. First, it has founded a regime which regards India simply as a land stocked with goods destined for Europe. If Muslims think of India as a land of Islam they are wrong; if Hindus think of it as the land of their mythical heroes, Laksman and Ram, they are deceived. India is merely Europe's warehouse, populated by loyal subjects of the British Raj.[7]

یہ بات غلط کہ ملک اسلام ہے ہند   یہ جھوٹ کہ ملک چمن و رام ہے ہند

ہم سب ہیں مطیع و خیرخواہِ انگلش   یورپ کے لئے بس ایک گودام ہے ہند

Those who support British ideas and values speak of them as the 'New Light' which brings *tahzib* or 'refinement' to those who embrace it. Sir Sayyid's influential periodical was called *Tahzib ul Akhlaq* – 'the Refinement of Manners' – 'manners' in the broader and more significant sense of the term. But Akbar cannot see how the light which only shows men how to exploit others can shed 'the radiance of refinement' nor will he give the name of human progress to the process which ruins a thousand men to advance the interest of a hundred.[8]

جس روشنی میں لوٹ ہی کی آپ کو سوجھے   تہذیب کی میں اس کو تجلی نہ کہوں گا

لاکھوں کو مٹا کر جو ہزاروں کو ابھالے   اس کو تو میں دنیا کی ترقی نہ کہوں گا

> The light that only lights the path to plunder
> I will not call 'refinement's radiance'.
> You ruin thousands to promote a hundred:
> I'll not call that 'humanity's advance'.

Not that he is always so grimly serious about it. In one verse[9] he contemplates the plight of the once well-to-do Muslim, deprived by the new regime of his former wealth, debarred by its puritanism from his former pleasures, and compelled by its new laws to give up his gun unless they grant him a licence to own one.

لذت چاہو تو وصلِ معشوق کہاں   شوکت چاہو تو زر کا صندوق کہاں

کہتا ہے یہ دل کہ خودکشی کی ٹھہرے   خیر اس کو بھی مان لیں تو بندوق کہاں

> You have no gold: how can you live in style?
> You have no mistress: how can you have fun?
> And if you want to end it all – alright –
> But then how can you when you have no gun?

In another verse[10] he contrasts the period of Muslim rule with that of the British. Its force depends on untranslatable play upon words:

پہلے تو حید تھی توابِ تفصیل   آگے غل ایک کا تھا اب دو کا

Tauhid – insistence upon the unity, the oneness, of God is contrasted with *tahsil* – the process of getting something from someone. The two words are parallel formations from two Arabic roots, and are identical in metrical weight. In the second half of the couplet there is a play on *ek*, which means 'one', and *do* which means 'two' – but also means 'give'. "'In our day," says Akbar, the stress was on God's *tauhid* – unity, and the cry was *ek*! – "one!" In their day the stress is on *tahsil* – extraction of wealth – and the cry is *do*! – meaning not "two" (although the word *can* mean that) but "Give!"'

The British established their rule by force, but they do not depend simply on force to maintain it. Unlike us, says Akbar[11]

مغربی اس کی طبیعت کو بدل دیتے ہیں مشرقی تو سرِ دشمن کو کُچل دیتے ہیں

We of the East break our opponents' heads
They of the West change their opponents' nature.

And perhaps their most effective weapon in this process is their system of education. First comes the gun, to break armed resistance, and then education to induce acceptance of the new order.[12]

جب لبوں لاہٹا تو رنداہے توپ چلی پر وفیسر یو پنچے

The guns have gone, and now come the professors.
The adze has done its work; now comes the plane.

They are bent on destroying us, but take steps to see that we don't feel it.[13]

قتل سے پہلے ہے کلوروفارم
شکر ہے اُن کی مہربانی کا

Before they murder us they chloroform us.
We ought to render thanks that they are kind.

The fact that there are ways in which Indians can benefit from the education which the British offer – and Akbar, as we shall see later, does not deny this – does not alter the fact that it was to serve their own interests and not their subjects' interests that the British introduced it. Akbar stresses its limitations in a whole poem leading up to the concluding couplet.[14]

تعلیم جو دی جاتی ہے ہمیں وہ کیا ہے فقط بازاری ہے
جو عقل سکھائی جاتی ہے وہ کیا ہے فقط سرکاری ہے

They give us learning – just enough for us to sell our services
And understanding – just enough for governmental purposes.

In fact, as he says in another verse:[15]

جس کے لائق تھی جو چیز اس کو ملی   ہے خدا ہی کی طرف ہر اک کا سورس

ان کا پاکٹ اور پیداوار ملک   حافظہ بندے کا اور کالج کا کورس

       All things receive the things most fitted to them
       God's will alone determines every source
       Their pocket holds the produce of our country
       Your servant's memory holds the college course

Along with education go other devices to reconcile you to your lot, like the pomp and splendour of durbars and other ceremonies of state. Akbar remarks rather sourly how kind it is of King George the Fifth, who besides being King of Great Britain, is also Emperor of India, to put himself out to spend ten whole days there.[16]

لندن سے دہلی آئے ہیں دس یوم کے لئے   یہ زحمتیں اٹھائیں فقط قوم کے لئے

One of his most famous longer poems describes an earlier durbar – the Delhi durbar of 1903.[17] At one point, after describing all the entrancing sights that meet his eyes he sums it all up in the words:[18]

آنکھیں میری ، باقی اُن کا

       My eyes are mine; the rest is theirs

And he imagines another Indian talking to him:[19]

پہننے کو تو کپڑے ہی نہ تھے کیا بزم میں جاتے   خوشی مگر بیٹھے کر لی ہم نے جشنِ تاج پوشی کی

       We had no clothes – how could we go to see the celebrations?
       We had to stay at home to celebrate the coronation.

Anyway, the whole thing is a lot of fuss about nothing. The rush and bustle of preparation remind you of the tumult of Judgement Day. But, he says:[20]

ہنگامۂ محشر کا تو مقصود ہے معلوم   دہلی میں یہ دربار ہے معلوم نہیں کیوں

       The tumult of the Day of Judgement has some purpose to it.
       But this durbar in Delhi now – what is *that* all about?

And in another verse[21] where, as often, he presses home an oft-repeated lesson with a neat topical reference, he calls upon his readers to see with what splendour the stars shine in the heavens, how God is an Emperor whose rule their illuminations celebrate every night, with a show that never fails to entrance you – and to which the angels admit everyone free, without ticket.

ملک پر شان و عظمت سے ستارے جگمگاتے ہیں   خدا کی سلطنت کی جو جلی ہر شب مناتے ہیں

یہی نظارہ ہم کو محو رکھتا ہے سدا اکبر   فرشتے بے ٹکٹ دیں نظرِ اعظم دکھاتے ہیں

Finally there is the sham – as Akbar thinks it – of consultation with the representatives of native opinion, membership of advisory councils, and so on. These are a sham because the British in any case can, and do, act they please – those who rule the country rule the councils, says Akbar[22]

کونسل تو ہے ان کی ہی جن کا ہے راج

– and the councils' only object is to enable publicity-seeking Indians to make a show and to keep them happy with the illusion that they are in some degree controlling their own destinies. That, says Akbar, is like judging the ways of English women by the ways of Indian women.[23]

وصل کا اس بت سے خود دیں سے کوئی ہنٹ کہاں   صرف بوسے میں بجلا سلف گورنمنٹ کہاں

Don't think it means the lady's going to sleep with you.
A mere kiss doesn't mean self-government.

Akbar would be more convinced of the benevolence of British rule if it produced an increase in the general well-being. What the British are doing is like giving medicine to a man who above all needs food.[24]

دوا ہے کالج اور کونسل سواس کی ہے فراوانی

غذا ہے راحتِ دل اور دولت) وہ بہت کم ہے

The medicines of colleges and councils flow abundantly.
The food – of peace and plenty – is in very short supply.

To 'honour' an Indian by making him a member of a council is like putting rouge on the cheeks of a starving woman.[25]

عزّت تِلی ہے شرکتِ کونسل کی شیخ کو

غازہ ملّا گیا ہے رُخِ فاقہ مست پر

And all the council's busy activities result in nothing substantial.[26]

رزولیوشن کی شورِش ہے مگر اس کا اثر غائب

پلیٹوں کی سدا سنتا ہوں اور کھانا نہیں آتا

Their resolutions make a din, but nothing ever comes of them
I hear the clatter of the plates, but dinner never comes.

The real nature of British rule becomes clear when you note the way in which
British officials treat their Indian fellow-subjects of the Crown. Akbar, here
again, ridicules the more gullible of his fellow-countrymen, who think that
solemn official proclamations mean what they say:[27]

کاغذ پہ اعتراف مگر دل میں کچھ نہیں

On paper they respect you; in their hearts they don't.

When Indians speak of themselves and the British as 'We' the British laugh at
them. He tells them:[28]

کہتے ہو تم جوڑی تو انھیں آتی ہی ہنسی   یعنی زبانِ شوق غلط لفظ میں کھنسی

When you say 'We' it only makes them laugh.
Your fervour brings the wrong words to your tongue.

What the British want are men who listen, not men who speak, even to ask
questions, much less to form judgements. Many lines, delivered, so to speak,
with a straight face, show that Akbar knows what is expected of him:

وہ کہتے ہیں یہ ٹھیک ہے ہم کہتے ہیں جی ہاں   بالفعل تو ہم اس کے سوا کچھ نہیں کرتے

They say 'This is correct.': we say 'Quite so.'
And, for the present, this is all we do.[29]

حکم خاموشی ہے اور میری زباں   آپ کی باتیں ہیں میرا کان ہے

The order to be silent binds my tongue
You have the right to speak, and I to hear.[30]

جھوٹ سے سچ کو کون چینتا ہے

آپ کہتے ہیں بندہ سنتا ہے

You don't think true and false concern me, do you?
Speak on: your humble servant listens to you.[31]

Even his Indian beloved, to whom he expresses the traditional complete sub-
mission demanded of the true lover, is familiar with his situation *vis à vis* the
British.[32]

میں نے کہا کہ اپنا سمجھتے مجھے غلام

بولا وہ بُت یہ ہنس کے فرنگی نہیں ہوا میں

I said to her 'Regard me as your slave.'
She laughed and said, 'I'm not an Englishman!'

And however respectful and subservient you may be, no Englishman is going
to treat you with anything but disdain. Among Indians, a fair complexion is
generally admired. But to an Englishman *all* Indians are blacks.[33]

میں کوں منہ لے کے انہیں شکل بکھلاؤں

گورے کو کہا جب یہ نگوڑا حبشی ہے

How can I have the brazenness to show my face before him?
He's said of fairer men than I, 'The fellow is a black!'

The most that you can expect is a curt greeting:[34]

اب اور چاہئے ینٹو کے واسطے کیا بات

یہی بہت ہے مشرف ہوئے سلام سے ہم

What greater honour could a native want than that?
Is it not plenty that he said 'Good day' to us?

A native counts for little, and an Indian native for less, and an Indian Muslim native for least of all.[35]

بھلا کیا پوچھنا ہے شانِ اکبر کا زمانے میں   کہ نیٹیو بھی ہے ہندوستانی بھی مسلماں بھی

Why ask what Akbar's standing is these days?
First, native; second, Indian; third, Muslim.

And in case you ever *should* think of stepping out of line, the police are there to watch you and control you:[36]

ہر گام پہ چند آنکھیں نگراں ہر موڑ پہ اک لیسنس طلب

at every step, eyes watching you, at every turn a demand to show a permit.

Some of Akbar's views of the police are perhaps rather startling to the average law-abiding British citizen, who, on the whole, tends to look upon the police as his protectors. But whatever they may be in Britain, they have perhaps never been that in India. Percival Spear has written of them[37] that they were 'undeniably unpopular....The stigmata of corruption and unnecessary brutality attached themselves to the police from the beginning and have not yet been shaken off.'

And to politically active Indians the '*khufia pulis*', the secret police or CID, have always been especially objectionable. Akbar, at any rate, doesn't find much to choose between them and the criminals they are supposed to pursue:[38]

شیخ جی کے دونوں بیٹے با ہنر پیدا ہوئے   ایک ہیں خفیہ پولیس میں ایک پھانسی پا گئے

The old man only had two sons; both turned out able fellows.
One went into the CID, the other to the gallows.

And in fact one of his objections to the CID is that it doesn't confine its efforts to checking real crime, but is equally busy checking those liberties on which the British profess to pride themselves:[39]

چوری نہ کبھی کی ہے نہ کرنے کا ارادہ   پھر بھی یہ ضرورت ہے کہ بھاگوں سوؤں سے

I never stole, nor do I plan to steal
And yet I have to run away from spies.

And, more bluntly still:[40]

پولیس خفیہ ہے انسدادِ جرم ہے ٹھیک   نہ چاہئے کہ وہ ہو انسدادِ گپ کے لئے

The CID is busily engaged in checking crime – alright.
It ought not to be busily engaged in checking talk.

And from all this – the contemplation of British power based in the last resort on force of arms which they are prepared to use, but sustained also by other methods, such as an education with moulds their subjects' outlook, trifling concessions which keep them happy, and many other things – Akbar concludes that there is nothing that Indians can do for the foreseeable future but accept British rule and make the best of it. In the true tradition of the classical Urdu *ghazal* which makes all manner of criticisms of society in words which cannot, when you look at them carefully, be conclusively *proved* to mean what they are correctly assumed to mean, he writes:[41]

بے سود آج تذکرۂ عدل و جور ہے   اپنا بھی ایک وقت تھا اُن کا بھی دَور ہے

Why talk today of justice and of tyranny?
We had our day; now they are having theirs.

where there is not much doubt that he is associating the idea of justice with Mughal rule, and the idea of tyranny with British rule, although the words do not quite unambiguously say so.

Or in the verse:[42]

ہم آہ بھی کرتے ہیں تو ہو جاتے ہیں بدنام   وہ قتل بھی کرتے ہیں تو چرچا نہیں ہوتا

If we so much as sigh we get a bad name.
They kill, and not a word is said about it.

Where the couplet *could* be taken in the context of the prevailing theme of the traditional *ghazal*, with its cruel mistresses to whose every act of tyranny their true lovers must submit without complaint – but where probably the 'They' of 'They kill' is a reference to the British.

Whatever your view of British rule, it is clear that you cannot stand against it. It is characteristic of Akbar that he combines his unpalatable advice to his fellow-countryment with ridicule of their Christian rulers' belief in the doctrine of the Trinity, a belief which, to the Muslim, is at best absurd and at worst blasphemous. He writes:[43]

یورپ والے جو چاہیں دل میں بھر دیں   جس کے سر پر جو چاہیں تہمت دھر دیں
بچتے رہیو اُن کی تیزیوں سے اکبر   تم کیا ہو خدا کے تین ٹکڑے کر دیں

The Englishman can slander whom he will
And fill your head with anything he pleases.
He wields sharp weapons, Akbar. Best stand clear!
He cuts up God himself into three pieces.

But, despite the joke, the essential point, as nearly always with Akbar, is a serious one: Akbar is arguing that Muslims must determine how best to live their lives starting from the fact that the British are now all powerful, and that Indians are going to have to live with this situation for a long, long time.

Opportunities and Dangers Under British Rule

Akbar does not deny that British rule has brought some benefits to India. What he ridicules is the idea that it was established for that purpose, and the accompanying idea that what India has lost by it – if indeed it has lost anything at all – is far outweighed by what it has gained. No, he says. The British won India by the sword – or, rather, by the gun – and they hold it by the gun, and hold it in their own interests. But it does not follow that all that they have done is bad; and where they have introduced useful things, it is simple good sense to take advantage of them. This general view leads him to his assessment of Sir Sayyid and the Aligarh movement. And despite much that has been written to the contrary by men who ought to know better (and in some cases undoubtedly *do* know better), that assessment is essentially a positive one. After Sir Sayyid's death in 1898 he wrote of him:[44]

ہماری باتیں ہی باتیں ہیں سَیّد کام کرتا تھا   نہ بھولو فرق جو ہے کہنے والے کرنیوالے میں
کہے جو چاہے کوئی میں تو یہ کہتا ہوں اے اکبر   خدا بخشے بہت سی خوبیاں تھیں مرنیوالے میں

> We only talk and talk and talk – while Sayyid used to work.
> Remember that to talk is not the same thing as do.
> Men may say what they like of him; what Akbar says is this:
> God grant him peace now he is dead. His virtues were not few.

And when he writes in this way he is not simply conforming to the conventional principle that one does not speak ill of the dead. His contemptuous epitaph on Sir Sayyid's British mentor, the English Principal of the Aligarh College Mr Beck, shows a complete disregard for this convention.[45] And there is more conclusive evidence in verses, some of them written during Sir Sayyid's lifetime, in which he praises his efforts and expresses his satisfaction with Aligarh's positive achievement. In 1892 when the College was in great financial difficulties, and the Nizam of Hyderabad came to its aid by doubling his monthly contribution to its funds – increasing this from Rs 1,000 to Rs 2,000 – Akbar wrote a poem of 15 couplets expressing his pleasure. The first seven are a generous tribute to Sir Sayyid, and there is not the slightest reason to doubt their sincerity. He writes:[46]

سب جلتے ہیں علم سے ہے زندگیِ رُوح   بے علم ہے اگر تو وہ انساں ہے ناتمام

بے علم و بے ہنر ہے جو دنیا میں کوئی قوم   نیچر کا اقتضا ہے رہے بن کے وہ غلام

تعلیم اگر نہیں ہے زمانے کے حسبِ حال   پھر کیا امیدِ دولت و آرام و احتشام

سیّد کے دل میں نقش ہوا اس خیال کا   ڈالی بنائے مدرسے کے خدا کا نام

All men know that the life of the spirit depends upon knowledge: without knowledge no man is a complete man: it is an inexorable law of nature that the nation which lacks knowledge and skills is destined to be the slave of others; and if education does not meet the needs of the age then all hopes of attaining wealth and comfort and honour are idle. This thought was engraved upon Sir Syyid's consciousness, and trusting in God, he laid the foundations of his college. He suffered setbacks, and disappointments, and the abuse of his opponents, but this servant of his nation kept to his task and showed the world what a stout heart and a powerful intellect can do – showed them what hard work really means. And because he worked sincerely God prospered him, and a splendid college was built.

Of all Sir Sayyid's teachings, his reinterpretation of religion was that which commanded least support; indeed the majority of his own most prominent supporters parted company with him in this field. (One of them, Nazir Ahmad, remarked caustically that trying to argue as he did was like trying to touch your buttocks with your ears.)[47] True, he shared with many Muslims of the old anti-British trend a puritan urge to revive the pristine simplicity of Islam; but an even more prominent aspect of his reinterpretation was his attempt, exceptionally bold in his day, to show a complete harmony between Islam and the findings of modern science. Akbar, like most of his contemporaries, had little sympathy for this part of Sir Sayyid's teaching. Yet in a poem about Sir Sayyid's religious doctrines,[48] Akbar stresses only the many features in them of which he approves, and says nothing of the others. The sting comes in the tail of the poem but it is most significant that the quite trenchant attack which it makes is directed not at Sir Sayyid, but at other exponents of the New Light with whom Akbar contrasts him.

In short, Akbar is not against progress. He knows that times are changing
and that the Muslims must change with them, learning new things and making
new adaptations to new conditions. He doesn't object in principle even to
changes which he considers unnecessary, and which he personally dislikes. If
you keep strong the faith by which you live, and obey the essential command-
ments of Islam, you may dress as you like, wear either a Western hat or an
Eastern turban just as you please,[49] eat what food you like in whatever company
you like,[50] and pay court to Anglo-Indian and British girls. There are verses in
which he declares his readiness to accept all these things, provided that the
commands of religion are heeded and not ignored.

قائم یہی بوٹ اور موزا رکھتے   دل کو مشتاق ہس ڈسوزا رکھتے

ان باتوں پہ معترض نہ ہوگا کوئی   پڑھتے جو نماز اور روزہ رکھتے

By all means wear your boots and socks
By all means woo your Christian miss
Just say your prayers and keep the fast
And no one will object to this.[51]

We need to bear these verses in mind when we read others in which he ridicules
new fashions. If he thinks them ridiculous he can say so; but that is not the same
thing as saying that they transgress the laws of religion, and Akbar *doesn't* say
that.

He does, however, express his fears and his misgivings about what Sir
Sayyid's teaching and Aligarh education may ultimately lead to. In one of the
relatively few verses directly critical of Sir Sayyid himself he questions how far
his vision really went.[52]

کیا جانتے سید تھے حق آگاہ کہاں تک

سمجھے نہ کہ سیدھی ہے مری راہ کہاں تک

Who knows how far Sir Sayyid saw the truth?
The end of his straight road was out of sight.

And for all his general approval of Aligarh education, he feels that there is an
emphasis upon material and secular things which obscures to a dangerous extent
the even greater importance of a strong faith in religion as the only sure guide
on life's journey.

A whole poem on the Aligarh College leads up to this point:[53]

خدا علی گڑھ کے مدرسے کو بتلا ام امراض سے شفا دے — جو رہے ہوتے ہیں رئیس زادے امیر زادے شریف زادے

لطیف و خوش منش چست و چالاک صاف و پاکیزہ شاد و خرم — طبیعتوں میں ہے ان کی جدت دلوں میں انکے نہیں کج ادا دے

کمال محنت سے پڑھ رہے ہیں کمال غیرت سے بڑھ رہے ہیں — سوار مشرق کی راہ میں ہیں ہی تو مغربی راہ میں پیادے

ہر ایک ہے ان میں کا بیشک ایسا کہ آپ اسے چاہتے ہیں جیسا — دکھائے محفل میں قدر و عنا جو آپ آئیں تو سر جھکا دے

قبیر باتخمیں تو صاف کہہ دیں کہ تو ہے معبود و جا ایک کھلا — قبول فرمائیں آپ دعوت تو اپنا سرمایہ کل کھلا دے

بتوں سے ان کو نہیں لگا و ٹھ مسوں کی لیتے نہیں وہ آہٹ — تمام قوت ہے صرف خوانذہ نظر کے جوہر میں دل کے سلا دے

نظر بھی آئے تو جو زلف پیچاں تو کہیں یہ کوئی پالیسی ہے — الیکٹرک لائٹ اس کو سمجھیں جو برق وحش کوئی مٹکرا دے

نکلتے ہیں کر کے غول بندی بنام تہذیب و درد مندی — یہ کہہ کے لیتے ہیں سب سے چندے ہمیں جو تم دو ہمیں خدا دے

انہیں اسی بات پر یقیں ہے کہ لبس ہی ہی اصل کار دیں ہے — اسی سے ہو گا فروغ قومی اسی سے جیکیں گے باپ دادے

مکان و کالج کے سب ہیں کیں ہیں ابھی انہیں تجربے نہیں ہیں — خبر نہیں ہے کہ آگے چل کر ہے کسی منزل ہیں کیسے جادے

دلوں میں ان کے ہے نور ایماں قوی نہیں ہے گرچہ تگباں — ہوائے منطق ادائے طفلی یہ شمع ایسا نہ بجھا دے

فریب دے کر ٹکلے مطلب سکھانے تحقیر دین و مذہب — مٹا دے آخر کو وضع ملت نمود ذاتی کو گر بڑھا دے

یہی بس اکبر کی التجا ہے جناب باری میں یہ دعا ہے
علوم و حکمت کا درس ان کو پر دفیسر دیں سمجھ خدا دے

Which, in slightly abridged translation, is:

May God confer on Aligarh a cure for every malady
And on its students, scions of the gentry and nobility.
Refined, and elegant, and smart, and clean, and neat, and radiant,
Hearts full of good intentions, minds blessed with originality,
They ride the highways of the East, and plod along the Western ways,
Each one of them, without a doubt, everything you would have him be.

No Indian fair, no English miss, diverts them from their chosen path;
Their hearts are innocent and pure; their books absorb their energy.
The lightning of a fair one's smile they take for electricity
And if they see a curling tress they think it is some policy.

All of them dwell in College, still without experience of life;
They do not know what lies ahead, nor what should be their destiny.
The flame of faith burns in their hearts, but those who guard it are not firm
And logic's winds may blow it out, or youthful immaturity,
Ensnaring them, and teaching them to hold religion in contempt
And, seeking fame, to bring to nought the ways of their community.

I pray then: May the boons of knowledge and of understanding be
Bestowed on them by their professors and their God – respectively.

Akbar does not want a situation in which the polish of Western learning and
Western manners cramps and restricts the free play of religious feeling. In an
apt metaphor he writes of one to whom this has happened:[54]

بہو صندل کا ہے مگر افسوس   دب گئی بو'' فرنچ'' پالش سے

His rosary is sandalwood. Alas!
Its fragrance is imprisoned in French polish.

He distrusts the emphasis which the spokesmen of the New Light put upon
reason and science, and their claim that religious truths can be proved one
hundred per cent by rational, scientific means. I am not a religious man myself,
and I feel a strong sympathy with the schoolboy who defined faith as 'believing
something which you know isn't true', but I must say that I think Akbar (and,
incidentally, in Sir Sayyid's own camp, Nazir Ahmad) was right in insisting that
religious belief involves recognition that reason and science can take you only
so far, and that the essence of religion is beyond their reach:[55]

خدا با ہر ہے حدِ دور بیں سے

God is beyond the range of telescopes

as he puts it. In the last resort, religion is a matter of faith, and long discussions
about it are pointless. He writes:[56]

خدا کے باب میں یہ غور کیا ہے
خدا کیا ہے؟ خدا ہے! اور کیا ہے

Why all this concentration on the problem?
You ask what God is? God is God. What else?

And, more sarcastically:[57]

مذہبی بحث میں نے کی ہی نہیں

فالتو عقل مجھ میں تھی ہی نہیں

I take no part when they discuss religion;
I haven't the intelligence to spare.

In fact, discussion of these questions is not only pointless, but positively
harmful. Akbar correctly foresaw that exaggerated claims for reason and science
would lead to a situation where, far from strengthening religious faith, they
would undermine and ultimately destroy it, and he warned his fellow-Muslims

سید صاحب سکھا گئے ہیں جو شعور   کہتا نہیں تم سے میں کہ ہو اس سے نفور

سوتوں کو جگا دیا انھوں نے لیکن   اللہ کا نام لے کے اٹھنا ہے ضرور

against this danger:[58]

Practice the ways Sir Sayyid's movement taught you
Nothing in them need give you cause for shame.
He woke you from your sleep; but now remember
When you arise, arise in Allah's name.

– a point which, addressing students directly, he makes in terms which .e thinks
will perhaps enable them to grasp it more easily. Their college course, he tells
them, leads up to the Convocation at the end of their student life where, if they
have worked as they should, they will get their degree. It's the same, he tells
them, with this life and the Day of Judgement:[59]

زندگی اور قیامت میں ریلیشن سمجھو   اس کو کالج اور اسے کانووکیشن سمجھو

Life and the Last Day bear the same relation –
(Mark this) – as College does to Convocation.

He feels that the leaders of the New Light, including even Sir Sayyid himself,
lack something fundamental, that instead of stressing the key importance of a
strong and all-pervading religious faith, which guides a man in every aspect of
his life, they ask you to put your trust in methods which are all too trivial to
achieve the substantial results the Muslim community needs:[60]

مسلمانوں کی خوش حالی کی بے شک دھن ہے سید کو

گر یہ کام نکلے گا نہ لیکچرے نہ چندوں سے

درستی تخت عزت کی کہاں اِن کیل کانٹوں میں

توقع شہ سواری کی نہ رکھو نعل بندوں سے

Sir Sayyid sought – no doubt of it – well-being for us Muslims.
But lectures and subscriptions? How can these set us on course?
Mere nails and tacks will not avail to mend the throne of honour.
Do not expect great horsemanship from him who shoes the horse.

And most of all he dislikes those in the Aligarh movement for whom the final unexceptionable formulation of what is good for the Muslims is what their British rulers say is good for them, who think that the will of God and the will of the British government are identical, and for whom, therefore, for all practical purposes the British *are* God. Get rid of the satirical exaggeration in all this, and it expresses accurately enough what was essentially Sir Sayyid's own stand. Akbar (and almost everyone else since his day resembles him in this respect) could not find it in him to say this bluntly, but we can be certain that it is Sir Sayyid's too pronounced partiality for the British that Akbar mocks in a fairly light-hearted way when he writes (in Persian, which he occasionally uses for his verse):[61]

عقلِ سید بود از انوارِ حکمت یافتہ   زورِ بازویش عدو را بیچارہ بر تافتہ

شکلے درپیش است اورا اگر گویم نبی   زانبیا ہرگز کسے نگر رشت پنشن یافتہ

Sir Sayyid had an intellect that radiated learning
And strength enough to vanquish any foe you care to mention
And I for one would readily have counted him a prophet
But that there never was a prophet yet who drew a pension.

However, the out-and-out attack on people who seem to regard the British as God is launched not against Sir Sayyid, but against other (unnamed) leaders of the modern school. In the poem referred to earlier, in which Akbar expresses his agreement with many of Sir Sayyid's religious beliefs, he turns in the end upon leaders of this kind:[62]

جواب حضرتِ سید کا خوب ہے اکبر ۔۔۔۔۔۔ ہم ان کے قولِ درست و بجا کو مانتے ہیں

ولیکن اس نئی تہذیب کے بزرگ اکثر ۔۔۔۔۔۔ خدا کو اور نئے طریقِ دعا کو مانتے ہیں

زبانی کہتے ہیں سب کچھ مگر حقیقت میں ۔۔۔۔۔۔ وہ صرف قوتِ فرماں روا کو مانتے ہیں

What our respected Sayyid says is good.
Akbar agrees that it is sound and fair.
But most of those who head this modern school
Neither believe in God, nor yet in prayer.
They *say* they do, but it is plain to see
What *they* believe in is the powers that be.

Other verses make the same point:[63]

مگر ہاں الشیخ جی کی پالیسی سے ہم نہیں واقف

اسی پر ختم کرتے ہیں کہ جو صاحب کی مرضی ہو

...But not for me the *shaikh ji's* policy
Whose final word is 'What the Sahib commands'.

As we saw earlier, Akbar knows that 'What the Sahib commands', he commands in the Sahib's interest, and it by no means follows that the Sahib's interest is the Muslim's interest too. He writes:[64]

روز افزوں ہے بلاشبہ برٹش اقبال

جو خلاف اس کے تصور کرے وہ وہی ہے

اپنا اقبال مگر اس نے جو سمجھا ہے اسے

یہ نئی روشنی کی سخت غلط فہمی ہے

With every passing day the fortunes of the British prosper. No doubt about it. And he who thinks otherwise is dreaming. But he who thinks that this is the same as *our* fortunes prospering is, like the apostles of the New Light, very much mistaken.

Akbar, then, shows a reluctance to attack Sir Sayyid personally; but the rarity in his verse of direct criticism of Sir Sayyid himself is due largely to another cause. It is important to remember that Akbar was, as near as makes no difference, a whole generation (twenty-nine years to be quite precise) younger than Sir Sayyid. Sir Sayyid achieved his great aim in life when the Aligarh College opened in 1877; and Akbar was already thirty-one years old in that year.

But he went on writing verse for more than forty years after that, that is, until twenty-three years after Sir Sayyid's death. And the main target of his attack is not so much Sir Sayyid's contemporaries as the subsequent generation of Aligarh graduates, in whom he sees very few of the virtues of Sir Sayyid's generation, and in their place all the weaknesses and deficiencies of the Aligarh pioneers accentuated and brought to fruition. He says of them:[65]

کہ آں مرحوم اکنوں درشمار شیخ می آید   گذشتندازآں قدر یاراں زحدِ سیدِ اے اکبر

So far have they transcended Sayyid's limits
That now they number him among the *shaikhs*

– the *shaikh*, or Muslim elder, being the symbol not only in Akbar's verse but in the whole long tradition of Islamic lyrical poetry, of the ignorant, bigoted, conservative pillar of orthodox religion. And in a long poem[66] (forty-six couplets) he enumerates the sins of this later generation and explicitly says that:[67]

ہم واسب کو تعجب کیوں ہوئیں یہ حالتیں پیدا

نہ تھا یہ مطلب سید کہ اس رُخ پر چلے دھارا

All are surprised to see these new developments.
It was not Sayyid's aim that things should take this course.

Akbar's Polemic Against the Ultra-Modern

It is against these unworthy sons of the Aligarh movement that perhaps the largest part, and certainly the most popular part, of his most significant verse is directed. Verses in which the tone is one of sorrow rather than anger describe what he thinks is the essence of their condition. He makes them say of themselves:[68]

جوا پنی گرہ میں ہے اسے کھو بھی رہے ہیں   جو بات مناسب ہے وہ حاصل نہیں کرتے

افسوس کہ اندھے بھی ہیں اور سو بھی رہے ہیں   بے علم بھی ہم لوگ ہیں غفلت بھی ہے طاری

We do not learn the things we ought to learn –
And lose what was already in our keeping;
Bereft of knowledge, plunged in heedlessness,
Alas! We are not only blind but sleeping.

And there is much truth in his words. Sir Sayyid and his contemporaries came fresh to the new learning of the West, but at any rate they came equipped with

all the traditional learning of their community behind them. Not so the next
generation. It was modern enough to regard the old learning as not worth its
attention, and yet not so truly modern as to put itself seriously to the task of
really mastering a new fund of knowledge and a new culture. It is again in
sadness more than in anger that Akbar speaks of them[69] as youngsters who have
set out on the long road to the West but have been robbed on the way – at a point
too far from home for them to be able to return and too far from their destination
for them to have any hope of reaching it. But he is not always so sympathetic,
especially when he contemplates those who don't even want any more for
themselves than the government wants them to have. He sees that the sort of
half-baked education which government colleges or government-approved
colleges supply suits British needs very well.

In the words of the couplet quoted earlier:

They gives us learning – just enough for us to sell our services
And understanding – just enough for governmental purposes.

What he *can't* see is how his fellow-Muslims, the descendants of a people
inspired by a dynamic faith, which had enabled them to change the course of
history and transform the lives of hundreds of millions of mankind, can be
content, and indeed proud, to have no horizons beyond a life of unthinking,
undistinguished subservience to a nation that has deprived them of all the power
and the honour they had once enjoyed, and whose representatives for the most
part look upon them with contempt.[70]

مٹاتے ہیں جو وہ ہم کو تو اپنا کام کرتے ہیں

مجھے حیرت تو اُن پر ہے جو اس پٹنے پہ مرتے ہیں

If they – the British – destroy us, they do it to serve their own purposes.
What astonishes me is that there are those among us who rejoice in our
destruction.

– like birds, who under the spell of the irresistible fowler, help tighten the snares
with their own beaks[71]

اپنی منقاروں سے علقہ کس لیے ہیں جال کا   ۔   طائروں پہ سحر ہے صیاد کے اقبال کا

He doesn't lose his sense of humour, but his contempt for these people's petty
ideals is quite unmistakable. He writes:[72]

ہم کیا کہیں احباب کیا کارنمایاں کر گئے   بی اے ہوتے نوکر ہوتے پنشن ملی پھر مر گئے

What words of mine can tell the deeds of men like these, our nation's pride?
They got their B.A., took employment, drew their pensions and then died.

Or in a more savage mood:[73]

چھوڑ لٹریچر کو پھر کر اپنی ہسٹری کو بھول جا

شیخ و مسجد سے تعلق ترک کر اسکول جا

چار دن کی زندگی ہے کوفتے سے کیا فائدہ

کھا ڈبل روٹی کلرکی کر خوشی سے پھول جا

Give up your literature, say I; forget your history
Break all your ties with *shaikh* and mosque – it could not matter less.
Go off to school. Life's short. Best not to worry overmuch.
Eat English bread, and push your pen, and swell with happiness.

For those who haven't quite forgotten their literature he recalls the story of the legendary Persian lover Farhad and his beloved Shirin. Farhad was promised Shirin if he would dig through a mountain. Like you, says Akbar, it was in pursuit of his own interests that he spent all his strength. But, *un*like you, he at any rate did it for something worth while:[74]

اعلیٰ مقصود چاہیئے پیشِ نظر   کوشش تری گو ہو لطفِ ذاتی کے لئے

فرہاد پہاڑ پر عمل کرتا تھا   شیریں کے لئے کہ ناشپاتی کے لئے

You need a lofty aim to set before you
Even if your own gain is all your care.
Remember, when Farhad dug through the mountain
He did it for Shirin, not for a pear.

Whereas you give up[75] your religion, abandon your people, change your appearance, and waste your days – all in the hope of getting a miserable clerk's job. What an impressive range of betrayal, and for what a contemptibly petty gain. And even so, not everyone gets what all these betrayals are calculated to achieve. The sahibs don't always reward their would-be humble servants in proportion to their expectations, and they are often genuinely at a loss to understand why. One such bewildered gentleman asks the British why their policy has to be so obscure when *his* policy is so clear:[76]

تمہاری پالیسی کا حال کچھ کھلتا نہیں صاحب   ہماری پالیسی تو صاف ہے ایماں فروشی کی

Your policy is quite obscure to us, Sahib.
Our policy is clear – to sell our faith.

Another, led to expect that learning English is a sure passport to advancement and to positions of responsibility, finds to his disappointment that this is not so. Akbar spells it out for him:[77]

نوکر کو سکھلاتے ہیں میاں اپنی زباں   مطلب یہ ہے کہ سمجھے ان کے فرماں

مقصود یہ نہیں میاں کی سی عقل و تمیز   اس نکتہ کو کیا وہ سمجھیں جو ہیں ناداں

They teach you English, he says, for the same reason that an English master teaches his foreign servant English – so that the man can understand and carry out the orders he receives. Only a fool thinks he does it to raise the servant's intelligence and understanding to the same level as his own. Another wonders why Sir Sayyid (whose English was in fact not all that good) did so well, while he (whose English is much better) isn't doing too well. Akbar explains the point:[78]

تم انگریزی داں ہو وہ انگریز داں ہے

True, you know English, but *he* knew the English.

In other words, it's not enough to learn the things the English want you to learn. Having done so you have to convince them also that they need your services. It seems that already in Akbar's day it was becoming increasingly difficult to do this, and that the problem of graduate unemployment was already emerging. He writes:[79]

کالج میں دھوم مچا رہی ہے پاس پاس کی

عہدوں سے آ رہی ہے صدا دور دور کی

The verse depends for its effect upon an untranslatable play on words. He says that the cry of the graduates is '*Pas! Pas!*' while the cry of the British is '*Dur! Dur!*' '*Pas*' has two meanings. In the indigenous Urdu sense it means 'near', but its English meaning, of a 'pass' in an examination, was already well established in Urdu by Akbar's time. '*Dur*' means 'far', and also, as an exclamation, 'Go away!' So, says Akbar, the graduates cry 'Near!' while the British cry 'Far!' – or, the graduates cry 'We've passed our examinations' and the British reply 'What of it? Go away!'

Because Akbar is a man of genuine human sympathies, a really bitter, savage tone is relatively rare in his verse. Often the tone is one of quite light-hearted mockery, as when, for example, he ridicules the dependence of the modern student upon written notes. Under the old system of education with its emphasis on memory and on learning by heart, when you knew a thing you knew it for evermore. But the habit of note-taking has destroyed all that. According to Muslim belief, when a Muslim is buried two angels come into the grave and question him about his faith and the kind of life he has lived. Akbar portrays a modern student in this situation:[80]

میں نے یہ چاہا کہ لکھوا دوں انہیں سب اپنا حال   جب نکیرین آئے میری قبر میں بہر سوال

یعنی کتی جو نوٹ بک وہ اس سفر میں کھو گئی   ہاتھ پاکٹ میں جو ڈالا مجھ کو حیرت ہو گئی

رہ گئی دنیا میں میری نوٹ بک مجبور ہوں   کہہ دیا میں نے کہیں اب ہر طرح معذور ہوں

When the angels both appeared inside the grave to question me
I myself intended to explain things comprehensively.
Delving in my pocket for my notebook, I was shocked to find
I had lost it on the way there – or, perhaps, left it behind.
Much confused I said, 'I really *must* apologise to you,
I have left my notebook in the world – there's *nothing* I can do.'

In a similar tone he defends the modern student's reluctance to believe in the throne of God:[81]

کیوں کر خدا کے عرش کے قائل ہوں یہ غریب

جغرافیے میں عرش کا نقشہ نہیں ملا

Poor fellows, how can they believe that there's a throne of God?
It wasn't on the maps they studied in geography.

Or he excuses their religious shortcomings by explaining how they have been led to think that access to such examples of modern technique as the British send their way enables them to solve all problems – not only here, he says, but in the next world too, where they will have such difficulties to face as the crossing of the bridge of Sirat – thin as a hair, and sharp as a sword – that leads to Paradise. That's no problem in their eyes, he says:[82]

بس کام ہے انہیں رو میش و نشاط سے   یاروں کو فکر روز جزا کچھ نہیں رہی

بائیسکل پہ گزریں گے ہم پل صراط سے   کہتے ہیں حرج کیا ہے جو باریک ہے وہ پل

No more they fear the day of retribution;
They concentrate on doing what they like.
What if the bridge to Paradise is narrow?
They say they'll ride across it on a bike.

Against the most daring of them, who have gone to the lengths of openly
abandoning religion, he speaks more trenchantly, but still humorously, sometimes appealing to their own strongest prejudices and beliefs in facetious proof
of his own propositions. Thus he tells an imaginary story:[83]

کہا میں نے صاحب سے با صد ملال   ہوا آج خارج جو میرا سوال

وہ جھنجھلا کے بولا جہنم میں جاؤ   کہاں جاؤں میں اب ذرا یہ بتاؤ

مگر اس تصور سے تسکیں ہوئی   یہ سن کر بہت طبع غمگیں ہوئی

کہ جب اہل یورپ میں بھی ذکر ہے

تو بے شک جہنم بھی ہے کوئی شے

Today when my petition was rejected
I asked the Sahib, feeling much dejected,
'Where shall I go to now Sir? Kindly tell.'
He growled at me and answered 'Go to Hell!'
I left him, and my heart was really sinking;
But soon I started feeling better, thinking,
'A European said so! In that case
At any rate there must *be* such a place!'

He makes a good deal of play with the theories of Darwin, still, let us
remember, newcomers to the scientific scene in the days when Akbar wrote,
and still disputed in Britain, let alone in India. Sometimes he uses them to point
the contrast between the world of Islam, with its strong tradition of spiritual
values, and that of the increasingly narrow materialism of the modern West. The
Muslim mystics sought to draw ever closer to God until the individual soul
merged with God and no longer had any separate existence. Mansur al-Hallaj,
the mystic hero of Persian and Urdu classical poetry, attained to this ideal, and
expressed it in the ecstatic cry of 'I am God!' Very different, says Akbar, are
the thoughts that inspire the Western scientist to ecstasy.[84]

ڈاروِن بولے بوزنا ہوں میں   کہا منصور نے خدا ہوں میں

Mansur in ecstasy cried 'I am God!'
Darwin's ecstatic cry is 'I'm an ape!'

There is a hint of the same argument in another verse in which he ridicules the blind, quite mindless imitation of everything British which characterizes the ultra-modern. In it he makes one of them – who is of course a believer in Darwin's theory – tell his British superior:[85]

هم تو انساں سے بنتے جاتے ہیں بندرانے حضور   آپ خوش قسمت تھے بندر سے جوانسان ہوگئے

Fate favoured you, kind sir: *you* grew from monkeyhood to manhood.
See *our* ill-luck: once men, we grow more monkey-like each day.

A sort of evolution in reverse.

A community of people that has forsaken all values of its own and lives in unthinking imitation of the ways of others isn't really alive. And if the East is subject to the power of the West, then in a way that is fitting, for it simply exemplifies the law that the disposal of the dead is in the hands of the living.[86]

مشرق بہ دستِ مغرب مردہ بہ دستِ زندہ

He takes an ultra-modern argument and uses it as a means of hitting them hard with this concept:[87]

بعدِ مُردن کچھ نہیں یہ فلسفہ مردُود ہے   قوم ہی کو دیکھتے مُردہ ہے اور موجود ہے

You say 'There's nothing after death?' What nonsense!
Just look at us. *We're* dead, and *we're* still here.

Some verses poke fun at those among the moderns who go a little too fast even for their fellow moderns. A short poem relates how a young man, recently graduated, approaches a young woman, also recently graduated, confident that their modernity and their higher education dispenses with the need to observe old-fashioned conventions. He says to her:[88]

میں بھی گریجویٹ ہوں تو بھی گریجویٹ
علمی مباحثے ہوں ذرا پاس آکے لیٹ

Both you and I have passed our graduation.
Lie down, let's have a learned conversation.

But, to his disappointment, she doesn't see things quite that way. But never mind. At any rate within the marriage relationship refinement, both of husbands and wives, is gaining ground rapidly. Akbar knows of a couple who have become as refined as anyone could wish:[89]

خدا کے فضل سے بی بی میاں دونوں مہذب ہیں

حجاب ان کو نہیں آتا انہیں غصہ نہیں آتا

Praise be! Both wife and husband are refined.
She feels no shame: he feels no indignation.

The quite fatuous importance which these gentlemen attach to things just
because they're European, British or British-approved, is a target of constant
mockery:[90]

چیز وہ ہے جو یورپ میں بنے   بات وہ ہے جو پائنیر میں چھپے

The things that signify are those that come to us from Europe
The words that signify, those printed in the *Pioneer.*

– the *Pioneer* being a famous English-language paper published from Akbar's
city of Allahabad, and taking a line which can fairly be described as more
viceregal than the Viceroy. Akbar's own opinion of the *Pioneer* was not a very
high one. He once remarked that Allahabad produced only two really good
things – and the *Pioneer* was not one of them. The two were Akbar – himself –
and *amrud* – guavas:[91]

کچھ الٰہ آباد میں ساماں نہیں بہبود کے   یاں دھرا کیا ہے بجز اکبر کے اغلا مرود کے

and while one might now wish to extend the list, these two items should indeed
appear on it. Akbar regarded the *Pioneer* as a British propaganda sheet,
concerned, like all propaganda sheets, to print not what the propagandist
believes, but what he wants his readers to believe. Akbar writes of it sarcastically:[92]

گھر کے خطوط میں ہے کہ کل ہو گیا چہلم اس کا

پائنیر لکھتا ہے بیمار کا حال اچھتا ہے

Letters from home have told us that his funeral rites are over:
The *Pioneer* reports his state as 'satisfactory'.

The ultra-modern, however, model their whole life style on abhorrence of what
is Indian and worship of what is Western, and Akbar doesn't spare them from
his sarcasm. Even the old conventional Muslim *shaikh*, he says, is affected by
this worship of the West, so much so that he modifies the Islamic prohibition

on wine:[93]

اب صرف منع کرتے ہیں دیسی شراب کو   مرعوب ہو گئے ہیں ولایت سے شیخ جی

> Even the *shaikh* has fallen to their spell.
> All he prohibits now is *Indian* wine.

How much *more* impressionable then, are the true products of the New Light:[94]

باپ ماں سے شیخ سے اللہ سے کیا ان کو کام

ڈاکٹر جنو لائے تعلیم دی سرکار نے

> What do they want with parents, or with maulvis, or with God?
> They owe their birth to doctors and their schooling to the state.

ہوئے اس قدر مہذب کبھی گھر کا منہ نہ دیکھا

کئی عمر ہوٹلوں میں مرے اسپتال جا کر

> So great is their refinement now, they've bid their parents' home goodbye.
> They spend their lives in restaurants and go to hospital to die.[95]

And, even more coldly:[96]

چند روزہ کھیل تھا آخر کو سب مر کھپ گئے   وضع بدلی، گھر کو چھوڑا، کاغذوں میں چھپ گئے

> They changed their fashions, left their homes, and got into the papers.
> But after all it doesn't last. Death ended all their capers.

'Got into the papers' – it always annoys Akbar no end that these people will sacrifice the last ounce of self-respect for a little publicity. The absurd pride which they feel at seeing their name in the press, receiving titles from the British government, or being nominated to a place in the British-controlled councils is ridiculed in hundreds of verses. Sometimes the point is made in metaphor, as when the owl is taken (as it always is in colloquial Urdu) as the symbol of a stupid man:[97]

جس سے مغرب نے کہا تو ازبری باز ہے   دیدے کے قابل اب اس الّو کا فخر و ناز ہے

> Look at the owl! What airs and graces! What a way to talk!
> Because the British told him he's an honorary hawk!

The crow too may aspire to similar distinction:[98]

پارک میں ان کے دیا کرتا ہے آپ مدح و ثنا

زاغ ہو جاتے گا اک دن آزری عندلیب

Perched in their park the crow makes loyal speeches
One day they'll make him honorary nightingale.

Sometimes the emphasis is slightly different – that of a man who goes into the councils not so much for the fame as for the material advantages he hopes for:[99]

حقیقت میں میں ہوں بلبل مگر جارے کی خواہش میں

بنا ہوں ممبر کونسل یہاں طوطی میاں ہو کر

I'm actually a nightingale, but since I want to eat
I pretend to be a parrot and accept a council seat

– where the metaphor of the parrot again stresses that in Akbar's view the members of the council do nothing more than mouth the words their British masters expect them to repeat. If you want to go in for such antics, he says, perform them at home, where at any rate the public can't see you. And refresh yourself with water from Banaras and guavas from Allahabad. You'll at any rate be performing in an Indian context and consuming Indian products – and all that will contribute more to Indian welfare than capering about in the councils.[100]

کیوں اپنے سر پہ زحمتِ بے سود لیجئے
کھلا پی کے گھر میں بیٹھئے اور گایئے بھجن
ہو وضع اپنے دلیس کی، مال اپنے دلیس کا

کونسل کے بدلے گھر میں اچھل کو دیجئے
کاشی سے جل، پراگ سے امرود لیجئے
بہتر ہے راہِ منزلِ بہبود لیجئے

In general, Akbar has a pretty cordial dislike for all public performers on the political stage, whether they act in parts assigned to them by the British or in the self-assigned role of national leaders fearlessly representing their nation's or their community's interests. There are so many of them, says Akbar, that they are like an army of generals, proud of their high rank, but apparently without any followers:[101]

لیڈروں کی معصوم ہے اور ف الله کوئی نہیں   سب تو جنرل ہیں یہاں آخر سپاہی کون ہے

And that is not surprising, for only the gullible take seriously their ostensible
concern for ordinary people:[102]

بہت مدتے وہ اسپیچوں میں حکمت اس کو کہتے ہیں

میں سمجھا خیر خواہ ان کو حماقت اسکو کہتے ہیں

He made his speech with copious tears – and that is known as 'policy'
I thought he was my well-wisher – and that is called 'stupidity'.

They sit in their great houses, burning with anguished love for their people:[103]

محل میں بیٹھ کر اب عشقِ قومی میں تڑپتے ہیں

More remarkable still:[104]

قوم کے غم میں ڈنر کھاتے ہیں مگر حکام کے ساتھ   رنج لیڈر کو بہت ہے مگر آرام کے ساتھ

In mourning for their nation's plight they dine with the authorities.
Our leaders suffer deeply for us, but they suffer at their ease.

Not that they forget their supporters:[105]

شکرادا کرنا ہے واجب ان کی طبع نیک کا

ہر ڈنر سے بھیجتے ہیں مجھ کو فوٹو کیک کا

I must not be ungrateful: see the trouble that he takes –
After each meal he eats he sends a photo of the cakes.

And some even make the supreme sacrifice:[106]

اک ڈنر میں کھا گیا اتنا کہ نکلی تن سے جان   خدمتِ قومی میں بارے جاں نثاری ہو گئی

He ate so much, his spirit left his body.
Such sacrifice! He gave his life for us!

If you can't be a political leader, be a journalist and edit a newspaper.
Leader is to editor as thief is to pickpocket:[107]

چورکے بھائی محرہ کٹ تو سٹا کرتے تھے   اب یہ سنتے ہیں ایڈیٹر کے برادر لیڈر

Numbers of both have grown rapidly:[108]

تمام قوم ایڈیٹر بنی ہے یا لیڈر   سبب یہ ہے کہ کوئی اور دل لگی نہ رہی

    The country swarms with editors and leaders
    Who can't find any other games to play.

And the one is about as effective as the other. He laughs at the idea that you can
effectively oppose a power that rules in the last resort by force of arms with
what in your gullibility you are pleased to call the power of the press, and mocks
at those who:[109]

جب توپ مقابل ہے تو اخبار نکالو

    Faced with a gun, bring out a newspaper.

or who demonstrate the bankruptcy of their much-vaunted 'national advancement' by arguing that if they can't deploy a regiment they can at any rate bring
out a *risala*:[110]

ملکی ترقیوں میں دو دالے نکالئے   پلٹن نہیں تو خیر رسالے نکالئے

    This is again a play upon words: *risala* means a detachment of cavalry; but
it also means 'a periodical'. But anyway, in their own eyes all is going well:[111]

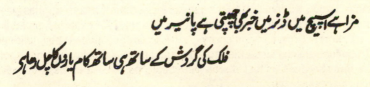

    They speak, they dine, their names get printed in the *Pioneer*.
    Day follows day: our friends draw nearer to their heart's desire.

He often stresses the distance they keep from ordinary people. In the later days
of more militant agitations than were common in the nineteenth century, when
it was quite common – and quite fashionable, says Akbar – for leaders to go to
gaol, he writes of them:[112]

ہم کر کروں سے کہاں راحت ہے ان کو میل میں

وہ تو ہیں اب وفد میں یا وعظ میں یا جیل میں

Mixing with us clerks? Oh, no! The greater pleasures must prevail
They must go on deputations, or to meetings, or to jail

And since it is these people who now lead the nation, the prospects as the end
of the nineteenth century approaches are, Akbar reflects, none too bright:[113]

مطلب کی کہوں تو پالیسی میں اڑ جائے   مذہب کی کہوں تو دل لگی میں اڑ جائے

غالب ہے کہ یہ بھی اس صدی میں اڑ جائے   باقی سر قوم میں ابھی ہے کچھ ہوش

Religious truths? They make a joke of them.
Sound sense? Oh no! That is not policy.
The nation still has *some* sense in its head.
That too may not outlast this century.

In fact the new century was to bring a new mood to the Muslims, leading
them to ways of thinking more in line with his own. But let us take stock of
Akbar's positive beliefs. We have seen what he was against: let us look more
directly for a while at what he was for.

What Akbar is For

One doesn't expect of a satirist that he should pay as much attention to what
men ought to do as to what they are doing and ought *not* to be doing, and some
critics, who perhaps bear too close a resemblance to the targets of Akbar's wrath
to feel comfortable with him, have belittled him for his so-called 'negative'
approach. 'If Sir Sayyid had never existed,' wrote one of them, 'Akbar would
never have been a a poet.'[114] But negative criticism always implies positive
comment. It surely doesn't take much wit to see that, for example, an attack on
hypocrisy implies a plea for sincerity. And secondly, while Akbar, like every
satirist, concentrates on attacking the vices and abuses that he sees in the society
around him, he does in fact directly advocate positive attitudes and positive
courses of action as well.

Professor Aziz Ahmad, of the University of Toronto, says of him[115] that he
is 'fiercely anti-Western, antipathetic to all modernisation'. But that is simply
not true. It is ture that some of Akbar's phrasing could at first sight give that
impression; and equally true that like men in all countries and all ages who are
dissatisfied with the present, he sometimes paints too rosy a picture of the past
– mistaking for a memory what is in fact an aspiration.[116] Take for instance the
line:[117]

نہ کتابوں سے نہ کالج کے ہے درسے پیدا

دین ہوتا ہے بزرگوں کی نظر سے پیدا

You cannot acquire it from books, nor yet from residence in College. You learn *din* – religion, a faith by which to live – from the vision of your elders.

That is only apparently a trite, conventional, conservative statement. If you look at the essence of it, Akbar is saying that you can go through university and read as many books as you like, but it is not so much the content of your academic course as the qualities of those who teach it that help you to learn how to live. Or as he put it in another verse:[118]

کورس تو لفظ ہی سکھاتے ہیں   آدمی آدمی بناتے ہیں

Courses only teach you words:
It's *men* that make you men.

In another verse he says:[119]

شعر میں اکبر یہی مضمون تو ہر بار باندھ

اے مسلماں سبحہ لے اے برہمن زنار باندھ

Akbar, in your verse repeat this theme again and again: Muslim, take up your rosary; Brahman, wear your sacred thread.

You could not want a more seemingly conventional, a more seemingly traditional and conservative verse. But whether it *is* so depends entirely upon what, for Akbar, the rosary and the sacred thread symbolize. And there are many verses that make it clear that what they symbolize is not an indiscriminate, unthinking adherence to ancient tradition, but a loyalty to all that is best in it, all that is valuable, and indeed essential, to the conduct of a moral and meaningful life. And it is this kind of loyalty that he means when he writes:[120]

ہم مصلحتِ وقت کے منکر نہیں اکبر   لیکن یہ سمجھ لو کہ وفا بھی ہے کوئی چیز

Akbar does not deny the need for moving with the times
But understand that loyalty has its importance too.

The verse implies a discriminating view of traditional values, changing those that need to be changed, and maintaining those which need to be maintained. One has to look at his verse to see which things fall into which of these two categories. And it is relevant to remember here that Akbar, like most Urdu poets, began as a writer of the *ghazal* – the traditional lyric form in which classical Urdu verse rises to the height of its achievement. (It has a tradition going right back to the fourteenth century and beyond in Persian verse, a tradition which Akbar and most cultured Indian Muslims of his day knew and valued.) And the *ghazal* tradition itself is one of rejection of the externals of piety and stress upon the true spirit of religion. There is abundant evidence that Akbar's thought continues this tradition. Thus he writes in one of his verses – and there are more like it – [121]

پنڈت کو بھی سلام ہے اور مولوی کو بھی

مذہب نہ چاہیئے مجھے ایمان چاہیئے

Away with pandits and with maulvis too.
I do not want religion, I want faith.

And, in more sarcastic tone he notes that anyway the new modernity is not incompatible with an empty observance of religious forms. He depicts the satisfaction of the aspiring modern who makes this discovery:[122]

نئی تہذیب میں دقت زیادہ تو نہیں ہوتی

مذاہب رہتے ہیں قائم فقط ایمان جاتا ہے

One can accommodate without much trouble to these modern ways.
Religions still remain – all that one loses is one's faith.

The outward sign of being a Muslim is circumcision, but Akbar ridicules the idea that circumcision itself entitles you to call yourself a Muslim. He writes ironically:[123]

ختنہ ہوتا بھی ہے مذہب میں بڑی چیز پر اکبر   بے نمازوں کو بھی دعویٰ ہے مسلمانی کا

It seems that circumcision is the essence of religion:
Men claim that they are Muslims who have never said their prayers.

Another *ghazal* tradition which he upholds – and this is again one which runs counter to conservative orthodoxy whether in religion or society or politics – is that of what I may call religious humanism. The *ghazal* poets always judge a man not by his religious professions – not by what he calls himself – but by what his conduct of life shows him to *be*. All men who love their God, no matter what the name they call Him by, and all men who love their fellow-men, regardless of creed and race and custom, are brothers to one another, and the pious Hindu who comes in this category is, so to speak, a better Muslim than the orthodox Muslim who hates the Hindu because he is an idolator. Akbar's verse abounds in expressions of this outlook:[124]

خدا ہی کی عبادت جن کو ہے مقصود اے اکبر

وہ کیوں باہم لڑیں گو فرق ہو طرزِ عبادت میں

Why should men fight, whose aim it is to worship God?
What matter if they worship him in different forms?

کعبے میں جلوہ گر وہی دیر میں مستتر وہی

کہتے ہیں ہم خدا کا نام کہتے ہیں رام رام بھی

His radiance fills the Kaba, *He* lies hidden in the temple.
It is to *Him* we cry, whether as Allah or as Ram.[125]

Ram being one of the many Hindu names for God. As in religion, so in politics. Akbar combats vigorously the kind of religious intolerance which holds up political advance:[126]

اگر مذہب ہو خلل انداز ہی ملکی مقاصد میں   تو شیخ و برہمن پنہاں رہیں دیر و مساجد میں

If their religion hinders us in working for our country's good
Shut up the *shaikhs* and Brahmans in their temples and their mosques.

As a Muslim, it is, quite properly, the Muslim advocates of hostility to other religious communities that he most often attacks. The couplet which was quoted earlier:

> But not for me the *shaikh ji's* policy
> Whose final word is 'What the Sahib commands'.

is the second of a short poem of only two couplets: and the first says 'Why should we quarrel with the Hindus. We share the same produce of the same land; and we too [that is, we Muslims] pray for their prosperity.'[127] To those Muslims (and there are still all too many of them) who think that because their ancestors conquered India they are superior to the Hindus, he points out that whatever role their ancestors played, *they* aren't playing that role today:[128]

اے بھائیو بابو صاحب سے کھسکنے کا نہیں ہے کوئی محل

گو نسل علاء الدین میں ہو مسکن تو تمہارا غور نہیں

> Ala ud Din may be your ancestor.
> What of it? *You* no longer live in Ghor.

and there is no reason for you to hold aloof from your Hindu fellow countrymen.

He has too much sense to think that Hindus and Muslims will never clash, but he says that such clashes need not shatter their essential unity. Both have to bear the blows of those who wield the rod of worldly power, but they should respond by being like water, on which the blows of a rod have only a momentary effect:[129]

اپنی اپنی روشش پہ تم نیک رہو   کہتا ہوں میں ہندو مسلماں سے یہی

موجوں کی طرح لڑو اور گر ایک رہو   لاٹھی ہے ہوئے در پانی بن جاؤ

> I say the same to Hindus and to Muslims:
> Be good, each as your faith would have you be.
> The world's a rod? Then *you* become as water.
> Clash like the waves, but still remain one sea.

He has the sense, too, to realize that in all probability the Hindu majority of Indian's population is likely to use its preponderance to claim more than its share; but even then, he says, good sense demands that the Muslims stand with them, and not in opposition to them, and so prevent the possibility of a situation arising in which the British and the Hindus join hands against them.[130] Of course there are inconsistencies. In the disputes between Hindi and Urdu, for instance, he suffers from the common Muslim illusion that Urdu is the common language spoken by Muslims and Hindus alike, and that Hindi is a pernicious invention designed to disrupt Hindu-Muslim unity. But even here he does his best. The quarrel between the two tongues, he says (he has a marked fondness for erotic imagery), is like the inter-twinning of the tongues of two lovers locked in a passionate kiss.[131] The language question, and the delicate question of the sacredness of the cow, he says, are the two main things that come in the way of Hindu-Muslim harmony, remarking ruefully that this *gao zaban* recipe is a troublesome one.[132] This is another pun. *Gao* mean 'cow', and *zaban* means 'tongue' or 'language', and *gao zaban* also means 'cow's tongue' – and a dish regarded as a delicacy by Muslims. On the language dispute he hasn't much to offer beyond an appeal to the Hindus to abandon their hostility to Urdu. On the cow he goes further, especially in verses written in the last period of his life when strong cordial feeling between the two communities reached a peak in their parallel, and allied, movements against their British rulers. Akbar expresses sympathy with Muslims who, inspired by this regard for Hindu suscep-tibilities, voluntarily abstain from beef. He gives an ingenious argument in support:[133]

حامی ہوا جو گائے کا ، بے شک ذہین ہے سمجھا یہ دل میں گائے کے سر پر زمین ہے

> If he supports the cow, he shows perception:
> He knows it is a cow that sustains the world.

– a reference to traditional Muslim cosmography, according to which the foundations of the earth rest upon the horns of a cow.[134]

Another metaphor makes the point that Hindus can hope to win Muslim goodwill, but not British goodwill, and that they should therefore make common cause with the Muslims against the British.[135]

بعض مسلم تو ایسے ہیں موجود منہ جو لحم بقر سے موڑتے ہیں

فرضی گورے مگر رکھیں کیوں کر جان بل کب گئے کو چھوڑتے ہیں

> There are some Muslims who abstain from beef
> Treating your tender scruples as their own.
> It's British Tommy who will not hold back,
> For how can John Bull leave the cows alone?

If Akbar's humanism finds expression in the traditional *ghazal* doctrine of mutual love between the sincere Muslim and the sincere Hindu, it finds expression also in another traditional *ghazal* theme – the theme of sympathy for the poor and hostility to the rich and powerful. It is worth remarking that unlike Sir Sayyid and his main lieutenants, Akbar was not an aristocrat, but the son of a respectable, but none too affluent, Muslim family from a country town,[136] and his sense of kinship with the ordinary man never left him. We have seen how he scourges the pillars of the New Light for being, as one of his verses puts it,[137] 'stiff with pride in the presence of their Indian brothers, but cringing like a coolie before the foreigner'. The poor make up the great majority of our people, he says – and yet the pillars of the New Light don't want to have anything to do with them. Their complacent aping of the West means nothing to the poor; while for them it is the be-all and end-all of their existence:[138]

غربا بھی ہیں مگر قوم کے اجزا اکثر غربا ہی سے تعلق میں ہی ان کو تو مفر

دور ہے ان سے خود آرائی مغرب کا اثر بحث ان کی بھی اسی بات پہ ختم مگر

They should not exaggerate the importance of *their* advancement to the advancement of their community:[139]

عہدے جو سو پچاس کو اچھے ملے تو کیا   تا نام نہ ہو گی قوم کبھی سو پچاس سے

In fifty to a hundred of them get good posts, what of it?
No nation yet was ever based on fifty to a hundred.

You too are 'natives', he tells them, just like us:[140]

نیٹو بھی رہو گے اور مرو گے بھی ضرور   کہتا ہوں کہ دعویٰ خدائی نہ کرو

Natives you are, and natives you will die.
Remember that, and don't think you are God.

And he uses a modern metaphor to remind them of one of the basic teachings
of their religion. Gentlemen, he says, don't despise those who travel third class.
It's the same engine that's hauling all of us to our destination. Your first and
second class last only to the terminus of the grave. After that a man's class will
be determined by the kind of life he has led.[144]

سمجھیں نہ حضور تھرڈ والوں کو حقیر   اِن جن تو دہی ہے جس کی ہم سب کو ہے آس

اسٹیشن گورنک ہے یہ فرسٹ و سکنڈ   بعد اس کے موافق عمل ہو گا کلاس

In much the same spirit he hits at the British too. In India, Afghanistan is
known as the country from which pomegranates come. When Lord Minto
invited the Emir of Afghanistan to visit India Akbar commented:[142]

جو سچی بات ہے کہہ دوں گا بے خوف و خطر اس کو   نہیں رکھنے کا میں ہرگز پری نرمے کہن ڈلے

انار آتے جو کابل کے تڑپتے سب کے حصے میں   امیر آئے تو ہم کو کیا مزے ہیں لارڈ منٹو کے

Akbar will always speak the truth boldly and fearlessly
And never hesitate to say what he thinks just and fair.
Afghanistan's Emir has come. That gives Lord Minto pleasure.
Had it been pomegranates we could *all* have had a share.

And in more serious tone he says that no man knows what is his role in God's
creation, but that heavenly reward lies concealed in the hunger and thirst of the
poor:[143]

ثواب کہتا ہے مل جائے گا کر ان کی مدد   چھپا ہوا ہے غریبوں کی بھوک پیاس میں ہوں

– that is, if you help those among you who hunger and thirst you will have your
reward in heaven.

Akbar then is concerned with *everyone*, not just with the rich and influential elites of his community. And he hopes for those changes in the thought and spirit of all of them which can alone give them a strong united will[144] and make them once more capable of becoming the masters of their own destiny. What his people need above all are firm principles,[145] without which one simply moves with the world and lacks all capacity for changing it. He asks the leaders of the New Light:[146]

ناز کیا اس پہ جو بدلا ہے زمانے نے تمہیں   مرد وہ ہیں جو زمانے کو بدل دیتے ہیں

Why feel so proud because the times have changed you?
True men are those whose efforts change the times.

and until they have the firm faith, and the sources of spiritual strength that enables them to do this, he says,[147]

قیامت تک وہ سرداری کے قابل ہو نہیں سکتے

Doomsday will come before they are fit to rule.

This faith they need can only be a religious faith, and that, too, of the kind which he and his predecessors in the *ghazal* tradition uphold – a faith which condemns formalism and bigotry, stresses the spiritual content of religion, and inculcates the love of *all* men as fundamental to the truly religious life. As often, he appeals to the experience of the West to support his argument. The British, whom you so admire, he tells the moderns, still have their Christian faith, while you, with your merely superficial Westernism, have lost yours:[148]

درس تھا ایکساں مگر وہ تو مسیحی ہی رہے
تجھ پہ مذہب کے عوض شیطان کا قابو ہو گیا
ایک ہی بوتل سے پی ہو تم نے دونوں نے شراب
لطف مستی ان کو آیا اور تو اوٹ ہو گیا

Taught the same lessons, he, the Christian, kept his faith
While you have lost yours, and succumbed to Satan's spell.
His the intoxication – yours the sottishness –
From wine from the same bottle, in the same hotel.

But his argument – just as well, perhaps – doesn't rest upon the appeal to British experience.

Clear principles and a unifying faith will teach the Muslims discrimination, a quality in which the champions of the Old Light and the champions of the New are both lacking, the first championing the old just because it *is* old, and the second championing the new just because it is new. He tells them both, in a verse about which you have to think a little before you see its point:[149]

بحثِ کہن و نو میں سمجھتا نہیں اکبر   جو ذرّہ ہے موجود ہے وہ روزِ ازل سے

Akbar, I do not understand this argument of old and new
For every atom that exists existed from eternity.

By which he means oldness and newness is no argument; what one has to decide is not between old and new but between good and bad. He feels himself very much caught between the anger of those who hate everything old and the equal anger of those who hate everything new, and expresses his predicament in a humorous verse:[150]

ہم دھوتی پہ ہے شبہ و حقارت کی نظر

پتلون پہ غصہ و شرارت کی نظر

بہتر ہے یہی برہنہ پھریئے اکبر

شاید پھر جائے انکی رغبت کی نظر

I wear a loincloth – and am looked at with suspicion and contempt.
I put on trousers – and arouse men's anger and hostility.
Perhaps I'd better drop them both and go around with nothing on.
Then maybe men will feel my charm and I shall feel their sympathy.

Many other verses make the same sort of point more seriously, attacking undiscriminating attitudes on both sides. He tells the indiscriminate advocates of reform:[151]

ہمیں گیرے ہوئے ہیں ہر طرف اصلاح کی موجیں   مگر یہ جس نہیں ہے ڈوبتے ہیں یا ابھرتے ہیں

Waves of reform are raging on all sides
But where are we? Sinking or surfacing?

Or, in another metaphor, he says that they are like men watching an operation, who are so fascinated by the movements of the lancet that they do not notice that the patient is dying:[152]

خوشی ہے سب کو کہ آپریشن میں خوب نشتر پیہ چل رہا ہے

کسی کو اس کی خبر نہیں ہے، مریض کا دَم نکل رہا ہے

We have already seen something of how *he* discriminates, how *he* decides what to accept and what to reject in the teachings of the modern school. Akbar criticizes the New Light not only because it rejects too much of the past but also because it contents itself with too little of the new. Some of his most savage verse is directed against those complacent 'brown Englishmen' who think that because they despise their own people, learn English, wear English dress, leave the 'native' city and live in a bungalow with the sahibs in their cantonment, they *are* virtually English. Really? Akbar asks them sarcastically. Does English blood run in your veins?[153] Do you think any Englishman can be your uncle?[154] Is the world as impressed with *you* as it is with the English?[155] If half your faults come from the senseless, wholesale rejection of everything in your own traditions and the equally senseless, wholesale enthusiasm for everything Western, the other half are due to the fact that you do not even begin to understand what are the things that have made the British a great and powerful nation, let alone acquiring those things yourself. A real grasp of modern science and modern skills, and a drive to develop trade and industry – these are the things that made the British great, and these are the things in which you must follow their example if you really want to become a modern people. And don't deceive yourselves: this isn't what the British want for you. You'll have to do it yourselves, and against British opposition. In much of his verse he uses the metaphor of the railway locomotive. The engine rushes past, puffing out clouds of smoke that darken the air – its speed and power symbolic of Europe's advance, and the smoke symbolic of the darkness of ignorance in which it wants to keep Asia sleeping.[156] Or in another view of the same scene,[157] the engine comes and passes us with a rush, and we hear some vague words from them about 'water and fire' and 'steam'. And for *this* they expect us to sing the praises of Europe's generosity to us! Akbar concludes:

No: let them teach us everything they know.
Then we will give thanks for their kindness to us.

انجن آیا نکل گیا زن سے   سن لیا نام آگ پانی کا

بات اتنی اور اس پہ یہ طومار   نقل ہے یورپ کی جاں نثانی کا

علم پورا ہمیں سکھائیں اگر   تب کریں شکرِ مہربانی کا

But they won't do that, he says. We are far from the shore, and the storms rage and the waves rise high and our ship is breaking up, but the British won't give us their steamships.[158] If you want to acquire modern knowledge adequately it will have be by your own efforts. *Make* that effort, and don't think that because you've got the money to buy cars to drive around in, that makes you a modern man. You'll have to exert yourself, face difficulties, go to other countries for the knowledge which the British deny you, and persist against all the pressures they can bring to bear to stop you. (And, here, he says, it would do no harm to learn something from the Hindus about the effectiveness of agitation.)[159]

عزم کر تقلیدِ مغرب کا ہنر کے زور سے   لطف کیا ہے لا دیئے موٹر پہ زر کے زور سے

غیر ملکوں میں ہنر کو سیکھ تکلیفیں اُٹھا   روکتے ہیں وہ اگر اپنے اثر کے زور سے

بابوؤں کا کام نکلا شور و شر کے زور سے   . . . .

This will lay the basis for your developing trade and industry. It is trade that makes the European nations so strong.[160] The trader (*tajir*) is king these days, for does he not wear the crown (*taj*) on his head? (that is, does not the word *taj* stand at the head (beginning) of the word *tajir*?)[161]

ہے تجارت واقعی اک سلطنت   زور یورپ کو اسی کا آج ہے

لفظِ تاجر خود ہے اس کا بڑا ثبوت   دیکھ لو تاجر کے سر پہ تاج ہے

When we turn our backs on trade and prefer government service we contribute to our own decline.[162] And industry will make your country prosperous 'Ply the mattocks of industry to clear the jungles of poverty.'[163] Not that you will be able to achieve all this before you are free,[164] for slavery saps the slave's morale,[165] but this is the path you must take.

And what, meanwhile, should be your attitude to the current realities of your situation? First to *recognize* realities, and not give yourselves illusions about them. For example, realize that the British hold all real power in their hands, and that you are nothing in comparison with them, for all your pathetic pride in your membership of committees and councils. He describes the situation of such a member puzzled because the British don't treat him with proper respect:[166]

جو پوچھا میں نے "حضرت میری عزّت کیوں نہیں کرتے"

تو وہ بولے کہ "تم اظہارِ قوت کیوں نہیں کرتے"

I asked him, 'Sir, why don't you show me honour?'
He answered me, 'Why don't you show your power?'

It's strength that alone commands respect, Akbar says:[167]

زورِ بازو نہیں تو کیا اسپیچ   ہاتھ بھی دے خدا زبان کے ساتھ

If you lack strength, what is the good of speeches?
God give us a strong arm, not just a tongue.

Secondly, maintain your dignity and self-respect. Rather than ride a mount whose reins are in the hands of another, it's better to walk.[168] Be yourself, and behave in the way your position demands:[169]

میں رعیت ہوں وہ شاہانہ دلیری ہے کہاں

مجھ کو کیوں رشک آتے وضعِ ملّتِ انگریز پر

I am their subject; why should *I* give myself lordly airs?
I do not need to envy them the way that *they* behave.

Well, but a man must live, they argue. Of course he must, Akbar replies, but do only what the need to earn a living compels you to do, and don't get involved in anything beyond that.[170]

طلبِ رزقِ ضروری سے تو مجبوری ہے   اس کے آگے ہے جو کچھ اس سے مجھے دوری ہے

Am I not to aspire to worldly success then? he is asked. There's not necessarily any harm in that, says Akbar, but your attitude to the world should be like the Englishman's attitude to the Indian – the 'native'. Some relationship is necessary, but the less you have to do with him the better.[171]

اکبر سے میں نے پوچھا اے واعظِ طریقت   دنیائے دوں سے رکھوں میں کس قدر تعلق

اُس نے دیا بلاغت سے یہ جواب مجھ کو   انگریز کو ہے نیٹو سے جس قدر تعلق

Conclusion

Beyond this we must admit that he hasn't much positive advice to offer. But then he's poet, not a politician; he defines general attitudes; he doesn't prescribe detailed courses of political action. This is partly because he is himself uncertain. He feels keenly the overwhelming preponderance of British power, and he knows that power is decisive in human affairs in *all* parts of the world, not just in India. In one verse he applauds the blunt way in which the German Kaiser stated this truth when he told the Pope.[172]

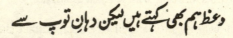

I too preach sermons – from the cannon's mouth.

He feels too not only the ineffectiveness, but the cheapness and lack of dignity in the policies that find favour with the Muslims. On the other hand the more militant behaviour of the Hindu politicians, while it occasionally appeals to him (as we saw a moment ago), generally frightens him, because it provokes an equally militant, and much more powerful reaction from the British.[173] He sometimes feels tempted to turn his back on public affairs, retire into his own shell and advise others to do the same. In one of his poems[174] he incorporates a famous verse of the fourteenth-century Persian poet Hafiz

رموزِ مملکتِ خویش خسروان دانند   گدائے گوشہ نشینی تو حافظا مخروش

The secrets of their states are known to kings alone
Sit in your corner, Hafiz. Why bestir yourself?

And in verse of his own he puts the alternatives like this:[175]

یا امیٹیشن کے صدقے جائے دودھ اور کھانڈ لے

یا ایجی ٹیشن کے بدلے تو چلا جا مانڈلے

یا قناعت اور طاعت میں بسر کر زندگی

رزق کی کشتی کو کھے، پتوار لے اور ڈانڈ لے

Go in for imitation and take milk and sugar and tea
Or take to agitation – and get sent to Mandalay
Or earn your bread and be content, and live as God commands.
Row your own boat; take up the oars; propel it on its way.

It was only perhaps in the last ten to fifteen years of his life that his attitudes began to change very markedly, and that, although never entirely free of misgivings, he began to look with sympathy on mass political activities, and indeed to cherish hopes of worthwhile results from them. This change came about under the impact of events outside India which changed the whole mood of Indian Muslims. From about 1910 there began a period of rapid expansion of European powers – not only, or even mainly, British, but French, Italian and Russian – against the Muslim countries of the Middle East, and Indian Muslims reacted with a growing anger and indignation which turned them more and more against their British rulers. Akbar's verses reflect their helpless rage. In one he writes (doing the same violence to the standard Urdu pronunciation of 'Turks' as we do in our translation to the standard English pronunciation of 'clerk'):[176]

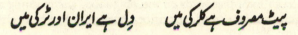

Our belly keeps us working with the clerks
Our heart is with the Persians and the Turks.

– 'our belly' meaning 'our need to earn a living'.

And he writes: 'We have no license to bear arms, no power to go and fight against Turkey's enemies. But we curse them from the bottom of our hearts, and pray that the worms may eat Italy's guns.'[177]

لائسنس ہتھیار کا ہے نہ زور

کہ ٹرکی کے دشمن سے جا کر لڑیں

تہِ دل سے ہم کوستے ہیں مگر

کہ اٹلی کی توپوں میں کیڑے پڑیں

Ideas which Akbar had pioneered now became more and more widely held. Mass feeling rose steadily from about 1910 to the early 1920s, culminating in the later years of the period in the Khilafat movement, and, in formal alliance with it, the first big non-cooperation movement of the Indian National Congress under Gandhi's leadership – the two allied movements forming together perhaps the first and the last modern mass movements to embrace Hindus and Muslims alike. Akbar responded with admiration, and even enthusiasm, both for the movement and for its leaders.

He says proudly:[178]

ہم وہ لقمہ ہیں کہ ہرگز نہ پچیں گے اُن کو

We are a mouthful they can *never* digest!

He knew quite well what forces had brought these united movements into being. (The 'Maulana' of the verse in which he states his judgement is almost certainly Maulana Muhammad Ali.) He writes:[179]

چلایا ایک ایک رُخ اُن کو فقط مغرب کی آندھی نے   دہ مولانا میں لغزش ہے نہ سازش کی ہے گاندھی نے

Maulana has not blundered, nor has Gandhi hatched conspiracies;
What blows them on the same course is the gale of Western policies.

Gandhi gets high praise as the man who can keep the lamp of the East burning even in the Western blast.[180] His very name is auspicious, for, says Akbar, from its letters you can form the words *an* meaning food, *gae* meaning cow, *dahi*, meaning yoghurt and *ghi* meaning clarified butter.[181] And he is changing the course of history:[182]

شاہ نامہ ہو چکا اب وقتِ گاندھی نامہ ہے   اِنقلاب آیا، نئی دُنیا، دنیا ہنگامہ ہے

Times change; new movements, a new world succeeds the old.
The tale of kings is ended; Gandhi's tale is being told.

But it does not last. Akbar reflects an increasing Muslim impatience and indeed contempt for what they see as Gandhi's lack of courage, his meekness in the face of British oppression and his readiness to abandon his allies to compromise with his, and their, enemies. He jeers at him and those who follow his lead:[183]

نہ صاحب کو مارو نہ صاحب سے بھاگو
چلاتے رہو غل، پٹو اور مانگو

Don't strike the Sahibs: don't run away from them.
Keep shouting, taking thrashings, and petitioning.

and, in a remarkable bitter verse:[184]

ایسے دشمن نصیب ہوں کس کس کو   ہوں مبارک حضور کو گاندھی
اور کھسک جائیں، جب کہو کھسکو   کہ پٹیں خوب اور سر نہ اٹھائیں

The British can have Gandhi, and most welcome!
What luck they have! – to find an enemy
Who'll take a thorough beating without stirring
And when they shout 'Away!' will slink away.

And he reaches the conclusion in the end:[185]

بے کی بھی صدا آئے گی تھچھے بھی بلیں گے   لیکن یہ سمجھ لیجئے صاحب بڑھیں گے

Let acclamations sound, and keep on spinning all you will
But mark my words: When all is done, the Sahibs will be here still.

The verse of Akbar's last period has been deliberately dealt with more briefly because taken as a whole it is of a piece with his earlier work, and simply expresses in new conditions the outlook which has already been described, wrapping, as always, the cloak of humour around the beauty of meaning to protect it from the cold, or, as he puts it in another verse, preferring to talk 'nonsense' that will attract people's attention and please them, rather than give sermons which are a trial to listen to:[186]

بار خاطر ہو تو واعظ کا بھی ارشاد بُرا

دل کو بہلا جاتے تو اکبر کی خُرافات اچھی

I hope we have said enough to show that he is *not* the wooden, unimaginative, unthinking, obstinate conservative that some have made him out to be – trying to hold back progress and even to put back the clock. There are indeed verses that can be interpreted in this way, and even a few – we would not attempt to deny it – which *must* be read in this way and cannot be interpreted in any other.[187] But these do not represent the essential Akbar. Essentially he is a man intensely aware of change, and of the irresistibility of change.[188] He knows the need for change and for adaptation to it – but he is aware also that when great changes take place in the life of a people much that is good is swept away with much that is bad. He accepts all that is good in the new, is more or less indifferent to what is in itself neither bad nor good but merely neutral, and exerts what effort he can bring to bear to preserve and carry forward into the new conditions all that he values in the old as well. In short he does what every sensitive, thinking person responding to great changes must try to do; and since most of the problems he confronts still confront us today, his verse still 'speaks to our condition'.

10. Iqbal and His Message

Iqbal's Importance

A Pakistani friend once said to me, 'Pakistanis have three articles of faith –
Islam, the Qaid e Azam[1] and Iqbal.' He told me that it was a legal offence in
Pakistan to publish any adverse criticism of the Qaid e Azam, and that there had
been moves to press for similar legislation about Iqbal. It is certainly the case
that Pakistanis take an immense pride in Iqbal. Many would hold that he is the
greatest of all Urdu poets, and nearly all of them feel that he is in a special sense
their poet.

They have good reason to feel that he is *their* poet. He was the first influential
Muslim thinker of his day to put forward in 1930 the idea that there should be
a separate political state for the Muslims of north-west India and to assert that
it was Muslims' common commitment to Islam which formed the all-important
bond between them. The relevant part of his 1930 speech reads:

> I would like to see the Punjab, North-West Frontier Province, Sind and
> Baluchistan amalgamated into a single state. Self-government within the
> British Empire, or without the British Empire, the formation of a consolidated
> North-West Indian Muslim state appears to me to be the final destiny of the
> Muslims at least of North-West India.[2]

But if Iqbal is in a special sense the poet of the Pakistanis, he is not the poet
of the Pakistanis alone. By the early 1920s he had become the most popular,
most influential poet of the whole Urdu-speaking community, and he continued
to hold that position until his death in 1938.[3] These were the decades in which
the people of South Asia were feeling their strength and preparing for the
decisive battle for freedom, and Iqbal's call for bold, proud, self-confident
action exercised a powerful appeal. Not only Muslims, but Indian nationalists,
Hindus and Sikhs, socialists and communists, all acknowledge his inspiration.
I too acknowledge it, and think that many others to whom his essential message
can be brought will find the same inspiration in it as Urdu speakers have done.

Iqbal's Message; the Power of Humankind

Iqbal wrote his verse not only in Urdu, but also, for reasons which I shall discuss
later, in Persian; and it is in four long Persian poems that his message is most
systematically expounded. These are *Asrar e Khudi* (Secrets of the Self),

published in 1915, *Rumuz e Bekhudi* (The Mysteries of Selflessness), published
in 1917, *Javed Nama* (entitled in one English translation *The Pilgrimage of
Eternity*), published in 1932, and *Pas chi bayad kard, e aqvam e sharq?* (What
then is to be done, O peoples of the East?), published in 1936.

As a Muslim writing primarily for Muslims, he cast his message in Islamic
terms. He sought to speak to the Muslims not only of South Asia but of that
whole vast area extending across Afghanistan, Iran, and Central Asia in which
until two centuries earlier Persian had been the language of administration and
culture. (He was perhaps under the illusion that it still served this function to a
much greater extent than was in fact the case.)

For Iqbal, two verses from the Quran were of key significance. In chapter
23, verse 14, God is described as *ahsan ul Khaliqin* – 'the best of creators'. It
is a verse to which, before Iqbal and to a great extent after him, few Muslims
have attached the importance that he did. Thus in Abdullah Yusuf Ali's
translation, which is abundantly annotated, the words used are 'the Best to
create', but there is no note on them, and most scholars have perhaps taken the
word 'best' as meaning simply 'supremely good'. Iqbal, however, drew from
the word the significant conclusion that if God is 'the best of creators' – not just
'the Creator' – then there must be other creators besides Him. And his most
important co-creator, thinks Iqbal, is man. (To what extent he would have
conceded that 'man' in this sense ought to include 'woman' is not certain, but
I think it is safe to say that he would have allotted her at best a subordinate role.)

He supports his view by a reference to another verse of the Quran – chapter
2, verse 30, where God, having decided to create Adam, says to the angels, 'Lo,
I will appoint a *khalifa* on the earth. *Khalifa* (caliph) is a word with whose
general sense every Muslim is acquainted. When the Prophet died it was felt
that the Muslim community needed to be headed by someone who, to the extent
that any lesser human being than Muhammad could do so, would act in his place,
guided by his commands and his example. Iqbal takes Adam as a symbol for all
humankind, and regards all humankind as charged by God with a similar trust.
Guided by God's commands, we must, as his *khalifas,* continuously take the
initiative in recognizing new situations, taking the appropriate measures to meet
them, and indeed creating new situations in which new possibilities arise for
fulfilling God's – and our – will. In this sense we co-create with God, and, as
we shall see, may even anticipate God's will. Iqbal translates *khalifa* in this
context by the rather unusual English word 'vicegerent' – one who *acts* on God's
behalf.

In order to play to the full the role that God has ordained for us, we must
develop our *khudi* – our 'self', a word by which Iqbal means in this context our
full potentialities for positive action. We need both to discover these potentialities and then to make full use of them. In a deservedly much-quoted couplet
from one of his Urdu *ghazals* he says:

خودی کو کر بلند اتنا کہ ہر تقدیر سے پہلے

خدا بندے سے خود پوچھے' بتا تیری رضا کیا ہے؟

Exalt your self so high that before issuing each decree of fate God
will himself ask you, His servant, 'Tell me, what is your wish?'[4]

He stresses that creation is a continuous and eternally continuing process,
and that we are, and always will be, called upon to work alongside God in the
work of creation. That is what 'life' truly means, and occasion may arise when
'to live' in the true sense of the world will mean to be ready to die for the cause
for which you live. To this spirit of complete dedication Iqbal gives the name
of *ishq* – love – often contrasting it with *aql* – rationality – which he regards as
an inadequate guide to selfless action. In his famous poem *Khizar e Rah* (The
Guide of the Way) (which I shall discuss at greater length below) he has a whole
section headed *zindagi* (life). In it he tells us:

Life is more than the calculation of gain and loss. Life sometimes means
going on living and sometimes means giving up one's life. Life is not to be
measured in todays and tomorrows. It is eternal, ever moving, ever young.
If you number yourself amongst the living, create your own world. Life is
the secret of Adam, the essence of God's creative command.

برتر از اندیشۂ سود و زیاں ہے زندگی

ہے کبھی جاں اور کبھی تسلیمِ جاں ہے زندگی!

تو اسے پیمانۂ امروز و فردا سے نہ ناپ

جاوداں پیہم دواں ہر دم جواں ہے زندگی!

اپنی دنیا آپ پیدا کر اگر زندوں میں ہے

سرِ آدم ہے ضمیرِ کن فکاں ہے زندگی!

In other words, you are truly alive only if you exert yourself to the utmost to
change for the better the conditions into which you were born. Only those days
count in the tally of life which are devoted to active struggle for such ideals.
Other days may have the same quota of twenty-four hours but they count as
nothing towards the tally of the *real* days of life. Moreover, such a life may call
upon you to make the supreme sacrifice, and if it does you must answer that call
without hesitation and count your very death as a sign that you are truly alive.

Such are the essentials of Iqbal's message, cast in terms which every Muslim understands, and supported by quotations from the Quran, which every Muslim believes is the word of God.

But it is a message which, can, without any distortion, be translated into terms capable of inspiring people of any other religion and (like myself) of no religion at all. In more general terms than those used by Iqbal one may state his message in these terms:

Man lives in a universe governed by laws which no one can escape. These laws (which Iqbal and all Muslims conceive of as the will of God) determine the limits within which we are free to act.

But provided that we understand these laws and do not attempt the impossible task of acting in violation of them, we have the freedom and the potentialities to determine the course of events and make our impact upon all humanity and upon inanimate nature.

To do this, we need to become aware of these potentialities, and to make it our aim in life to use them in the service of humanity, ready even to die in pursuit of this aim.

Love (*ishq*) is the power that enables us to fulfil this duty. Mere rationality (*aql*) is not enough.

In only one respect would I regard his message as too limited. I would agree with Iqbal in despising and condemning the narrow, practical, self-seeking 'rationality' expressed in the unarticulated thought that follows the 'but' when people say, 'Principles are all very well, but....' But that is a very limited conception of rationality. *Aql,* rationality, is not in itself limited, but on the contrary, is something that can and should work in complete harmony with *ishq,* and to the same ends.

Nationalism versus Internationalism

Iqbal has another important message to deliver. He grew up in a period when feelings of national pride and a desire to assert national rights were on the increase. The feeling was becoming widespread, in India as elsewhere, that the bond of common nationality could and should take precedence over every other bond that unites individuals and forms them into a community. Those who embraced this view often did so with an almost religious fervour. To them their motherland was everything, and nothing except the glory of the motherland mattered. There was a time when Iqbal too felt something of this fervour. In one of his early poems, *Naya Shivala* (A New Shrine), he calls for the abandonment of the old traditional religious attitudes which teach their followers to hate their fellow-countrymen and declares:

خاکِ وطن کا مجھ کو ہر ذرّا دیوتا ہے

Every grain of the dust of my country is a god to me.[5]

One of his most famous poems of this period, still popular in India, is his *Tarana e Hindi* (Indian Anthem) which begins:

سارے جہاں سے اچھا ہندوستاں ہمارا

Our India is the best country in the world.[6]

This childish sentiment is felt by millions of people in every nation – not of course because they have studied all the countries of the world and after careful thought concluded that theirs is the best. No, the mere fact that it is *their* country *means* that it is the best. There is hardly a line in this eighteen-line poem which rises above this childish level.

This poem was written some time before 1905.[7] Within a matter of years he had come to feel very differently. The third section of his first collection of Urdu verse comprises poems written 'from 1908 to....' The date is significant; 1908 was the year in which Iqbal returned home after a three-year sojourn in Europe – mainly in England and Germany – where he saw clearly the catastrophe to which national rivalries were heading. In this section there is a poem *Tarana e Milli* (Anthem of the (Muslim) Community) which begins:

چین و عرب ہمارا، ہندوستاں ہمارا

مسلم ہیں ہم وطن ہے سارا جہاں ہمارا

China and Arabia are ours, India is ours
We are Muslims; the whole world is our country.[8]

The poem was clearly written to resemble *Tarana e Hindi* as closely as possible in form–the metre is the same; the rhyme scheme is the same, and some of the words the same. The *'hindostan hamara'* (our India) ends the first line in both poems; the words *'sara jahan'* (the whole world) occur in the first couplet of both poems, and through out the poem words used in *Tarana e Hindi* are repeated. And this clearly stressed community of form serves to bring home all the more sharply the totally different content of the two poems. The opening line startles the reader, and was intended to. The whole poem could be read as a call to Muslims to conquer the world (and no doubt *is* so read by many readers). But the very next poem (*Vataniyat*) indicates that this is not the thought that is uppermost in Iqbal's mind. Its full title is *Vataniyat (yani vatan ba-haisiyat ek siyasi tasavvur ke)*. *Vataniyat* is a difficult word to translate. *Vatan* means the place or country of one's birth, and *vataniyat* 'country-of-one's-birth-ism'; but we capture Iqbal's essential point if we translate his title as 'Nationalism' – that is 'nation' as a political concept. He begins by saying that this age has fashioned new idols, new gods, and the most powerful of them is 'the nation', after which the very next words are

جو پیرہن اس کا ہے وہ مذہب کا کفن ہے

The 'nation's' garment is religion's shroud.[9]

In other words, to worship the nation is to deny religion. The last verse says:

اقوامِ جہاں میں ہے رقابت تو اِسی سے

تسخیر ہے مقصودِ تجارت تو اِسی سے

خالی ہے مدافقت سے سیاست تو اِسی سے

کمزور کا گھر ہوتا ہے غارت تو اِسی سے

اقوام میں مخلوقِ خدا بٹتی ہے اِس سے

قومیّتِ اسلام کی جڑ کٹتی ہے اِس سے

> If there is rivalry between the nations of the world, this *vataniyat*
> is the cause of it.
> If the object of trade is conquest, this is the cause of it.
> If politics is devoid of sincerity, this is the cause of it.
> If the home of the weak is destroyed, this is the cause of it.
> It is this that divides God's creation [humankind] into nations.
> It is this that severs the root of the community of Islam.

Once again, Iqbal, as a Muslim, expresses his message in Islamic terms. And once again it is a message which, expressed in universal terms, can inspire people of any religion and of no religion at all. It asserts that the bond of common nationality must never transcend that stronger and nobler bond of common dedication to a high ideal, and that dedication to the greater glory of one's own nation as the supreme ideal in life brings nothing but disaster. The senseless slaughter and suffering of the First World War was soon to provide a powerful argument in Iqbal's favour, and world politics has continued to provide such arguments ever since. In Iqbal's own part of the world, India and China, the two most populous countries of the world, accounting together for something like half of the world's population and living in friendly relationship for a decade, transformed that friendship into an enmity which has continued ever since and, inspired by 'national rights', went to war for a tract of territory which was, and is, of almost no conceivable practical use to either of them.

It is important to note that Iqbal's emphatic rejection of nationalism (love-of-country-ism' as a political concept) by no means implied that one should not love one's country and feel a common bond with all those who live in it. Iqbal felt that bond with his country and his fellow countrymen all his life. In particular his poetry is free of all hostility to Hindus. The one line of his *Tarana e Hindi* which says anything really significant is:

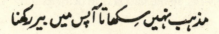

Religion does not teach us to fight one another.

One of his early poems *Aftab* (The Sun)[10] is a translation of the hymn to the sun in the Vedas, the earliest religious writings of the Hindus. The second collection of his Urdu verse is introduced by an Urdu version of a verse of Bhartrihari, the Sanskrit poet

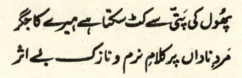

The heart of the diamond can be cut open by the leaf of a flower,
On the fool, soft and delicate poetry can make no impression.[11]

– by which he means not that you can in fact cut a diamond with a leaf, but that even those who could fancy that this might be possible must realize that the possibility of making an impression on the mind of a fool is absolutely inconceivable. And in *Javed Nama* he honours both Bhartrihari and *Jahan-dost* – the Persian translation of the name Vishramitra, who in Hindu legend was the teacher of Rama, the hero of the great Hindu epic the *Ramayana*, an epic which, we are told, he intended to translate into Urdu.[12]

Iqbal's Message to the Poor and Oppressed

Iqbal, then, sees it as the task of humankind to exert its full strength to change for the better the world in which we live, and that this task demands that we rise above considerations of narrow national interest and unite with others all over the world to carry our task to completion.

We shall see now what else he thinks it demands. He believes that just as we need to fight to end the oppression of nation by nation so too must we fight to end the oppression of the poor by the rich. These ideas find powerful expression in his famous poem *Khizr e Rah*, (The Guide of the Way). He wrote this poem in 1921, and recited it under the auspices of the *Anjuman i Himayat i Islam* ('Society for the Support of Islam') at its 37th annual meeting in April 1922, to an audience of twenty thousand. Eye witnesses have described the copious tears with which he recited it, and the impact which it made. Khizr (or Khizar) is the mysterious figure in Islamic legend who found and drank the water of life, so that he will never die. It is said that he appears to travellers who have lost their way and guides them back on to the right path; and he gives spiritual guidance too. The unnamed figure in the Quran who explained God's purposes where these were unintelligible to Musa (Moses) is generally understood to be Khizar.

It is worth while looking at this poem in some detail. It comprises eleven long stanzas; these vary in length, and the argument often runs on from one stanza to the next. In the first and second stanzas Iqbal describes his meeting with Khizar and the questions which he puts to him, and the remaining nine stanzas give Khizar's replies. Here I select from them only those themes which are relevant to the present context.

Khizar begins his reply to the poet with a paean of praise to a life spent roaming the deserts. To those brought up in the tradition of Urdu poetry the parallel between what he is saying and the constant theme of the Urdu *ghazal* is immediately evident. I may remark in passing that the fairly common practice of contrasting Iqbal's message to that of the classical Urdu *ghazal* is in my opinion a profoundly wrong one. On the contrary, Iqbal's message deserves to be seen as a continuation of that of the Urdu *ghazal* in every essential respect. The lover in the Urdu *ghazal* 'roams the deserts' – the words are used metaphorically – for the same reason as Khizar does, in pursuit of a high ideal for which he is ready to sacrifice every material comfort. However, there is an emphasis, and a very correct emphasis, in this section upon the concept of life as unceasing activity, unceasing movement, unceasing search, for ever-fresh significant truth. Khizar's very first remark to the poet is 'This continuous movement is the proof of life'.

$$ یہ تگ و پوئے دما دم زندگی کی ہے دلیل $$

– that is, only those who are engaged in constant search are really alive.

This thought is elaborated even more beautifully in the second section of the poem, which plunges in right away to depict what Iqbal considers the essence of life, in lines which I have already quoted above.

In another stanza – *saltanat* (imperial rule) – he describes the wiles which ruling nations use to keep other nations in subjection, employing apparently democratic deceptions which merely serve to veil the undiminished power of the capitalist. (The poem belongs to a period when constitutional changes in India were being proposed.) Iqbal calls for the rejection of the authority of all such rulers. 'Dominion', he says, 'belongs only to God. Do not disgrace your free nature by accepting slavery. If you recognize any man as your master you are more of an infidel than the Brahmin himself.'

سروَری زیبا فقط اُس ذاتِ بے ہمتا کو ہے

حکمراں ہے اک وہی، باقی بُتانِ آذری

از غلامی فطرتِ آزاد را رُسوا مکن

تا تراشی خوخستہ از برہمن کافِ برتری

The stanza which immediately follows is headed 'Capital and Labour', and makes a parallel point – that workers produce wealth which their masters appropriate, accepting as wages what is in fact no better than alms given to the poor. Concepts of race, nationality, church, empire, culture and colour are all used by the capitalist rulers of the West to hoodwink their subjects and to keep them quiet. Iqbal calls upon the labouring people of the West to recognize that their day is dawning and that they must rise up, destroy the old system, and build a new world.

Finally comes the section on the world of Islam. Iqbal describes how the peoples of the Muslim world have been subjected to the will of the West, sometimes by force and sometimes by guile. He calls upon them to renew and strengthen their faith, trusting in God's promise and confident that if they enter the struggle they will ultimately be victorious. He commends to them the words of Rumi, the great Persian poet, that in order to create a new world, old foundations must first be completely destroyed. It is in this section that Iqbal calls upon all Muslims to reject all those concepts which have strengthened the power of the Western nations, and above all to reject narrow sectarianism and narrow nationalism. 'From the shores of the Nile to the soil of Kashgar he who makes distinction of colour and blood shall be destroyed.' Whether he be a Turk dwelling in a palace or an Arab of noble family, his Muslim faith takes precedence over these considerations. The Muslim community is a single, united, worldwide community, and only if it maintains that character can it emerge from its present troubles.

Once again it is relevant to make the point that while Iqbal, as a Muslim, addresses his fellow Muslims, his essential message is applicable to Muslims and non-Muslims alike. That message is: Devote your lives to the pursuit of high ideals, rejecting all distinctions of blood and colour, nation and class, and uniting with all those all over the world who share your ideals and struggle to realize them.

It is a striking fact that in this poem there is no specific mention of those hundreds of millions of peasants that constitute perhaps the major part of the poor and oppressed of the world. But other poems do speak of them, and convey the same essential message. The most famous passage comes in the poem *Farishton ka Git* (The Angels' Song) – in the part headed *farman e khuda farishton se* (God's command to the angels) and beginning

اُٹھو میری دنیا کے غریبوں کو جگا دو

Rise, and arouse the poor of my world[13]

and calling upon them to take 'that field that does not provide sustenance for the peasant' and 'burn every ear of corn' that grows in it.

The Limitations of Iqbal's Thought

Iqbal's message is an inspiring one. But it must be said that he himself is not always true to its spirit.

In an article published in December 1909 Iqbal's older contemporary Nazir Ahmad had spelt out with great and justified emphasis what the concept of humanity as God's *khalifa* involved (I have summarized this article in the chapter 'Nazir Ahmad and the Aligarh Movement' and need not repeat it here.)

In Iqbal's mind these implications are much less clear than they were in Nazir Ahmad's, and before Nazir Ahmad, in the minds of the great *ghazal* poets of Urdu and Persian. For them, people *as people* are important, and there is constant insistence that those who serve God truly, and fulfil, wholeheartedly and at every cost, God's command that they love their fellows are the true worshippers of God, no matter what they call their religion and no matter whether they call God Ram, as many Hindus do, or Allah, as Muslims do, or any other name. Iqbal was, of course, thoroughly familiar with this tradition, and sometimes echoes it. For instance, in *Javed Nama*[14] he writes:

کافرِ بے دار دل پیشِ صنم

بہ از دینداری کہ خفت اندر حرم

The infidel with a wakeful heart [bowing down] before an idol,
Is better than a religious man asleep in the mosque.

But this sentiment does not often recur in his verse, and one constantly feels that when Iqbal pictures to himself man as God's *khalifa* he thinks not of all mankind but of that part of mankind which is also Muslim. And even within these limits his thought is not always clear and consistent. On the one hand he advances the concept of *mard e momin*, 'the man of the true faith', defining him as one who wholeheartedly accepts Iqbal's concept of Islam as the only true one, and lives his life accordingly. Of the traditional spokesmen of Islam, the mullah and the *pir* (spiritual guide), he speaks scathingly, mockingly, and often angrily, attacking them for the way they exploit their credulous followers.[15] He fulminates again and again against kings and kingship.[16] And yet in general he seems tacitly to accept the view that anyone who calls himself a Muslim *is* a Muslim, and that too a *mard e momin*, and that those Muslim potentates of the past and present that Muslims regard as great men *are* great men.

He tells us how the true Muslim develops his *khudi* and exerts it to change the world, but here too his concepts are blurred. W. Cantwell Smith wrote very aptly of him, '...he was less devoted to enunciating what one ought to do than to lashing one into doing it with all one's might'[17] – but that is an understatement of Iqbal's position. There are times when he clearly regards any man who does what he wants to do with all his might as one to be admired and emulated – provided he is one who calls himself a Muslim. The most blatant example of this is his praise in *Javed Nama* of the Iranian king Nadir Shah and his Afghan successor Ahmad Shah Abdali[18] – both of them cruel, ruthless, tyrannical rulers who in the eighteenth century repeatedly invaded India, plundering and killing its people, including thousands of Muslims, on a grand and revolting scale. The *mard e momin* of Iqbal's ideal, far from praising them, should regard them as a disgrace to the name of Islam, and if Iqbal had been true to his own ideals he should have had no difficulty in recognizing this.

The late Aziz Ahmad (whose *Iqbal, Nai Tashkil* I regard as one of the best studies of Iqbal) was once asked, 'Why do you Pakistanis make so much of Iqbal?' He replied, 'Because he made us feel good.' Like many off-the-cuff remarks, this stated a truth of a kind less commonly and less openly expressed in academic writing. Iqbal did indeed make them feel good, and it is not difficult to see why.

His whole view of history is, to say the least of it, a simplistic one. One often feels that he thinks that he is still living in the eighteenth century. He writes in Persian, thinking that Persian is still a language which will give him access to vast areas of the Islamic world.

He sees the king of Afghanistan as one who can still decisively influence the fate of Indian Muslims, as in the eighteenth century Abdali could. (Many Indian Muslims in Abdali's time looked to this ruthless killer and plunderer to restore their fallen fortunes, and Iqbal, two centuries later, still sees him in this light – unlike his poetic forebear Mir, who hated Abdali and rejoiced in his humiliation at the hands of the Sikhs.)

In famous lines in *Javed Nama* he calls '(Mir) Jafar of Bengal and Sadiq of the Deccan'

$$ننگِ آدم، ننگِ دیں، ننگِ وطن$$

– a disgrace to mankind, a disgrace to religion, a disgrace to their country'[19] because they sided with the British in the power struggles of the eighteenth century. He thinks that they ought to have known, what nobody in the eighteenth century did know, that the British were the future enslavers of the whole of India and must be resisted accordingly. In reality, however, those who chose to fight the British were inspired by motives no different and no more noble than those who chose to take the British side. Both were out to maintain their own power, and calculated their course accordingly. And the resisters, no less than the others, were examples of the kind of ruler that Iqbal condemns, 'kings' to whose domination he says no true Muslim should submit. He feels indignant against the British and their allies not so much because they enslaved India as because they ousted its Muslim rulers. And while he condemns Mir Jafar, there is no similiar condemnation of Sir Sayyid Ahmad Khan, who was still alive when Iqbal was a young man (he died in 1898, when Iqbal was in his early twenties), although Sir Sayyid dedicated his whole life to reconciling the Muslims to British rule and trying to turn them into its enthusiastic supporters.

He has nothing substantial to say about Muslims' duties to non-Muslims under their rule. He says of the triumph of the Sikhs over their Muslim rulers in Panjab that they 'snatched away the sword and Quran' from the Muslims because these Muslim 'lions of the Lord' had 'taken to the ways of the fox' (whatever that means)[20] whereas the fact is that the Muslims never abandoned the sword, but found it no match for the stronger sword of their one-time subjects, driven to revolt by the oppression of their Muslim rulers – that is, doing exactly what Iqbal says everyone who is oppressed should do.

To Iqbal, Muslim conquest is a glorious thing. (As I said earlier, his *Tarana e Milli* – 'China and Arabia are ours, India is ours; we are Muslims; the whole world is ours' - *could* be interpreted as a call to conquer the world.) He says that Muslim rule in Spain showed its astonished subjects a new phenomenon – that of rulers who came not to rule but to serve,[21] ignoring the obvious fact that, even assuming that they did serve, they needed first to establish and maintain their power to command in order to do so. And whatever the Muslim rulers of Spain did or did not do, history is full of Muslim rulers who commanded all right, but somehow never got around to serving.

He is the implacable enemy of imperialism, but in his eyes Turkish imperialism was not imperialism at all, because the Turks were Muslims. In the days of the Khilafat movement he shared the almost universal illusions of the Indian Muslims, which I have already described.[22]

To Iqbal it seems obvious that in any territory ruled by Muslims right and justice would automatically prevail; so it never occurs to him that there is any need to raise questions of Muslim policy towards non-Muslims. In his 1930 speech foreshadowing the demand for Pakistan he calls for a state comprising, along with other provinces, Panjab – not just the Muslim majority areas of Panjab, but simply Panjab, where Muslims were only a little over half of the population. (And incidentally, for all his insistence that Muslims must conceive of 'nation' as meaning the community of Muslims, untrammelled by geographical definitions and by other people's false ideas of nationality, he has nothing to say about the Muslims of the north-east of India, more numerous than those of the north-west, whose homeland later became East Pakistan and, later still, Bangladesh.)

In short, Iqbal all too often shares, and appeals to, the deplorable chauvinism that affects the Muslim community no less powerfully than Hindu chauvinism affects the Hindus and British chauvinism the British. For Muslims affected by it every 'great man' that Muslim history has produced is regarded with pride and admiration. The last great Mughal emperor Aurangzeb is admired because in his reign the Mughal empire reached its greatest extent, because he insisted upon Muslim observances more strictly than his predecessors, because he copied out the Holy Quran with his own hand, and so on and so forth; and the fact that he imprisoned his father and killed his brothers in order to secure the throne for himself is not thought of as relevant. Similarly in our own day, the royal rulers of Saudi Arabia, whose wealth and dissipation are as well known to Muslims as they are to everyone else, are admired because they prohibit alcohol and inflict the Islamic punishments for crime – and admired by people who simultaneously proclaim that Islam does not permit monarchy and that the true Muslim lives the simple, austere life that the Prophet did.

Conclusion

But none of this alters the fact that Iqbal's essential message is a noble and inspiring one. The millions of non-Muslims whose imagination it captured were right in seeing it as tinged by, but by no means dominated by, Muslim chauvinism. And if there is vagueness, obscurity and inconsistency in his expression of that message it must be said to Iqbal's great credit that he himself was to some extent aware of it, and frankly avowed it – though at times he also defended it. He wrote in his notebook in 1910, 'I like an element of obscurity and vagueness in poetry, since the vague and obscure appear profound to the emotions.'[23] Like so much of what he said, the words can bear more than one interpretation. If he means that poetry ceases to *be* poetry if it limits itself too narrowly to the expression of thought and feeling applicable only to one specific situation, then he is right. And if he means that poets should deliberately express themselves in terms that can only mystify the reader, then he is advocating something quite unacceptable. More valuable, less ambiguous, and more evidently sincere are the words of a Persian poem which he wrote towards the end of his life.

> When I packed my provisons for the journey from this earth,
> everyone said, 'We knew him!' But no one knew this traveller –
> What he said, and to whom he said it, and from where he came.[24]

In the 'no one' he had once included, and perhaps still included, himself. An early poem (of the period 'up to 1905') ends with the words

اقبال بھی اقبال سے آگاہ نہیں ہے

کچھ اس میں تمسخر نہیں، واللہ نہیں ہے

Iqbal too does not know what Iqbal is –
I swear to you by God, I am not joking.[25]

It is perhaps this inadequate self-knowledge that gave rise to the ambiguities and contradictions which I have described. But these should not obscure for us the value of the best of what he has to say.

Part 3
Literature and the People
(1920s onwards)

11. Achieving Independence, and After

At the beginning of the section on classical poetry, I wrote that in studying Urdu literature it is the Muslim view of South Asian history that concerns us; and similarly the introduction to the second section was headed *The Raj and the Muslim Response*. But from the early 1920s onwards an important change took place: the best Urdu literature ceased to concern itself mainly with the Muslim community and began to reflect the thought and feeling and aspirations common to the people of all communities, Muslim, Hindu and Sikh alike. At the same time Urdu literature ceased to be overwhelmingly the work of Muslim writers. The greatest prose writer of the 1920s and early 1930s was Prem Chand, a Hindu, and after him, alongside Muslim writers like Ismat Chughtai and Saadat Hasan Mantu, came the Hindu Krishan Chandar and the Sikh Rajindar Singh Bedi. But even to label these writers Hindu or Sikh or Muslim is not really appropriate, for, to them and to us, what is important is their common humanity, and not the religious community into which they were born. Their deepest sympathies – and ours as we read their work – are with the people they portray as people, regardless of the community to which they belong; and such a portrayal was a new phenomenon in Urdu literature.

There had been non-Muslim writers before these who had made significant contributions to Urdu literature. Outstanding among them was Sarshar, but it is a striking fact that in nearly all of his work, and in all of his best work, it is the experience of the Muslim community that he portrays.

From the twenties onwards neither non-Muslim nor Muslim writers confine themselves in his way.

All of them are, of course, entirely familiar with South Asian Muslim cultural traditions, as any writer must be whose literary medium is Urdu. It is perhaps worth noting at this point which classes of non-Muslims did habitually write in Urdu.

Among the Hindus of the Urdu/Hindi speaking area two groups were thoroughly at home in the Muslim milieu. One was the Kashmiri Brahmins – Kashmiri in the sense that they had originally come from Kashmir to settle in their new homeland. Sarshar belonged to this group. The other was the Hindu Kayasths, a caste of people whose traditional profession had been service in the middle and lower ranks of the Mughal administration. This had made them fluent in Persian, and, when Urdu replaced Persian, in Urdu too. Prem Chand was a Kayasth, and began his literary career as a writer in Urdu. He continued to write in Urdu all his life, though he soon began writing in Hindi too, so that all his work is available in both languages and he is a major figure in both literatures.

The other major nursery of Urdu writers was the Panjab. Here, for historical reasons that need not concern us, Urdu was until long after the coming of independence in 1947, the language of literature not only for the Muslims but for the almost equally numerous non-Muslim Panjabis, the Hindus and Sikhs. For all of them their native Panjabi was the language of familiar, everyday conversation – and not of anything else; and it was as natural for Krishan Chandar and Rajindar Singh Bedi to write in Urdu as it was for their Muslim fellow Panjabi Saadat Hasan Mantu. This is no longer the case in the Indian Panjab. The Sikhs now use Panjabi not only as the language of the home but of all areas of public life, and have developed a rich and flourishing Panjabi literature; and for the Hindus, Hindi has replaced Urdu as the language of literature. But until the 1940s Urdu held the position that I have described.

Urdu literature from the twenties onwards reflects the very great change that now took place in the life of the country. Nearly forty years earlier, in 1885, the Indian National Congress had been formed to represent to the British rulers the aspirations of those Indians who, while accepting British rule, wished to be allowed to play a greater part in national affairs. British reluctance to meet these aspirations drove them more and more into opposition to British policies, and from about 1905 onwards an influential section within the Congress began to press for complete independence, though it was not until 1929 that the Congress as a whole put forward this demand.

Congress had from the start committed itself to secular ideals and appealed for support to Hindus, Muslims, Sikhs, Christians – in short, to the whole population, regardless of religious allegiances. Influential sections of the Muslims had responded to that appeal, but these were based mainly outside the Urdu speaking heartland; there it was Sir Sayyid's voice that prevailed. His uncompromising stand that the Muslims must identify themselves completely with the British involved vigorous and consistent opposition to Congress, and during his life time and for some years after his death most Muslims followed his lead.

As we saw in the previous section, this situation changed drastically in the first decades of the twentieth century, when the Muslims moved into active opposition to the British. In addition the emergence of Gandhi as the undisputed leader of the national movement in the years immediately following the First World War marked a new stage in the struggle. It was he who for the first time brought the mass of the Indian people into the political arena. When he launched the non-cooperation movement of 1920-22 a militant mass movement of Muslims against their British rulers was already sweeping the country, and Gandhi's alliance with it brought into being a powerful, united Hindu-Muslim front on a scale that the country had never before seen. That unity was shattered by the events of 1922, when, as the movement was reaching its climax, Gandhi called it off because it was, here and there, assuming violent forms of which he did not approve. Hindu-Muslim unity was never again restored, but this by no means signified a reversion to the situation that had formerly prevailed. Within a few years independence from British rule became the common aim of non-Muslims and Muslims alike, and millions of people all over the subcontinent were ready to move into action whenever Gandhi and the other Congress leaders called upon them to do so. And if Muslims increasingly held themselves aloof from the Congress-led movement, this was not because they did not want independence but because they were more and more preoccupied with the problem of how to safeguard their interests once independence was achieved, and with it the rule of a non-Muslim (and, as they feared, anti-Muslim) majority. In short, almost everyone wanted independence, and even among those who felt no strong desire for it the realization had grown by the end of the twenties that independence was coming and that they had best prepare themselves for it.

The thirties saw further significant developments. In the early years of the decade another mass movement, under Gandhi's control, was launched. It proved to be a protracted and, on the whole, an inconclusive one, and it produced among the politically articulate a dissatisfaction with Gandhian methods and a sympathy for more modern left-wing Marxist-influenced political policies.

As the decisive battle for independence drew near, the leaders of the movement were prompted by the need to mobilize still more extensively the mass support of the people (and, in many cases, by a deep and genuine sympathy for them) to pledge themselves not only to the cause of freedom but to that of a freedom which would radically change the social order and bring happiness and prosperity to the poor in town and countryside. Nehru was the most influential spokesman, but by no means the only spokesman, of this ideal, and the ideas of socialism and communism began to influence wider and wider sections of the population. A further major development occurred when in 1937 provincial elections were held, and Congress gained victories which enabled it to take office in most of the provinces.

All this is the background to a political climate of a kind rarely experienced in the modern history of the West. The nearest parallel that the West can offer is perhaps provided by the years from mid-1941 to the end of the Second World War. In those years the necessities of the war against fascist Germany, Italy and Japan, fought in alliance with the Soviet Union and with China, in which nationalists and communists were formally in alliance, made revolutionary views respectable and evoked ardent expressions of radical populism from even the most unlikely quarters.* In India in the middle thirties there was a similar sense of a common goal; the final battle for independence was clearly approaching, and in such a situation politics is dominated by this one central issue – often, one feels, to the almost total exclusion of all others. All who espouse the cause of independence, both at home and abroad, are welcomed into the all-embracing alliance which all see as the essential guarantee of victory. In India, revolutionaries and moderates came together. On the international scene the Soviet Union, with its declared policy of support for colonial liberation, attracted the sympathies of many who were far from being on the left, and this in turn enhanced their readiness to co-operate with the radicals and the revolutionaries.

---

* Those who are old enough will know that this was so; and those who aren't will discover its correctness if they will look up and study the public speeches of British and American statesmen of the time.

It was this desire for independence, sympathy for the poor, and an increasing feeling that the solution of the problems of the poor must be sought not only in liberation from foreign rule but in opposition to the Indian rich, that found reflection in the Urdu writing of this period. Even in the writers from the Muslim community, there was little or no reflection of an outlook which was concerned mainly or exclusively with the Muslims. Religious fervour was not in evidence, and communal prejudice completely absent.

It was in Urdu prose writing that these trends found their clearest expression, but poetry too was affected by them. Here Iqbal continued until his death in 1938 to dominate the field. As we have seen, his message, though cast in Islamic terms, stressed the power of human beings to make their own future and inspired in them the courage to do so, and so naturally appealed to readers in every community who were determined to do just that and to free their country from foreign rule and domestic oppression.

The extension of the range of poetry which Hali had pioneered and Iqbal had carried further continued. New forms, too, gained general acceptance. From the middle thirties free verse established itself, with prose poems following a good many years later.

The *ghazal* too continued to flourish. In Chapter 5, 'The Raj and the Muslim Response', I described how well its traditions met the needs of the first mass, united struggle against the British at the end of the First World War. They continued to meet the needs of this period too. Hasrat Mohani, one of the most courageous of the fighters for freedom, continued to write *ghazals* until his death at the age of 76 in 1951, and *ghazals* formed a significant part of Iqbal's verse too. The poets of the Progressive Writers' Movement, which was launched in the middle thirties, included some who regarded the *ghazal* as an obsolete medieval form, and vigorously propagated this view. But others, of whom Faiz was the most notable, never subscribed to it, and wrote *ghazals* along with verse in other forms; and the *ghazal* increasingly regained popularity even with poets who had once been hostile to it.

As in Europe after the Second World War, so in India after independence in 1947 the wide ranging unity that had brought victory could not be maintained once victory had been won. But Urdu writers in general continued to stand by the ideals their work had proclaimed. When the appalling communal massacres of 1946 and 1947 that preceded and accompanied independence broke out, these writers took their stand against the communal frenzy and used their literary power to oppose it, and in the decades that followed continued to express the strongly humanist values that had given them their appeal and made their name.

In poetry the new trends continued, but the *ghazal* too has maintained its place. This should not occasion any great surprise. For the last sixty years and more the social and political conditions of life in the subcontinent have provided a setting which can well sustain the *ghazal* as a vehicle of much of the thought and emotion of poets and audience alike; and on present indications, they may well continue to do so. Many people have felt that social and political power has been in the hands of forces alien and hostile to them, whether these were identified with the British or with their successors in independent India and

Pakistan, and they have been in the position of the lover-hero of the *ghazal*, oppressed and persecuted, but valiantly maintaining the stand which he believes to be the true one. In present-day Pakistan, where Islamic fundamentalism is still strong, and in India, where Hindu, Sikh and Muslim chauvinism still flourish, there are many who would see themselves as being in essentially the same position as the lover in his mystic or quasi-mystic role, maintaining strongly humanist values against the bigotry of the orthodox. The *ghazal* form is clearly not one which meets the needs of Muslims alone. Its continuing importance in Hindi films testifies to its great popularity with a predominantly non-Muslim population; it is a form which can express the emotions of all people who commit themselves firmly to the values in which they believe, in the face of the misunderstanding and hostility which they evoke in others in the community to which they belong. So long as these situations continue – and they seem unlikely to disappear in the short- or middle-term prospect – the *ghazal* too is likely to continue as a mode in which Urdu speakers express their response to the conditions in which they live.

12. Prem Chand and the Short Story

Prem Chand is one of the greatest writers of twentieth century India. He has two especial distinctions: firstly, that he is one of the very few non-Muslim writers who stands in the first rank of the writers of Urdu literature;[1] and secondly, that he is a figure of equally great importance in two literatures – that of Urdu and that of Hindi. For he wrote in both and produced versions in both of virtually everything he wrote.

I well remember the deep impression that his writing made on me when I first began to read it as a student in 1946. I was reading the first chapter of his early novel, entitled in its Urdu version *Bazar i Husn* (literally, 'The Beauty Market' – that is, the prostitutes' quarter), and can remember what an impact its description of landlord oppression made on me. It is not his greatest novel by any means, but I felt sure that none of the English writing about India could possibly have made the impact which Prem Chand did, writing as he did from within Indian society and speaking of what he knew intimately from his own life experience. I had always looked forward from that day to the time when some of his best writing could be presented and published in English translation, and when many years later this wish was realized it was a matter of very great satisfaction to me.

Prem Chand's first collection of short stories was published before the First World War, but it is his writings of the 1920s and early 1930s, up to his early death in 1936, which are the solid basis of his fame. His American translator, David Rubin, writes in the preface to his selection of Prem Chand's short stories (*The World of Prem Chand*) that Prem Chand 'virtually single handed...lifted [Urdu and Hindi] fiction...from a quagmire of aimless romantic chronicles to a high level of realistic narrative...' That, with due respect to David Rubin, was not Prem Chand's achievement. At least, it may have been his achievement where Hindi was concerned (I am not competent to judge on this point), but it is quite untrue where Urdu is concerned. Even before Prem Chand was born, Urdu prose fiction had already produced realistic writing of a high order and at least one novel, Mirza Rusva's *Umrao Jan Ada*, had developed the Urdu novel to a height of perfection which in my view Prem Chand never attained.[2] Prem Chand's achievement was something else – to bring into the pages of literature the ordinary people of India, and particularly that large majority of them which lives in the villages in which he himself spent much of his life and which he knew so well. This was a tremendous achievement, and one not less significant than that which David Rubin, erroneously in my opinion, ascribes to him.

His output was considerable – some twelve novels and nearly three hundred short stories. In them one finds an unparalleled picture of the life of Indian people. The general opinion is that his short stories are technically superior to his novels, and it is true that already in stories written during the years of the First World War he shows a well-developed mastery of his craft. He is without doubt the first Urdu writer to produce short stories comparable in standard to, say, those of Guy de Maupassant, and for nearly two decades, until the short-story writers of the Progressive Writers' Association began to make their mark, he was virtually alone in this field.

A good many of his stories are available in English translation. David Rubin's *The World of Prem Chand* is a collection of twenty-four of them which well represent the total range, and there are a number of Indian paperback translations by Indian translators.[3]

In them one can trace his development from a rather naive nationalist, on through one greatly influenced by Gandhi's deep concern for the poor and oppressed, to one who in his last years abandoned the sometimes rather sentimental ideas which go with Gandhism and portrayed with many-sided realism the social conflicts of his time, and was clearly influenced by the theories of socialism. Those who rightly admire his later work have been, in my view, too adversely critical of his earlier stories. In earlier and later stories alike he writes vividly, with humour, frankness, a deep sympathy for the poor and an uninhibited admiration for the true nobility which the poor can show.

It is this last quality which has evoked most of the adverse criticism which I consider unjust. I can best explain what I mean by taking an actual example and say a word or two about his famous story *Namak ka Darogha* (The Salt Inspector), published in 1915. It is a story of the days when the British rulers of India had just introduced legislation to make the production of salt a government monopoly. (Many will know of this iniquitous act from Gandhi's famous Salt March of 1930.) The opening words tell us that 'when the Salt Department was established and everyone was prohibited from using this God-given blessing', this opened the doors to widespread corruption. The opportunities for bribe-taking were such that people would give up much better posts to get the most menial jobs in the Salt Department. The actual story begins when a young man, Bansi Dhar, having completed his education, is ready to look for a job and is advised by his old father to go for one in the Salt Department on the explicit grounds that he will be able to make much more than the income that goes with the job by taking the bribes that will be offered him. Bansi Dhar gets the job of Salt Inspector.

One night he is at his post on the river bank when he is awakened by the sound of a train of carts arriving ready to cross. He goes out to investigate, and learns that they carry goods belonging to an influential Brahmin landlord, Pandit Alopi Din, and when he investigates further he discovers that, as he had suspected, the carts are loaded with contraband salt. He summons Alopi Din, who has lived a life which has made him thoroughly accustomed to what his wealth and influence can achieve.

Alopi Din was the largest and most distinguished landlord in those parts, a man of great influence, who had the ear of the authorities. Important British officials would accept his hospitality and go hunting and shooting on his lands.

He obeys the summons good-humouredly, thinking that the Inspector is a new boy who doesn't yet understand how things are done, and is surprised when his offer of a 'gift' is rejected and the Inspector puts him under arrest. With mounting alarm and anxiety he repeatedly increases the value of the bribe he offers until it reaches forty thousand rupees, but the Inspector is unmoved, and his staff, though deeply shocked by his order to take the great man into custody, arrest him.

By morning the news has spread like wildfire. 'The world was asleep,' says Prem Chand, 'but the world's tongue was awake,' and crowds gather to see Alopi Din taken in handcuffs to court.

But he only had to wait to get to the court. In these boundless waters Pandit Alopi Din was a crocodile. The authorities revered him. Their staff were his humble servants, the lawyers and officers of the law his servile orderlies, and the watchmen and court attendants his slaves.

Predictably, the court finds that there is not sufficient evidence to convict, and in its judgement rebukes the Inspector for his excessive zeal.

Within a few days Bansi Dhar is dismissed, and returns home penniless to his father. His father is furious, and vents his anger on his son. His mother and his sister too, who had built great hopes on the prospect of his 'earnings', are angry with him, and his wife for several days has nothing good to say to him.

A week later a handsome carriage draws up at the door. It is Alopi Din's. The father rushes to ask Alopi Din's pardon for his son's conduct, and says he would rather have been childless than have such a son, but Alopi Din cuts him short and says, 'Don't say such things.' The father replies, 'What else should I say of such a son?' And Alopi Din replies emphatically, 'That he is the pride of your house; that he has brought lustre to his ancestors' name; that you give thanks to God for giving you such a son.' He then addresses the son, telling him that he has drawn up an agreement which requires his signature, and says, 'I am a Brahmin. Until you agree to my request I shall not move from this spot.' Bansi Dhar reads the document. It appoints him at a salary of six thousand rupees a year, plus day to day expenses, to take full charge of all Alopi Din's property. Bansi Dhar signs, and the two men embrace.

Critics have said that the character of the Salt Inspector is too good to be true, and that moreover the complete change of heart on the part of the villain of the piece who attempts to corrupt him is totally unconvincing. This story, they say, is an example of Prem Chand's naive idealism, a crude propagandist piece written under the influence of an over-simple concept of Gandhism. In my opinion this criticism is totally unjustified. It is true that modern fiction in the West tends to fight shy of portraying wholly noble characters. But that does not mean that such characters do not exist. G.K. Chesterton has pointed out that the novel's claim to be interested in individuals, whereas narrative before the advent of the novel was not, cannot be justified, and that a more accurate judgement of the modern novel would be that it is interested only in unusual, complex individuals.[4] But there are in India, and (I should say 'By the grace of God' if I were a religious person) perhaps in every country in the world people who in similar circumstances would, to their eternal credit, behave exactly as the Salt Inspector behaves in this story; and to accuse Prem Chand of naivety or lack or realism because he chose to portray such a character is ridiculous. The second part of this common criticism is just as untenable. The concluding part of the story is presented almost entirely in the form of dialogue on which Prem Chand himself makes no comment; and Alopi Din does indeed present himself as having undergone a change of heart. But the reader can surely not fail to see that, whether the change of heart is sincere or not, Alopi Din would have been quick to realize how valuable, when he himself is corrupt and is surrounded on all sides by corrupt people, a totally honest man could be to him.

Prem Chand's uninhibited admiration for admirable people continues strongly in evidence in his later stories too. One such story, published in 1932, seventeen years after *Namak ka Darogha* is entitled *Shikva Shikayat* (Complaint) and takes the form of a long monologue in which a wife complains of her husband. His kindheartedness and his unvarying readiness to put himself (and her) out to help lame ducks is recounted with example after example. He always buys the household provisions from struggling shopkeepers who barely make a living and whose stocks are therefore never fresh. Nothing that she can say can make him mend his ways. In one cold winter the sweeper asks for some cast off clothing to keep him warm. She says:

In these times of unemployment who has any clothes to spare? Maybe the rich do, but we don't even have all the clothes we need. You could pack up his majesty's (= my husband's) complete wardrobe in a parcel and send it through the post. And that winter we hadn't been able to get new clothes made. I turned him down flat. It was extremely cold. I could feel that myself; and I knew very well that the poor must be suffering. But what can you or I do except feel sorry for them? When the rich and influential have clothes enough to fill a goods wagon then of course the poor have to suffer the tortures of nakedness. Anyway, I refused. And what did *he* do? He took off his coat and gave it to him. I was furious. It was the only coat he had...But he doesn't mind going about in rags. If people laugh at him, let them. *He* doesn't care. *I* could die of shame... In the end I couldn't bear it any longer and I got a coat made for him. It was the last thing I *wanted* to do. I felt like making him put up with the cold until he'd had a bellyfull, but I was afraid he might fall ill; and then we'd be in even worse trouble. After all, he's the breadwinner.

I expect he thinks himself a model of virtue and modesty... *I* don't ... *I* call him a simpleton and a fool. I've several times seen that sweeper he gave his coat to the worse for drink; and I've pointed him out to *him* too. Why should *we* pay for others' bad habits? And if he was so virtuous and so generous, he would show his generosity to his own family. Is all his generosity reserved for others? Shouldn't his family get even a tiny part of it?

At one point their old servant leaves and they have to employ a new one. The wife is persuaded against her better judgement to take on a man her husband feels sorry for and who he assures her will be an excellent servant. Predictably, he turns out to be lazy, or incompetent, or both. In particular he never gets the main room swept and clean ready for the day's activities. She gives him an ultimatum. By such and such a time on the next morning either the room is spick and span or he is sacked. When she comes to look at the room the next morning she is astonished to find it *is* swept and clean. Her husband laughs and says:

He swept the room early this morning. I had a word with him. You don't explain to him how to do his work; you just scold him.

Everyday after that she finds that the room is clean – until one morning she gets up earlier than usual...'I come into the room,' she says, 'and what do I see? Ghura [the servant] standing in the doorway and his majesty sweeping the room himself.'

The climax comes when it is time to arrange the marriage of their seventeen-year-old daughter. He will not hear of her being married into any family that demands a dowry. At last a match is made with a family that does not raise the question of a dowry, though the girl's mother is convinced that they expect one. The time comes when at the wedding the traditional ceremony of *kanyadan* (literally, 'gift of a maiden') is to be performed. The father is expected to perform this ceremony, but he absolutely refuses – as he has refused to allow every other traditional marriage ceremony to be performed. She says:

Night came, and it was time for the *kanyadan* ceremony. He's always objected to this. He says, 'It's absurd. Is a girl something that you give as a present? Money can be a present; an animal can be present; but to give a girl as a present is ridiculous.' All my pleading left him unmoved....In the end I had to perform the ceremony myself. He didn't even put in an appearance. And the best of it is that *he* was cross with *me* and wouldn't speak to me for months.

She ends her monologue with words that begin, 'But the odd thing is that in spite of all these things I can't bear to be parted from him for a single day....If I were offered instead someone who had all the learning and intelligence and beauty and wealth in the world I wouldn't even look at him...' – and ends, 'I think perhaps I am even ready to regard all his faults as virtues.'[5]

Similar in tone is his story (in the same collection that *Shikva Shikayat* appeared in) entitled *Masum Bacca* (An Innocent Child). In it he honours the simple goodness of a servant whose innocence (in the best sense of the word) is mocked by his sophisticated master (the narrator of the story) as 'naivety', until he sees that it is nothing of the sort. The servant leaves his job to marry a destitute, homeless woman who has already been married three times and has three times run away from her husband. His master asks him whether he really thinks that such a woman can ever be a good wife. He replies that she is a good woman.

Those people [her husbands] probably thought they'd done her a big favour by marrying her. They wanted her to devote herself to them heart and soul. But, sir, you can't make another person yours until you make yourself hers.

Some months after their marriage she again disappears. Her husband searches everywhere for her and ultimately finds her in a hospital in a distant city where, six months after his marriage to her, she has given birth to a son. He comes back radiant with joy to his old master, proudly carrying the child in his arms. His master says sarcastically that it's the first time he's ever heard of a child being born six months after marriage, implying pretty plainly that this fellow is such a fool that he doesn't realize that the child is not his. The servant replies:

Sir, I didn't even think about that. It was because she felt ashamed that she ran away. I said to her, 'Gomati, if you don't love me, leave me, I will go away at once and never come near you again. Anything you need I'll do all I can to send you...I love you as much as I ever did; no, I love you *more* than before... If you have not stopped loving me, come with me. I will be true to you for as long as I live. I didn't marry you because you were a goddess but because I love you, and because I thought you loved me too. This child is *my* child, my own child. If I'd bought a sown field would I abandon its crop because someone else had sown it?

And he laughs aloud.

You feel that here is a man, as real as such men are rare, for whom *every* child is his own child, and that the narrator is right when this reply overwhelms him with shame at what has been his attitude towards him.

Prem Chand is also by the early thirties not afraid to describe, without comment and without adverse judgement, characters who behave in ways that most of his contemporaries, including many who would pride themselves on their broad-mindedness, would condemn. In the same collection he has a story, *Nai Bivi* (The New Wife). The main characters are an elderly *banya* (grain merchant-cum-moneylender), his young wife Asha, and a young manservant. The servant feels a cordial contempt for his master, and motivated both by his sexual desire for the young wife and by sympathy with her plight, makes advances to her. The story ends with the words they exchange with each other when the *banya* has gone out. The last words in the story are:

[The servant is speaking] 'All the things you do for him are things a mother would do. *That's* not what a wife's for.'
'What *is* a wife for, then?'
'I'm only your servant. Otherwise I'd tell you what a wife is for.'

They heard the sound of a car stopping. For some reason Asha's *anchal** had slipped off her head down to her shoulders. She quickly drew it over her head

---

* That part of the saree which a woman draws forward to cover her head as a sign of modesty.

again and said as she went to her room, 'When he's had his meal and gone out again, come to see me.'

Prem Chand makes no comment, and ends the story at this point.

Thus the range of his writing extends more widely as the range of his understanding of the society in which he lives extends. He trusts more and more in his reader to draw conclusions, and no longer thinks it necessary to include among his characters even one who is wholly admirable. His greatest novel *Gaodan* (The Gift of a Cow), written in the years between 1932 and 1935 and published in June 1936, shortly before his death, bears striking testimony to his maturity. Its story is difficult to summarize. Its central character is Hori – a poor peasant who has less than an acre of land; the story describes his relationships with his two brothers, his wife Dhaniya and his son and two daughters (the only survivors of six children), and the landlords, moneylenders, police and others who ruthlessly exploit and oppress the village poor. His dearest wish is to own a cow, and when he dies to make a gift of it to a Brahmin, for this will guarantee his salvation. He manages to acquire one, but his two brothers react with insane jealousy, and one of them poisons it. He sinks deeper and deeper into debt as his life goes on, and in the end dies with only a few small coins in his possession, earned by making ropes. The novel also portrays something of industrial life in the cities, where Hori's son goes to work in a factory.

But if Hori is the hero of the book, and one for whom the reader feels a deep sympathy, he is far from being a wholly admirable character, and his defects and undesirable qualities are depicted quite frankly. The book presents a detailed picture of the life of the peasantry of Uttar Pradesh (then United Provinces) which it would be difficult to surpass. Some of the criticisms commonly made of this book – for instance that the urban characters are less well-drawn than the rural characters and that urban scenes are not fully integrated into the structure of the novel as a whole – are justified. But this does not detract from the book's very great achievement.

I would remark at this point that Prem Chand has often suffered from the application by the English-educated of canons of literary criticism allegedly embodying world standards, but in fact derived wholly from the modern literature of Europe and North America. These standards assert, for example, that the novel is the highest and only really perfect form of prose narrative fiction, and that whatever work of fiction, either in the early literature of Europe or in the literature of other countries, does not conform to the requirements of the modern novel is an inferior piece of work. There are welcome signs that even in the modern West in recent years the impertinence of this view is beginning to be recognized. Some years ago I was delighted to read a book by the Americans Scholes and Kellogg entitled *The Nature of Narrative*,[6] in which they say that they wrote their book with the aim of 'putting the novel in its place'. This is a very apt phrase, for by it they mean both putting the novel in its place in the whole tradition of prose narrative fiction, and also demoting it from the unwarrantably exalted position that critics have claimed for it. The fact that Prem Chand's *Gaodan* does not meet the exacting requirements of the modern novel as narrowly defined by such critics should not at all mean that we can deny its rightful claim to being a major work of twentieth century prose fiction.

In 1935, the year in which he completed *Gaodan*, he wrote a short story entitled *Kafan* (The Shroud). Many would think that this story represents the peak of his achievement. In no other story of Prem Chand that I have read does one find writing which makes so tremendous an impact. The story opens with a father and son, belonging to the very poorest sections of village society, conversing about the impending death of the son's wife in childbirth. You are struck by the matter-of-fact and unfeeling way in which they speak of the dying woman, with only an occasional conventional comment on her goodness. When she finally dies they turn their attention to collecting the money to buy a shroud, and having at length with great difficulty raised it, go into a liquor shop on their way and spend the money they have collected. The story ends with their half-drunken conversation as they come out of the liquor shop.

Clearly they are not heroes. But equally clearly they are not (to use the modern term) anti-heroes either. The reader cannot help feeling a most profound sympathy with them, and the more often you read this story the more strongly you feel that what Prem Chand is saying is, 'Yes, these people are degraded and unadmirable, but what has made them so?' And one knows that the answer is, 'The inhuman exploitation to which people such as they are subjected throughout their lives has made them what they are; and until that exploitation is destroyed for ever their good human qualities can never be brought out.'

This story marks a new stage in the development of Prem Chand's social and political views, and his adoption of an outlook strongly influenced by modern socialism. A year later he consented to preside over the first session of the newly formed Progressive Writers' Association in 1936. I shall speak in more detail of the PWA and of Prem Chand's relation to it in the following chapter. For the present it is enough to say that for two decades before its foundation Prem Chand had blazed the trail for the best of the prose fiction that the PWA writers were to produce. The artistic power of *Kafan* is so great that one can only feel the keenest regret the Prem Chand died shortly after writing it. If he had lived only a few more years one can feel sure that he would have produced work markedly superior to the great work which we already have and by which he will be remembered, not only in his country but, as translations into other languages make his work available in other continents, throughout the world.

13. The Progressive Writers' Movement

In the 1930s developments occurred which culminated in 1936 in the formation of the Progressive Writers' Association – PWA for short. It was an all-India association and included in its ranks writers of a number of India's major languages, but in no other language did it exert so great an influence as it did in Urdu, and writers who joined the Association or sympathized with its aims made new contributions of lasting value to the stock of Urdu literature. Before giving some account of these it is sensible to say something of the early history of the Association and of the historical conditions in which it arose.

The first major practical move towards the formation of the Progressive Writers' Association seems to have been made in London, in the Nanking Restaurant in Denmark Street, in November 1935 – or perhaps in 1934: the date is not certain. It was there that a number of radical Indian students and intellectuals met, discussed and formulated its original manifesto and made plans to establish the movement in India. They included Mulk Raj Anand (at that time one of the very few Indian writers in English to have made an impact upon the English reading public), Sajjad Zahir, Jyoti Ghosh, Promod Sen Gupta and M.D. Tasir. Through friends, who after completing their studies in London, Oxford, Cambridge, Paris and elsewhere had now returned home, contacts were made with sympathetic circles in India, and when Sajjad Zahir returned to India shortly afterwards – he was the first of the London circle to return – he set about establishing the basis for an organized movement there.

He went taking with him the 'Manifesto of the Indian Progressive Writers' Association, London' dated 'London, 1935' and printed in the London *Left Review* of February 1936. The first part of it reads:

> Radical changes are taking place in Indian society. Fixed idea and old beliefs, social and political institutions are being challenged. Out of the present turmoil and conflict a new society is arising. The spirit of reaction, however, though moribund and doomed to ultimate decay, is still operative and making desperate efforts to prolong itself.
>
> It is the duty of Indian writers to give expression to the changes taking place in Indian life and to assist the spirit of progress in the country. Indian literature, since the breakdown of classical culture, has had the fatal tendency to escape from the actualities of life. It has tried to find a refuge from reality in spiritualism and idealism. The result has been that it has produced a rigid formalism and a banal and perverse ideology. Witness the mystical devotional obsession of our literature, its furtive and sentimental attitude towards

sex, its emotional exhibitionism and its almost total lack of rationality. Such literature was produced particularly during the past two centuries, one of the most unhappy periods of our history, a period of disintegrating feudalism and of acute misery and degradation for the Indian people as a whole.

It is the object of our association to rescue literature and other arts from the priestly, academic and decadent classes in whose hands they have degenerated so long; to bring the arts into the closest touch with the people; and to make them the vital organs which will register the actualities of life, as well as lead us to the future.

While claiming to be the inheritors of the best traditions of Indian civilisation, we shall criticize ruthlessly, in all its political, economic and cultural aspects, the spirit of reaction in our country; and we shall foster through interpretative and creative work (with both native and foreign resources) everything that will lead our country to the new life for which it is striving. We believe that the new literature of India must deal with the basic problems of our existence today – the problems of hunger and poverty, social backwardness and political subjugation, so that it may help us to understand these problems and through such understanding help us to act.

After this preamble it sets out an ambitious list of organizational tasks which it proposes that the Association take up, and of cultural and literary objectives for which it proposes to organize support. One of these tasks is:

To produce and to translate literature of a progressive nature and of a high technical standard; to fight cultural reaction, and in this way, to further the cause of Indian freedom and social regeneration.

The formidable commitment of time and energy necessary to bring into being an organization with such ambitious aims was made primarily by Sajjid Zahir and a number of his associates. Sajjid Zahir was a communist, and made no secret of his views; his closest colleagues too were either already communists or were shortly afterwards to become communists. But within a matter of weeks it became clear that remarkably wide support for the aims of the projected Association would be forthcoming, and within months some of the most prominent writers of verse, prose-fiction, and literary criticism had declared their sympathies for the movement, including not only those on the left, but Congress supporters of predominantly Gandhian outlook, people who, though sympathetic to nationalist sentiment, had held aloof even from the Congress, and others with no very articulate political views at all. The basis for this exceptionally wide-ranging support has already been explained in the introduction to this section.

In Urdu the ground for the success of the new movement had been prepared to some extent by the publication in 1932 of a collection of stories entitled *Angare* (Burning Coals). Of its ten stories five are by Sajjad Zahir, two by Rashid Jahan, two by Ahmad Ali, and one by Mahmuduzzafar – and all of these except Ahmad

Ali were communists. Its publication raised an uproar, as a result of which the book was banned; and one has only to read it to see quite clearly why this happened. Nearly all the stories include accounts of intimate sexual relationships which even today, nearly two generations later, would still shock most Urdu readers; and there are satirical attacks not only upon religious leaders but on religion – and one story in which God himself is portrayed in scathing and sarcastic terms. It is a matter for regret that the overall character of the book and the scandal which it caused have obscured the fact that two of Sajjad Zahir's stories and both of Rashid Jahan's are good pieces of writing which could not cause offence to any serious reader who appreciates good literature.

Because *Angare* was seen as a challenge to accepted literary values, its appearance is regarded as a landmark in the history of Urdu literature. Yet it was never reprinted, and has never been translated into English. To give the reader some idea of its themes and styles of writing, I give here brief outlines of a few of the best stories in the collection.

Sajjad Zahir's most effective story is entitled *Garmiyon ki ek rat* (A Night in the Hot Season). Barkat Ali, a clerk in a government office in Lucknow, has offered his mid-evening prayer and is walking home through Aminabad Park. The scene is vividly described – the groups standing around the sherbet-sellers' shops, the cries of the newspaper boys and the tonga-man soliciting fares, and the hawkers of garlands of sweet-smelling flowers; the people sitting on the benches or lying on the grass....He has a garland in his hand, and as he passes a bench hears his name called out. It is his head clerk, sitting on the bench with some of his hangers-on sitting on either side of him. He makes fun of his subordinate, hinting that the garland means that he has some secret romantic purpose in mind. Barkat Ali dutifully joins in the laughter at his expense, and moves on, grumbling to himself at all he has to put up with.

> A wife and children: sixty rupees a month, and extra income [from bribes] not to be relied on, though I did manage somehow to get a rupee to-day....These villagers get more knowing by the day; you have to talk for hours before they'll put their hand in their pocket. And when they do they think they've bought you....And if you're caught, you're dismissed. That doesn't happen to the big shots. If *they're* caught the worst that happens to them is that they're transferred elsewhere.

At this point he hears someone call his name. It is Jumman, the messenger in his office. He soon guesses what he wants. Jumman tells him all his troubles, but before he can come to the point Barkat Ali says,

> 'Yes, these are all signs that Judgement Day is near....Yesterday after the Friday prayers the *maulana*[*] preached a sermon about it....It's a punishment

---

[*] *maulana* - a title of respectful address for a learned man, and more particularly for one well-versed in Islamic learning.

for our sins – and look what calamities the children of Israel had to suffer for less than this....'

Jumman knows nothing about the children of Israel and Barkat Ali seizes the opportunity to instruct him, and so prevent him saying what it is he wants.

'Jumman, you, a Muslim, and you don't know about the children of Israel? The Holy Quran is full of stories about them....'

But Jumman is not to be put off for long. He comes to the point and asks Barkat Ali to lend him a rupee, promising that he will pay it back as soon as he gets his pay. Barkat Ali replies,

'Jumman, I know you're in trouble, but you know yourself the situation I'm in. I can't afford to give you anything, let alone a rupee. If I'd had the money you wouldn't even have needed to ask. I'd have offered it you myself....'

Jumman does not let go. But by now they have reached a cinema. One showing is over, and as people come out Barkat Ali is recognized by one of them, an old college friend from quite a wealthy family, who at once invites him to get into his car and come and spend the evening with him. He has hired a famous singer and dancer for a private performance. Barkat Ali does not take much persuading. He no longer gives Jumman a thought, but gets into the car; as the car moves off he sees Jumman still standing there.

A second story is entitled *Phir yih hangama*....(This turmoil too...). The words are taken from a famous verse of Ghalib:

جب کہ تجھ بن نہیں کوئی موجود

پھر یہ ہنگامہ اے خدا کیا ہے؟

> When all is You, and nought exists but You
> Tell me, O Lord, why all this turmoil too?

The piece describes all sorts of unrelated incidents, where good fortune or bad befalls those involved without the slightest rhyme or reason. The reader is silently, but pretty clearly, invited to conclude that if there *is* a God, then he is one who is indifferent to the demands of common justice and humanity.

The inclusion in *Angare* of the woman writer Rashid Jahan's two pieces was something new in Urdu literature. There had been women writers before her but none who portrayed so bluntly the callousness and injustice women suffer at the hands of their menfolk. The first of her pieces is *Dilli ki sair* (A Trip to Delhi), in which a Muslim woman from Faridabad (twenty miles from Delhi) made the trip with her husband, travelling by rail for the first time in her life. The other women flock to hear her tell them all about it. When they had reached Delhi station her husband had met 'some wretched station master' and gone off with him, leaving her sitting in her *burqa* on their luggage – alone, afraid, and hungry. 'And Delhi station is huge; even the Red Fort can't be so huge as that.' And she goes on to describe the everyday scenes of a big railway station as though they were the wonders of the world. Two hours later her husband returns and asks her off-handedly, 'Are you hungry? Shall I bring you some *puris* or something?' She replies, 'For God's sake take me back home. I wouldn't go with you on a trip to Paradise. A fine trip *this* has been!' The Faridabad train is standing there. Her husband sulks and says, 'All right, if that's what you want. If you don't want to see the sights of Delhi, don't.'

The other is a much longer piece entitled *Parde ke piche* (Behind the veil), a one-act drama, and simply relates a conversation between purdah-women recounting in grisly detail all the things they have to put up with from their husbands.

Whether the *Angare* writers had intended the book to be the forerunner of an organized movement, I do not know. But part of their response to the storm it raised was to urge progressive writers to come together. In April 1933, after the banning of the book, Mahmuduzzafar issued a press statement on their behalf in which he said that they made no apology for what they had done and called for the immediate formation of a Progressive Writers' League, appealing to all who agreed with them to contact them for this purpose.[1] It was not until 1936 that this aim was realized, but it is clear that the response to *Angare* was by no means uniformly hostile, and that many who felt that the *Angare* writers had gone too far nevertheless sympathized with their desire to break the taboos which had hitherto excluded important areas of life from literature and had muted justifiable social and political protest. So that when the PWA provided a channel for a more moderate realization of that desire it met with a widespread welcome.

The antecedents of the PWA go further back, and are more respectable, than the London manifesto of 1935 would have us believe. Its picture of a literature which 'Since the breakdown of classical culture' had 'become anaemic in body and mind' is a far from accurate one. (These rather curious words were introduced into the 1938 revision of the manifesto.)[2] At any rate where Urdu literature is concerned quite the reverse is true. Since the emergence of new, Western-inspired literary forms in the nineteenth century, Indian literature, including Urdu literature, had experienced a vigorous and healthy development, which the progressive writers were now to continue. The writers of the Aligarh school would have subscribed to a great many of the ideas expressed in the 1935 draft manifesto, and the concept of literature as something which should teach its readers sound personal and social morality is one familiar from a very much earlier period. In the Indian and Islamic traditions alike, literature had always been didactic in one way or another, and indeed its readers would have been puzzled and surprised by any suggestion that it ought not to be. Nevertheless the stories written in the atmosphere of the Progressive Writers movement have a much more universal appeal than, for instance, the prose writing of the Aligarh movement. Though both saw literature as serving a social, moral purpose, the morality which the Aligarh writers preached was not one which Westerners, or many of today's South Asians, easily identify with; whereas the social concerns evident in both Prem Chand's stories and those of the PWA express values common to people in many cultures.

But this change in emphasis was not a sudden one. Already by the 1920s some of the foremost poets and prose writers of Urdu had, unmistakably and forcefully, expressed their support for movements of resistance to imperialism and for fundamental social change, and that too not only in South Asia but on a world scale. Hasrat Mohani, perhaps *the* greatest *ghazal*-writer of the first two decades of this century, had been from his earliest days a fiery worker for India's full independence, and had by the middle twenties deduced from Islamic premises that communism was the answer to India's and the world's needs. More importantly, the most influential Urdu poet of the twenties and thirties, Iqbal and the outstanding prose fiction writer of the same period, Prem Chand, though less extreme than Hasrat, had raised their voices against imperialism and in favour of the poor and the oppressed. They too looked beyond the boundaries of India. Iqbal made sympathetic reference to Marx, implicitly including him as one of the *ahl i kitab* (people of the book) – that is those who, like Muslims, Jews and Christians, have a religion founded on a holy book. 'Marx', he said, 'is not a prophet, yet carries a book [*Capital*] under his arm';[3] he has 'the heart of a believer and the brain of an infidel'.[4] He also expressed sympathy for Lenin in such poems as *Lenin in the Presence of God*[5], and said of communist atheism that it is a step in the right direction, because it has already accepted the first part of the Islamic profession of faith, 'There is no god...' and needs now only to accept the second part '...but God'.[6] Prem Chand's views were expressed in an article written in Hindi, only a few months before his death, entitled *Mahajani Civilisation*[7] (Moneylender's Civilisation). In it the features of capitalist society – detestable to him – which exalt the greed for money above everything else, are contrasted on the one hand with the more humane relationship between man and man which, he says, preceded the impact of capitalism, and on the other hand (and even more strongly) with the new socialist society, which he believes has been established in the Soviet Union, though (perhaps to avoid attracting the attention of the authorities) he nowhere mentions the Soviet Union by name.

It is not surprising, then, that Prem Chand welcomed the formation of the PWA and gave the presidential address at its first conference in Lucknow in 1936. His death only a few months later was a heavy loss to the movement.

There was reason to hope that Iqbal too might well give his support. Sajjad Zahir tells us that he visited Iqbal at the beginning of the hot season of 1937. Iqbal spoke of his interest in socialism, declared his general sympathy with the progressive writers' efforts, and asked them to keep in touch with him. Sajjad Zahir says that he resolved to have a fuller discussion with him when he next visited the Punjab, but Iqbal died (20 April 1938) before this could take place.

Hasrat Mohani gave his support to the new movement, as did other poets

who had made their name after Iqbal but before the formation of the PWA –
Josh Malihabadi, the self-styled 'poet of revolution' (*Sha' ir i inqilab*) and Firaq
Gorakhpuri, who, like Prem Chand, was a man of eminence in the Hindi as well
as in the Urdu literary world.

In literary criticism and literary scholarship Abdul Haq, secretary of the
long-established Society for the Advancement of Urdu (*Anjuman i Taraqqi i
Urdu*) and already known as *baba i Urdu* (the Grand Old Man of Urdu) was the
figure whose adherence to the new movement most enhanced its appeal. In the
Presidential Address which he sent to be read out to the conference of Hindi and
Urdu progressive writers held in Allahabad in 1937 (he was prevented by illness
from coming in person), he exhorts the progressives to do for Indian society
what the Encylopaedists had done for France in the eighteenth century.

The movement, once launched, went on from strength to strength. Jawaharlal
Nehru (who spoke Urdu well and fluently) attended and spoke at a conference
in 1938, and the movement scored an even greater triumph when Sajjad Zahir
succeeded in getting a declaration of support and a message to the conference
from Rabindranath Tagore, whose fame and prestige were perhaps greater than
that of any other Indian writer of that period. His message carried a correspond-
ing weight. It said in part,:[8]

> To live in seclusion has become second nature to me, but it is a fact that the
> writer who holds himself aloof from society cannot get to know mankind.
> Remaining aloof, the writer deprives himself of the experience which comes
> from mingling with numbers of people. To know and understand society, and
> to show the path to progress, it is essential that we keep our finger on the
> pulse of society and listen to the beating of its heart. This is only possible
> when our sympathies are with humanity, and when we share its sor-
> rows....New writers must mix with men, and recognize that if they live in
> seclusion as I do they will not achieve their aims. I understand now that in
> living apart from society for so long I have committed a grave mistake....This
> understanding burns in my heart like a lamp, and no argument can extinguish
> it.

He then goes on to express in his own words the same sentiments as the PWA
manifesto had expressed, calling upon writers to dedicate themselves selflessly
to the service of their country and their people.

The new writing made a very great impact, and the movement soon produced
new writers who deservedly won the regard of a readership considerably more
extensive than those who shared their progressive views. There were some in
whom the quality of their literary work was not commensurate with the clarity
of their political outlook. Among these were the communist poets, Ali Sardar
Jafari and Kaifi Azmi. But Kaifi Azmi, whom few would regard as a first-class
poet, was one of the sophisticated poets who knew how to appeal to new
audiences, such as those who attended the 'revolutionary *mushairas*' which the
PWA organized among the Urdu-speaking industrial workers of Bombay. Other
poets closely associated with the PWA were Makhdum Muhiuddin, Asrar ul
Haq Majaz, whose best work reaches appreciable heights, and, most important

of all, Faiz Ahmad Faiz, to whom a separate article in this collection is devoted.

However, the field in which the movement scored its greatest achievement was that of the short story. Krishan Chandar, Rajindar Singh Bedi, Saadat Hasan Mantu and Ismat Chughtai are the major names. It is worth stressing that three out of these four – Krishan Chandar, Bedi, and Mantu – were Panjabis and the first two were non-Muslims. (Krishan Chandar was a Hindu and Bedi a Sikh.) This highlights the fact that before independence and for a decade or two after it Urdu was the literary language of the Panjab, for Muslims, Hindus and Sikhs alike.[9]

These and other short-story writers of the PWA developed to an even higher level the qualities which Prem Chand had pioneered – in particular, the ability to portray vividly, and with great sympathy, the lives of ordinary people. They exhibit great technical skill, and the story form is itself a universal one and so poses no obstacles to readers from other literary traditions. These qualities taken together make the PWA short stories perhaps the best starting point for readers in the West who want to sample some of the varied wealth of Urdu literature. Since only a handful of them are available in good English translation, I have selected a few from each of the major writers, and outline them here.

[handwritten marginal note: no longer true]

Krishan Chandar, who died in 1977, was the most prolific of these, and the one who did most to realize the PWA's aim of bringing the arts 'into the closest touch with the people'. Sometimes the results do not (to say the least of it) rank high as literature. According to a recent study of his work[10] he wrote more than five thousand stories, and judging by the relatively rather small sample I have read, I would think that perhaps 80 per cent of them could be destroyed without literature suffering any great loss thereby. But the best of his stories are excellent. More than those of any of his contemporaries, they make a direct, simple, almost naive appeal to his readers' deepest human sympathies, and stories of this kind are numerous enough to ensure him a permanent place among the great writers of Urdu literature.

All these qualities are clearly evident in a story called *Mahalakshmi ka Pul* (Mahalakshmi Bridge). Krishan Chandar presents himself as a worker who lives in the slum where many other industrial workers live, on one side of the railway line at Mahalakshmi, a station on a Bombay suburban line. He, like others, is waiting for the Prime Minister's train to arrive on its way to Bombay, where the Prime Minister is to address a large meeting. On one side of the line is the slum, and on the other the racecourse, where the rich come to 'worship in the temple of Lakshmi' (the goddess of wealth and prosperity) and win and lose large sums of money. On the bridge that crosses the railway are six faded, patched and threadbare sarees hung out to dry, and the narrator says, 'It's quite a while yet before the train is due. Let me pass the time by telling you the story of the owners of these sarees. I know all of them well.' He then does so, with pathos and with humour. As he finishes the last story he sees the Prime Minister's train approaching. The story ends:

But the Prime Minister's train didn't stop. He went to make his speech at Chowpatti [a wealthy district of Bombay] and so wasn't able to see these six sarees. So I want to tell him now, 'If some time your train passes this way again, do look at these six sarees hanging on the left on Mahalakshmi Bridge. And then look at the bright coloured silk sarees that the washerwomen have hung out to dry on the right, sarees that come from houses where the owners of factories with high chimneys and people who draw high salaries live. Look at both sides of the bridge and then ask yourself which way you want to go. Please note: I'm not asking you to become a communist or preaching class war to you. I just want to know: are you on the right side or the left side of Mahalakshmi bridge?

Though Krishan Chandar spells out the moral that he wants his readers to draw, the descriptions of the lives of the poor women are so vivid and appealing that you feel that when he does this he is doing no more than giving expression to what you yourself have already come to feel, and you do not feel in the least oppressed by it. The same is true of another of his best stories, *Kalu Bhangi* (Kalu the Sweeper). Like *Mahalakshmi ka Pul* – and, in fact, like much of his best writing – it is told in the first person.

In *Kalu Bhangi* the narrator is presented as Krishan Chandar himself, the son of a doctor (as indeed he was) who has already made a name (as indeed he had) as a short-story writer. Every time he sits down to write he sees in his mind's eye an old sweeper, Kalu (Blacky – so called because he has the very dark complexion commonly found amongst untouchables), who comes and stands hovering by him. When Krishan Chandar asks him what he wants he says he would like him to write a story about *him*. The story goes on to detail all the questions Krishan Chandar asks him in an effort to get material interesting enough to form the basis of a story. He says:

In the days when I had just begun to write, to help my study of character I would sometimes question him, keeping a fountain-pen and pad by me to take notes.

'Kalu Bhangi, is there anything special about your life?'
'How do you mean, Chote Sahib'*
'"Anything special, out of ordinary, unusal?'
'No, Chote Sahib.'

(A blank so far. Well, never mind. Let's persevere. Perhaps something may emerge.)

'Alright, tell me then; what do you do with your pay?'

'What do I do with my pay?' He would think. 'I get eight rupees. I spend four rupees on flour, one rupee on salt, one rupee on tobacco, eight annas on

---

* 'Little Sahib', because his father, the doctor, is the 'Big Sahib'.

tea – four annas on molasses – four annas on spices. How much is that, Chote Sahib?'

'Seven rupees.'

'Yes, seven rupees. And every month I pay the money-lender one rupee. I borrow the money from him to get my clothes made, don't I? I need two sets a year; a blanket I've already got, but still, I need two lots of clothes, don't I? And Chote Sahib, if the Bare Sahib would raise my pay to nine rupees, I'd really be in clover.'

'How so?'

'I'd get a rupee's worth of *ghi* and make maize *parathas*. I've never had maize *parathas*, master. I'd love to try them.'

Now, I ask you, how can I write a story about his eight rupees?

Then when I got married....

'Kalu Bhangi, haven't you got married?'

'No, Chote Sahib.'

'Why?'

'I'm the only sweeper in this district, Chote Sahib. There's no other for miles around. So how *could* I get married?'*

Another blind alley. I tried again.

'And don't you wish you could have done?' I hoped this might lead to something.

'Done, what, Sahib?'

'Don't you *want* to be in love with somebody? Perhaps you've been in love with some one and that's why you don't marry?'

'What do you mean? – been in love with some one, Chote Sahib?'

'Well, people fall in love with women.'

'Fall in love, Chote Sahib? They get married, and maybe big people fall in love too, but I've never heard of anyone like me falling in love. And as for not getting married, well I've told you why I never got married. How *could* I get married?'

(How could I answer that?)

'Don't you feel sorry, Kalu Bhangi?'

'What about, Chote Sahib?'

After that I gave up, and abandoned the idea of writing about him.

Krishan Chandar then thinks of the kind of life that the other employees in the hospital live – for instance the ward orderly or the compounder (the man who makes up medicines to the doctor's prescription). *They* have had experiences out of which you *could* make a story, and he relates some of these

---

* He could only marry someone of his own caste.

experiences. In between times he recalls things that have struck him about Kalu Bhangi – how well he roasts corn on the cob, how the animals – the doctor's cow and the compounder's goat – love him, how he would like to get the cow to lick his bald head for him, and so on; and he concludes that there is really absolutely nothing else he can say about him. At this point he tells us of how Kalu Bhangi had suddenly fallen ill and died. He goes on thinking about him – and after much thought concludes that he knows now why Kalu Bhangi has been so persistent:

Now I know what it is you want. You want to hear the story of something which never happened, but which *could* have happened... I know that when you get the cow to lick your head, in your imagination you see your wife passing her fingers through your hair and stroking your head until your eyes close and your head nods and you fall asleep in her kindly embrace. And when you roast the cob for me so gently over the fire and look at me so kindly and affectionately as you give it me to eat, in your mind's eye you are seeing that little boy who is not your son, who has not yet come into the world, and while you live never will come, and yet whom you have fondled like a loving father, and held in your lap while he played, and kissed on the face, and carried about on your shoulder saying 'Look! this is my son!' And when you could have none of these things, then you stood aside and scratched your head in perplexity and all unconsciously began to count on your fingers, one, two, three, four, five, six, seven, eight – eight rupees. I know the story of what could have happened. But it didn't happen, because I am a writer, and I can fashion a new story, but not a new man. For that I alone am not enough. For that the writer, and his reader, and the doctor, and the compounder, and Bakhtyar and the village *patwari* and headman, and the shopkeeper, and the man in authority, and the politician, and the worker, and the peasant toiling in his fields, are all needed – the united efforts of every one of those thousands and millions and hundreds of millions of people. On my own I am powerless; I can't do anything. Until all of us join hands to help one another, this task cannot be carried out....
Never mind! Go on standing there. It's better that you should; then perhaps the day will come....

In both these stories Krishan Chandar's aim is clear: he wants to evoke in the reader a sympathetic understanding of the lot of the poorest sections of Indian society, and a determination to change their condition. It is rare for writing which is so clearly didactic to be also so effective. Many of the techniques by which he succeeds in moving the reader are simple, even obvious. One that he uses in many stories is constantly to repeat a key phrase or sentence, which becomes a sort of refrain, deliberately playing on the reader's emotions. For example, the emptiness of Kalu Bhangi's life is stated in a succession of simple facts, but stated again and again, and continually contrasted with the more fortunate lives of others, these simple facts convey a keen sense of the tragedy of such a life. Krishan Chandar makes no attempt to disguise what he is doing – and perhaps that is why as a reader you do not feel in the least manipulated.

There are other stories in which he makes no such overt attempt to tell the reader what to think. A good example is *Mujhe Kisi se Nafrat Nahin* (I Don't Hate Anyone). It describes an incident in the lives of a group of people struggling to make a living on the fringes of well-off Bombay society. It is told in the first person by a reasonably popular poet who is a little better-off than most of his friends because he gets a modest fee from his participation in *mushairas*. One day he visits a friend who is always thinking up quick ways of making a fortune and is currently preparing to launch upon the market a product called *tel dhara* – 'a fragrant, compound oil which is a certain cure for every illness'. As they are talking they are joined by two other friends – both of them hard up and looking for some means of earning some money. One of these is trying to get into the Bombay film world, but complains bitterly that the field is dominated by Abbas and his hangers on, and that they make it impossible for anyone else to get a look in. He goes on and on about this, and it seems that he *hates* Abbas.

Meal time approaches, and the poet feels himself in some difficulty. He had come intending to take the inventor of *tel dhara* out to a slap-up lunch, and now here are these other two. He waits until it is nearly three o'clock, hoping they will go away, but they don't, and in the end he decides to invite them too, but perforce go to a much cheaper restaurant. They size up the situation pretty well and, out of consideration for their would-be host, advance plausible reasons for declining the invitation. The aspiring film-worker is most emphatic of all, declaring that he has already had his midday meal, but in the end both he and the other accept, and all four of them go off to the restaurant. The film man eats more than all the others – twenty-five *puris* as against the others' ten, twelve and fifteen – and a number of other dishes besides. After they have finished, the other two go off and only the poet and the film man are left. The film man says, 'It was three days since I'd had anything to eat.' The poet invites him to have coffee at another restaurant, where he washes, combs his hair, and generally spruces himself up. As they sit enjoying their coffee, the poet asks him, 'Why do you hate Abbas?' He replies, 'Hate him? I don't hate him. I don't hate *anyone* – I'm not hungry now.'

The poet tells the story in a tone of good-humoured mockery, and its moral is both obvious and effective.

Many of Krishan Chandar's stories were written not for an audience with any literary education, but for people whose reading tastes were of the simplest, and indeed for those who could not read at all but who came to meetings at which the stories were read aloud. Much of his writing of this kind cannot, in my and most other people's view, be included in the category of good Urdu literature, but it nevertheless represents an achievement which commands admiration. I knew him personally, and liked and respected him. When in 1950 I expressed to him my criticisms of one of his most popular stories in this category he was not in the least offended, named two other progressive writers (Ismat Chughtai and Rajindar Singh Bedi) whose stories he thought would be more worthwhile translating into English than his own were, but said that he had read this and other stories like it to mass audiences, that they had been very popular, and that he wished to continue writing for such audiences. It seems to me that this stand is quite unobjectionable. During the terrible Hindu–Muslim riots he wrote story after story driving home the message that all decent people must abhor the communal killings and do their best to stop them. And if these stories are not great literature it is to be hoped nevertheless that no thoughtful and humane person will wish to deny that he performed a service to humanity in writing them.

One of Rajinder Singh Bedi's earliest stories which won great acclaim was a very simple one called *Garm Kot* ('Warm Coat' – that is, an overcoat). It is about a junior clerk, his wife and their small son and daughter, and revolves around the problem of how to use the ten rupees which is all he has left after he has paid his monthly bills. He badly needs a new overcoat, and his wife wants him to spend the money on buying the cloth for this. But his daughter needs cloth for her sewing lessons at school and the little boy is clamouring for a toy tricycle. One evening he is passing a confectioner's shop and is suddenly overcome by a craving to eat something. When he puts his hand in his pocket to get out the ten-rupee note, all he finds is a hole. He has to go home to tell his wife. There is nothing to be done abut it....The next day he is talking to two of his friends when he feels something in the lining of the coat. It is the ten rupee note that he had thought he had lost. He goes home joyfully to his wife, prepares to go out to buy the things his children needed, and then suddenly feels afraid he might lose it again. So he asks his wife to instead while he looks after the children, regaling them with the prospect of their mother's return with the things they want. She eventually comes back with a parcel. They open it. It is the cloth for his coat.

The great charm of the story is the picture it gives of the great love that unites the man and the wife and their children.

In general, Bedi's stories reflect his keen interest in the complex psychology of the characters he portrays, an interest which seems to have steadily increased over the years. He excels among male writers in his keen and sensitive perception of Indian women's characters and feelings. This is already evident in *Garm Kot*, and in two of his best stories women characters, beautifully portrayed with the deepest sympathy, play the central role. One of these is *Apne Dukh Mujhe Dedo* (Give Me Your Sorrows). It is the story of Indu, a girl from a simple village background, and of the development of her relationship with her husband, Madan, son of a post office clerk. On her wedding night Indu tells Madan that she wants him to promise to give her something; when he asks her what it is, she surprises him greatly by saying, 'Give me your sorrows.' She proves to be a model wife, a model daughter-in-law, a model mother, and a model manager of the whole household, and the greater part of the story is made up of incidents vividly described in which all these qualities become evident.

The last section of the story takes place after fifteen years have gone by. Madan seems to have lost interest in her and is spending all his time away from home. (The implication is that he is running after other women.) One day when he comes home he is astonished to see his wife wearing make-up, dressed to kill, and looking extremely attractive. They talk, and eventually she says, 'Do you remember that on our wedding night I asked you something?'

'Yes,' Madan said. '"Give me your sorrows."'

'You didn't ask *me* for anything.'

'Me?' Madan asked in astonishment. 'What was there for me to ask you for? You gave me everything....'

'You should have said, "Give me your joys."'

Madan at last understands that she wants to be not just his wife, but his lover. He realizes that he too wants this, and the story ends at this point.

Only two things mar the effectiveness of this story. The first is a lack of realism in the portrayal of the episode that forms the climax. Bedi draws a picture of Indu successfully banishing all traces of fifteen years of motherhood and of the ravages of the hard life she has led and transforming herself into the replica of a beautiful young woman; and not only is so complete a physical transformation unbelievable, it is not required by the development of the story. The other fault is a choice of words and of turns of phrase which seem to be inspired simply by a desire to show off. For instance at one point in the story he speaks of 'The moon, which guides the waves and the blood of women' where the context demands no more than 'the moon', and elsewhere he seems to want to demonstrate that, although Urdu is not his mother tongue, he commands a formidable range of literary vocabulary; and this leads him on occasion to use high-falutin words when more common ones would have suited his purpose much better.

Another excellent story, and one which is free of these jarring features, is *Lajvanti**, a story about events in the Hindu community in the period immediately after the winning of independence. The story begins:

> Partition was completed; countless numbers of people rose up and wiped the blood from their wounds; and then all together turned their attention to those whose bodies were whole but whose hearts were wounded.

Refugees were resettled, and a movement began to recover women who had been abducted and to restore them to their homes. The orthodox were strongly opposed to reinstating these 'defiled' women, and many of the less orthodox too could not bring themselves to take back wives and daughters who had been 'defiled' by other men. A committee is set up to run a campaign to combat these ideas and to create an atmosphere in which the women would be received with love and dignity. Foremost among its members is Sundar Lal, whose own wife had been abducted. He leads the processions to mobilize support for the campaign and works day and night for its success.

He had never been a model husband himself. His wife was a country girl. He had caught sight of her when he went to her village with a friend who was going

---

* This is both the name of the main woman character and of a plant called in Urdu chui mui (meaning '(you) touch (it and it) which closes up when touched.

to be married there, had taken a fancy to her, and had subsequently been able to arrange his marriage to her. But he was a quick-tempered man, would often lose his temper with her, and quite often beat her. She on her side didn't regard such treatment as anything very unusual.

Like other village girls she knew that that's what men do; and in fact if any of the women folk rebelled against it the girls themselves would say, 'What sort of a man is it who can't keep his woman under control?'
[Lajvanti herself] couldn't keep still for long, and even after the most violent quarrel Sundar Lal had only to smile once and she'd be unable to restrain her laughter, would run to him, fling her arms round his neck and say, 'If you hit me again I won't speak to you' – and it was at once obvious that she no longer gave a thought to the beating he'd given her.

One day she is brought back, dressed in Muslim style and in fear and trembling in case Sundar Lal should refuse to take her back. But the slogan of his movement was '*dil men basao* – 'make them a home in your hearts' – and Sundar Lal had said to himself, "Only let Laju [Lajvanti's nickname] come back and I will really and truly make her a home in my heart.'

Now he no longer calls her Laju, but addresses her as *devi* – literally 'goddess', but a standard Hindu mode of respectful address. He resolves never even to ask her what her experiences had been when she had been abducted. All he had ever asked her about her experience was:

'Who was it?' Lajvanti had lowered her eyes and replied 'Jumman.'
'Did he treat you well?'
'Yes.'
'He didn't beat you?'
Lajvanti laid her head on Sundar Lal's chest and said, 'No.' Then she said, 'He didn't beat me, but I was more afraid of him than I was of you. Even when you beat me I was never afraid of you....You won't beat me any more?'
'No, *devi*, I won't beat you any more.'

But Lajvanti doesn't want to be his *devi*. She wants to be his wife, just as she was before.
The story ends:

Sundar had made her feel as if he thought she was made of glass....She settled in, but was desolate....Sundar Lal did not see her tears or hear her sighs....

Bedi's primary intention in the story is to highlight the plight of women in a society in which men are obsessed by concern for their own honour and the women's deepest feelings and needs are felt to be irrelevant to this. But, typically, he is also concerned to show how complex are people's emotional needs and capacities. So Sundar Lal, who vigorously opposes the traditional attitudes, is at the same time a man who does not realize what his wife needs from him. And his wife is portrayed as having been happiest in a situation where she had been regularly beaten by her husband.

Saadat Hasan Mantu's stories have an appealing quality of a sort of informal, often ironical, and yet sympathetic and unjudgemental approach to his characters. One of his early stories is *Naya Qanun* (The New Law). It is about a tonga-driver who hears that on 1 April 1937 a new law is coming to bring independence to India. (This 'new law' is in fact the 1937 India Act which granted very limited powers to provincial assemblies elected on a narrow franchise.) He is delighted, and when 1 April comes he proceeds at once with great enthusiasm to repay in kind the insufferably arrogant behaviour of one of the British tommies who form a large part of his clientele – and ends up in jail.

Another, *Kali Shalvar* (The Black Shalvar) is a story of prostitutes. It focuses on an incident in the life of Sultana, a prostitute from Ambala who has recently moved to Delhi. In Ambala she had started living with Khuda Bakhsh, an enterprising man with no resources except his own shrewdness, who had managed to learn photography, gradually acquired the necessary equipment, and set himself up as a photographer. Both have been doing well until, at Khuda Bakhsh's wish, they move to Delhi. There neither of them prospers. Sultana has very few customers, and Khuda Bakhsh begins to spend all his time away from the house. Sultana, bored and listless and anxious about her lack of trade, spends a lot of her time on the balcony, contemplating the engines in the shunting yard opposite. One day a passer-by looks up at her, and she beckons him to come up. He stays where he is for a while, and then comes up.

Sultana finds the way he behaves both disconcerting and oddly attractive. The story continues:

Sultana invited him to sit down on the carpet, and he did. To start the conversation she said, 'You were afraid to come up.'

'What makes you think that?' he said. 'What's there to be afraid of?'

'I thought so because you stayed where you were for quite a while, and then decided to come up.'

'You're mistaken. I was looking at the flat above yours. There was a woman there who was taunting some man, and that amused me. Then a green light came on on the balcony, and I stopped to look at it. I like green light. It looks very pretty.'

He started to size up the room, and after a while stood up.

'Are you going?' Sultana asked.

'No,' he said. 'I want to look over your house. Come on, show me all the rooms.'

Sultana showed him the three rooms one after another and he looked them over without saying a word. When they got back to the room where they had been sitting he said, 'My name is Shankar.'

Sultana for the first time took a good look at him...[her impression of him and his appearance is then described]. Then she said, 'What can I do for you?' Shankar had been sitting there. Now he lay back and said, 'Do for me? *I* don't want anything. What can *I* do for *you*?'

When Sultana didn't reply he said, 'Oh. I see! Now listen to me. I know what you were thinking, but you thought wrong. I'm not the sort of man who gives you something when he goes. I charge fees, like a doctor. You called me up, and you'll have to pay me.'

Sultana was flabbergasted, but she couldn't help laughing.

'What do you do?' she asked him.

'I do what you lot do,' he replied.

'What's that?'

'What do *you* do?'

'I...I...I don't do anything.'

'I too don't do anything.'

Sultana said crossly, 'That doesn't make sense. There must be *something* you do.'

'And there must be something *you* do,' Shankar calmly replied.

'Yes, I waste my time.'

'I too waste my time.'

'Come on then, let's waste time together.'

'I'm at your service. But I never *pay* to waste time.'

'Use your head...This isn't a charity.'

'No, and I'm not a volunteer.'

Sultana hesitated. 'Who are these volunteers?' she said.

'Bloody fools,' said Shankar.

'Well, *I'm* not a volunteer.'

Sultana hesitated. 'Who are these volunteers?' she said.

'Bloody fools', said Shankar.

'Well, *I'm* not a bloody fool.'

'No; but that Khuda Bakhsh who lives with you – he's a bloody fool.'

'Why?'

'Because he's been going for days to a holy man, hoping that he'll change his fortunes – when he hasn't a hope of changing even his own....'

They go on chatting for a little while until at last she says,

'God knows what nonsense you talk. Are you going to stay, or not?'

'Only on the condition I told you.'

Sultana got up. 'On your way, then,' she said.

Shankar got up, entirely at ease, and thrusting his hands in his trouser pockets said as he left, 'I come this way every now and then. Whenever you need me, call me. I can do a lot for you.'

While all this has been happening Muharram, the month of mourning for the martyrdom of the Prophet's grandson Husain, has been approaching. Sultana badly wants to be dressed appropriately for Muharram, and would like above all to have a black shalvar, like the one her friend Mukhtar has; but she has no money left to buy it with, and all her small pieces of jewelry have been sold to pay their day to day living expenses – except for a pair of cheap silver earrings. She gets desperate, and one day tells Khuda Bakhsh that somehow or other, by fair means or foul, he has got to get her a black shalvar. Then she goes out on the balcony to cool down. She has stood there for nearly an hour watching the scene below when Shankar appears. He looks up at her, and without thinking she beckons him to come up. When he does, she doesn't know what to say. He lies down and after a while says:

> 'You can call me up as often as you like and send me away again as often as you like. I never mind such things.' They chat inconsequentially and then she says, 'Tell me plainly, what do you want of me?'
>
> 'The same as the others want,' he says.
>
> In the end she agrees. 'But I tell you this must be the first time anyone's agreed to your conditions.'
>
> 'You're quite wrong,' he says....
>
> As he leaves afterwards she says, 'Shankar, will you do something for me?'
>
> 'First tell me what it is.'
>
> She feels embarrassed. 'You'll think I'm demanding payment, but...'
>
> 'Go on; why have you stopped?'
>
> Sultana plucks up courage and says, 'The thing is that Muharram's coming, and I haven't got any money to get a black shalvar made.'
>
> After some talk he promises to get her one and bring it to her on the first day of Muharram. 'There, are you happy now?' Then he looks at her earrings and says, 'Can you give those to me?'
>
> She laughs. 'What do you want with them? They're only ordinary silver. Worth five rupees at the most.'
>
> 'I asked for the earrings,' he says. 'I didn't ask you what they were worth.'
>
> 'Take them,' she says. She regrets it afterwards, but he has already gone.
>
> She has no expectation that he will keep his promise, but on the morning of the first day of Muharram he turns up, with trousers creased and hair dishevelled, looking as though he has just got out of bed, and hands her a parcel. She opens it. It is a black satin shalvar.
>
> The story ends with a scene that takes place that same afternoon:
>
> Just as she'd finished dressing there was a knock at the door. Sultana opened it an Mukhtar came in. She looked at Sultana....and said, 'That shalvar's new. When did you get it made?'
>
> Sultana said, 'The tailor delivered it today,' - and as she was speaking she noticed Mukhtar's earrings.
>
> 'Where did you get those earrings?' she said.
>
> 'I bought them today.'
>
> Whereupon they both fell silent.

The part of the story which I have told at some length occupies only the last nine of its eighteen pages. The first nine are devoted to providing the setting and, in a sense, nothing happens. But the writing is so vivid and appealing that you never feel, 'When is he going to start on the story?' Sultana's life in Ambala, her handling of the British tommies who are her main customers, Khuda Bakhsh's history, Sultana's panic-stricken first encounter with a flush toilet in their new Delhi flat, her interest in the shunting yard across the road – all these things hold your attention from the start. When in the 1940s a number of writers were each asked to contribute a story to a volume *Mere Bihtarin Afsane* (My Best Stories), this was the one that Mantu chose. After its publication he continued to write for another thirteen years, until his death in 1955, but I would still rate *Kali Shalvar* as one of his very best stories.

When *Kali Shalvar* was published Mantu was accused of obscenity. There is in fact nothing obscene (whatever that term means) about it, but the mere fact that it is a story about prostitutes and that he did not sit in judgement upon them was enough to make many critics think it so, or profess to think it so. Mantu responded to them with justifiable anger – but with a rather dubious argument. He quotes, whether with a real or feigned disgust it is impossible to tell, passages from the erotic *masnavis* of the classical poets Mir, Dard and Momin and says (quite correctly) that there is nothing like that in *his* stories. Be that as it may, he was more than once tried on charges of obscenity. He seems to have responded by saying to himself, 'Alright, if I'm to be condemned anyway, let me give them something to condemn me for' – and some of the resulting stories are, to say the least of it, unedifying. He was similarly provoked by many of the stories written at the time of the horrifying, large-scale mutual massacres of Muslim and non-Muslims (Hindus and Sikhs) that preceded and accompanied the partition of the country in 1947. Such stories portrayed *either* the Hindus *or* the Muslims as virtuous, innocent victims, or the writer was at pains to show a sort of mathematical equality in the praise and blame allotted to each side. It seems to have been in annoyed reaction to such stories that he published his collection *Siyah Hashiye* ('Black Margins' – but 'margins' often means 'marginal notes'). It recounts with a sort of black humour incidents that occurred in the riots, and one cannot help feeling some repugnance when events of such inhumanity and horror are used as materials for humour. On the other hand some of his stories of this period, published in other collections, are superb. One of the most famous is *Toba Tek Singh*. It begins:

> Two or three years after Partition it occurred to the governments of India and Pakistan that....there should also be a transfer of the insane. Muslim lunatics in Indian lunatic asylums should be sent to Pakistan, and Hindu and Sikh lunatics in Pakistani lunatic asylums should be handed over to India.
>
> I don't know whether this was a sensible idea or not; but anyway in accordance with the decision of the experts high-level conferences were held at various places and finally a day was appointed for the transfer of the lunatics to take place. Careful investigations were made. Muslim lunatics whose relatives were still in India were allowed to stay, and the rest were despatched to the border. On this side, in Pakistan, since practically all the Hindus and Sikhs had left, the question of keeping anyone didn't arise. All Hindu and Sikh lunatics were brought under police protection to the border.

Mantu goes on to describe what happened in a Lahore asylum when the news of the transfer became known. Most of its inmates had very little idea of what Partition was all about. Even those who were not insane – for example, murderers whose relatives had bribed the police to declare them so and in this way save them from the gallows – had very little idea of what was going on. The warders too were ignorant illiterates. All sorts of explanations, each more absurd than the last, were being bandied about....

There was a Sikh lunatic who had been in the asylum for the last fifteen years. He talked completely unintelligible nonsense, never slept, day or night, and never lay down. From constant standing his legs were always swollen. When he was asked his opinion about the transfer he answered with his usual nonsensical words, adding at the end, however, 'of the Pakistan government.' Later he changed this to 'of the Toba Tek Singh government', and began to ask the other inmates where Toba Tek Singh was. But nobody knew whether Toba Tek Singh was in India or in Pakistan. They tried to explain, but they themselves were puzzled by the fact that Sialkot used to be in India, but now, according to what they had heard, was in Pakistan. Who could tell whether Lahore, now in Pakistan, tomorrow might go to India; or whether the whole of India might become Pakistan: or Pakistan and India one day vanish into thin air?

This Sikh lunatic was quite harmless. All the staff of the asylum knew about him was that he came from Toba Tek Singh, where he had several holdings of land. One day he had suddenly gone mad, and his relatives had put him in heavy chains and had him admitted to the asylum.

His name was Bishan Singh, but everybody called him Toba Tek Singh. His relatives would come to visit him once a month, but after Partition their visits cesaed....

When he heard of Partition he began to ask whether Toba Tek Singh was in India or in Pakistan. But no one could tell him....One day Fazal Din, an old Muslim neighbour from Toba Tek Singh, came to visit him. He told him that all his family had reached India in safety, and had asked him, Fazal Din, to visit him from time to time....Bishan Singh listened and then asked, 'Where is Toba Tek Singh?'

Fazal Din was a bit puzzled. 'Toba Tek Singh?....Where is it?....It's still where it was.'

'In India? Or in Pakistan?' Bishan Singh asked.

'In India....No, no....in Pakistan.' Fazal Din was all confused. Bishan Singh muttered some unintelligible nonsense....

The day of the transfer arrived. Most of the lunatics were against it, and couldn't see why they should be moved from where they'd always been to some unknown place. One by one they were called to have their particulars taken. When Bishan Singh's turn came he asked the official, 'Where is Toba Tek Singh? In Pakistan? Or in India?'

The official laughed. 'In Pakistan,' he said.

Bishan Singh ran back to his companions and refused to move. People told him, 'Look, Toba Tek Singh's gone over to India now. Or if it hasn't it'll be sent there at once.' But nothing could move him. They tried to use force to make him cross the border, but he stood there on his swollen legs as though no power on earth could shift him.

And since he was harmless they left him where he was and got on with other things. Before the sun rose he let out a heart-rending cry. Several officials came running – and saw that he, who for fifteen years had never lain down, was lying face down on the ground. Toba Tek Singh lay on ground between the barbed wire beyond which in one direction lay India and the exactly similar barbed wire beyond which in the other direction lay Pakistan.

You finish reading the story asking yourself, 'Who are the lunatics? The inmates? Or those who are arranging their transfer?'

Another story of Partition days, *Khol Do* (sensibly entitled *Sakina* in Hamid Jalal's translation, because the Urdu title cannot, in this context, be satisfactorily translated), tells the story of men who use their declared mission of rescuing abducted women and restoring them to their families as a cover for satisfying their own lust on these women. To publish stories like these at the time he did took considerable courage – a quality in which he was never found wanting – and confidence, a confidence based upon the perfectly correct assessment that he was a great story writer. He expressed this confidence in an impudent epitaph he wrote for himself only a year before his death – he virtually drank himself to death in 1955, at the age of forty-two: 'Here Saadat Hasan Mantu lies buried – and buried in his breast are all the secrets of the art of story writing. Even now, lying under tons of earth he is wondering whether he or God is the greater story-writer.'[11]

Ismat Chughtai is, at her best, the most powerful of all these writers. Her mother tongue is Urdu, and she has an unrivalled range of vivid, homely, idiomatic language. The themes of her best stories are drawn from the lives of women and are told largely in the specific language of women, a language which, since women live in a world so largely separate from that of the men, has long had its own vocabulary and turns of phrase. Its appropriateness to her themes is obvious, and it works powerfully to bring her readers closer to the people she is portraying and to make them feel that they are real. One feels sometimes that she overdoes this use of the specific language of women, using words so unfamiliar that they distance her readers from her characters rather than bring them closer. Her performance is rather uneven. She is not strong on narrative, and while it is often the case that her themes so rivet the attention of the reader that the lack of narrative development doesn't matter, this is not always so. Finally she seems to have reacted to some extent as Mantu did to unjustified criticism of her so-called 'obscenity' and written stories about things no one had dared to write about before simply *because* no one had dared to write about them before, not realizing that this does not in itself guarantee good writing. But her best work is free of these faults. She depicts vividly, ruthlessly, and at the same time with the deepest sympathy the lives of women in Urdu-speaking society, writing with an authenticity which no male writer could have matched. One of her best stories is *Nannhi ki Nani* (Tiny's Granny). It is hardly a 'story' at all, in that there is very little development in it. But its vivid pictures are unforgettable, and the cruel implications of facts and events simply presented without comment come across with greater force than any comment could convey. The story begins:

God knows what her real name was. No one had ever called her by it. When she was a little snotty-nosed girl roaming about the alleys people used to call her 'Bafatan's kid'. Then she was 'Bashira's daughter-in-law', and then 'Bismillah's mother'; and when Bismillah died in child-birth, leaving Tiny an orphan, she became 'Tiny's granny' – and she remained 'Tiny's granny' to her dying day.

There was no occupation which Tiny's granny had not tried at some stage of her life. From the time she was old enough to hold her own cup she had started working at odd jobs in people's houses in return for her two meals a day and occasional cast-off clothes. Exactly what the words 'odd jobs' mean, only those know who have been kept at them at an age when they ought to have been laughing and playing with other children. Anything from the uninteresting duty of shaking the baby's rattle to massaging the master's head comes under the category of 'odd jobs'. As she grew older she learned to do a bit of cooking, and she spent some years of her life as a cook. But when her sight began to fail and she began to cook lizards in the lentils and knead flies into the bread, she had to retire. All she was fit for after that was gossiping and tale-bearing. But that also is a fairly paying trade. In every *muhalla* there is always some quarrel going on, and one who has the wit to carry information to the enemy camp can be sure of a hospitable reception. But it's a game that doesn't last. People began to call her a tell-tale, and when she saw that there was no future there, she took up her last and most profitable profession: she became a polished and accomplished beggar.

At meal-times Granny would dilate her nostrils to smell what was cooking, single out the smell she liked best and be off on its track until she reached the house it was coming from.

'Lady, are you cooking *aravi** with the meat?' she would ask with a disinterested air.

'No, Granny, The *aravi* you get these days doesn't cook soft. I'm cooking potatoes with it.'

'Potatoes! What a lovely smell! Bismillah's father, God rest him, used to love meat and potatoes. Every day it was the same thing: "Let's have meat and potatoes," and now (she would heave a sigh) I don't see meat and potatoes for months together.' Then, suddenly getting anxious, 'Lady, have you put any coriander-leaf in with the meat?'

'No, granny. All our coriander was ruined. The confounded water-carrier's dog got into the garden and rolled all over it.'

'That's a pity. A bit of coriander-leaf in with the meat and potatoes makes all the difference. Hakimji's** got any amount in his garden.'

'That is no good to me, Granny. Yesterday his boy cut Shabban Mian's kite-string and I told him that if he showed his face again he'd better look out for himself.'

---

* *aravi*: a root vegetable
** Hakimji: a practioner of the traditional Muslim (originally Greek) medicine.

'Good heavens, I shan't say it's for you.' And Granny would gather her *burqa* around her and be off with slippers clacking to Hakimji's. She'd get into the garden on the plea of wanting to sit in the sun, and then edge towards the coriander bed. Then she'd pluck a leaf and crush it between her finger and thumb and savour the pleasant smell and as soon as the Hakimji's daughter-in-law turned her back, Granny would make a grab. And obviously, when she had provided the coriander-leaf she could hardly be refused a bite to eat.

Ismat goes on to describe her remarkable sleight of hand in stealing food, hiding it about her person, and denying brazenly that she had done so, and adds, 'Granny was not only a tale-bearer, thief and cheat. She was also a first rate liar.' She does her best to provide for her grand-daughter – the 'Tiny' of the story's title – and gets her a job at the 'Deputy Sahib's' house. ('Deputy' presumably means Deputy Collector, the second-in-command in the administration of a large district.) The Deputy Sahib rapes her (she is only fifteen and barely understands what is happening) but no one dares to speak out against him. Tiny goes to the bad, and eventually runs away. After losing her, Granny's most loved possession is her pillow, and this and the scraps of stale food she gathers, she has to defend against the monkeys.

Granny's life-long enemies were the monkeys – 'the confounded, blasted monkeys'. They had been settled in the *muhalla* for generations and knew all about everyone who lived there. They knew that men were dangerous, and children mischievous, but that women were only afraid of them. But then Granny too had spent all her life among them. She'd got hold of some child's catapult to frighten them with, and when she wound her *burqa* round her head like a great turban and pounced upon them with her catapult at the ready, the monkeys really did panic for a moment before returning to their usual attitude of indifference towards her....

....The monkeys must have acquired a personal grudge against Granny. How else can you explain the fact that they turned their backs on everything else the world had to offer and concentrated all their attacks on Granny's scraps of food? And how else can you explain the fact that a big, rascally, red-behinded monkey ran off with her pillow, which she loved more than her life? Once Tiny had gone, this pillow was the only thing left in the world that was near and dear to her. She fussed and worried over it as much as she did over her *burqa*. She was for ever repairing its seams with stout stitches. Time and again she would sit herself down in some secluded corner and start playing with her pillow like a little girl playing with a doll. She had none but the pillow now to tell all her troubles to and so lighten her burden. And the greater the love she felt for her pillow, the more the stout stitches she would put into it to strengthen its seams.

And now see what a trick Fate played on her. She was sitting leaning against the parapet with her *burqa* wrapped round her, picking the lice out of her waist-band, when suddenly a monkey flopped down, whipped up her pillow, and was off. You would have thought that some one had plucked

Granny's heart out of her breast. She wept and screamed and carried on so much that the whole *muhalla* came flocking.

The monkey proceeded with the greatest enjoyment to peel the manifold coverings off the pillow as though he were peeling the successive skins off an onion – those same coverings over which Granny had pored with her weak and watering eyes, trying to hold them together with stitching. As every fresh cover came off Granny's hysterical wailing grew louder. And now the last covering was off, and the monkey began bit by bit to throw down the contents.

It turns out that the pillow contained, among the other things, all the 'stock of stolen property that Granny had got together by years of raiding'.

Granny's shrieking suddenly stopped. Her tears dried up, her head dropped, and she stood there stunned and speechless....She passed that night sitting on her haunches, her hands grasping her knees, rocking backwards and forwards, her body shaken by dry sobbing, lamenting and calling the names of now her mother and father, now her husband, now her daughter Bismillah, and her grand-daughter Tiny. Every now and then, just for a moment, she would doze, then wake with a cry, as though ants were stinging an old sore. At times she would laugh and cry hysterically, at times talk to herself, then suddenly, for no reason, break into a smile. Then out of the darkness some old recollection would hurl its spear at her, and like a sick dog howling in a half human voice, she would rouse the whole *muhalla* with her cries. Two days passed in this way....

[On the third day]: Early in the morning, when the water-carrier came with his water-skin he saw that Granny was sitting on her haunches on the stairs. Her mouth was open, and flies were crawling in the corners of her half-closed eyes. People had often seen Granny asleep just like this, and had feared she was dead. But Granny had always started up, cleared her throat and spat out the phlegm, and poured out a shower of abuse on the person who had disturbed her. But that day Granny remained sitting on her haunches on the stairs. Fixed in death, she showered continuous abuse upon the world....

Granny was shrouded just as she was, squatting on her haunches. Her body had set fast, and no amount of pulling and tugging could straighten it.

Ismat concludes the story with the only words in which she allows herself to express all she feels about her subject:

On Judgement Day the trumpet sounded, and Granny woke with a start and got up coughing and clearing her throat, as though her ears had caught the sound of free food being doled out....Cursing and swearing at the angels, she dragged herself somehow or other, doubled up as she was, over the Bridge of Sirat and burst into the presence of God the All-Powerful and All-Kind... and God, beholding the degradation of humanity, bowed his head in shame and wept tears of blood. And those divine tears of blood fell upon Granny's rough grave, and bright red poppies sprang up there and began to dance in the breeze.

Many of Ismat Chughtai's stories are, like *Nannhi ki Nani*, hardly stories at all in the traditional sense, but depictions of situations which she draws so vividly that she holds the reader in her spell. One shorter piece, *Sas* (Mother-in-law) tells how an aged mother-in-law is driven almost to desperation by her vivacious, active, childlike fifteen-year-old daughter-in-law. And one of her masterpieces, *Dozakhi* (literally, 'The Hellish One'), which is not written as a story, is a pen-portrait of her brother Azim Beg Chughtai, a writer of light-weight humorous stories popular in the twenties, a portrait in which her combination of complete bluntness and deep sympathy is profoundly moving.

The progressive writers made their greatest contribution in the period from 1936 to the early years of independence in the late forties. Thereafter the PWA could no longer maintain the broad unity which came relatively easily when independence was still an unrealized aim, and it began to disintegrate. But the writers who had made their name under its aegis continued to produce work of excellent quality even after the organized movement had virtually ceased to exist. Krishan Chandar, after a period in which he wrote very little of value, re-emerged in the early sixties with an excellent collection of semi-autobiographical stories *Meri Yadon ke Chanar* (The Chenar Trees of my Memories). Both Ismat and Bedi too continued to write stories which won critical acclaim.

The great contribution of these writers was to enlarge the range of the themes of prose narrative, breaking the taboos which their predecessors had accepted and portraying vividly and with great artistic skill all the new social realities of the thirties and after. With them, Urdu prose fiction entered a new stage of its development, and much of their writing will always have a place in the stock of what Urdu has to offer to the world.

14. Faiz Ahmad Faiz – Poetry, Politics and Pakistan

The poetry which the Progressive Writers' Movement produced did not reach the heights which the short story did. But one poet secured for himself an important place in Urdu poetry and upheld some of the major values of the progressives for nearly half a century, from the middle thirties right up to his death in 1984. This was Faiz Ahmad Faiz. By the middle fifties he was already recognized as the leading Urdu poet of Pakistan, and rapidly became the most popular Urdu poet of the whole subcontinent.

As we shall see, it was not solely the excellence of his poetry that won him this position, but his poetry is nonetheless his most important legacy to us and demands our main attention.[1]

Faiz began his career as a poet at a time when different categories of poets catered for different, and often conflicting, tastes. First were those, mainly *ghazal* poets, who were content to continue virtually unchanged the classical tradition and regarded any departure from it as a departure from poetry itself. Two other groups wrote in conscious response to what they felt to be the demands of new times and new conditions. One comprised the progressives and their sympathizers, whose viewpoint has been discussed in the previous chapter, and the other those equally self-conscious innovators whose major organization was the *Halqa i Arbab i Zauq* (Circle of Men of Good Taste, or, more literally, Circle of Possessors of Taste). The tone of this somewhat pretentious title captures very well the lofty disdain that they generally felt for their numerous contemporaries who had not been blessed with 'good taste'. Their quarrel with the progressives stemmed from their view that art and propaganda were mutually exclusive, and that art must be for art's sake alone. (It must be said that some of the progressives provided ample fuel for this fire, producing verse which, if clearly progressive, was equally clearly not poetry. However, it should also be said that some of the 'men of taste' made the opposite mistake and assumed that anything that was presented as a poem and was clearly not propaganda must therefore be art.) The progressive school included some whose hostility to the 'men of taste' was matched by a hostility to the *ghazal*, which they regarded as an outmoded, medieval form.

Faiz from the very beginning held himself aloof from all these extreme views. His poetry of all periods shows a certain catholicity of taste and a command of a wide range of skills which enabled him to win acceptance and esteem from the audiences for all three trends. *Ghazals*, poems on overtly progressive

themes, and 'modern' poems which do not, however, express anything inconsistent with progressive values – all are to be found in his collections of verse.
So too are poems in the tradition of the *qavvali* – popular devotional Muslim
verse – and of the *tarana* – rousing verse embodying the sentiments appropriate
to popular political campaigning. Faiz maintained this breadth of range to the
last, and it is one of the bases of his exceptional popularity.

Eight collections of his verse were published in his lifetime. The first, *Naqsh
i Faryadi*,[2] was published in 1941, and includes poems dating from 1928-29
onwards. The last dated poem in his last collection, a *ghazal*, was written in
November 1984, only a matter of days before his death. *Poems by Faiz*, a good
selection of poems with parallel verse translations by V.G. Kiernan, was
published under the auspices of UNESCO in 1971. Almost all the poems,
Kiernan says, 'were chosen by Faiz himself, and all the translations have been
discussed with him,'[3] and Kiernan has added an introduction[4] and notes. The
selection covers the first four collections, and a few poems from (at that time)
uncollected verses. Although these four collections comprise only about half of
Faiz's total output, most of the poems I discuss in this chapter are taken from
them. There are two main reasons for this. The first is that Faiz's best-known
poems (and in my view almost all his best ones) are included in these first four
collections, while the last four have relatively few. And a second, rather more
mundane one, is that *Poems by Faiz* (which was recently republished[5]) provides
the maximum help both to those who are able to study his verse only through
the medium of English and to those whose study of Urdu is still in its relatively
early stages. Kiernan's translations are appreciably better, and certainly closer
to Faiz's originals, than any of those by subsequent translators, and for students
of Urdu, there is the help afforded by the Roman transliterations and the literal
translations which the book provides.

Three of the first four collections include forewords by Faiz himself, and in the
forewords to the first and the fourth *(Dast i Tih i Sang)* he tells us something of
their themes and of the varying backgrounds against which they were produced.
Almost all the poems of the period 1928-29 to 1934-35 were the product (to use
the coy words of his introduction to his first collection) of a *muayyan* ('established') emotion. One guesses that by 'an established emotion' he means one
generally recognized as being commonly experienced – that is, love – and this
is confirmed by his description of this in the introduction to his fourth collection,
where, speaking of these same early poems, he describes them, in words only a
trifle less coy, as springing from 'that affliction of the heart which befalls most
people in their youth.' Numbers of these, not surprisingly, are in the *ghazal form*.

The earliest of his most famous poems, *mujh se pahli si muhabbat, meri
mahbub, na mang*, 'my beloved, do not ask of me my former kind of love' (No.
6 in Kiernan's translation where it is entitled *'Love, Do Not Ask'*) begins the
second part of *Naqsh i Faryadi* and marks, he tells us, the beginning of a new
consciousness, an awareness that a man's love for a woman cannot be the be all
and end all of life, and that he must be aware of, and deeply affected by, the

suffering of the poor and exploited. A better poem is 'To the Rival' (No. 7 in Kiernan). In the traditional *ghazal* the rival is a stock character, the type of the false lover whose professions of love, all too often accepted by the poet's beloved as sincere, are in fact a deception, practised to achieve his own selfish ends. In Faiz's poem by contrast he is one whose love is as sincere as the poet's own, and one with whom the poet feels a common bond, and indeed a common bond stronger than he could feel with any other, since both he and his rival have forged it from identical experience. Faiz goes on rather abruptly to say that from this experience 'I learned to be the friend of suffering creatures' and that now whenever he thinks of the suffering and the exploitation that is their lot, a fire over which he has no control sets his heart aflame. In *Poetry's Theme* however, (No. 12 in Kiernan) he declares that, aware as he is that the sufferings of the poor afford themes for poetry, the charms of his beloved are such that only they can be the theme of *his* poetry. But it seems that he did not always feel like this. Only a few poems before *Poetry's Theme* comes one of his best directly political poems, *Speak*. In Kiernan's translation (No. 11 in his selection) it reads:

Speak, for your two lips are free;
Speak, your tongue is still your own;
This straight body still is yours –
Speak, your life is still your own.

See how in the blacksmith's forge
Flames leap high and steel glows red,
Padlocks opening wide their jaws,
Every chain's embrace outspread!

Time enough is this brief hour
Until body and tongue lie dead;
Speak, for truth is living yet –
Speak whatever must be said.

I shall return to this poem below.

Naqsh i Faryadi was published in 1941.[6] A second collection, *Dast i Saba*,[7] did not appear until eleven years later, in 1952, and presumably includes all the verse he had written over these eleven years. These were years in which he had acted on the conclusions he had reached in the mid-thirties and played an active part in social and political movements. He had been a leading light in the Progressive Writers, Association from the start. In June 1942, convinced now that with the entry of the Soviet Union into the Second World War it was the duty of progressives everywhere to support the war effort, he joined the army, in which he served until December 1946, leaving with the rank of Lieutenant-Colonel, and (in 1943) having been awarded the MBE. From February 1947 to March 1951 he edited simultaneously two progressive daily papers, the English-language *Pakistan Times* and the Urdu *Imroz* – the duties of an editor in Pakistan being perhaps rather less onerous than Western readers might suppose. He also publicly identified himself with the trade union movement, and in 1951 was Vice-President of the Pakistan Trade Union Federation. In the relatively free political conditions that prevailed up to 1951 he also served in posts to which he was appointed by the Pakistan government, going to San Francisco in 1948 and Geneva in 1949-50 as a member of the Pakistan government delegations to the International Labour Organization (ILO).[8]

But independence had not brought into being the kind of regime that could maintain the unity of all those who had fought for it, and, both in India and Pakistan, the new rulers began to turn with increasing ruthlessness against the mass of the people whose support had brought them to power. The strength and depth of Faiz's feelings on political issues had evidently increased over the years, and in *Dast i Saba* poems on political themes occupy a prominent place. Despite his earlier disclaimer in *Poetry's Theme*, he has now found in these themes the inspiration which produces true poetry no less effectively than themes of love. In 1952, when this collection appeared, only five years had passed since the political settlement of August 1947 which brought independence to the subcontinent and its simultaneous partition into the two states of India and Pakistan. Two of Faiz's best poems express the widespread disappointment which the aftermath of independence had brought.

To a Political Leader (No.14 in Kiernan's selection) reproaches the type of leader at whose call his followers have fought against almost impossible odds to achieve their aims, whose whole political capital consists of this heroic, self-sacrificing support – and who now wants to curb the forces which he himself had mobilized, even if by so doing he jeopardizes all the gains that have been won. *Freedom's Dawn* (No.19 in Kiernan's selection) speaks directly of the August 1947 settlement, described in its first line as

یہ داغ داغ اُجالا' یہ شب گزیدہ سحر

'This much stained radiance, this night-bitten morning', and goes on to say that this is not the dawn that those who had fought for freedom had laboured so hard to bring. Our new rulers, says Faiz, tell us to rejoice because the struggle is over now. Not so, he says,

> Night's heaviness is unlessened still, the hour
> Of mind and spirit's ransom has not struck;
> Let us go on, our goal is not reached yet.

These two poems, and the earlier poem *Speak*, exemplify a marked characteristic of Faiz's progressive poetry. He never speaks, as some of his contemporaries do, in the strident tones that raise the hackles of all except the converted, but maintains what I have called the universality of the traditional *ghazal*, which enables it to speak to different people's different conditions. (And indeed this is a quality of much of the world's great poetry.) I have read (somewhere that I cannot now recall) that *Speak* was written soon after the outbreak of the Second World War, and reflects the very widespread indignation of politically articulate

Indians at Britain's high-handed declaration of war on India's behalf, and at the restrictions of political liberties imposed in the name of wartime needs. But nothing in what the poem actually says restricts it to that situation (and in the notes, Kiernan, quite properly, does not think it necessary to tell us anything of the circumstances in which it was written). Moreover, the poem tells its audience to speak, but doesn't tell it *what* to speak. And so it remains a spirited call to all free men, in any country and any age, to speak out boldly what free men have a duty to say, even though they risk imprisonment if they do so. *To a Political Leader* has the same sort of universality. Readers encountering it for the first time when *Dast i Saba* came out in 1952 would almost certainly assume that it was addressed to the leaders of the new post-independence states. But Kiernan's note tells us that it was the mass uprisings of August 1942 that had inspired it.[9]

Freedom's Dawn has the same universal quality. Some of Faiz's left-wing critics have criticized it for an alleged ambivalence, arguing that *anyone* who is dissatisfied with the post-independence regimes of India and Pakistan can identify with it. But that view is quite untenable. The poem's theme is the disappointment of those who had fought for independence – and not of anyone else; and it captures admirably the sort of helpless restlessness after 1947 of millions of people who had felt that independence would see the birth of a brave new world without quite knowing what that brave new world would be like, and who now felt that whatever independence ought to have brought, it was certainly not this. Faiz's left-wing critics would presumably have wanted him to produce a poem which would have told its readers *why* independence had not brought the results they had hoped for and what must now be done to remedy the situation. But I know of no Urdu poem which has done this, and I very much doubt whether this kind of demand is one that poetry can meet. Poetry demands what one may call a certain generality; greater specificity belongs to the domain of prose.

It is about half-way through *Dast i Saba* that we find the poem in which he at last completely harmonizes the love one feels for a lover, with its demand for self-sacrifice, with the wider, more inclusive love that makes similar demands. In *Two Loves* (No.29 in Kiernan) Faiz expresses his equal dedication to his mistress and to his still recently established country, Pakistan, speaks of all that he has suffered in his love for both, and concludes

> Yet my heart feels no regret for either love
> My heart bears every scar but that of regret.

This stand is one which thenceforth he never abandoned. And though *Two Loves* does not explicitly say so, it is clear from other poems that when Faiz speaks of his commitment to his country he means first and foremost commitment to the cause of the poor and exploited masses of its people.

The poetry of the years to 1952 constantly reflects an awareness of dangers that lie ahead, speaks of the risks of suffering, imprisonment and even execution that those who fight for the cause of the people will be obliged to face, and calls upon them to be steadfast in the fight. By the time it was published Faiz was himself in gaol. In March 1951, he, a number of leading communists, and a group of army officers had been arrested and charged with taking part in a conspiracy to overthrow the Pakistan government. It was not until just over four years later, in April 1955, that he was released on bail. (He was acquitted in September 1955.) Most of the poems in *Dast i Saba*, and all the poems of Faiz's third collection, *Zindan Nama* (Prison Writings), published in 1956, were written during his imprisonment. One of Faiz's fellow-'conspirators' in the Rawalpindi Conspiracy Case, as it was called, was Major Muhammad Ishaq, and in a long and valuable introduction to *Zindan Nama* he gives us a fairly detailed account of Faiz's imprisonment. He was arrested on 9 March 1951, and for three months held in solitary confinement in Sargodha and Lyallpur (now Faisalabad) Gaols and deprived of writing materials. Then, until July 1953, he was in Hyderabad gaol. The 'conspirators' were then split up and sent to different prisons. Faiz and Muhammad Ishaq were among those who were allocated to Montgomery gaol, and it was from there that Faiz was released in April 1955.

Faiz, in a short essay prefaced to his fourth collection *Dast i Tih i Sang*,[10] has described what the experience of imprisonment did for his development as a poet. He says that the verse he wrote in gaol continues that strand in his poetry which began with *Love, Do Not Ask,*

> But the experience of imprisonment, like that of love, is in itself one of fundamental significance, and opens up new windows of thought and vision. Thus in the first place, all one's sensations are again heightened, as they had been at the onset of youth, and the sense of wonder at the coming of day, the shades of evening, the deep blue of the sky, and the feel of the passing breeze comes back once more. Another thing that happens is that the time and distance of the world outside become unreal. Things that are near seem far away, and far away things seem near, and the distinction between tomorrow and yesterday vanishes so that sometimes a moment seems like an eternity and things that happened a century ago seem to have happened only yesterday. And thirdly, in the leisure of isolation from the world outside, one finds time for thought and study, and time to devote more attention to adorning the bride of poetry.

– in other words, time for polishing one's verse.

Both Faiz and Ishaq speak of different distinctive periods ('moods', as Ishaq calls them) of the verse of these four years of imprisonment. The first, says Ishaq, was that of the three months of solitary confinement, where Faiz composed and memorized the short poem that now stands first in *Dast i Saba*. Kiernan's translation of it reads (No.17):

> If ink and pen are snatched from me, shall I
> Who have dipped my finger in my heart's blood complain –
> Or if they seal my tongue, when I have made
> A mouth of every round link of my chain?

and his note on it tells us that it is 'one of several poems that Faiz composed in solitary confinement, when deprived of writing materials, and was only able to write down several months later.' Ishaq says 'Faiz Sahib used to say that in those days he felt greatly inspired and all manner of themes would come to mind; some poems he could not remember afterwards, but those he could are included in *Dast i Saba*.' He then lists seven of them. Kiernan's selection includes three of these, numbers 17 (just quoted), 25 and 28. All three express courage in the face of every danger, and confidence in what the future will bring. Thus in *Tauq o Dar ka Mausam*, This Hour of Chain and Gibbet (to use Kiernan's title), he calls the time

> This hour of chain and gibbet and rejoicing
> Hour of necessity and hour of choice.

and tells his captors

> At your command the cage, but not the garden's
> Red rose-fire, when its radiant hour begins;
> No noose can catch the dawn wind's whirling feet,
> The spring's bright hour falls prisoner to no net.
>
> Others will see if I do not, that hour
> Of singing nightingale and splendid flower.

For some reason Faiz himself in the essay just quoted is silent about these first three months, and speaks of only two periods – the Hyderabad one (June 1951 to July 1953) and the Montgomery one (July 1953 to April 1955).

He says of the verse of the two-year Hyderabad period that it is dominated by the – "sense of wonder", and instances one of the last poems in *Dast i Saba*, A Prison Nightfall, (No. 33 in Kiernan's selection) as an example.

> Step by step by its twisted stairway
> Of constellations, night descends
>
> Graciously on that roof's high crest
> The moonlight's exquisite fingers gleam;
> . . . . .
> One thought keeps running in my heart –
> Such nectar life is at this instant,
> Those who mix the tyrants' poisons
> Can never, now or tomorrow, win....

Ishaq says of this period that 'all the physical comforts that are possible in jail were provided,' and that although there were a number of charges against them that carried the death penalty, the 'conspirators' were in excellent morale and confident that somehow victory would be theirs. But Faiz, on 14 July 1952, suffered a heavy blow when his brother, who had come to visit him in gaol, died of a sudden heart attack.

In July 1953 when Faiz, Ishaq and others were allocated to Montgomery Jail, Faiz was first sent for two months to Karachi to undergo medical treatment, and it was not until September 1953 that he began his almost continuous stay in Montgomery. (For three weeks in March 1954, Ishaq tells us, they were sent to

Lahore to have their teeth attended to.) Faiz says that these years were a period of 'boredom and fatigue'. Almost all the poems in *Zindan Nama* were written during these two years.

Ishaq says that Faiz felt the constraints of prison life in Montgomery all the more keenly because in hospital in Karachi he had been relatively free. 'His friends had no difficulty in coming to see him [and] these were reasons why he came to feel intensely the blessings of freedom.' When he came to Montgomery Gaol, therefore, he felt the extremity of the contrast. He began, too, to feel more keenly what must be the plight of other political prisoners in other countries. He salute to the freedom fighters of Africa, *Africa, Come Back*, belongs to this collection. Already in *Dast i Saba* he had written *To the Students of Iran Who gave their Lives in the Struggle for Peace and Freedom* – expurgated in Kiernan (No.30) to read *To Some Foreign Students....* and to omit all references to Iran (and with an anxious note "...this poem should be taken in a general sense, not as referring to any particular place or time."[11]) Ishaq says that in Montgomery gaol they read in the American periodical *Time* an account of the shooting of Iranian students in prison, printed alongside pictures of the place where they had been killed. 'Faiz feels a special love for (Iran), the country of Sadi and Hafiz. He was upset and disturbed for several days,' and eventually gave expression to his feelings in a poem *The Last Night*, in which he portrays the ...'thoughts that pass through the mind of a prisoner on the night before his execution next morning.' (This poem for some reason is, as far as I can ascertain, not included in any of Faiz's collections.)

In *Zindan Nama* too is a poem, *We Who Were Killed in the Dark Street*, written in May 1954 after reading the letters of Julius and Ethel Rosenberg, the American couple who were executed, despite worldwide protests, after being found guilty (wrongly, as many believed) of betraying atomic secrets to the Soviet Union. Ishaq regards the poem *Darica* (The Window) as the most complete expression of Faiz's mental state at this time. Faiz himself singles out *O City of Lights* as typical of this period. Both are included in *Poems by Faiz* numbered respectively 36 and 35.

The Window begins

In my barred window is many a cross

and goes on to list some of the things that are crucified on these crosses

On one the heaven's spring cloud is crucified
On one the radiant noon is crucified

Yet every day they return, revived to be crucified again.

Zindan Nama is only the third of Faiz's eight collections of his poems, but the first three collections provide ample materials for a study of all that is best in his poetry, and I shall make only occasional references to later poems.

I have hitherto spoken mainly of Faiz's political poems, because I believe these to be his best. But as I said at the outset, there are also poems of other kinds. Some of the best are his love poems, often, though not always, in *ghazal* form. The very first poem in *Naqsh i Faryadi*, comprising only two couplets and headed simply *Ashar* (Couplets) but in Kiernan's translation entitled *Last Night*, is one such poem. This translation reads:

> Last night your faded memory filled my heart
> Like spring's calm advent in the wilderness,
> Like the soft desert footfalls of the breeze,
> Like peace somehow coming to one in sickness.

Another short poem, also in *Naqsh i Faryadi*, is in Kiernan's translation (No.22) headed *Her Fingers* and reads:

> The softness of her fingers is in this dawn-wind's hand;
> And as it stirs, the fancy comes today to my mind
> That her soft hands are searching through the ranks of our friends
> To find what are their heartaches, to feel where are their wounds.

A *ghazal* of five couplets in *Zindan Nama*, unusually simple in its language and with a long, strongly rhythmic line

$$ - - \smile - - | - \smile - | - - \smile - - | - \smile - $$

begins

> When are you not with me in memory? When is your hand not in mine? A
> thousand thanks that as night follows night, no night is a night of separation.

The *ghazal* ends

> If you gamble in the game of love, stake as much as you like – why be afraid?
> If you win, what happiness! And even if you lose, all is not lost.

Another poem of two couplets in *Dast i Tih i Sang* is headed *Tanhai* (Solitude) and reads:

> Today loneliness like a well-tried friend
> Has come to be my evening wine-pourer.
> We sit together waiting for the moon to rise
> And set your image gleaming in every shadow.

Finally there are poems which are neither political poems nor poems of love. It is a striking feature of his poetry that he is not afraid to portray in a poem any emotion that he feels deeply. Such poems are clearly not 'propaganda' (and this allows the 'Men of Good Taste' to approve of them) and though most have nothing in them to offend progressives either, some of them do. For progressives – or at any rate the most puritanical among them – it is a cardinal sin to despair. Well, Faiz sometimes felt a keen sense of despair, and since he felt it, he expressed it. His poem *Yas* (Despair) is on that theme and nothing else, and contains no sop to the puritan progressives (such as, for example, an expression of regret, confession of weakness and so on); it belongs to the late 1920s, the days of the great world economic crisis, days in which, says Faiz, graduates looked in vain for employment, 'days when suddenly children's laughter died, when ruined peasants left their fields to work as labourers in the cities, and when respectable women took to prostitution.' It was written in the period before Faiz became a revolutionary, but he quotes it in his foreword to his fourth collection, *Dast i Tih i Sang* published in 1965, without any adverse comment, and evidently did not include it in those poems of his youth which (as we shall see) he regarded as not reaching a 'tolerable' standard.

Faiz himself says that 'The period after *Zindan Nama* was one of some mental turmoil. I had lost my profession of journalism. I had again to go to gaol. The period of martial law arrived....' (In September 1955 Faiz had resumed his post as editor of the *Pakistan Times*, but in December 1958, in the early days of Ayub Khan's martial law regime, he was again imprisoned and the *Pakistan Times* and associated newspapers were in 1959 taken over by the military regime.) Faiz continues, '...and in the mind and atmosphere of that environment alike, conditions gave rise to a feeling that once again the road ahead was to some extent blocked and one must look for other ways forward.' It was a period, he says, of 'stagnation and waiting'. He is writing, presumably somewhere around 1964 or 1965, because although the piece is not dated it appears as a sort of foreword to *Dast i Tih i Sang* and, one imagines, was written to serve as such. He continued to live and write for another twenty years, and one wonders whether he ever really emerged from the mental state he describes. At all events, 1955 marks the beginning of a new period. To the best of my knowledge he never wrote any account of his development over these years to continue his account of the period 1928 to 1955; so we do not know what he thought about it.

I have already said that I shall not in this chapter discuss more than an occasional example of his verse of this period. I shall, however, say something of his role both as a poet and as a prominent figure in the public life of Pakistan; and this requires some further discussion of the 1934 to 1955 period as well.

At the beginning of this chapter I said that it was not solely the excellence of his poetry that won him the pre-eminent position he came to occupy. We should note here some of the other factors that contributed to his standing. Generalizing them, one might say that Faiz was always, both in politics and in literature, sufficiently identified and sufficiently *un*identified with a number of different groupings to get the best of a number of worlds. To say this is not to question his sincerity – a quality which is not the exclusive property either of the committed or of the uncommitted – but simply to state a fact. Let us first take the literary field.

Faiz was a Panjabi, but like most Panjabi Muslim writers, he always chose to write in Urdu which, since the decline in Persian, has been *the* dominant language of culture of the Muslim community throughout the subcontinent. (The few poems which he wrote in Panjabi towards the end of his life do not significantly alter the picture.) His attainments in Urdu were such as to excite both the pride of his fellow-Panjabis and the admiration of the *ahl-i-zaban* – the people of Urdu mother tongue. The first were proud that one of them could write

Urdu well; the second admired the exceptional attainments of one who was *not* one of them; and no poet of Urdu mother tongue could have won this kind of esteem from both publics.

Secondly, as we have already seen, he wrote in a way which enabled him to appeal to each of the (broadly speaking) three different audiences for poetry.

Two factors outside the field of poetry also contributed to his prestige. Firstly, in 1941 he married an English wife; and secondly although his sympathies were with the poor, he was not one of them, and lived a decent, respectable, reasonably comfortable life which his respectable contemporaries recognized with a feeling of satisfaction as being very much like their own. (In my experience these essentially snobbish attitudes held by people in South Asia – and, for that matter, elsewhere – are not perceived as being in any way inconsistent with advanced revolutionary views.)

Faiz's imprisonment as one of the accused in the Rawalpindi Conspiracy case brought, along with the hardships, an enhanced fame; so that when he came out of gaol he had a larger and more appreciative public than when he went in.

Finally, by this time he was *the* leading progressive poet in Pakistan, a sort of personal embodiment, unique in Pakistan, of the by now virtually defunct Progressive Writers' Association.

Thus conditions that came into existence independently of his will or his contriving, brought him to the fore. He was a highly intelligent man and, as the words I have quoted above imply, now began to take stock of his new position.

It seems to me that from the time of his release after the Rawalpindi Conspiracy trial Faiz made up his mind that he was not again going to do anything that could land him in prison, and that he was going to lead as comfortable a life as possible, proclaiming the same message in his poetry as he had always done, remaining in the limelight, but refraining from any dangerous political activity. At all events, he suffered imprisonment only once after that, when Ayub Khan established his martial law regime in 1958. (He was in gaol from December 1958 to April 1959.) I am told that far from being imprisoned on Ayub Khan's instructions, he was gaoled without Ayub Khan's knowledge by an over-zealous subordinate who thought that Faiz's imprisonment would please the Americans, and that pleasing the Americans was an important part of Ayub's policy. My informant tells me that when the officially approved organization of Pakistani writers protested, Ayub Khan told them that he had given no orders for Faiz's imprisonment and gave immediate instructions for his release. After that, until the end of his life, Faiz lived a life of considerable material comfort, surrounded by rich and influential friends who would entertain him lavishly and treat him to the whisky of which he was so fond.

His position in the political and social life of Pakistan was somewhat similar to his position in poetry – one of an avoidance of full commitment to any clear cut stand and one which therefore enabled him to steer clear of anyone's strong disapproval. Always on the left, but never either a Communist Party member or so close a fellow-traveller as to be identified with it, his stand may be fairly described as a blend of Marxism with a kind of secular Pakistani nationalism, a blend of a kind which made him close enough to the communists to win their praise and respect, but not so close as to forfeit the friendship of the more liberal elements of the Pakistani establishment, or indeed of that establishment as a whole in its more liberal moments. In international politics too he came to occupy a similar position, especially during the years when Pakistan moved from its one-time stand of clear and uncomplicated alignment with the West in the early days of the Cold War. Thus, Faiz indeed contributed, both as a poet and as a citizen, to the cause of peace and friendship between nations, but one doubts all the same whether he would have been awarded the Lenin Peace Prize in 1962, and whether Pakistani opinion would have been so pleased at his receiving the award, had he been either closer or less close to either of the two positions between which he stood. His standing internationally contributed further both to his fame and to his comfort. During his sojourns in the Soviet Union he was provided with all the comforts of the life to which he had accustomed himself – and so also, though less frequently, in China, Cuba, the USA and other countries he visited.

Other features of Faiz's behaviour contributed to this sort of blurring of the lines. Kiernan says that in his personal relationships he is famous for his silences (p.26) and one could say the same of him in the political field. Even his friends would, I think, find it hard to tell how far these were the silences of uncertainty and how far the deliberately ambiguous silences of political tactics. His travels abroad had something of the same character, so that one of our mutual acquaintances once said to me in some exasperation, 'When Faiz ought to stay in Pakistan he comes out, and when he ought to stay out he goes back.'

His acceptance of government posts, in the conditions of relative political liberty which existed until 1951, is, I think, both understandable and justifiable. His continuing acceptance of them in later years is, to say the least, rather less so. Under the Bhutto regime of 1971-77 he was Cultural Adviser to Bhutto and continued to hold this post until Bhutto's overthrow by Zia ul Haq, long after Bhutto's savage and vindictive nature was inflicting imprisonment, torture and humiliation of the most shameful kind upon those who crossed him. In 1977, when General Zia ul Haq again established martial law, Faiz thought it best to leave the country; but nobody forced him to: he went of his own free will to take up a well-paid post of editor of a Soviet-supported literary journal. He remained abroad until returning to settle in Lahore in November 1982, two years before his death.

All this brings one back to his role as a poet; for this sort of ambiguity represents, in a way, a somewhat novel development of an old tradition. In the old quasi-feudal autocratic society the *ghazal* poet was, amongst other things, the licensed critic of the establishment, and was protected by two generally accepted conventions. The first of these was the nature of the *ghazal* itself, which permitted many of its verses to be interpreted simultaneously on several planes of meaning, some more 'dangerous' than others. The second was the convention that *in his poetry* he had a right to be as unambiguously rebellious as he pleased–but at the price of having his words regarded as 'only poetry', and not to be taken seriously outside the poetic symposium – the *mushaira* – where they were uttered. Faiz took full advantage of this time-honoured convention. But he did more than that. Whether by conscious design or not, he in some degree succeeded in extending the range of operation of this convention beyond the bounds of the *mushaira* into society at large, and brought into being a situation in which his role as a poet enhanced his role as a politician, and his role as a politician enhanced his role as a poet – but in politics too, reaping the same advantages and paying the same price for them as the classical poet did in his more restricted field of operation. (Not that he pushed his luck too far. I was intrigued when a banker, a co-speaker with myself at a condolence meeting for Faiz in London soon after his death, said that he disagreed with Faiz's political views – views which, however, he had never heard him express except in poetry.) Given the present stage of development of Pakistani society, to do what Faiz did was not too difficult a task, but Faiz's success was all the same remarkable. And having said all that, one must add that Faiz's poetry reflects very faithfully the feelings of vast numbers of his radically inclined fellow-countrymen, including most of those whose favourite arena of radicalism is the drawing-room.

This, as it may appear, rather harsh-sounding judgement can be supported both by the similar judgement of his close friend and fellow-'conspirator' Muhammad Ishaq, which I shall quote below, and, more importantly, by reference to his poetry.

There is a lot of Faiz's poetry that does not appeal to me; but I should hasten to add that I can say the same of almost all the poetry I have ever read. I read a poet's work, feeling as I do so that much of it is eminently forgettable, and some is enjoyable – and, occasionally, with a thrill of delight, '*This* is real poetry.' I feel this, for instance, in reading Mir, whose *best* poetry I love; and I think that it is a poet's best poetry that he deserves to be judged by. Mir's best poetry puts him in the first rank of poets. I don't think that Faiz's does.

To do him justice, Faiz was of the same opinion, at any rate about his first published collection *Naqsh i Faryadi*. He begins his foreword:

> The publication of this collection is a sort of admission of defeat. A few of its poems are perhaps tolerable, but a few tolerable poems don't make up a publishable book. In principle I should have waited until I had accumulated poems of this kind in sufficient number, but it has begun to seem pointless to wait any longer.

Later in the same foreword he speaks of 'the commercial reason' for not omitting his early verse. He says that the poems in the first part of the collection (occupying 36 pages of its total of 72) are mostly love poems (described, as we have seen, as a *muayyan* ('established') emotion which made it easy to write in established forms). He says that he experienced it when he was young, and adds that 'the roots of the experiences of youth are not deep' – on which one feels inclined to comment, 'the roots of the experiences of youth are not deep' – on which one feels inclined to comment, 'Speak for yourself'. However, the roots of the experiences which these early poems of Faiz express are indeed not deep, and one feels that when he and Kiernan made a selection for the UNESCO-sponsored translation they were right to exclude almost all of them. Even the few that they included cannot for the most part be numbered among his best poems.

This seems to be the point at which to say that 'commercial reasons' continued to weigh with Faiz throughout his life. The sort of ambiguity which one encounters in every aspect of his life is in evidence here too. He wrote verse which appealed, and, one feels, was consciously designed to appeal, to each of the three audiences I have described, and perhaps all the more so to the first two – the 'traditional' and the 'modern' – because in general he took his stand with the progressives, and his 'traditional' and 'modern' poems therefore made a greater impact than would have been the case if *all* his verse had been in a single style.

Of poetic tradition he wrote towards the end of his preface to *Naqsh i Faryadi*, 'I have not thought it appropriate to depart unnecessarily from traditional styles', adding that he had made only minor departures from the traditional rules of metre and rhyme. 'Quite right!' one thinks. 'He has had the good sense to reject the view that the traditional forms, and above all the *ghazal*, are outmoded, "feudal" forms that no progressive poet should employ.' But when one looks at his *ghazals* one cannot help feeling that along with good and effective ones in which the best *ghazal* traditions are used to express age-old but still powerfully relevant feeling, or are without violence adapted to wholly contemporary themes, there are others of the kind that any competent versifier could have written at any period of the *ghazal's* history. One such *ghazal* is that in *Zindan Nama* which begins

گلوں میں رنگ بھرے باد نوبہار چلے

Let colour fill the flowers, let the breeze of early spring blow.

It is one in the repertoire of one of South Asia's most popular *ghazal* singers, Mehdi Hasan, and, one feels, finds a place in it because it expresses in easily intelligible language, well-worn and wholly unremarkable themes to which any popular audience can at once respond. Any *ghazal* which singers as popular as Mehdi Hasan sings gains a currency which contributes substantially to the fame of its author, and one feels of not a few of Faiz's *ghazals* that he wrote them for him, and a number of other famous singers, with that sole aim in view and not because he had anything much to say in them.

One has much the same mixed feelings about poems on which Faiz's appeal to the moderns must have been based. Faiz knew very well that a progressive poet has emotions which are shared by others who would not call themselves progressive but are not the less valid and not the less valuable for that, and that these can often be most successfully expressed in forms (including free verse) which had no place in the classical canon. Poems like *Solitude* (No.8 in Kiernan) and *Despair*, which I have already quoted, are good examples of the best that he produced in this style. But in others the 'modern' trappings seem to be everything. Thus in *Evening*, the overall impression is one of outlandish, obscure, and pointless comparisons – 'Every tree is like a temple, a ruined... temple'...'The sky is like a (Hindu) priest...It is as though some magician is seated behind a curtain...' Here and in other poems Faiz seems to be imitating the unnecessarily difficult diction, and the fashionable, pretentious, culturally snobbish and pointless obscurity which characterizes the worst of Ezra Pound, T.S. Eliot and their imitators, and where what is said, wherever it is intelligible, seems to be not worth saying. And there is no doubt that there were, and are, among Faiz's readers quite a number who like this kind of poem for exactly these spurious qualities. Faiz himself evidently liked this poem, for he included it in the selection which Kiernan translated. Kiernan, perhaps, was less impressed, for he notes on the comparison of the sky with a Hindu priest, 'I give the meaning as explained by Faiz, but the image, taken straightforwardly, is a curious one.'

Faiz's poetic diction, one feels, is often just a bit too much. What is wrong with it is well illustrated by his remarks already quoted, that the enforced leisure of imprisonment gave him the opportunity 'to devote more attention to adorning the bride of poetry.' This pretentious manner mars a lot of his verse. Many in the audience of a popular poet are dazzled by poetry that abounds in Persianized vocabulary and Persian constructions, and Faiz is all too fond of high-flown language; and the result is sometimes ridiculous, as where the barking of dogs is expressed as *ghogha e sagan* which may be reasonably translated as 'the clamour of canines.' Even in his best poems one finds this kind of thing. To describe freedom's dawn as *shab-gazida* ('night-bitten') is disconcerting rather than striking. If he had left 'the bride of poetry' to exercise her appeal by beauty unadorned we should have had better poetry.

The content of his verse, too, leaves one with a sense of something lacking. I have already remarked on his comment that the roots of youthful love are not deep. Where Faiz is concerned, judging by his poetry *his* love never did become deep. His beloved is, to me, a singularly unattractive person. In the appealing *ghazal* in *Zindan Nama* which I quoted above there is a couplet that reads:

> The field of love is not a king's court. Here no one asks your name and lineage. The lover has no 'name' and love knows no caste.

But if this was Faiz's view of the lover he seems to have taken a different view of the beloved. His beloved is not simply a woman; she is a lady – a lady with plenty of money and plenty of leisure to spend on make-up, fine clothes and rare perfume, and it is these rather than any intrinsic qualities (for he rarely mentions any) that Faiz seems to find attractive. No wonder that in *Freedom's Dawn* it is the restraining arms of rich ladies reclining in their sumptuously appointed bedchambers (*khvab-gah*) that tried to hold him and his comrades back from participating in the freedom struggle. Nor does Faiz's discovery announced in *Love Do Not Ask* impress me much. The realization that there are other things in life besides love of women which must engage a mature man's attention, and that no one can be forever insensitive to the sufferings of the poor and oppressed is surely not so world-shaking that it needs to be announced with a fanfare of trumpets. However, my rather lukewarm response to this poem reflects my own personal development, in which concern for the poor and oppressed preceded the experience of passionate love for a woman, and it never at any time occurred to me that there was any conflict between the two. I realize that this is not everyone's experience, and that others who are not lacking in the capacity for wider human sympathies can go through a stage in which these sympathies are dormant, and love for a woman can be so all-consuming that nothing else seems to matter – even in a country where stark poverty confronts one inescapably on every side, as it does not, or need not, in the developed countries of the world. I suppose that I also expected more of a poet who was at home in the *ghazal* tradition, in which love is all-embracing and it is taken for granted that love for woman (or man), love for humankind, love for God, love for high ideals – all these are aspects of a single, indivisible love. Faiz seems to attain to this realization rather tardily in *Two Loves*, and that too after the relapse announced in *Poetry's Theme*.

The other of his 'Two Loves', his country and its poor and oppressed inhabitants, is portrayed, like his lady beloved, in terms of external appearances; and in this portrayal Faiz shows a propensity to dwell upon scenes that evoke disgust rather than on things that arouse sympathy – let alone that admiration and solidarity which are the indispensable basis of the revolutionary social change that Faiz preaches. Thus in *Love, Do Not Ask* what he contrasts with the charms of his beloved are diseased bodies, with pus flowing from festering sores. In *Dogs*, where dogs are clearly a (not very apt) symbol of miserable, oppressed humanity, the picture is one of people who live and die in filth, begging and stealing in order to live, bearing every humiliation, and when they fight at all, fighting one another.

Ishaq, then, is right when he says that 'the blood and sweat of the working people of Pakistan' is not much in evidence in Faiz's poetry, and that 'his poetry still has to emerge from the drawing room, the school and the college and spread to the streets, markets, fields and factories.' It is in the drawing-rooms and colleges that Faiz felt most at home, where it is my experience that revolutionaries (both those who see themselves as such only in fantasy and those who are more fully committed) rarely want to know the real human beings whose cause they champion and whose role they seem to see (consciously or unconsciously) as that of admiringly applauding them and doing as they tell them.

Faiz's rather lukewarm style of loving and his concern never to commit himself too unequivocally seems to have entered into his soul, so that even in poems where the expression of stronger feeling would have posed no risk, that feeling is surprisingly absent. His poem on Iqbal, an incomparably powerful influence both for good and bad, says almost nothing, though it was written after Faiz had formed his progressive outlook. A literal translation reads,

To our country came a sweet-voiced *faqir*. He came, and passed through singing his *ghazals* in his own style. He filled the empty roads with people, and the deserted taverns began to come to life. Only a few had the vision to penetrate to him, but his song went deep into the hearts of all. Now that king in beggar's clothing has gone far away, and the roads of our country are again despondent. A few dear ones have one or two visions, but his song dwells in the hearts of all. The beauties of that song will never fade. Its exuberance, its fervour, its deep feeling – this song is like the fierce flame of a volcano. Caught in its leaping fire, the heart of the wind of non-existence melts [whatever that means]. It is like a lamp that does not fear the rage of the desert wind, like a candle oblivious of the coming of morning.

A poem, in short, that could apply to any poet who exercised a great influence on his contemporaries, and tells us nothing whatever about the qualities which made him great and influential or about Faiz's assessment of him and his message.

Even where we would expect the expression of deeply felt personal emotion one does not find it–and if Faiz felt it, he did not succeed in conveying it. His 1982 poem in memory of his comrade in imprisonment, Major Muhammad Ishaq, has echoes of Ghalib's lament for his dearly loved adopted son Arif, with its *radif 'koi din aur'*, and abounds in stilted phrases that convey no real emotion.

Faiz did not rely simply on fortunate circumstances to maintain and enhance his popularity. He and his admirers created myths about his political commitment in which truth mingles with stories which, if not wholly untrue, include substantial elements of 'suppression of the true and suggestion of the false.'

Thus, there is much popularity to be gained outside Pakistan if people know that, in Kiernan's words, Faiz had been jailed 'sometimes' (p.283, n.17) 'in solitary confinement...deprived of writing materials', and on one occasion on a charge that could have carried the death penalty (p.284, n.25). These things make a special appeal in Britain, for once a subject people has actually been victorious in its struggle for independence the British generally feel a retrospective sympathy for that struggle which they were far from feeling at the time; and in the same way they have a ready sympathy for political prisoners when it is no longer they who are doing the imprisoning. This is a deserved popularity – and it remains unalloyed if one does not know, what is also true, that the conditions in which he lived in jail were, for three-and-three-quarters of his four-year term, not anything like as harsh as Kiernan's words would naturally lead his English readers to suppose. They would be surprised to learn what Faiz's fellow-prisoners, Sajjad Zahir and former Major Muhammad Ishaq, tell their Urdu readers in their foreword to *Zindan Nama*. Thus Sajjad Zahir recalls how when Faiz's second collection of verse *Dast i Saba* was published, 'we got permission from the authorities to hold a party in which all of us prisoners congratulated Faiz on its publication.' Ishaq writes of conditions in Hyderabad Jail, where they were held during the first stage of court proceedings against them.

The court building was inside the jail. The court sat from 8 a.m. to 12 noon. Saturdays and Sundays were free. In the afternoon our lawyers would come to consult us from time to time, but the rest of the time was our own....We made our own provision for our meals. Two prisoners...who were excellent cooks had been assigned the duty of cooking for us, and we ate in regular style, as though we were dining in the officers' mess....In the evenings we would play volley ball or badminton....*Mushairas, qavvalis* and dramas generally took place in our compound. When we went to see Sajjad Zahir on our free mornings he would entertain us to coffee and biscuits and we would talk about literature and politics.

I have already quoted his statement that in Hyderabad Jail 'we had every bodily comfort which is possible in a goal.' In Montgomery Jail, he says, 'we had pretty well all the facilities we had had in Hyderabad.' I shall say more about all this below.

Similarly, the impression has been given that Faiz was forced into exile when Zia ul Haq came to power, though this was not so.

An almost ludicrous example of what can result from this myth-making can be found in Naomi Lazard's introduction, headed 'Translating Faiz', to her recently published translations of Faiz's selected poems.[12] After a greatly exaggerated picture of Faiz's standing throughout the South Asian subcontinent ('Anyone who knows any poetry at all in that vast region knows of Faiz') she says:

Faiz became a spokesman for his people in another way too. Instead of struggling for a literary career, instead of taking high posts as lecturer or professor, he dedicated himself to teaching illiterate people. He was blasé in his disregard for the blandishments of life. He identified himself with the masses of the poor, the exploited, the victims.

Such statements, based, one must presume, on what Naomi Lazard was told by Faiz himself, can only provoke sarcastic laughter in those who know the truth.

Faiz was also at pains to conceal as far as possible personal habits which he thought potential admirers would disapprove of. In the sense which 'everyone' bears in such statements, everyone knew that he drank; but he was at pains not to let this general knowledge become more general than it already was. When Kiernan was preparing his translation for publication I was shown a draft of his introduction in which there was a very mild reference to Faiz's drinking. I spoke of this to Faiz, who told me that there would be no such reference in the finally approved draft; and, sure enough, the published introduction includes no such reference.

All of this has given rise to some bitterness in those progressives who avowed the same political views as Faiz but were denied, or denied themselves, the opportunities to combine this avowal with a life of such material comfort as he enjoyed. One of them told me emphatically, 'Faiz has absolutely nothing to do with the mass of the people,' and another, 'Faiz will never set foot in any house where the floors are not covered with the most expensive carpets.' When he was approaching the end of his self-imposed exile some young progressives in Islamabad alleged to me that he had now begun to write poetry in which there was nothing to which General Zia ul Haq could object.

I have written these last pages because I think that they deal with an aspect of Faiz and his place in the cultural and political life of Pakistan which needs to be understood. But having said that I would stress that there are even more important things that should be understood.

Firstly, even if Faiz can be fairly accused of a too wholehearted concern with building his own image and seeking his own safety and comfort, it ill becomes people who have never had to experience imprisonment for their political beliefs or lived under the threat of a death sentence to adopt a lofty moral tone towards one who has. Those who have not undergone the stress of that experience can only *hope* that if they did they would have the strength to emerge from it ready to react with more consistent courage than Faiz seems to have reacted. If for most of the years of his imprisonment he lived in relative comfort, imprisonment is nevertheless imprisonment; and moreover not all his time in prison was spent in such comfort. The solitary confinement in which he had been held for a full three months, Ishaq tells us, 'had had so profound an effect upon him that even after he came to Hyderabad he could not bear to be alone.'

Secondly, the most important thing about Faiz is his poetry. It is Faiz the poet, much more than Faiz the man, that has made a more significant impact on Pakistanis, both in Pakistan and in the numerous other countries where they have settled, and upon thousands of others in the Urdu-speaking community; and there is no reason to think that this impact will not continue many years after his death.

Thirdly, if the best poetry is written by those who, like Mir, for example, live a life in which they consistently feel, think and act as they and their audience would wish them to, and somehow convey this unmistakably in what they write, there are also poets who present themselves not as they are but as they wish they *could* be, and where that aspiration is strongly and sincerely felt, the poetry it inspires is, or can be, good poetry.

And finally if Faiz's warmest admirers are not the effective revolutionary force one would like them to be, they are nevertheless, in the Urdu phrase – *ghanimat* – a good deal better than nothing. Faiz's poetry gives their feelings and aspirations the expression that they need and deserve, and it will long continue to inspire others with a hatred of oppression, a sympathy with the downtrodden, and the desire for a better world.

Suggestions For Further Reading

Some of you may want to make a more thorough and comprehensive study of Urdu literature, and this note is written for the guidance of those who do. You will need to use libraries to get many of the titles I shall list, since many of them have long been out of print. In Britain, the library of the School of Oriental and African Studies, University of London, will probably have all the books you need, but you do not need to join it; your local library can borrow its books for you under inter-library loan arrangements.

General Accounts

It is a good idea for you to begin with short, summary accounts of the literature, and then go on to the more detailed ones, leaving the most voluminous until last.

If you want to see Urdu literature set within the perspective of South Asian literature as a whole, read the article by Ian Raeside and myself in *A Guide to Eastern Literature*, (ed.) D.M.Lang (Weidenfeld and Nicholson, 1971) pp.215-49. For a fairly full outline account of Urdu literature itself, begin with my article in the 1967 edition of the *Encyclopaedia Britannica*. Aziz Ahmad gives a useful, though here and there pretentious and misleading, summary account in the new *Cambridge History of Islam* (Cambridge University Press, 1967) Vol.2, pp.695-701, and a rather fuller one in his *An Intellectual History of Islam in India* (Edinburgh University Press, 1969) pp.91-111. There are good accounts of literary institutions (for example the *mushaira*) and of some major literary figures in Muhammad Mujeeb, *The Indian Muslims* (Allen and Unwin, 1967).

Histories of Urdu literature

Of the separately published volumes on Urdu literature, by far the best short account is D.J.Matthews, C. Shackle and Shahrukh Husain, *Urdu Literature*, (Urdu Markaz, London, 1985). I have given my opinion of this and other histories in *How Not to Write the History of Urdu Literature* (see Ch.3, note 1). The great defect of *all* other histories in English is that they are full of repeated, irrelevant and unhelpful comparisons between Urdu literature and English literature – invariably to the detriment of Urdu. T.Grahame Bailey's *History of Urdu Literature* (Calcutta, 1932) is a concise account, but for the most part it gives too much detail about quite unimportant writers and too little about important ones; and it is so dry and unimaginative that it is difficult to read. All the same it helps in reinforcing the factual framework. R.B.Saxena's *History of Urdu Literature* (Allahabad, 1927 and at least one subsequent reprint) is fuller, and a good deal more readable than Grahame Bailey's, though pretty limited in its understanding. Muhammad Sadiq's *History of Urdu Literature* (Oxford University Press, Pakistan, 1st edition, 1964, 2nd augmented edition, 1984) is, unfortunately, still the only full length general history. Comments on Sadiq's interpretation appear also in *Understanding the Urdu Ghazal*.

Other Reference Works

The *Encyclopaedia of Islam* has entries on more writers than any other general reference work of this kind. Refer also to the notes in David Matthews and Christopher Shackle, *An Anthology of Classical Urdu Love Lyrics* (Oxford University Press, 1972). These give better and more adequate short accounts of the major *ghazal* poets than you will find in the general histories.

Files of the periodical *Mahfil*, published in the United States in the 1960s, include, along with accounts of other South Asian writing, articles on, and translations from, Urdu. So do those of its successor, *The Journal of South Asian Literature*, published semi-annually by the Asian Studies Center, Michigan State University, East Lansing, Michigan 48824. C.M.Naim's *Annual of Urdu Studies*, of which six issues have appeared, is well worth reading; it is available from him at 1130 E.59th Street, Chicago, Il., 60637, USA. The emphasis is on contemporary or near-contemporary literature, but some articles deal with earlier writers too. A similar publication, *Urdu Canada*, edited by W.A.Shaheen, is published by Urdu Canada Publications, Post Box 2276, Station D, Ottawa, Ontario, Canada, K1P SW4.

Translations

In general, you will learn things from translations, even where these are not of first-rate quality, which you cannot learn from writing *about* Urdu literature. Readers in Britain can find translations, especially of works by contemporary writers, often in paperbacks published in India, at shops in or near London, of which at the time of writing the best-stocked is Books from India, 45 Museum Street, London, WC1A 1LR, tel. 071-405-7726 and 071-405-3784. The quality of the English is often poor, but this should not deter you from reading them.

The Annual of Urdu Studies and *Urdu Canada* generally include some translations from Urdu short stories and poetry (again, mainly of modern and contemporary writing) and other occasional publications from the USA sometimes have materials on Urdu. In March 1962 C.M.Naim published *A Bibliography of English Sources for the Urdu Language and Literature*, and subsequently an undated *Addendum* was published in *Mahfil*, Vol.1, No.1. Gopi Chand Narang's *Bibliography of Urdu Short Stories in English Translation*, with a long supplement by Mary Seidlinger, appeared in *Mahfil*, Vol.4, No.2, Winter 1968. The 162 pages of Frances W.Pritchett, *Urdu Literature, a Bibliography of English Language Sources,* Manohar, New Delhi, 1979, is still, to my knowledge, the most comprehensive, and very valuable, guide. Useful lists of this kind will probably continue to appear from time to time.

Reading relating specifically to different periods of the literature is suggested under the relevant headings that follow. I do not generally repeat here information already provided in the notes and references; so you should refer to these too.

Classical Poetry

Ralph Russell and Khurshidul Islam, *Three Mughal Poets* (Harvard University Press, 1968; and Allen and Unwin, 1969) has three chapters devoted to Mir, and treats more fully of the eighteenth century background. It also gives a chapter each to Sauda and Mir Hasan. Sauda was a good *ghazal* poet but is most famous in Urdu literary tradition for his powerful *qasidas*. In *Three Mughal Poets* we have concentrated on his best and most vigorous writing, found in his vituperative, Rabelasian satires. The chapter on Mir Hasan gives an extended summary of his *masnavi, Sihr ul Bayan* (The Enchanting Story), which is still, two centuries after it was written, deservedly popular. The chapters on Mir also include summary translations of several of his *masnavis*.

In the first half of the nineteenth century *masnavis* by the Delhi poet Momin and the Lucknow poet Navvab Mirza Shauq reach the same standard. Shauq's best *masnavi, Zahr i Ishq* (The Poison of Love), has been translated into English prose by Shah Abdus Salam *et al.* (DK Publications, Delhi, 1982). The most comprehensive work on the *marsiya* in English that I have seen is Syed Ghulam Abbas, *The Immortal Poetry and Mir Anis* (sic) (Majlis-e-Milli, Karachi, 1983). Pages 229 to 339 of this book carry the Urdu text, and parallel English verse translation, of one of the *marsiyas* of Anis, the greatest exponent of this genre.

For other *ghazal* poets of the classical period the best short account in English is in Matthews, Shackle and Husain, *Urdu Literature* (mentioned above). In the first half of the nineteenth century both Delhi and Lucknow produced *ghazal* poets of distinction, and translated examples of their work are included in the book. It also gives a good brief account of Nazir Akbarabadi, a remarkable major poet of the late eighteenth and early nineteenth centuries whose major work is not in any of the classical forms. He is the one poet of the period whose poetry, but for the barrier of language, would be readily intelligible and make an immediate appeal to the modern English reader. He writes mainly of the everyday life of his native Agra, of the seasons, the festivals and entertainments of its citizens, and describes all these with a zest and a down-to-earth humanism which are very appealing. But effective translation which would capture the music and the strong and varied rhythms of his verse is extremely difficult, and the few samples of translation of his work given in *Urdu Literature* are the only successful ones I have seen.

For those of you who know some Urdu, Matthews and Shackle's *Anthology of Classical Urdu Love Lyrics* (see above) will be useful. Literal English translations, designed to help you understand the original, face the Urdu text. *The Golden Tradition: An Anthology of Urdu Poetry*, selected, edited and translated by Ahmed Ali (Columbia University Press, 1973) covers the eighteenth and the nineteenth centuries. The quality of the translations is uneven, and the accompanying accounts of the poets less reliable than those in Matthews and Shackle.

For Ghalib, the fullest treatment is in the books by Khurshidul Islam and myself, *Ghalib – Volume I: Life and Letters*, (Harvard University Press, 1969; and Allen and Unwin, 1969) and the forthcoming *Volume II: Urdu and Persian Ghazals*. Short treatments are fairly numerous. One of the best is M.Mujeeb, *Ghalib* (Sahitya Akademi, New Delhi, 1969).

Literature in Reaction to British Rule, 1857-1922

A book that gives a good general background for the period, with fairly substantial references to literature, is W.Cantwell Smith, *Modern Islam in India* (Minerva Bookshop, Lahore, 1943; and Gollancz, 1946). His equation of the Aligarh movement with the expression of a Muslim bourgeois outlook is quite untenable, but this can easily be ignored. For Indian nationalist views of much the same period see S.Abid Husain, *The Destiny of Indian Muslims*, (Asia Publishing House, London, 1965), and the relevant chapters of M.Mujeeb, *The Indian Muslims* (Allen and Unwin, 1967).

Once you have some understanding of the general background, I cannot stress too strongly that you will learn more from the translated writings of poets and writers of this period than you will from books about them. Aziz Ahmad and G.E.von Grunebaum (eds.) *Muslim Self-Statement in India and Pakistan, 1857-1968* (Otto Harrassowitz, Wiesbaden, 1970) include useful extracts from the verse of Hali and of Iqbal. (See also the books noted in notes 19, 21 and 31 on Chapter 7. Details of the book referred to in note 31 are given in the main text.)

For further study of particular authors and/or intellectual leaders of this period there is no lack of materials available.

There are two biographies of Sir Sayyid Ahmad Khan – that of Graham already mentioned (Ch.6, note 21), and Hali's *Hayat i Javed*, first published in 1901, only three years after Sir Sayyid's death. A translation of the major part of it by David Matthews and Khalid Hasan Qadiri was published in 1979.

C.F.Andrews, *Zakaullah of Delhi* (Heffer, Cambridge, 1929) is an excellent sympathetic study of an important supporter of the Aligarh movement to whom too little attention has been paid.

Muhammad Sadiq, *Muhammad Husain Azad* (Lahore, 1965) is a good informative study.

Khalid Hasan Qadiri, *Hasrat Mohani* (Delhi, 1985) covers the whole span of Hasrat's long life, from 1880 or 1881 to his death in 1951, and is particularly interesting not only because it takes in the whole history of modern India's (and Pakistan's) struggle for independence but also because Hasrat was a *ghazal* poet of a high order, steeped in the best traditions of classical culture and devoted to the *ghazal* ideals, and we see him carrying his ideals into the struggle against British domination of the Aligarh scene, against Hindu and Muslim communalism, and for communism as he understood it. The book is therefore relevant to the last section '(Literature and the People, 1920s Onwards)' as well as to this one.

A good account of the novel and short story (relevant, again, to the last section of this book as well as to this one) is Suhrawardy's (details in note 4 to Ch.7). The author's enthusiasm for her subject makes it enjoyable reading, and is a most refreshing change from the negative attitudes of most writers in English on Urdu literature. It sometimes leads her to make amusingly naive statements, such as that on p.41 where she says that *Mirat ul Arus* 'is the first real novel in Urdu, and still the best.' There are also some surprising gaps in the book, but in general it is very well worth reading.

Iqbal has been the subject of an extensive literature, but two brief accounts of his life and work are an adequate preparation for reading his own writings. The British Library publication (1977) *Allama Sir Muhammad Iqbal*, by Q.M Haq and M.I.Waley is a very good concise account, and so is the earlier Iqbal Singh, *The Ardent Pilgrim* (Orient Longman, 1951). But after reading them turn to Iqbal himself. He has been particularly well served by English translators. His three major Persian works are all available in translation – R.A.Nicholson's translation of his 1915 poem *Asrar i Khudi*, under the title *Secrets of the Self*, first published in 1920 (revised edition, Lahore 1940); A.J.Arberry's translation of the 1918 *Rumuz i Bekhudi*, entitled *The Mysteries of Selflessness* (London, 1953); the same translator's version of the 1932 *Javid-Nama* (Allen and Unwin, 1966). In addition *Payam i Mashriq* (1923) was translated into English verse by M.Hadi Husain under the title *A Message from the East* (Iqbal Academy, Lahore, 1977); Parts I and II of *Zabur i Ajam* were translated by Arberry (*Persian Psalms*, Lahore, 1948). *Pas chi bayad kard e aqvam i sharq* (1936) has been translated by B.A.Dar (What Should then be Done, O People of the East? Iqbal Academy, Lahore, 1977.) Only rather smaller selections of his Urdu verse have been translated, but V.G.Kiernan's *Poems of Iqbal* (London, 1955) is a good selection well translated. Arberry translated his famous *Shikva* and *Javab i Shikva* (Complaint and Answer, Lahore, 1955) and there have been other translations by Pakistanis and Indians, the most recent of which is Khushwant Singh's verse translation (Oxford University Press, Delhi, 1981. Reprinted with corrections, 1982) sandwiched between Urdu script and Hindi script versions of the original. For a number of different, thought-provoking assessments of his verse and his message, go to the three books listed above – Cantwell Smith's, M.Mujeeb's and Syed Abid Husain's. All have interesting things to say about Iqbal. Cantwell Smith's assessment is still, in my view, the best and most comprehensive of the relatively concise accounts.

Literature and the People, 1920s onwards

Many of Prem Chand's short stories, and two of his novels, have been translated into English. Details of some are: *A Handful of Wheat and Other Stories*, (trans). P.C.Gupta, (New Delhi, 1972); *The Shroud and Twenty Other Stories*, (trans). Madan Gopal, New Delhi, 1972; *The Secret of Culture and Other Stories*, (trans). Madan Gupta, Bombay, 1960; *Twenty-four Stories by Premchand*, (trans). Nandini Nopany and P.Lal, (New Delhi, 1980); *The World of Prem-chand*, (trans). David Rubin, (London, 1969). Rubin's translations are in my opinion the best.

Gordon C. Roadarmel translated *Gaodan* under the title *The Gift of a Cow* (Allen and Unwin, London, 1968) and David Rubin has translated *Nirmala* (Orient Paperbacks, New Delhi and Bombay, 1988).

Two good full-length biographies of Prem Chand in English are Madan Gopal, *Munshi Premchand, a Literary Biography* (Asia Publishing House, London, 1964) and a better one by Prem Chand's son Amrit Rai, *Prem Chand, a Life*, translated from the Hindi by Harish Trivedi (People's Publishing House, New Delhi, 1982). The preface tells us on p.v that this was 'published in a fuller version in Hindi in 1962'.

For the short stories of later writers see the introductory note to Ch.14 and references listed above under *Translations*. Frances W.Pritchett, *Urdu Litera-ture*....(mentioned above) has a separate section (pp.27-34) on translations of short stories published before 1979. Ranjana Ash (ed.) *Short Stories from India, Pakistan and Bangladesh* (Harrap, 1980) includes my translation of a story by Ahmad Nadim Qasmi.

A selection of Mantu's stories (eleven in all) was translated by Hamid Jalal and published under the title *Black Milk* (Lahore, n.d. (1956). The Summer, Fall 1985 issue of the *Journal of South Asian Literature* (Vol.XX, No.2) was devoted to Mantu and gives 13 stories in translation, together with essays by Linda Wentink and Leslie A.Fleming. The latter's *Another Lonely Voice* (University of California, Berkeley, 1979) is an extended study of his work. Another selection of 24 stories, selected and translated by Khalid Hasan, *Kingdom's End and Other Stories*, was published by Verso, London, 1987.

Bibliography of the Author's Writings on Urdu

In this bibliography Ralph Russell's writings on Urdu are listed in the order in which they first appeared. Readers who are interested can find a detailed account of his contribution to Urdu studies in: 'Ralph Russell: Teacher, Scholar, Lover of Urdu', by Marion Molteno, in C.M. Naim (ed.), *Annual of Urdu Studies*, 6 (1987).

* indicates that substantial portions of the article/book have been included in this volume.

1950: *'Urdu ka mustaqbil'* (The future of Urdu) in *Nai Raushni* (Delhi) 4:1.
1951: *Urdu Studies in England* (unpublished)
1955: *Urdu literature* in *Encyclopedia Britannica*; revised 1964.
1959: *'Translation of Krishan Chandar's story, 'Kalu Bhangi' in *Indian Literature*, 2:2.
    *'Tiny's Granny', translation of Ismat Chugtai's story, *Nannhi ki nani* in *Contemporary Indian Short Stories* (Sahitya Akademi, Delhi); reprinted in *Truth Tales* (Kali, New Delhi; and The Women's Press, London, 1986).
    'An eighteenth-century Urdu satirist' in *Indian Literature*, 2:1.
1960: Some problems of the treatment of Urdu metre in *Journal of the Royal Asiatic Society*.
1966: Reviews of *A history of Urdu Literature* by Mohammad Sadiq in *Journal of the Royal Asiatic Society, pts. 1 and 2* and *Asia Major*, Wl. X11, pt. 1.
1968: With Khurshidul Islam, *Three Mughal Poets – Mir, Sauda and Mir Hasan* (Harvard, Cambridge; and Allen and Unwin, London, 1969).
    *The Rise of the Modern Novel in Urdu, in *New Orient* (Prague) 7:2, 33-39.
    'The Development of the Modern Novel in Urdu' in T.W. Clark (ed.), *The Novel in India* (Allen and Unwin, London).
    *'Themes of eighteenth century Urdu lyric poetry in the verse of Mir' in *Sasibhusan Dasgupta Commemoration Volume* (ed.) R.K. Dasgupta and Sisit Kumar Das (Calcutta).
1969: With Khurshidul Islam, *Ghalib Volume, 1: Life and Letters* (Harvard, Cambridge; and Allen and Unwin, London).
    *'The Pursuit of the Urdu Ghazal' in *Journal of Asian Studies* 29:1; 107-24.
    'On translating Ghalib' in *Mahfil* (East Lansing) 5:4; 71-87.

'Poet of Humanity' in *The Illustrated Weekly of India* (New Delhi) 90:8; 34-5.

'Ghalib and the Revolt of 1857' in *Mainstream* (Delhi) 7:26; 31-33.

*'Ghalib's Urdu Verse' in *Mainstream*, 7:28; 17-25 (subsequently republished in *Ghalib, the Poet and his Age*, 1972).

Articles on Ghalib, Ghazal, and Iqbal in *The Penguin Companion to Literature, Volume IV: Classical and Byzantine, Oriental and African*, (ed.) D.R. Dudley and D.M. Lang (Penguin, Harmondsworth).

1970: *'The Urdu Ghazal in Muslim Society' in *South Asian Review*, 3:2; 141-49.

Translations of selected stanzas of Musaddas-e-Hali in *Muslim Self-Statement in India and Pakistan*, (ed.) Aziz Ahmad and G.E. von Grunebaum (Otto Harrassowitz, Wiesbaden) 95-99.

Notes on Urdu for BA students entering the 2nd year course (unpublished).

1971: *Essential Urdu – a course for learners in Britain* (published by the author).

'When I was Little' translation of Rajinder Singh Bedi's story, *Jab main chota tha* in *Adam*, 355-60; 145-51.

The Shore and the Wave, translation of Aziz Ahmad's novel, *Aisi Bulandi, Aisi Paisti* (Allen and Unwin, London).

With I. Raeside, 'Indian and Pakistani Literature' in *A Guide to Eastern Literatures*, (ed.) D.M. Lang (Weidenfeld and Nicholson, London; and Praeger, New York, Washington) 213-49.

1972: Ghalib: 'A Self-Portrait' and *'Ghalib's Urdu Verse' in Ralph Russell (ed.), *Ghalib: the Poet and his Age* (Allen and Unwin, London).

*Strands of Muslim Identity in *South Asian Review*, 6:1; 21-32.

Review of D. Matthews and C. Shackle, *An Anthology of Classical Urdu Love Lyrics* in *South Asian Review*, 6:1; 78-80.

*'Poetry and politics in Pakistan' review of *Poems by Faiz* translated by Victor Kiernan, in *Modern Asian Studies*, 6:3; 353-78.

1973: 'Review of Matthews and Shackle' (see above) in *Journal of the Royal Asiatic Society*, 1; 75-77.

1974: 'The British Contribution to Urdu Studies' in *Oriental College Magazine* (Lahore) Centenary number, 50; translated and republished as '*Angrezon ki Urdu-dosti*' in *Afkar* (1981) 133; 422-30.

*With Khurshidul Islam 'The Satirical Verse of Akbar Ilahabadi' in *Modern Asian Studies*, 8:1: 1-58.

Review of *Ghazals of Ghalib*, (ed.) Aijaz Ahmad, in *Journal of the Royal Asiatic Society*, 1: 78-82.

Articles on Urdu literature in *Dictionary of Oriental Literature*, Vol. 2, (ed.) D. Zbavitel (Allen and Unwin, London).

A primer of Urdu verse metre (published by the author).

Notes for undergraduates beginning the study of Urdu (unpublished).

1976: With Jogindar Shamsher 'Panjabi Journalism in Britain: A Background' in *New Community*, V.3: 211-21.

1977: **Reflections on Khizar-i-rah*, Iqbal centenary celebrations. (Lahore) (unpublished).

*Leadership in the All India Progressive Writers' Association, in B.N. Pandey (ed.) *Leadership in South Asia* (Vikas, Delhi).

1978: 'Islam in a Pakistan Village: Some Impressions', in *Perspectives on World Religions*, (ed). Robert Jackson (SOAS, London) 221-325.

With Jogindar Shamsher, 'Panjabi Poetry in Britain', in *New Community* VI:3: 291-305.

Readings in everyday Urdu (published by the author).

Urdu teaching, immigrant communities, and SOAS (unpublished).

1979: With Jogindar Shamsher, 'The Panjabi Short Story in Britain', in *New Community*, VII:2; 233-246.

Exercises in Prose Translation (English–Urdu), (published by the author).

1980: 'Compulsions', translation of Ahmad Nadim Qasmi's story *'Bandagi Becharagi'*, in *Short Stories from India, Pakistan and Bangladesh*, (ed.) Ranjana Ash (Harrap, London).

Ethnic minority languages and the schools, with special reference to Urdu (Runnymede Trust).

*'Prem Chand', in *The Asian*, III: 6 and 7: 12-13.

With Khalid Hasan Qadiri and Aqeel Danish, *Urdu translations of English passages* (published by the author).

Urdu teaching in Glasgow (published by the author).

1980-82: *A new course in Hindustani for learners in Britain* Part 1 (SOAS, London) Parts II and III, 1981; Part IV, 1982.

Revised edition of Part I, see 1986.

1980-86: *Urdu teaching newsletter* (published by the author/editor).

1981: *'Urdu shairi men Islam ka tasavvur'* (The concept of Islam in Urdu poetry), in *Jang* (London) December 1980 to January 1981.

1982: *Urdu in Britain* – Reports of the first and second national Urdu conferences, 1979 and 1981 (ed.) (Urdu Markaz, London).

'Urdu in Britain: a note', in *Pakistan studies*, 1,2.

1983: Aziz Ahmad, South Asia, Islam and Urdu, in *Islamic Society and Culture* (ed.) Milton Israel and N.K. Wagle (Manohar, New Delhi) 59-68.

1984-86: With Khalid Hasan Qadiri, translations of numerous children's books for dual-text (English/Urdu editions).

1985: *South Asian Radicals and Britain's South Asian Languages* (published by the author).

With M. Molteno and R. Maqbool, *Working with Urdu teachers in supplementary schools in Nottingham* (published by the authors).

Letters to Khwaja Hasan Nizami written in 1949, published in the newspaper *Ravi* (Bradford) August 1985.

'Translating the Issues', in *Issues* (London) Spring 1985.

Report on work for Urdu teaching in Britain prepared for the Pakistan Embassy (unpublished).

The educational needs of Pakistani children, speech given in the Pakistan

Centre, Nottingham (published by the author).

Urdu teaching in British schools (London Borough of Newham).

'The Urdu Language', in *Language and Culture Guide: Urdu* (CILT:Centre for Information, on Language Teaching and Research, London).

1986: *A new course in Urdu and spoken Hindi*, part I (SOAS, London).

Ralph Russell ki taqrir (Ralph Russell's speech), speech given to an event organized and printed by the newspaper, *Ravi*, in Bradford, September 1986.

The last four years of Urdu in Britain – a personal statement (National Language Authority, Pakistan) with Urdu translation by Inamul Haq Javaid.

1987: 'How not to write the history of Urdu literature', in C.M. Naim (ed.) *Annual of Urdu studies*, 6, 1-10; reprinted in *Jang* (London), 25-26 July 1989.

1988: With Marion Molteno, 'Community languages', in *Languages in schools from complacency to conviction*, (ed.) D. Phillips (CILT, London).

Note on Pronunciation and Transliteration

For the consonants, you can in most cases use the sounds that the English letters indicate, though there are in fact substantial differences between the consonant systems of the two language. For your purposes:

gh is near enough to 'g' and
kh is like the final sound in 'loch'

q is near enough to 'k'

The vowel sounds in Urdu do not in most cases correspond completely to English sounds. The following are, however, approximate equivalents;

'a' is like the 'a' in the 'attire'

'ā' is like the 'a' in 'father'

'i' is like the 'i' in 'him'

'ī' is like the 'i' in 'keen'

'u' is like the 'u' in 'put'

'ū' is like the 'u' in 'rule'

'e' is like the 'ay' in 'day'

'o' is like the 'o' in 'hole'

'ai' is like the 'a' in 'hat'

'au' is something like 'awe'

I have deliberately not used the elaborate transliteration that scholarly works generally use, since the scholars of Urdu will know that, for example 'Hali' stands for what they would write as 'Hālī', while all that other readers need to know is what 'Hali' is enough to tell them – that the second letter is 'ā', and not 'a'. I have not marked final vowels, since you can assume that all these are long.

Notes and References

Chapter 1

1. The story is quoted by Ghalib in a letter to Chaudhri Abdul Ghaffur and the full passage is translated in Ralph Russell and Khurshidul Islam, *Ghalib: Vol.1: Life and Letters,* Harvard University Press and Allen and Unwin, 1969, pp.288-89.

2. See Hanīf Naqvi, *Tazkira i Nikāt ush Shu 'ara* in *Ājkal,* Delhi, issue dated July 1962.

3. The suggestions for further reading at the end of the book tell you where you can find more detailed accounts and/or samples of the works of other poets in translation.

Chapter 2

This chapter is based on an article originally published as 'The Pursuit of the Urdu Ghazal', in the USA *Journal of Asian Studies,* XXIX, I, 1969, but I have incorporated in it and in Chapter 4 material from *Themes of 18th Century Urdu Lyric Poetry in the Verse of Mir,* a revised version of a paper read in December 1962, to a seminar at the School of Oriental and African Studies, University of London, which was published in *Sasibhusan Dasgupta Commemoration Volume,* New Age Publishers, Calcutta, n.d. (?1968).

Throughout this chapter I write with the *ghazal* poets of the eighteenth and nineteenth centuries in mind. The *ghazal* continues to flourish to the present day (see *Achieving Independence, and After,* pp.193ff.) but some of my generalizations would need some slight modification to be made fully applicable to the twentieth-century *ghazal* too.

1. 1st edition, p.19, 2nd edition, p.20. For further discussion of this book see my article 'How Not to Write the History of Urdu literature' in C.M. Naim (ed.), *Annual of Urdu Studies 6* (1987), pp.1-10.

2. I still hold this to be a correct statement, despite the common assertion of some Urdu critics that the best *ghazals* do show a unity of mood throughout. And cf. note 28 below.

3. Cf. Ralph Russell, 'Some Problems of the Treatment of Urdu Metre', *Journal of the Royal Asiatic Society,* April 1960, pp. 48-58; and *Primer of Urdu Verse Metre,* (published by myself, 1974).

4. See *Changing attitudes to poetry – Azād and Hāli* (pp. 121ff.).

5. *The Allegory of Love*, New York, Oxford University Press, paperback, 1958, p.13.

6. This is dealt with at length in Ch.4 of Ralph Russell and Khurshidul Islam, *Three Mughal Poets,* Harvard University Press, 1968, and Allen and Unwin, 1969, and in the introduction to our forthcoming, *Ghalib, Volume 2: Urdu and Persian Ghazals*.

7. In her Introduction (p.15) to her translation of *The Song of Roland*, Penguin Books, 1957.

8. Act III, Scene 3.

9. In *Three Mughal Poets* this point was not made. Frances Pritchett later drew my attention to it.

10. There are also many which are not on themes of love at all.

11. Ch. 7, vv.1 ff.

12. Penguin Books, 1956, p.139.

13. Dorothy Sayers, in the Introduction to her translation, has a passage, too long to quote here, in which she gives an admirably lucid explanation of this parallel. (*The Divine Comedy, I: Hell*, Penguin Books, 1949, pp.67-68.)

14. *The Waning of the Middle Ages*, Penguin Books, 1955, p.119.

15. *Kulliyāt i Mīr,* (ed.) in 5 volumes by Kalb i Ali Khān Fāiq, and published by Majlis i Taraqqi i Adab, Lahore, 1976-82. This verse is from the first *dīvān* – Vol.I, p.347.

16. *Kulliyāt*, Vol.I, pp.242-43.

17. *Zikr i Mīr*, (ed.) Abdul Haq, Aurangabad, 1928, p.39.

18. Nazīr Ahmad, *Mauiza i Hasna*, (ed.) Iftikhār Ahmad Siddīqi, Majlis i Taraqqi i Adab, Lahore, 1963, Letter No.99, pp.199-200.

19. *Poems from the Divan of Hafiz* (trans. Gertrude Bell), London, 1897, p.51.

20. Ibid., pp.62-63.

21. Cf. J.B. Broadbent, *Poetic Love*, London, Chatto & Windus, 1964, pp.31-32.

22. Dent, Everyman's Library, 1908, p.285; first published in 1836.

23. p.2.

24. It follows that the study of a particular *ghazal* poet needs to some extent to proceed from an attempt to answer the question, who and/or what does 'beloved' mean to him? I have attempted to answer this question in the chapters 'Mir-the Poet and the Man' (pp.53ff.) and (more comprehensively) 'The Ghazals of Ghalib' (pp.63.ff)

25. *Umrāo Jān Ada,* Majlis i Taraqqi i Adab edn., Lahore, 1963, p.108; first published 1899.

26. Cf. *The Discarded Image*, Cambridge University Press, paperback, 1964, p.190 (and cf. also p.162).

27. Hāli, *Muqaddima She'r o Shāiri*, Ram Narain Lal, Allahabad edn., 1931, pp.195-96; first published in 1893.

28. I am aware of the ingenious argument by which Professor G.M. Wickens has sought to establish the existence of a subtle unity in the Persian *ghazal*, and note that Mr Carlo Coppola, in a review of a translation of selections from

Ghalib's Urdu verse, apparently accepts this argument for Urdu too (*Literature East and West*, Vol. XI, No.2, pp.203-06). I claim no competence to judge the issue where Persian is concerned. The strong argument against it by Dr (now Professor) Mary Boyce, in her article 'A Novel Interpretation of Hafiz' (*Bulletin of the School of Oriental and African Studies*, Vol. XV, Part 2, 1953), would appear to be convincing, especially as, so far as I am aware, Professor Wickens has never made any attempt to refute it. But where Urdu is concerned I would most definitely assert that the typical *ghazal* has no unity of content, and that the mode by which it was (and is) transmitted to its audience is in itself adequate explanation of why this should be so.

29. *Kulliyāt*, Vol. I, p.259.

30. *The Story of an African Farm,* London, 1896, p.172.

31. I was struck by this point in a lecture by my colleague Dr (now Professor) V.L. Menage. He tells me that he owes it to a Turkish writer.

Chapter 3

Ideally, the previous chapter should have been followed by a full account of the *ghazal* poetry of Mir, the first and perhaps still the greatest, of the *ghazal* poets of Urdu. But such an account extends over three chapters of another book, Ralph Russell and Khurshidul Islam, *Three Mughal Poets* (Harvard University Press, 1968; Allen and Unwin, London, 1969), shortly to be republished by Oxford University Press, India, and I must content myself here with referring readers to that. The present chapter quotes relatively short extracts from it, but in the main addresses a question not directly addressed there. This chapter is based mainly on the article 'Themes of....Poetry in the Verse of Mir', full details of which are given in the introductory note to Ch. 2.

1. For further details see *Three Mughal Poets*.

2. By Francis Pritchett.

3. In *Three Mughal Poets* we assumed that these two poems referred to the same woman, but Nisār Ahmad Farūqi's research shows that this was not the case.

4. References for quotations are to the *Kulliyāt* (see note 15, Ch.2). These words are in I.265, 5, which means line 5 of *ghazal* No. 265 in the first *divān*. Subsequent verses quoted here are similarly indicated.

5. I.407,1.

6. *Twilight of the Mughals*, Cambridge University Press, 1951, p.9.

7. Sir Jadunath Sarkar, *Fall of the Mughal Empire*, Vol.2, Calcutta, 2nd edn., 1950, p.93.

8. I.116,4,5.

9. IV.222,5.

10. VI.119,6.

11. I.382,5.

12. III.201,10.

13. In *Zikr i Mīr*, ed. Abdul Haq, Aurangabad, 1928, pp. 101-02.

14. This and the anecdote following are both taken from the chapter on Mīr in Muhammad Husain Azād, *Āb i Hayāt* – in the edition I have (Lahore, 14th edn., n.d.) they are on pp.216-18.

15. See the article quoted under note 2, Ch.1.

16. *Āb i Hayāt*, p.215.

17. III.1,5.

Chapter 4

This chapter is reproduced, with minor changes, from a paper presented in 1969, when the centenary of Ghalib's death was celebrated at the School of Oriental and African Studies, University of London. It was subsequently published, along with others, in a volume which I edited, entitled *Ghalib, the Poet and his Age* (London, George Allen and Unwin, 1972).

Nearly all quotations are taken from Ralph Russell and Khurshidul Islam, *Ghalib – Volume I: Life and Letters*. Page references are to this book, except where otherwise stated.

Readers who know Urdu may wish to check references to original Urdu and Persian sources. They will need to use libraries, and go in the first place to *Ghalib, Vol. I*, where full references to sources are given. References in it to Ghalib's Urdu *dīvān* are to the first edition. The second edition (n.d., but the preface is dated March 1971) differs to some extent. But verses are not too difficult to find in any of the numerous editions of the Urdu *dīvān* because the *ghazals* in a *dīvān* are arranged in a way which groups them together according to the final letters of the couplets (though within each group alphabetical order is not followed); and the poems on other forms are separately grouped in the *Kulliyāt* and are not so numerous that any particular poem is difficult to find. Ghalib's Urdu letters have been published in numerous editions, but it should not be difficult to find extracts, whichever edition you are using. The letters are arranged according to whom they are addressed, so the name of the addressee and the date will be sufficient to enable you to find them. Where a date is conjectured the conjecture is that of Ghulām Rasūl Mihr.

1. p.249.

2. See 'Understanding the Urdu Ghazal', p.41.

3. p.354.

4. *Kulliyāt* Vol. I, p.434.

5. p.312.

6. p.264.

7. p.362, where, however, the verse is not quoted.

8. See *Three Mughal Poets*, p.183, n.15.

9. p.279.

10. p.226.

Chapter 5

Some of the material in this chapter is adapted from 'Strands of Muslim Identity in South Asian' *South Asian Review*, Vol.6, No.1, October 1972.

Chapter 6

A shorter version of this chapter first appeared in *The Novel in India*, ed. T.W. Clark, Allen and Unwin, London, 1970.

1. Ataullah Pālavi, *Tazkira i Shauq*, Maktaba Jadīd, Lahore, 1956, pp.55, 105.

2. For a full account see *Three Mughal Poets*, Ch.3.

3. Ram Gopal, *Linguistic Affairs of India*, Asia Publishing House, London, 1966, pp.163-64.

4. Shaista Akhtar Banu Suhrawardy, *The Development of the Urdu Novel and Short Story*, Longmans Green and Co., London, 1945, pp.14-15.

5. 'Translate' is perhaps too percise a word for what they did.

6. The title means 'The Garden and Spring'. As very frequently with Urdu works, it gives no indication of what the book is about. It is chosen because, read as a chronogram, it gives the date of composition of the book.

7. W.H. Allen, London, 1862.

8. See note 10 below.

9. The information about *Fasāna i Ajāib* is taken from Sayyid Masūd Hasan Rizvi Adīb's edition of Sarur's *Fasāna i Ibrat*, Kitāb Nagar, Lucknow, 1st edn., December 1957.

10. The catalogue of Hindustani books in the India Office Library, published in 1900, lists an edition of *Fasāna i Ajāib* published in Lucknow in 1845. There is then a gap until 1866, but between that date and 1889 sixteen different editions are listed, of which, however, only the last was published outside the Delhi – U.P. area (from Bombay).

But, significantly, the editions of Mīr Amman's *Bāgh o Bahār* are even more numerous: and its popularity clearly starts earlier and spreads further afield. Most of the early editions were published outside the Delhi – U.P. area. Then, from 1850, it clearly becomes very popular in the Delhi – U.P. area also. Finally, in the 1870s, its popularity spreads to Bombay and then the South. Precise figures are as follows:

From 1804 to 1847 – eight editions, of which only two (Cawnpore, 1832 and 'Delhi, 1845?') are from the Delhi – U.P. area.

From 1850 to 1871 – twelve editions, *all* from the Delhi – U.P. area.

From 1872 to 1879 – sixteen editions, of which eleven are from the Delhi – U.P. area, the other five being from Bangalore (1872), Bombay (1874, and two in 1877), and Madras (1876).

An edition in Devanagari (Hindi) characters appeared as early as 1847, and there are other Devanagari editions in 1852, 1869, 1870 and 1879. There is also one in Gujarati characters published from Bombay in 1877.

I have left out of account editions and translations by English scholars – mostly published in London – clearly intended for the use of English students; also a translation into French published in Paris.

11. The account of the Dastan of Amir Hamza derives mainly from Raz Yazdani's Urdu *dāstānon* par *kām kā tajziya aur tabsīra*, published in the Indian government periodical *Ājkal*, Delhi, issue dated July 1960.

See also Abdul Halim Sharar's account in Ch. 12 of his *Guzashta Lakhnaū*, (many editions). An English translation of this work, somewhat abridged, was published in 1975 – translated and edited by E.S. Harcourt and Fakhir Hussain, under the title *Lucknow: The Last Phase of an Oriental Culture*, Paul Elek, London, 1975. The relevant passage on the dastans is on pp.91-92.

12. The Newal Kishore Press (see below) itself made this claim. See, for example, the announcement on p.2 of the cover of the second volume in the series, *Nausherwān Nāma*, Daftar i Awwal, Jild i Duwam. Lucknow, 3rd edn., 1915.

13. Cf. Firoz Husain, *Life and Works of Ratan Nāth Sarshār*, 1964 (unpublished Ph.D. thesis, University of London), p.99.

14. Rāz Yazdānī. See Note 11 above.

15. Cf. also Sharar's account referred to in Note 11 above.

16. Rāz Yazdānī statement, and that of the letter which he elicited from the successor of the Newal Kishore Press, is not accurate in every detail. Ghalib, in a letter to Nawwab Kalb i 'Ali Khan of Rampur dated August 1865 (see *Makātib i Ghalib*, ed. Imtiyāz ali Ārshi, Rampur, 1937) speaks of a Persian work *Rumūz i Hamza*, and says that it was written in the days of Shah Abbas II (1642-66).

In 1965 Qāzī Abdul Vadūd of Patna showed me detailed notes which he had made on this work. It is a relatively short single volume. He told me that *Tilism i Hoshrubā*, which is in his view indeed the best part of the Indian *Dāstān i Amīr Hamza*, owns little or nothing to *Rumūz i Hamza*. The remark of the 'translator' who departed from his Persian original was drawn to my attention by Firoz Husain (see note 13 above); but, regrettably, I failed to note the reference. Cf. also Muhammad Hasan Askarī's introduction (p.20) to his selection from *Tilism i Hoshrubā*, Maktaba Jadid, Lahore, 1953, on new material avowedly introduced by the *dāstān-go*.

17. For a full account of Sarshār see Firoz Husain, op. cit.

18. Cakbast, *Mazamin i Cakbast*, Shaikh Mubarak Ali, Lahore, n.d., Essay on Pandit Ratan Nāth Sarshār, p.24.

19. *Addresses and Speeches relating to the Mahomedan Anglo-Oriental College, in Aligarh...1875-98*, ed. Nawab Mohsin-ul-Mulk, Institute Press, Aligarh, 1898, *Tamhīd*, p.2.

20. Cf. *Selected Speeches*, ed. G.M. Young, Oxford University Press, World's Classics series, 1935, p.359.

21. Urdu text in *Musāfirān i Landan*, ed. Shaikh Muhammad Ismāīl Pānīpati, Majlis i Taraqqi i Adab, Lahore, 1961, pp.183-84. English translation quoted from G.F.I. Graham, The Life and Work of Sir Syed Ahmed Khan, K.C.S.I., London, Hodder and Stoughton, 1909 edn., pp. 125-26.

22. *Fasāna i Āzād,* Vol. I, 9th edn., Newal Kishore Press, Lucknow, 1949, pp. 69-70.

23. Once again, the picture is perhaps closer to reality than the modern reader might think. Thus Edward Lear comments on 'the enormous meat meals, especially the immense quantities of roast mutton, that English people were accustomed to eat in India at that time....' See Angus Davidson, *Edward Lear,* Penguin Books, Harmondsworth, 1950, p. 212.

24. pp. 418-20.

25. See note 34 below.

26. *Rasm ul Khat,* 5th edn., Delhi, 1919, p.l. Nazīr Ahmad's Preface is dated 1912.

27. Dībāca to *Mirāt ūl Arūs.* But Iftikhār Ahmad Siddīqi's authoritative study, *Maulvi Nazīr Ahmad, Ahvāl o Āsār* Majlis i Taraqqi i Adab, Lahore, 1971, shows that Nazīr Ahmad's account is largely untrue, and that the book was written on the pattern of an earlier one by another author, and written to be submitted (successfully) for a prize then being offered by the provincial government for works of this kind. (In this chapter factual detail about Nazīr Ahmad and his works is taken from Iftikhār Ahmad Siddīqi's book.)

28. Footnotes in the preface to its sequel Banāt un Nāsh tell us that by 1888 it had been published in editions totalling more than 100,000 copies, and had been translated into Bengali, Braj, Kashmiri, Panjabi and Gujarati. (*Banāt un Nāsh,* Delhi, 1888 edn., p. 1, fns. 11 and 12.)

29. Cf. Dibaca to *Mirāt ul Arūs,* but this too may well be untrue.

30. p. 51.

31. Here and in the passage quoted below, the translation is Ward's.

32. pp. 62-63.

33. It was published in 1872.

34. These are respectively, *Taubat un Nasūh* (The Repentance of Nasūh), published in 1874; *Mohsināt* (also known as *Fasana i Mubtala* (The Tale of Mubtala)), 1887; *Ibn ul Vaqt* (A Son of the Age), 1888; *Ayyāma,* 1891; and *Rūya i Sadiqa* (a title with a double meaning – Sadiqa's Dream or A True Dream), 1892. For a brief account of most of them see Suhrawardy (op. cit., p.104 – see note 4 above), pp.53-65. For some reason she does not mention *Ruya i Sadiqa;* nor does she give dates of publication.

35. *Taubat un Nasūh,* Ch. 1.

36. *Ibn ul Vaqt,* Ch. 2.

37. *Taubat un Nasūh,* Ch. 1.

38. *Badr un Nisā ki musībat.* Suhrawardy describes this book on pp. 82-84. Neither she nor Sadiq gives the date of publication. The earliest edition in the British Museum is dated 1897.

39. See note 11 above.

40. Muhammad Sadiq, *A History of Urdu Literature,* London Oxford University Press, 2nd edn., revised and enlarged, 1984, p. 430.

41. There have been numerous editions of *Flora Florindā,* as of most of Sharar's novels. That which I have used was published by Maktaba i Urdu, but bears no date or place of publication. I obtained it from Pakistan in about 1960.

Occasional page references are to this edition.

42. Faiz Ahmad Faiz, *Mīzān*, Nāshirīn, Lahore, 1962, p. 229.

43. Ch. 4, p.38.

44. pp. 326-27 (towards the end of Ch. 28).

45. p. 24.

46. Cf. Ch. 20, p.202, and Ch. 24, pp.264-65.

47. p.229.

48. *Zāi i Sharīf*, Ashrafi Book Depot, Lucknow, n.d. (?1963), pp.3-4.

49. The concluding sentence of *Zāt i Sharīf*.

50. Or, perhaps, she recognizes the verse.

51. Mirza Rusvā, *Umrāo Jān Adā,* ed. Zahīr Fatehpūrī, Majlis i Taraqqī I Adab, Lahore, 1963, pp. 321-23.

52. p.263.

53. The great Persian poet. The verse quoted is not in fact one of Hāfiz, but it has become proverbial.

54. pp. 280-81.

55. By Oriental Longmans Ltd.

56. *Zāt i Sharīf*.

57. *Sharīfzāda*.

Chapter 7

1. In what follows, the factual information is taken wholly from Iftikhār Ahmad Siddīqi's excellent book (see Ch. 6, note 27). There is much in this book that contradicts accounts given in earlier works. Where it does, the author has argued his case for new conclusions thoroughly and convincingly. All page references are to this book.

2. Provinces (or, in independent India, states) were, and are, divided into districts, which are subdivided into *tahsīls*. The administrative and judicial head of a district is popularly known as a Collector, and that of a *tahsīl* a *tahsildār*.

3. p. 27.

4. Later Sir Richard Temple, famous today for his great compilation, *The Legends of the Punjab*.

5. p. 105.

6. A description of Nazīr Ahmad's tales has already been given in the previous chapter and is therefore not repeated here.

7. p. 47.

8. But elsewhere Iftikhār Ahmad Siddiqi seems to suggest that he began to write these booklets from about 1871.

9. p.88. But p. 347 gives the date of writing as 1873 and of publication as 1874.

10. p. 138.

11. p. 247; and cf. p. 179.

12. p. 251.

13. I have read *Ibn ul Vaqt*, a tale in which Nāzir Ahmad's exposition, through

the character of Hujjat ul Islām, of his interpretation of Islam occupies a substantial part, and some shorter pieces, including the very remarkable essay of December 1909 on the vicegerency of man to which I make detailed reference below. I have also studied Iftikhar Ahmad Siddīqi's critical account of Nazīr Ahmad's religious writings.

14. and 15. p. 297.

16. Iftikhar Ahmad Siddīqi reproduces the full text on pp. 444-46.

Chapter 8

1. Aslam Farrukhi, *Muhammad Husain Āzād*; Hayat aur Tasanif, Anjuman i Taraqqi i Urdu, Karachi, 1965. This is a work in two volumes. Vol. I (440 pages) deals with Āzād's life; Vol.II (792 pages) deals with his works. In Vol.II, ch. 1, which runs to p.340, is devoted to *Ab i Hayat*. The survey of the *tazkiras* is in Vol.II, pp.28-58.

2. p.7, n.4.

3. This conversation occupies the last part of Ch.9.

4. *Yādgār i Ghāib*, (ed.) Khalīl ur Rahmān Dāudi, Majlis i Taraqqi i Adab, Lahore, 1963, pp.9-10.

5. *Maktūbāt i Sir Sayyad,* (ed.) Shaikh Muhammad Ismāīl Pānīpati, Majlis i Taraqqi i Adab, Lahore, 1959, p.312.

6. 9th impression, 1970, pp. 124-25.

Chapter 9

This chapter first appeared as an article in *Modern Asian Studies,* 8, 1, 1974. An abridged Urdu translation (by Nurul Hasan Naqvi) was included in Muhammad Zāhid (ed.), *Akbar Kī Tanziya aur Zarīfāna Shāiri,* Educational Book House, Aligarh, 1979, pp.36-109.

To prepare the article Khurshidul Islam and I worked together in the way described in the Author's Preface to *Three Mughal Poets* (Harvard University Press, 1968; and Allen & Unwin, London, 1969). Khurshidul Islam read the whole of the four volumes of Akbar's *Kulliyāt*, and made a comprehensive selection, which we then studied and discussed together. The editing of the *Kulliyāt* leaves much to be desired. Some attempt at dating has been made in Part I, but only within very broad limits. In general, all four parts seem to include verse of all periods, Parts II and III being, in effect, substantial supplements to Part I, presenting verse which had been missed when Part I was compiled. Part IV, however, seems to comprise mainly the verse of Akbar's last years. It is possible that some of the verses included were not published during his lifetime, but, if so, this is not indicated. The footnotes are quite often incorrect. In Parts I and III, the poems are numbered: in Parts II and IV they are not. References are given thus: II, 54, 3 means Part II, page 54, line 3, and references to Part IV are given in the same way. But I, 70, 4 means Part I, number 70 (not page 70), line 4; and similarly with Part III.

The present article deals only with his topical verse and excluds the bulk of his *ghazal* poetry; this too would repay serious study. Akbar, like his older contemporary Hāli, is one of those poets whose achievement in the *ghazal* has been overshadowed by the greater popularity of their other verse.

A full study of Akbar is long overdue, and a good deal of material for such a study is available in the various collections of his letters and the reminiscences of him by, among others, Abdul Mājid Daryābādi, Khwaja Hasan Nizāmi, Tālib Ilāhābādi, and Qamar ud Dīn Ahmad.

The English text of the chapter is mine and is an expanded version of a lecture I gave at the Oriental Centre, Institute of Contemporary Arts, London, on 30 November 1971; but it represents the views of both the authors.

1. III, 1064.
2. I, 1076, and cf. (e.g.) III, 1242, 1 and 1061, 3.
3. II, 48, 4.
4. I, 125, couplets 1,2,4,6, and 9. Cf. also (e.g.) IV, 30, 4.
5. I, 35.
6. III, 578, 2.
7. I, 868. He makes a similar point in III, 1357, about Englishmen who go home to England when they retire instead of staying on in India.
8. I, 53.
9. I, 1099.
10. I, 1037, 2.
11. I, 124, 1.
12. III, 580.
13. I, 54, 10.
14. III, 1402.
15. IV, 97, 1-2.
16. II, 90, last line.
17. I, 593.
18. Line 34.
19. I, 179, 4.
20. I, 115, 3.
21. II, 79, 13-14.
22. III, 1218, 6.
23. III, 1333.
24. I, 245, 2 and cf. I, 534, 2.
25. I, 74, 2.
26. III, 28, 1.
27. II, 91, 10.
28. II, 91, 5.
29. I, 194, 2.
30. I, 265, 14.
31. IV, 52, 14.
32. I, 915.
33. I, 279, 8.

34. I, 104, 14.
35. III, 1437.
36. II, 94, 3-4.
37. *India, Pakistan and the West, 4th edn., Oxford University Press, 1967,*
p.81.
38. III, 1438.
39. III, 866, 4.
40. III, 626.
41. IV, 53, 19.
42. I, 299, 6.
43. I, 1097.
44. I, 674.
45. I, 922.
46. I, 622, 1-7.
47. Nazīr Ahmad, *Mau'iza-i-Hasna*, Delhi, 1308 A.H. (A.D. 1890/1) letter
99, p.175. The book was first published in 1887. As we have seen, he applies
the same comparison to those who try to interpret the whole of Hafiz in a mystic
sense.
48. I, 623.
49. I, 152.
50. I, 638.
51. II, 86, 6-7. Many more verses could be quoted. II, 75, 8-19 – a poem of
eleven couplets – gives a long list of all the things that can be allowed provided
that religious obligations are observed. Cf. also II, 23, 13; 80, 13-14 and 21; and
83, 15.
52. I, 99, 1.
53. I, 640.
54. III, 772.
55. II, 46, 3.
56. III, 728, 1.
57. III, 447, 1.
58. I, 463.
59. I, 923, 1.
60. I, 260, 5-6.
61. I, 928.
62. I, 623, 14-16.
63. II, 59, 9-10. And compare note 65 below.
64. II, 82, 3-4.
65. I, 67. '*Shaikh*' here carries the connotation which I explain in the text. I
should add that it does not always mean quite that. It can be used of any Muslim
leader, in the political as well as in the religious field, who claims more
importance and authority than the poet thinks he deserves. This is the sense in
the line quoted earlier (see note 63). Below (note 73) it has no pejorative sense
at all, but means simply the Muslim elder who imparts religious instruction to
the young.
66. I, 594.

67. Line 23.
68. I, 755.
69. II, 66, 6:

راہِ مغرب میں یہ لڑکے لٹ گئے   واں نہ پہونچے اور ہم سے چھٹ گئے

70. II, 78, 18.
71. II, 71, 9.
72. II, 64, 19.
73. II, 51, 5-6. And compare note 65 above.
74. I, 579.
75. I, 151, 3:

مذہب چھوڑو ملّت چھوڑو واصورت بدلو مگر گنواؤ
صرف کفر کی کی اُمید اور اتنی مصیبت توبہ توبہ

76. I, 179, 2.
77. I, 907.
78. I, 656, last line.
79. I.1008, last line
80. III, 1217.
81. III, 1314.
82. I, 1192.
83. II, 69, 7-10.
84. III, 1212, 2.
85. II, 35, 15.
86. III, 539.
87. II, 90, 10.
88. III, 1210, 1.
89. III, 28, 2.
90. II, 62, 7.
91. II, 66, 5.
92. I, 243, 3.
93. III, 1120, 2.
94. III, 733, 5.
95. I, 875, 1.
96. II, 98, 5.
97. IV, 53, 9.
98. II, 10, 3.
99. I, 1062, 4.
100. III, 1129.
101. III, 996, 3.

102. II, 55, last line.
103. III, 1335.
104. III, 1349.
105. II, 70, 15.
106. III, 963, 2.
107. IV, 18, 1.
108. II, 89, 19.
109. III, 1430.
110. I, 765.
111. II, 37, 20.
112. IV, 32, 9.
113. I, 578.
114. The exact words (translated from Urdu) are 'If Sir Sayyid Ahmad Khān and *Avadh Punch* had not existed, Sayyid Akbar Husain Sāhib would not have been a poet.' *Avadh Punch* was the humorous periodical in which Akbar published much of his verse. Sayyid Akbar Husain was Akbar's full name. The words are those of Muhammad Yahyā Tanhā, as quoted by Shaikh Muhammad Ikram in *Mauj i Kausar*, 5th edition, 1963, Ferozsons Ltd, Lahore, etc., p.213. We cannot find the passage in Tanhā's *Siyar ul Musannifin*, and in his *Mirāt ush Shuarā*, Vol. II, Shaikh Mubarak Ali, Lahore, n.d. (1950), pp.60-61, his statement is a much more qualified one. Perhaps this was an earlier, and more rash, version of the judgement expressed there. The words quoted by Ikrām are in any case a fair summary of the fairly widely held view of Akbar's 'negativeness'.
115. Aziz Ahmad, *An Intellectual History of Islam in India*, Edinburgh University Press, 1969, p.105. His earlier assessment, in his *Islamic Modernism in India and Pakistan, 1957-1964*, Oxford University Press, 1967, pp.101-02, is rather less sweeping.
116. Cf: H.W.C. Davis, *Medieval Europe*, Williams & Norgate, London, n.d., p.23.
117. I, 23, 1.
118. III, 462.
119. I, 152, 2.
120. I, 90, 3.
121. II, 48, 20.
122. II, 47, 14.
123. IV, 3, 6. And compare II, 54, 16.
124. II, 79, 16.
125. II, 85, 15.
126. II, 79, 4.
127. II, 59, 7-8.
128. I, 893, 3.
129. I, 516.
130. I, 1155.
131. For example, I, 1149, 2; and 1159.
132. I, 1111.

133. IV, 52, 16.

134. Indian Muslim tradition was that the earth rests on the horns of a cow. Cf. (e.g.) Mīr Anīs, Marsiya beginning *jab qat's kī musāfat i Shab āftāb ne*, stanza 167 in Masud Hasan Rizvi's text in *Rūh i Anis*, 2nd edn., Kitab Nagar, Lucknow, 1956, p.253, and footnote 3.

135. III, 1421.

136. Qamar ud Din Ahmad, *Bazm-i-Akbar*, Anjuman-i-Taraqqi-i-Urdu, Delhi, 2nd edn., 1944, pp. 15-17.

137. I, 948, 1.

138. II, 61, 5-6.

139. II, 87, 16.

140. I, 1135, 2.

141. III, 1190.

142. III, 1455.

143. III, 364, 2.

144. II, 26, 14, and I, 534, 1.

145. II, 26, 17-18.

146. I, 124, 2.

147. II, 26, 18.

148. I, 844.

149. I, 240, 7.

150. I, 1059.

151. II, 96, 5.

152. II, 37, 10.

153. I, 576.

154. I, 201, 2.

155. II, 92, 13.

156. I, 1143.

157. I, 54, 12-14.

158. II, 52, 3-4.

159. II, 87, 7-9.

160. I, 644, 2. Cf. II, 63, 9.

161. I, 644, 3.

162. II, 31, 2.

163. I, 687, 60.

164. II, 26, 15.

165. III, 819.

166. IV, 47, 21.

167. III, 540, 1.

168. I, 813. And cf. I, 1205, 4.

169. I, 875, 2.

170. II, 108, 17.

171. III, 1068.

172. I, 975.

173. I, 739.

174. I, 617, 3.

175. I, 790.
176. III, 1420.
177. II, 57, 14-15.
178. IV, 64, 11.
179. IV, 48, 4.
180. IV, 91, 10-11.
181. IV, 48, 3.
182. IV, 46, 1.
183. IV, 40, 7.
184. IV, 42, 4-5.
185. IV, 51, 7-8. Cf. also his despondent reflections on the shooting at Amritsar, IV, 78, 5-6 and 96, 8-11.
186. I, 166, 10.
187. The most celebrated is I, 1030, in which he complains of having to drink piped water and read printed type. Cf. also his complaint against electric light, IV, 65, 16.
188. Cf. (e.g.) II, 83, 4-5, and the complete poem (13 couplets), I, 247.

Chapter 10

1. 'Great Leader'–ie Muhammad Ali Jinnah, the inspirer and leader of the movement for the creation of Pakistan, and its first Governor-General.
2. Quoted in Q.M. Haq and M.I. Waley, *Allama Sir Muhammad Iqbal*, British Museum Publications Ltd, London, 1977, p. 28.
3. Thus the consideration of Iqbal takes me beyond the '1922' which I have given as the closing date of this period. But Iqbal's message had already been formulated by then and his later writing adds little to it.
4. *Bīl e Jibrīl*, p. 55. In this and subsequent references I give the page numbers of each collection, as included in the Urdu and the Persian centenary editions of Iqbal's *Kulliyāt*.
5. *Bāng e Darā*, p. 88
6. Ibid., p.83.
7. Another, much better, poem *Hindostanı Baccon ka qaumı gıt* (Indian children's national song) belongs to the same period. It is better because it at any rate lists the blessings that India has given to the world. See *Bāng e Darā*, p. 87.
8. *Bāng e Dara*, p. 159.
9. Ibid., p. 160.
10. Ibid., p. 43.
11. *Bal e Jibrīl*, p. 3.
12. Q.M. Haq and M.I. Waley, 1977, op. cit., p. 27.
13. *Bal e Jibrīl*, p.109.
14. Line 614, p.39.
15. For example, in *Bāng e Dara*, pp. 59-60, *Bal e Jibrīl*, pp. 109-10, 117-18, 158-59, 166, *Zarb e Kalīm*, pp. 35-36.

16. See (e.g.) *Bang e Darā*, p.262, *Bal e Jibril*, pp. 123, 128, 146, 162.
17. In *Modern Islam in India*, Lahore, 1943, p.122.
18. pp.171-72.
19. p. 142.
20. p. 157.
21. *Bal e Jibrīl*, p.98.
22. See *The Raj and the Muslim Response*, above.
23. Quoted by Arberry in his introduction to his translation of *Javid-Nama* (Iqbal, *Javid-Nama*, translated from the Persian with introduction and notes by Arthur J. Arberry. Allen and Unwin, 1966, p.13.)
24. *Armughan e Hijāz, p. 139.*
25. *Bāng e Dara*, p.60.

Chapter 12.

This chapter is a considerably extended version of a speech delivered in 1980 at a meeting held to celebrate the centenary of Prem Chand's birth.

1. Others are, in the 19th century Sarshar and in the 20th Krishan Chandar.
2. See *The Development of the Modern Novel.*
3. For details see 'Suggestions for Further Reading'.
4. G.K. Chesterton, *The Victorian Age in Literature*, London, n.d., p. 98. I am not, however, quoting his exact words.
5. The husband in this story is to some extent Prem Chand himself. See Amrit Rai, *Premchand, a Life*, translated from the Hindi by Harish Trivadi, People's Publishing House, New Delhi, 1982, p. 244, where Prem Chand's stubborn refusal to perform the *kanyadan* for his own daughter is described.
6. Robert Scholes and Robert Kellogg, *The Nature of Narrative*, Oxford University Press, 1966, p.3.

Chapter 13

The first part of this chapter is based upon my contribution to B.N. Pandey (ed.). *Leadership in South Asia*, Vikas, New Delhi, 1977, entitled *Leadership in the All-India Progressive Writers' Movement, 1935-1947.*

Two of the stories treated at length in the article were translated by me and published in India. That of Krishan Chandar's *Kālu Bhangi* appeared in *Indian Literature*, April-September 1959, and that of Ismat Chughtai's *Nannhi ki Nāni* in *Contemporary Indian Short Stories, Series I*, Sahitya Akademi, New Delhi, 1959. This translation has been reprinted a number of times, most recently in *Truth Tales* (The Women's Press, 1987).

I include translated extracts in my outline of the stories, and all the translations are my own. Even where I summarize, I have taken care to do so using wherever possible the words of the original; so these passages too are more in the nature of condensed translation than retellings.

1. I am indebted for this information to Shabana Mahmud, who has prepared *Angāre* for republication and written an excellent and informative introduction to it.

2. This was reproduced in *New Indian Literature*, No. 1, Lucknow, 1939, pp. 116-17.

3. *Jāved Nāma*, line 1072 (p. 64, line 2).

4. *Armughān i Hijāz*, in the poem *Iblīs ki Majlis i Shūra*.

5. In *Bāl i Jibrīl*, p. 106.

6. *Pas chi bāyad kard...*, the chapter headed *lā illāh lil illāh* (There is no god but God).

7. Published under this title in English translation by Ravi Bakaya in *Indian Literature*, No. 1, 1952, pp. 26-33. Amrit Rai in *Premchand, A Life*, pp. 363-64 gives details of the circumstances in which this, his last essay, was written.

8. I retranslate from Sajjād Zahīr's Urdu version.

9. All three communities were united in regarding Panjabi as a language which one used only in the home or in informal conversation. Most Panjabi Muslims and Hindus still do take this view. It is only the Sikhs who (especially since Independence and the later (1966) redrawing of the old provincial boundaries to make Panjab an overwhelmingly Panjabi-speaking state) have accorded Panjabi the status of a modern literary language.

10. Jīlānī Bānū, *Krishan Chandar*, Sahitya Akademi, New Delhi. 1987.

11. *Dastāvez* – a selection of Mantu's writings (ed.) Balrāj Menra, New Delhi, 1986. The epitaph is printed immediately after the title page.

Chapter 14

1. Faiz was not only a poet, but a literary critic of more than average perceptiveness. His collection of critical essays, *Mīzān*, and particularly its outstandingly good article on Sharar (see Ch. 6 and note 42 above), deserves more attention than it generally receives.

2. The titles of Faiz's eight collections defy translation, and I give their titles in the original mainly for the convenience of readers who know Urdu and already have some acquaintance with Faiz's work. Nearly all – perhaps all – are words quotes from, or based upon, an Urdu or Persian couplet of another poet. *Naqsh i Faryādi* (Which Kiernan translates as *Remonstrance* but which carries something of the sense of an appeal against injustice) combines the first two words of the first *ghazal* in Ghalib's Urdu *dīvān*.

3. *Poems of Faiz*, p. 9.

4. The introduction is more reticent than one would like, partly for reasons I shall discuss below and partly because *Poems by Faiz* was sponsored by the Pakistan government, and it was evidently thought necessary to tread delicately in order not to jeopardize its chances of publication. All the same it has much useful information.

5. Jointly published by Vanguard Books, Lahore; and South Publications, n.d.

6. Kiernan gives the date 1943. It seems he worked from a second edition, with added poems (Nos. 14, 15 and 16) which now, in Faiz's collected verse, are included in the second collection.

7. *Dast i Saba*, 'The hand of the breeze', aptly translated by Kiernan as *Fingers of the Wind*, is a reference to a couplet of Hāfiz which Faiz quotes immediately after his foreword, and which means 'The breath of the breeze of morning will bring fragrance, and the old world will again become young.'

8. The information in this paragraph is taken from an extract from an article prefixed to the complete (or nearly complete) collection of Faiz's verse published under the title of *Nuskhahāe Vafā* (roughly, Records of Commitment) by Educational Publishing House, Delhi, 1986.

9. I wonder whether this is in fact so. Both Faiz and Kiernan were in India at the time (as I was), and had the political awareness to understand what was happening. The leaders of the Indian National Congress had resolved to start a mass struggle against the British, but before they could organize it they were all imprisoned, and the powerful movement which erupted was deprived of their leadership. This is not the situation which this poem describes.

10. *Dast i Tih i Sang*, 'The hand (trapped) under the stone'. Kiernan gives it the English title *Duress*. The words are taken from a verse of Ghalib which is quoted in full to form the concluding couplets of one of Faiz's own poems.

11. This is the most deplorable example of the voluntary reticence and self-censorship which is discernible in the Introduction and elsewhere in the book. Iran would almost certainly have vetoed the publication of a book containing such a poem.

12. *The True Subject*, selected poems of Faiz Ahmad Faiz, Princeton University Press, 1988. The two quotations are both from p. xi.

Index

Zed Books Ltd

is a publisher whose international and Third World lists span:

- **Women's Studies**
- **Development**
- **Environment**
- **Current Affairs**
- **International Relations**
- **Children's Studies**
- **Labour Studies**
- **Cultural Studies**
- **Human Rights**
- **Indigenous Peoples**
- **Health**

We also specialize in Area Studies where we have extensive lists in African Studies, Asian Studies, Caribbean and Latin American Studies, Middle East Studies, and Pacific Studies.

For further information about books available from Zed Books, please write to: Catalogue Enquiries, Zed Books Ltd, 57 Caledonian Road, London N1 9BU. Our books are available from distributors in many countries (for full details, see our catalogues), including:

In the USA
Humanities Press International, Inc., 165 First Avenue, Atlantic Highlands, New Jersey 07716.
Tel: (908) 872 1441;
Fax: (908) 872 0717.

In Canada
Garamond Press, Suite 408, 77 Mowat Avenue, Toronto, Ontario M6K 3E3.
Tel: (416) 516 2709.

In Australia
Peribo Pty Ltd, 26 Tepko Road, Terrey Hills, NSW 2084.

In Southern Africa
David Philip Publisher (Pty) Ltd, PO Box 408, Claremont 7735, South Africa.